LIFE WITH ROSE KENNEDY

"THE ROSE KENNEDY I KNEW, AND WHOM I WANT TO SHARE WITH THE WORLD, WAS . . . A SPUNKY OLD LADY WHO COULD BE FULL OF VIM AND VINEGAR, AND I THINK SHE WAS PROUD OF THE FACT."

—from *Life with Rose Kennedy*

*   *   *

"REQUIRED READING IF YOU STILL BELIEVE IN CAMELOT . . . fascinating . . . revealing . . . priceless for its insider's look at the Kennedys at play in Palm Beach and Hyannis Port."

—*Milwaukee Sentinel*

*   *   *

"THE AUTHOR SPARES NO ONE. . . . There are wonderful tidbits about the entire family, and it's juicy indeed to read about which Kennedy members are nice and which abuse their power. All Kennedy watchers will delight in this insider's view, carefully written and very readable."

—*Ocala Star Banner*

*   *   *

About the Authors

Barbara Gibson served as Rose Kennedy's personal secretary and close confidante in the 1970's. She previously worked on Capitol Hill as a secretary for a congressman. A mother and grandmother, she currently lives and works as a Realtor Associate in Florida.

• • • •

A Manhattan-based author, Caroline Latham is the author of *Michael*, the bestselling biography of Michael Jackson, *Priscilla and Elvis: The Priscilla Presley Story* and numerous other books.

LIFE WITH ROSE KENNEDY

BARBARA GIBSON
with Caroline Latham

WARNER BOOKS

A Warner Communications Company

Warner Books, Inc.
666 Fifth Avenue
New York, N.Y. 10103

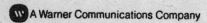 A Warner Communications Company

Printed in the United States of America

This book was originally published in
hardcover by Warner Books.
First Printed in Paperback: December, 1986

10 9 8 7 6 5 4 3 2 1

When Mrs. Kennedy once suggested to me that I keep a diary of my days working for her, she said, "It will be nice for your children to have, to look back on." And so, as Mrs. Kennedy suggested, I would like to dedicate this book to
my children, Kathleen and Kevin, and to their children, and to posterity.

Contents

1

Remembering Rose Kennedy

The last real conversation I had with Rose Kennedy was early in the summer of 1982. Although I had visited her only a few months before, I was shocked at the change in her. Her body seemed shriveled and terribly thin. The knuckles of her hands were so swollen that her wedding ring had been cut to help ease it off. Her memory was spotty, and I feared that perhaps she wouldn't remember me.

Her granddaughter Sydney Lawford took me out to the terrace of the Palm Beach house, where Mrs. Kennedy was sitting in the sun, swathed in several layers of clothes despite the balmy temperature. When Sydney told her grandmother I was there, it was obvious that she didn't recognize my name. But, seconds later, it was equally obvious that she did recognize my face. I gave her a kiss on the cheek and we began chatting.

I told Mrs. Kennedy about my current job as a private secretary to a wealthy Palm Beach businessman. I intended simply to be entertaining, but after she listened quietly for a few minutes, she remarked, "I can tell you don't like him by the expression on your face." I was surprised that she was still able to read my expressions so clearly. After all, it had been several years since we mutually agreed that she really needed a nurse/maid/companion more than a secretary and I left her employ.

I answered that it wasn't so much that I didn't like him as it was that I didn't approve of the way he lavished gifts on his children and spent extravagantly on luxurious living. Mrs. Kennedy quickly responded, "Well, of course, that's personal. If he has a lot of money, he probably worked hard for it, so he should be able to spend it the way he chooses." I thought the comment humorous, in view of what I knew about her own spending habits and idea of thrift.

I had moved since the last time I stopped by to visit, so I told Mrs. Kennedy all about my new apartment and how much I was enjoying it. She didn't seem to recognize the address, but when I told her it was near the Seminole Golf Club, she perked up. "Oh, yes," she said enthusiastically, "the President used to play there. Mr. Kennedy played there also. We used to pack up the car with a picnic lunch and go there to spend the day." Her face lighted up as the memories came back to her.

At her age, it was not surprising that the past held more interest than the present or future. Yet she didn't indulge herself for long in looking back. She asked questions about a book I had read lately, and we discussed a report in the paper that in an upcoming TV movie about the Kennedys, the role of Rose Kennedy would be played by Katharine Hepburn. It amused me to think how frequently tall women were chosen to play the part of my former employer, who was just barely over five feet tall. It must be the power of her personality that made it seem appropriate to portray her as statuesque.

Sydney came back to remind Mrs. Kennedy that it was nearly time for the evening news on television. Although she was then in her early nineties, Mrs. Kennedy apparently kept up her interest in world events and maintained her customary clockwork schedule. She invited me to stay and watch the news with her; when I pleaded a previous engagement, she suggested I come back another day and swim with her. I was amazed and impressed to learn that she was still going in the pool every day. What an iron will she had!

I told her I would stop by again soon, and she

squeezed my hand. As I walked back across the terrace, she suddenly called out to me, "Oh, Barbara, what was it you did for me?"

"I was your secretary, Mrs. Kennedy."

She answered thoughtfully, "Is that so . . ." and then there was a long pause.

"I seem," she said, "to remember a very pleasant association."

That's the way I remember it, too.

Working as secretary to Rose Kennedy was a job unlike any other. It made big demands, and it brought big rewards. There were times when I felt I would never understand my employer, and other times when I felt I understood her all too well. When I first began to work for her, I found her surprisingly easy to talk to, but difficult to feel close to. But as time passed, our relationship grew. Mrs. Kennedy was a feisty and independent woman who had never acknowledged that she needed anyone and wasn't going to start just because she was a frail octogenarian. Yet I recognized that she valued the closeness and companionship that developed between us, as did I. I never doubted that it was a privilege to share the candid thoughts of this spirited and critical old lady.

Today, whenever I meet people who know that I was once Rose Kennedy's personal secretary, they always ask the same question: "What's she really like?"

When I started working for Mrs. Kennedy, I knew no more than the mix of legend and history that everyone else knows. I knew that Mrs. Kennedy had once been Rose Fitzgerald, the beautiful daughter of Boston's turn-of-the-century mayor, John F. Fitzgerald, who was affectionately known to his constituents as "Honey Fitz" in honor of his persuasive way of speaking. Rose was still in her teens when she met Joseph Patrick Kennedy, only son of a Boston Irish publican who was also active in city politics, sometimes as Honey Fitz's ally and sometimes as his rival. Rose's father was opposed to the match, and the couple had to wait seven years before they could marry.

By the time of their marriage, Joe had already become a bank president. True, it was a small bank, and his father was one of the major stockholders, but it was still an early demonstration of Joe's business acumen and proved to be the first step in a long process of amassing wealth and power. Joe Kennedy was a stock speculator, a deal maker, a manipulator of stock prices (back in the days when such tactics were legal). He is rumored to have made money selling liquor during Prohibition, and it's certainly a fact that he made a considerable amount of money in the movie business.

While Joe was out conquering the world, Rose was at home raising the children. They had nine of them, so she was kept busy. The oldest child, Joseph P. Kennedy, Jr., was their pride and joy. According to most reports, Joe Jr. was a natural leader and like his father an aggressive man. The family expected great things of him, but their hopes were destroyed abruptly and painfully when Joe Jr. was killed on a dangerous bombing mission near the end of World War II.

The second child was John F. Kennedy. A somewhat frail and bookish child, he nevertheless did his best to live up to his parents' expectations and become a keen competitor in all arenas. When his older brother died, Jack became the focus of family hopes, and he began his political career as a congressman not long after World War II. The fact that he was a veteran, and a hero to boot—decorated for his efforts to save his crew when his PT boat sank in the South Pacific—didn't hurt his appeal to the voters. The rest is history, from the shining moments of Camelot to that dreadful day in Dallas and the sorrow the Kennedy family shared with the world. Although his widow, Jackie, remarried (to Greek shipping tycoon Aristotle Onassis), she and her two children, Caroline and John, remained a part of the Kennedy circle.

The third child was Rosemary, a beautiful girl who also brought her parents heartbreak. Early in her childhood, it became apparent that her development was unnaturally slow, and the Kennedys had to face the fact that Rosemary was retarded. They did their best to look for cures and help, and they also did their best to camouflage her condition. Eventually they had to admit defeat, and Rosemary was permanently placed in a convent, where she could be looked after by the nursing sisters.

The fourth child was Kathleen, a bright and vivacious girl who was always surrounded by friends and admirers. Kathleen had a great social success in London when her father was ambassador there, and finally she married the heir to the greatest English dukedom. Her husband was killed in action in World War II, only a few brief weeks after their marriage. Kathleen stayed with her family for the rest of the war, but as soon as peace was declared, she returned to live in England. She was killed a few years later in the crash of a small private plane during bad weather.

The fifth child was Eunice. She was a smart, tough, courageous girl; many observers thought that if she had been a boy, she would have been the most successful of all the Kennedy children. Eunice married Sargent Shriver, who at that time was employed by her father as the director of the Merchandise Mart, a huge retail complex in Chicago. Eunice and Sarge had five children: one daughter (Maria, now a cohost of *CBS Morning News*) and four sons. Sarge, who was the director of the Peace Corps during his brother-in-law's administration, was later appointed ambassador to France by Lyndon Johnson. He was George McGovern's running mate in 1972 and made an attempt to run on his own for the presidency in 1976. Since then, his political career has been in abeyance. Eunice remains extremely active in charitable affairs for the retarded, especially those sponsored by the Kennedy family foundation.

Sixth in line was Patricia. Pat married actor Peter Lawford, and the couple lived for some time in southern California. They had four children: one boy and three girls. The children were still relatively young when the marriage ended in divorce. Pat now lives in New York, where she is one of the stars of that city's social elite.

The seventh child was Robert F. Kennedy. As a small boy, he was doggedly determined to keep up with his older brothers, no matter how much effort it took. He made it into the Navy at the very end of World War II and then went to law school. Bobby was a devoted family man, very much in love with his wife, Ethel, and always trying to spend as much time as possible with his children. They had eleven of them, ranging from Kathleen Hartington Kennedy, who was the oldest of all the Kennedy grandchildren, down to daughter Rory, who was born months after Bobby's death. Bobby was his brother's attorney general and the one who inherited much of his political legacy when President Kennedy died. After a long struggle with an innate reluctance to step into his brother's shoes, Bobby finally decided to run for the presidency in 1968 . . . and tragically became the second Kennedy to fall victim to an assassin's bullets. Ethel and the younger children still occupy the same house in suburban Virginia and spend their summers at the Kennedy compound in Hyannis Port.

The eighth child of Joe and Rose Kennedy was Jean. She married Steve Smith, a shrewd businessman who became his father-in-law's right hand, helping him run the family business empire and taking over after his death. Jean and Steve have four children, two boys and two girls, and they live in New York, where they are socially prominent.

The ninth and last child was Edward M. Kennedy. The much-loved and often spoiled baby of the family, he grew into a charming and gregarious man, with a touch of the natural Irish political instincts of his grandfather. Ted also went to law school, and in 1962, while his brother was in the White House, he was elected U.S. senator from Massachusetts. Ted and his wife, Joan, had three children: Ted Jr., Kara, and Patrick. Ted seems to have weathered more tragedy than any one man could be expected to survive. Beyond the deaths of all three of his brothers, Ted has coped with a long

period of hospitalization after a plane crash that left
doctors convinced he would never walk again; the
unfortunate events at Chappaquiddick that left Mary
Jo Kopechne dead and his political career shadowed; the heartbreak of discovering that his son
Teddy had bone cancer, which necessitated the am-
putation of his leg; and his wife's alcoholism, which
required more support than perhaps he was able to
give at the time. Ted and Joan were divorced in the
early 1980s, but she still has the house only minutes
away from the Kennedy compound in Hyannis Port,
and Ted remains close to his children.

The raising of all her children was Mrs. Kennedy's chief concern. Her husband was away for
long periods of time, occupied with business matters
and, according to rumor, having affairs with a number of women, including a long and passionate one
with Gloria Swanson. It was Rose who took the
children to church, worried through their illnesses,
meted out discipline for offenses such as unfinished
homework or rude behavior. Years later, when her
son became President, Mrs. Kennedy often told reporters about how she kept track of the major events
in her children's lives by using an index card system
on which she jotted down such things as dates of
inoculations and their heights and weights on each
birthday.

Through all this, the public came to have an
image of Rose Kennedy that was, finally, too good

to be true. At least she herself never took the public's conception of her too seriously, as I learned when I worked for her. I remember particularly one day when I picked her up after church (the chauffeur, as so often happened, was otherwise occupied). She was just inside the church doors, and as I walked in, she flicked me with a few drops of water from the small stoup nearby. "They tell me I'm a saint," she said wryly, "so this is my blessing." It is certainly true that many books and articles about the Kennedy family make Rose Kennedy out to be a minor saint, perpetually uncomplaining and self-sacrificing. But the Rose Kennedy I finally learned to know after years of living and working with her closely was considerably more interesting than that. Deeply religious and wholeheartedly dedicated to her family, she was nevertheless fully human, with the foibles and follies that condition implies for all of us.

One minute Rose Kennedy could step into the limelight, beautifully dressed and elegantly groomed, looking authentically glamorous and much younger than her eighty-odd years. Then this woman, who was revered by millions all over the world, would go off for her solitary walk, her solitary swim, her solitary trip to mass, spending most of her daily life all alone. She could be outspokenly critical, and yet she would never tell anyone when she felt sad or depressed. She worked her emotions out in the swimming pool, dog-paddling furiously from one end to the other as she tried to escape her sorrows. She could give away millions to the retarded and then try to return used bottles of nail polish for credit.

In other words, Rose Kennedy was a complex person. And I believe she wanted people to know it. She never fell for her own publicity, and in the end I think she wearied of it. She was a spunky old lady who could be full of vim and vinegar, and I think she was proud of the fact. I'm sure she would not like to be remembered as nothing more than saintly and silent. What about the headstrong woman who could glare at you for long minutes and then say fiercely, "Do as you're told"? What about the octogenarian who loved to dance and who sang Irish ballads at the top of her voice in kitchen duets with the cook? What about the woman who wore false eyelashes even when her hands were so shaky with age that it was hard to put them on? Those were a part of Rose Kennedy, too, and I think what I liked best about her was that she never tried to hide it.

Perhaps that was why she made such a point of encouraging me to keep a diary of my experiences in the years I was with her. "You'll never have another job like this one," she advised me, and she wanted to be sure I was keeping a record of it. At her urging, I did keep a diary, and I did save many boxes of papers and memorabilia. At the time, I was dubious about the usefulness of such records, but now I am glad I have them, because they help me jog my memory so I can paint an accurate picture of the real Rose Kennedy.

Mrs. Kennedy was quite aware of the fact that even when I worked for her, people frequently asked me what she was like. I remember one conversation we had about it: When I confirmed that it was true that people often asked me about her, she asked me eagerly what I said! I answered that she was too complex a personality to describe in a few short sentences. It would take a book. . . .

Here then is my answer to the question. See for yourselves the charming, aggravating, amusing, maddening, admirable woman who was Rose Kennedy.

2

What Does "the Secretary" Really Do?

As I pulled into the driveway of the Kennedy compound in Hyannis Port one summer day in 1974, I thought about my coming interview with Rose Kennedy, who was looking for a new private secretary. My own feelings about the job, then as now, could best be described as ambivalent.

How do you get to be the personal secretary of one of the world's most famous women? In my case, it was entirely accidental.

I had gone to live on the Cape in 1967 after my marriage ended. Our family had known happy times there during summer vacations, which is per-

haps what made it attractive to me at that moment.
I bought a comfortable house big enough for myself
and my two children, Kathleen and Kevin, then
school age. The cozy familiarity of life in a small
town on the Cape seemed like just what we needed,
after years of moving with my husband to such
disparate places as Cleveland, Ohio, and Tokyo,
Japan. We had all learned a lot from the traveling
we had done, but I felt it was now time to put down
some roots.

As soon as the three of us were settled, I began
to look around for some kind of work to keep me
busy and to supplement my income. When I was
single, I had worked as a secretary in Washington,
first for the FBI and then in the office of a congressman. My experience on Capitol Hill had prepared me for virtually anything . . . or so I thought
until I met Mrs. Kennedy.

I found a part-time job doing secretarial work
for a prominent local businessman; the convenient
hours made it possible to see my children off to
school in the morning and be there when they got
home in the afternoon. There was a part-time bookkeeper in the office, who mentioned that she had
formerly worked for ''the Ambassador,'' as Joe
Kennedy always liked to be called. Since his stroke
in 1961, there had been no need for the large business staff he had once employed, but she still kept
in touch with the remaining clerical staff at the com-

pound. She knew that they were often overburdened by the work load of that busy family, especially in the spring of 1968, when Bobby was making his bid for the presidency.

Then came the tragic news of Bobby Kennedy's assassination at his victory celebration in the California primary. The increased volume of mail and renewed press attention on the entire family made it impossible for Mrs. Kennedy's secretary to keep up. Would I consider taking some work on?

The circumstances seemed ideal. I could pick up the typing work and do it at home in the late afternoons and evenings. It would bring in some extra money, and it might be fun, too; once again I would feel connected to world events. I told the bookkeeper I was interested.

Only a few days later I got a call from Mrs. Kennedy's secretary, Denise Smith, asking if I could come to her house that evening to pick up some work. When I got there, I thought the poor woman looked positively exhausted. Denise said she had been working six or seven days a week, and yet she was still far behind. Unwilling to keep up the demanding pace any longer, Denise was resigning. But she wanted at least to clear up the backlog of correspondence before a new secretary came on the scene. She gave me a pile of routine letters that needed only standard replies and dictated more personalized answers to other letter-writers. As I staggered to the door with my assignment, she cautioned me, "No one at the compound knows about this. I cleared it with the Kennedys' New York office, and you'll be paid directly by them. Don't tell Mrs. Kennedy!" It was by no means the only time I was to hear that warning.

Together we worked to clear up the backlog, and by the end of the summer, Denise was able to leave. The Kennedys, as usual, went to Palm Beach that fall, and I remained to winter over in gray Hyannis. But the following spring, I got a call from Mrs. Kennedy's new secretary, Diane Winter. Like Denise, she urgently needed help. I understood why as soon as I walked into the charming cottage the Kennedys had rented for her in Hyannis Port, just around the corner from the compound. Her entire living room was filled with stacks of file folders, unopened mail, packages, and newspapers. Diane moaned that some of the filing that needed to be done was more than two years old.

For the first few weeks of that summer, I went to Diane's house three nights a week to help her try to cope with the overflow. But someone must have decided that it was all right to tell Mrs. Kennedy about the work I was doing, because Diane soon suggested that I start coming to the Kennedys' house to do typing and filing there. A makeshift office was set up for me across the hall from Diane, in a little first-floor nook the family called the Golf Room because it was where they kept their clubs and golf shoes. I did my typing on an antiquated steno desk someone had dug up and my filing on the floor, where I could sort things into piles.

I was then only a secretary's secretary, but occasionally I caught sight of my real employer, Mrs. Kennedy. The first time she passed my door, she looked in and said, "Good afternoon. Diane tells me that you have two children. How lovely! How are they? Thank you for coming," and walked quickly on without waiting for a reply. She was dressed in a wide-brimmed straw hat, Bermuda shorts, white bobby socks, and funny black shoes that looked old-fashioned and "sensible." On most occasions when I subsequently caught sight of Mrs. Kennedy, she was on her way through the hall where I worked to the garage to get into her green Buick sedan and dash off to do an errand or play a round of golf.

At other times, I would catch sight of her walking across the wide front lawn that sloped down to the sea. Her small figure—Mrs. Kennedy was only about five-one—was almost obscured by the confusion of dogs, grandchildren, nurses, and domestics, yet she always seemed to be the focal point of the composition. She habitually acted calm and cheerful. Even in periods of great stress, her attitude was "business as usual." I remember that I had to go to the compound on the Sunday morning after the news of Chappaquiddick broke, to drop off eighty-five letters I had typed that needed Mrs. Kennedy's signature so they could go out Monday morning. Of course, I had heard the shocking news of Ted's accident on the radio that morning—or at least the sketchy details that were first released —and I was a bit apprehensive about what I would find when I got to the Kennedy house.

To my surprise, Mrs. Kennedy appeared quite serene. She and her daughter Pat were having breakfast together and talking normally about nothing in particular. Then I caught sight of Senator Kennedy walking out of Ethel Kennedy's house with a man whose face was unfamiliar to me, and the Senator was smiling in his usual jovial manner. It was my first glimpse of the famed Kennedy ability to remain outwardly unruffled no matter what the crisis. I would have thought it was just another summer Sunday at the compound if I hadn't later seen those same two men, now looking very worried, pacing the beach in coats and ties, quite obviously discussing the situation and how it should be handled.

My recollections of that summer of 1969 are nearly all pleasant ones. My office was packed with interesting memorabilia, including a charming painting by Jackie of all the children at Hyannis Port, standing on the jetty waving at the Ambassador's plane as it circled overhead. There were family snapshots and the framed historical treasures of a check signed by Thomas Jefferson and the first airmail letter flown into Surinam by a young pilot named Charles A. Lindbergh. The house was full of people coming and going, and out of the corner of my eye, I could watch the passing parade: Joan Kennedy looking very pretty and very pregnant; Bobby and Ethel's children Joe, Bobby, and David stopping by to see their grandparents; dogs passing in and out; the Senator striding through the front door of the house and calling out to his mother. Through my office window, which was adjacent to the kitchen, there wafted wonderful smells of baking cookies and big family feasts being prepared. Outside, there was the well-kept lawn, the blaze of flowers, and always the noise of children having fun.

Yet, in retrospect, I realize that the summer of 1969 was a hard one for Rose Kennedy. First there was the news of Jacqueline Kennedy's marriage to Aristotle Onassis, which brought a flood of correspondence, much of it hostile. Then there was Chappaquiddick, another event that created public dismay and private sorrow as well, both for the tragedy of the life lost and for the career shadowed. And underlying all the news of that summer was the obvious decline in the Ambassador's health. For years after his stroke, although he was unable to either walk or talk, Joe Kennedy remained very much the master of the house. Things were done his way; his comfort and convenience were the overriding imperatives; and his pleasure and approval were still anxiously sought. But by the summer of 1969, it was obvious that he was sinking, and that fact dominated the emotional atmosphere of the entire compound.

By the time the Ambassador died that fall, I was no longer working for the Kennedys. Discouraged by the heavy burden of Mrs. Kennedy's correspondence, I had found a full-time job elsewhere. My daily routine was now much calmer, but occasionally I missed the excitement of the days at the Kennedy compound. Still, I had never really known anyone there very well, neither family nor staff. The Kennedys were just another memory, a good topic of conversation at parties, a remembered highlight of my life, like the time some twenty years earlier when I had a chance to meet the Duke of Kent while on a skiing holiday in Austria.

I did make a point of keeping up with the news of the Kennedy family through Joe Gargan, who was a vice-president of the Hyannis bank where I later went to work. Joe was Rose Kennedy's nephew and Teddy Kennedy's companion since boyhood. Once or twice he had mentioned that the full-time job as Mrs. Kennedy's secretary was available (there seemed to be quite a turnover). But with my two children at home, the travel involved was impossible. And I still remembered the terrible burden of the work there.

Then, in the summer of 1974, Joe once again asked me if I would consider working as Mrs. Kennedy's secretary. At this point, the notion appeared more feasible. Since my children were now away at school, I would be able to travel back and forth between Palm Beach and Hyannis Port. But did I want to take on something as strenuous as the job of Rose Kennedy's secretary? I remembered those former secretaries who were virtually buried under the heavy load of the work involved. Surely the rapid turnover in that position was no mere coincidence. When I expressed these qualms to Joe Gargan, he reassured me. "Since Uncle Joe died and Aunt Rose had her stroke last February, things have definitely slowed down. It's a different job these days."

Just how different I was soon to learn for myself.

At Joe's urging, I called the latest secretary, Jay Sanderson, to set up an appointment to see Mrs. Kennedy. Jay had recently become engaged and was anxious to locate a suitable replacement so she could leave to be married. She said she was sure I would find the job much easier these days than I remembered it and suggested that she schedule an interview for me with Mrs. Kennedy right away. "Let's make it for some time after work," she said. "Mrs. Kennedy will be impressed with the fact that you are too hardworking and prudent to take time off from your present employer.''

I dressed for that 8:00 P.M. interview with great care, hoping my navy blazer and white skirt would strike the right balance between professionalism and the modesty appropriate to secretaries. Instinct told me to enter the house through the rear service entrance, as I had always done when I worked there before. I was greeted by a maid, who introduced herself as Jeannette and added, to forestall confusion, that Mrs. Kennedy always pronounced her name "Janet." She showed me into the living room, and then I heard Mrs. Kennedy's familiar voice call down from the head of the stairs, "Is the guest here?"

She came down immediately. I stood and smiled as she made her entrance, dressed in a short-sleeved white suit I recognized from a picture of her on the cover of *Look* a few years earlier, along with suitable costume jewelry and what seemed like a lot of makeup for an elderly lady. I stepped forward and offered my hand. She grasped it warmly, saying, "Sit here with me on the couch, dear." I learned later that the couch was held in high esteem, since it was the one in the Kennedy house in Bronxville, New York, on which Cardinal Pacelli had sat when he came to tea a few years before he became Pope Pius XII. To Mrs. Kennedy, it was ever after a treasured memento.

I had been somewhat nervous about this interview with the famous Rose Kennedy, who had always before seemed so distant, and it didn't help that she turned up looking exactly like a picture on a magazine cover. Yet, to my great surprise, I found her very easy to talk to. She quickly made me feel comfortable, and the questions she asked me about myself seemed interested rather than threatening. She mentioned, as she looked at my résumé, that she didn't remember I had worked there in the past. I said it was in the summer of 1969 (the labors of 1968 were still a secret). She replied, "Of course, that was the year Mr. Kennedy died," and then her voice trailed off and she looked into space for a few minutes as the burden of memories came back to her.

Suddenly snapping back to the present, Mrs. Kennedy mentioned that her need was for a social secretary. Would my business experience be appropriate for dealing with the kind of correspondence I would have to handle? I suggested that to give her reassurance, I would type up a sample letter. To do so, we walked through the back hall to the secretary's room, where I went to the desk and took out a piece of Mrs. Kennedy's gray stationery, engraved by Cartier's. This familiarity surprised her, especially in view of her own repeated protest that she knew nothing about the "office."

Mrs. Kennedy gave me a hypothetical case of

someone who had invited her to attend a luncheon and asked me to write a letter declining the invitation. She was happy with my finished letter, but I wasn't, for I noticed how faint the ink was. "There's something wrong with the ribbon on this typewriter, Mrs. Kennedy," I said. "It's so pale, I think it needs to be changed." She took the letter again, adjusted her glasses to look at it more carefully, and agreed, "Yes, you're right, it does." She seemed delighted that I had discovered a flaw, and from that moment, it was clear that she wanted me to be her secretary.

"The hours are nine to five. Mr. Kennedy always liked the secretaries to be in the house all day, so Janet will fix lunch for you here." She paused, and her next words seemed just a bit disgruntled. "I don't know what the pay is. You'll have to settle all that with the New York office." With that, the business discussion was over. "Do you think you'll enjoy going to Florida in the winters?" she asked almost teasingly.

"It should be nice to escape the winters on the Cape," I responded, "and I have relatives there I'll enjoy seeing."

In a flash, the atmosphere changed. "Yes, well, of course, that's personal," she said distantly. For Mrs. Kennedy, there was a wall of privacy around any personal matter—mine, hers, or anyone else's—and she didn't intend to see it breached.

After a moment, she showed me politely to the door (the rear door, so I knew I had guessed right about the status of "the secretary") and said she would like me to start as soon as possible.

Later, when I replayed the conversation in my mind, I worried about whether I was doing the right thing in accepting the job. Would the work be too much for me? Would Mrs. Kennedy? Still, I had by this time worked in enough offices to know how dreary a more conventional job could be. I hoped working for Mrs. Kennedy would give me an occasional taste of fun and the chance to meet some interesting people. Moreover, the compensation, when finally discussed with the New York office, sounded good. Not only would I get a reasonable salary, but the New York office would provide a place to live in both Palm Beach and Hyannis Port; I could sell or rent my own house and live rent free. They would also pay me for the mileage put on my car doing errands for Mrs. Kennedy and driving back and forth from Massachusetts to Florida. So I decided to take the job—and do my best to get all the fun out of it that I could.

I have to admit that my brave resolution was a bit shaken when I got together with the departing secretary for dinner before she left. Jay gave me a long set of instructions about how to handle the job. And my employer.

"Your day starts at nine o'clock when you

arrive at the post office. And be sure you leave on
the dot of five," Jay said sternly. "Otherwise, you'll
find that your hours simply get longer and longer.
Establish the precedent that you go out to lunch
every day. There's never anything to eat in the refrigerator, and the maid will *not* cook for you. And
whatever you do, don't agree to live in the house
or in the apartment over the garage, even for a short
period, or your life will never be your own."

Jay explained that the last few secretaries had
made some changes to lighten the work load. Many
letters could be answered with a simple engraved
card one of them had devised, which said: "Mrs.
Kennedy appreciates your interest and regrets that
she is unable to answer her mail personally." She
mentioned that after Mrs. Kennedy's stroke in 1973,
the doctor had decided it was necessary to protect
her from any worry. So I was to show her only three
or four pieces of mail a day—just the ordinary personal correspondence she would enjoy—and handle
the rest myself without telling her. She was to see
only bills under thirty-five dollars. Everything else
I was to approve and send directly to New York,
where it would be paid out of Mrs. Kennedy's account.

I got the feeling there was more Jay could have
told me. But she was anxious to leave and be married, and I was supposed to start immediately. So

she wished me good luck and assured me that I would learn all about the job as I went along.

She was right. But what I learned was not exactly what I had expected.

My first few days on the job were extremely puzzling. For one thing, I couldn't understand what had happened to the staff I had seen in the house back in 1968 and 1969. In those days, the bustling household was supported by a cook, two maids, a gardener, a chauffeur, a secretary, and of course a round-the-clock nursing staff for the Ambassador. Now the elderly Jeannette turned out to be the sole person working inside the house. She alone did the cooking and all the cleaning for the fifteen-room house and its occupants, and she also looked after Mrs. Kennedy and her clothes. The extent of her chores clearly explained why she told me firmly she would not cook for me no matter what Mrs. Kennedy's instructions were about eating my lunch at the house. How could she spare the time? With all the work she had to do, it wasn't surprising that she put her foot down about taking on more. Outside, there was only Arthur, who served as gardener, chauffeur, handyman, and keeper of the keys for all three of the houses in the compound: Mrs. Kennedy's, Ethel's, and Jackie's. He, too, had his hands full, especially since Mrs. Kennedy had given up

driving herself, after a minor accident that frightened everyone in the family. Occasionally men were
hired by the day to do heavy cleaning and odd jobs,
but day in and day out, the work of taking care of
that big place fell on just two people. According to
the local gossip, Mrs. Kennedy had fired the entire
staff after her husband's funeral, saying she could
no longer afford to keep so many people on the
payroll.

Another thing that puzzled me was why Mrs.
Kennedy was alone so much of the time. It was
July, the height of the summer season, and the whole
family was gathering in their respective homes. Ethel
was next door with all of her younger children, and
Jackie was at her house with its backyard bordering
on Ethel's. The Shrivers were only a few minutes'
drive away, and Teddy and his family were at Squaw
Island, out at the tip of Hyannis Port yet still within
walking distance for the active Kennedy family. Yet
with all those people around, Mrs. Kennedy still
spent most of her day by herself and ate her meals
alone.

Most puzzling of all was the total lack of security at the compound, and most particularly at
Mrs. Kennedy's house. During the peak of the tourist season, the town posted a guard on weekdays
only, at the head of the dead-end street that leads
into the compound, motivated at least as much by
a desire to prevent traffic jams of goggling tourists

as to protect the Kennedys. In the daytime, Arthur might be around to deal with intruders, unless he was driving Mrs. Kennedy somewhere, or way down at the other end of the property doing yard work. At night, there was no one in the big old house except for Mrs. Kennedy and Jeannette, who slept in—two elderly women all alone. The house was rarely locked; and even when it was, there were so many doors and windows in this oversize cottage by the sea that breaking in would have been child's play (as some of the grandchildren were later to demonstrate).

All in all, Mrs. Kennedy seemed curiously un-protected for a woman whose family had been the subject of public interest and private fantasy for so many years. One day, when Jeannette was off, Mrs. Kennedy and I were chatting in the kitchen as she made her own lunch of reheated creamed chicken (after refusing my offer of help). The two of us were alone in the house. Arthur was nowhere to be seen, and no one else appeared to be around the compound. "Mrs. Kennedy," I asked impulsively, "doesn't it worry you to be alone like this? Anyone could just walk in on you here in the kitchen."

"Nonsense," she replied with spunk. "No one would try anything with me." Then she added more thoughtfully, "I am an old woman, and the con-sequences would not be that great." She closed the conversation by strolling over to the refrigerator and taking out a dish of cold custard, which she promptly devoured with good appetite. Taking a few of her favorite sugar cookies from the tin on the counter, she went upstairs for her afternoon nap. Clearly she had no fears for her own safety . . . but I wondered if maybe the rest of the family sometimes worried about her there alone.

A few weeks later, my concern about this issue intensified, when it was discovered that a young woman was following Mrs. Kennedy back and forth to church and also trailing her on her long late-afternoon walks. One morning I found the woman sitting on the porch of the house that had been rented for me a few blocks away from Mrs. Kennedy's. When I got into my car, I found some papers she had left there—incoherent notes full of underlinings and exclamation marks. It turned out that she was an emotionally disturbed person who had decided she had to talk to Senator Kennedy about saving the world, and she thought his mother could lead her to him. The next time Teddy came to the compound, the woman caught sight of him. Having been briefed on the situation, he talked with her quietly for a few minutes in his car. Not long after that, she was taken away for psychiatric observation. I always thought it was both brave and kind of the Senator to talk to her, which made the eventual denouement all the more surprising: The young woman's father attempted to sue the Kennedy family for causing his daughter's emotional problems.

Gradually I began to realize how little of my time with Mrs. Kennedy would really be devoted to secretarial tasks. Although my day always began at the post office as I picked up the mail (the quantity sometimes required several trips back and forth to the car), it turned out that the mail was only the first and not the most important task of the day. I tried to sort it out roughly when I first came in, at the same time that Mrs. Kennedy returned from morning mass and had her breakfast in the dining room. By the time she was back upstairs in her bedroom, I had found the few personal letters I thought she might be interested in, and I was ready to go up to her room when she buzzed for me on the telephone intercom. That was the last moment of my day that could even be called routine.

From then on, the schedule was up to Mrs. Kennedy—and the results could definitely be unexpected. She might tell me to look up a word in the dictionary and type up the definition on a sheet of paper for her to memorize so she would be sure to use the word correctly. Or she might want to review some sketches she had requested from Paris designers for outfits she would buy on her trip there in the fall. She might issue instructions to call Eunice, Pat, and Jean and ask them to come look at some Sandwich glass they might like to have. She often asked me to drive her into town, where she would shop for underwear, or get her hair done, and perhaps attend midday mass if for some reason she had missed her regular morning attendance. There was a thank-you note to write to the nuns of the Sacred Heart convent who had sent her a cake (angel food, of course); an appointment to arrange for someone who wanted to take a picture of the needle-point piano bench cover made by Mrs. Kennedy's mother so it could appear in a book written by a friend of Jackie's; Pat Lawford's glasses, which she had left on her last visit, to be packed up and sent to her; a frantic search for the keys to Jackie's house when her burglar alarm suddenly went off at an incredible volume that could be heard all over Hyannis Port. Such crises were all in a day's work.

I also learned that I was sometimes going to have to act as Mrs. Kennedy's bodyguard. One afternoon I was working peacefully in my office when I heard loud noises coming from the dining room. I walked into the hall, and to my consternation saw a tall black man—I'm sure he couldn't have been shorter than six-five—strolling toward me. I drew myself up to my full five feet two inches and demanded to know who he was and how he had gotten into the house. He said he was collecting for charity and that when no one answered his knock at the rear door, he had simply walked in. Using the calmest voice I could manage under the circumstances, I told him this was a private residence and that he should speak to the gardener about any solicitation. Unfortunately the intruder showed no signs of departing. To my great relief, Arthur himself appeared at that moment, with the guard from the corner in tow. Their joint presence convinced the man to leave, and I breathed a sigh of relief.

Suddenly Mrs. Kennedy appeared at the head of the stairs, nostrils dilated and eyes blazing—a look I was to become quite familiar with. "I thought I told you to call me in time for my appointment," she said angrily. I looked at my watch and realized that she was right, I was several minutes late. Not wanting to alarm her unduly, I simply said that someone had come to the door and I had to make sure he was taken care of. She snapped, "I'm supposed to know about everything here. This is my house and that's what I'm here for." As I apologized, I thought to myself she seemed to intuit that something untoward had happened. As I was to learn in forthcoming years, it was not easy to deceive Rose Kennedy, no matter how kindly one's motives.

As time went by, I began to think of my position as being not so much that of secretary as of a lady-in-waiting. For example, since there was no maid to help Mrs. Kennedy with her clothes, I was the one to assist her in dressing when she made a public appearance: do up the tiny buttons, give an opinion about the choice of hat, perhaps help smooth out the rouge if she had applied it with too heavy a hand. Often I walked her to the car and waved her out of sight; just as often I myself might drive her where she was going. I tried to make a point of greeting her when she returned from some public event and helping her hang up the expensive Paris originals she wore for such occasions before she settled in for a restorative nap. Sometimes it seemed like a court ritual we were playing out.

Even when I accompanied Mrs. Kennedy, my lady-in-waiting status decreed that I tactfully remain a few steps behind. Jeannette had made this aspect of my duty clear from the outset. "If Mrs. Kennedy asks you to go into church with her some morning, be sure to sit in one of the pews at the back. She doesn't like to have people sitting up in front with her." In fact, she rarely asked me to attend with her, but she did sometimes ask that I come along and wait outside until she emerged. The church had both a front and a side door, and Mrs. Kennedy used them interchangeably, so I often incurred her wrath by being at the wrong door. I was the one who was supposed to be standing there waiting, not her!

Nowhere was that lady-in-waiting feeling stronger than in Mrs. Kennedy's own house. Apparently it had long been a custom for her children and grandchildren to stand as she entered a room. So when she and I would set off to do an errand or check up on something around the house, visitors would bob up and down as we passed—me always walking a respectful distance behind Mrs. Kennedy. This happened even when she went out to the pool. All the relatives lounging around would suddenly leap to their feet to acknowledge her presence as I followed carrying her towel and robe. I am not exaggerating when I say that even the people *in* the pool tried to stand up.

A lady-in-waiting was supposed to supply companionship when it was needed and, just as important, to recognize when it wasn't. It was only my second day on the job when Mrs. Kennedy asked me if I would like to swim with her. I said I would love to, but I didn't have a bathing suit with me. When she assured me that she could find an old suit that would fit me, I realized that she was genuinely eager to have company.

Together we walked down that famous path to the sea, where the Kennedys had so often been photographed. As we waded into the water, I began to have second thoughts. It was after all only early July, and the North Atlantic waters of Nantucket Sound were still rather chilly. When I shivered and squealed, Mrs. Kennedy said firmly, "Posh, this isn't cold. I grew up swimming in the Maine waters, and this feels warm by comparison." I wondered about the advisability of her swimming in such cold water, for I knew she had had a stroke the year before and I had seen in the files instructions from her doctor that she was not to swim in water colder than eighty-six degrees. Yet there she was, bobbing happily around in the calm ocean. So I plunged in to paddle by her side. She was very gay and light-hearted that afternoon, and I thought to myself, "It would have been fun to know her when she was younger." I had the feeling the young Rose Kennedy would have made a good friend, the kind who could turn even ordinary everyday life into a bit of a lark. That afternoon was the first time I heard her endearing, really quite girlish giggle—a sound I would grow to cherish.

We often swam together after that, especially in Palm Beach, where there was rarely a member of the family to go in with her. I enjoyed it because she was a good companion during those times. Besides, what office job can offer you the perk of a daily swim, either in the ocean or an Olympic-size heated pool? And in addition to the health and beauty benefits, I got to chat familiarly with Rose Kennedy—not a bad way to spend an hour of a working day!

Shortly after we began to swim together, Mrs. Kennedy one day suggested that I have lunch with her. It was lovely sitting at the old polished table, carefully placed in front of the dining room windows to get the best view of the sea, and chatting with Mrs. Kennedy throughout our leisurely hot meal of broiled chicken and rice and pureed carrots. But that day proved to be my only opportunity for such enjoyment. Jeannette, who had silently set a place for me when instructed to do so by Mrs. Kennedy, caught me almost immediately after lunch to protest. She didn't intend to wait on other staff members, she reiterated, and if the matter came up again, she would complain to Mrs. Kennedy. I didn't want to turn the situation into a crisis, so the next time Mrs. Kennedy asked me to join her for lunch, I said that I thought Jeannette didn't like it and I would go out for lunch as usual. She made some sharp remark about how she would run her own house any way she wanted to. But in fact she dropped the matter, and no further lunch invitations were proffered. I had the feeling she would have liked the company but she knew she would pay dearly for disturbing the domestic equilibrium.

That incident illustrated one of the difficult aspects of the job. As Mrs. Kennedy's private secretary, I necessarily became acquainted with many intimate details of her life. I saw her private face rather than her public one, and that inevitably made me feel emotionally involved. It was not easy to think of working for Mrs. Kennedy as just another job, or one of the world's most respected women as just another boss. By the end of my first week,

I had already grown very protective of Mrs. Kennedy and very concerned about her welfare. I became upset when I thought people were not considering her wishes or looking after her health properly. It was necessary to work at reminding myself that Mrs. Kennedy was not a favorite elderly aunt but rather my current employer.

I believe Mrs. Kennedy, too, found it difficult to maintain the emotional distance of an employer. Yet she knew the dangers of becoming attached to people whose presence was only temporary, for the one or two or three years they might remain in her employ. In many ways, Mrs. Kennedy was a very warm and very caring human being, and that inner warmth often prompted her to disregard the fact that I was "the secretary" and reach out to me with friendly gestures. Then she would remember that I just worked there and that, like the long string of secretaries before me, I would probably be leaving in a matter of months. So she would bend over backward to establish the difference between personal and professional.

An example came that first summer in Hyannis Port when Carol Channing, who was appearing at the Cape's Melody Tent, paid a visit to Mrs. Kennedy. Carol was a friend of Mrs. Kennedy's daughter Eunice. She was always very nice about offering tickets to everyone in the compound, including the staff, who wanted to see her show. Thanks to her kindness, I had tickets to see it later in the week, so I was looking forward to getting an up-close glimpse of the star herself.

Mrs. Kennedy, Eunice, and Carol sat chatting in the big wicker chairs on the veranda, enjoying the sunshine and the wonderful view of the sea. After a while, Ethel came over with two of her children, Joe and little Rory, to join the group. While they were all gathered outside, I happened to walk by the maid's dining room, where I spotted Jeannette sitting tranquilly. I asked her if she was going to serve them something to drink, like lemonade or ice tea. "No," she answered flatly. "I'm not a serving maid. I don't have the right uniform. Besides, I'm too busy doing everything else around the place." I had read in a magazine somewhere that Carol Channing was a health-food addict who always brought her own food and drink along with her when she went to parties. For her sake, I hoped she had brought something with her on this visit, because it was obviously the only way she was going to get any nourishment.

After a while, Mrs. Kennedy brought Carol in to look at the family photos and mementos that covered every available inch of wall space in the sun-room. Since my office not only adjoined the sun-room but actually had a door opening into it, I was excited by the prospect of getting a chance to see the star in person. I heard footsteps approaching my door—and then, to my chagrin, I saw Mrs. Kennedy's hand reach across and close it firmly. The incident made me realize that whatever kind of personal rapport Rose Kennedy and I might succeed in establishing, there would always remain in Mrs. Kennedy's eyes a gap in our roles. To her, we were employer and employee, madam and staff.

It was interesting to see how the rest of the family regarded my status. Both Ethel and Jackie were extremely courteous, not just at our first meeting but always. Ethel, trimly dressed in navy slacks with a matching cardigan tied around her shoulders, introduced herself and shook my hand. Jackie, whom I first met as she came strolling back from the beach in a small but very becoming bikini, said, "Oh, you must be Gramma's new secretary, Barbara," and went on to make a few minutes of polite conversation.

This was in marked contrast to the reception I got from the Shrivers. The first time I met Eunice, I was sitting in Mrs. Kennedy's bedroom discussing a letter. Eunice ran in and without apology interrupted our conversation to ask her mother about plans for her upcoming birthday celebration. She was wearing shorts and an old white T-shirt, and she had apparently just washed her hair without bothering to take the time to comb out the tangles or smooth it away from her eyes. When their conversation was finished, she simply turned on her heel and left the room as abruptly as she'd entered it. I was surprised she didn't nod or glance in my direction; she came and went as if I weren't there at all. Her husband, Sarge, had an even odder response to meeting me, when I ran into him one day in the hallway. I knew who he was, of course, from photographs, but I assumed he didn't know who I was and that the proper thing to do would be to introduce myself. "Hello," I said, smiling, "I'm Barbara Gibson, Mrs. Kennedy's new secretary." He glanced at me briefly. "Well, lah-dee-*dah*," he said, and kept on walking.

By my second week on the job, I had met nearly all the members of the family, as they gathered in Hyannis Port to celebrate Mrs. Kennedy's birthday on July 22. There was to be a big clambake on the front lawn, and the plans and preparations were swirling all around me. The volume of mail suddenly picked up, as friends and strangers sent their best wishes. I counted more that 450 cards alone, not to mention the constant deliveries of presents and flowers. I showed a stack of cards to Mrs. Kennedy, who said with a glint of triumph, "I should be the one who's running for office!" The morning of the day itself, when the tour boats passed in front of the compound, they each dropped anchor and all the tourists aboard sang "Happy Birthday." She enjoyed stepping out on the porch to acknowledge the tribute with a wave.

I commented on all the excitement her birthday seemed to be creating, and she said sagely, "All this will soon calm down. . . . and then something else will happen. This is a big family, and there is always some kind of excitement."

Most of the time I spent with Mrs. Kennedy was very rewarding. I loved to listen to her comments on current events. That summer was the time of the Watergate scandal, which she followed closely and with great interest. Rather than rejoicing in the Republican scandal, she thought about the personal tragedies. "All those men," she said to me one day, "what will their families do?" Later she remarked approvingly, "Mrs. Ford has a very nice smile. They make a nice-looking couple." Prince Charles was much in the news that summer, and about him she said simply, "Everyone has their own destiny. They just have to work it out."

In fact, she was a keen observer of everything that passed before her. From her windows at "the big house" in the compound, she was able to see everything that was going on, and she was quick to comment. Once, after seeing Sandy Eiler, the stout man whom the Shrivers had for several years hired as a sort of athletic director for all the kids in the summer, she dictated this note to Sarge: "Please tell Sandy to start wearing a shirt. I am sick and tired of looking at his navel. Every year it becomes more prominent.'' She watched Ethel's children pedaling around the circular drive in front of her house in a small open racing car. ''Call Ethel's house,'' she asked me, ''and tell them to please put that contraption away in the garage. I told them last summer I did not want to see the children playing in it because it is too dangerous, and I'm not going to tell them again.'' I made the call to Ethel's secretary and relayed the message, and almost immediately there was no small vehicle to be seen.

Although Mrs. Kennedy was sometimes a bit imperious, she could also be very warm and friendly. I was touched by her evident enjoyment of our conversations about the latest fashions or some new kind of makeup that was being advertised for its revolutionary benefits. Sometimes I had to pinch myself to remember that this was a woman in her eighties, because she was still so interested in every detail of her appearance. At times, Mrs. Kennedy could also be rather maternal. On one of the rare days when she didn't feel up to swimming, she encouraged me to go in alone, which I did, enjoying the soothing motion of the summer-warm ocean. When I emerged from the water and headed up the path toward the house, I saw Mrs. Kennedy waving to me from the porch. ''Yoo-hoo,'' she called, ''are you all right?'' She had put off taking her nap so she could watch over me all that time. I felt both happy and embarrassed (especially since this whole episode was being avidly watched by a boatload of tourists passing in front of the compound).

One day when Mrs. Kennedy and I were enjoying the bright sunshine as we paddled around in the bay, I told her how much I appreciated the chance to swim with her regularly and what a pleasure it was to have so varied a routine on the job. But I added that I was worried that I would slip behind in the typing and filing and correspondence. She looked at me with a wonderful sparkle in her eye and said, "Don't worry about the mail or the filing. Just keep me happy."

I tried my best.

3

Mrs. Kennedy and "the Children"

To my surprise, Mrs. Kennedy's children seemed to be almost as much in awe of her as I was. The more I watched their behavior in her presence, the more convinced I became that they, too, respected her greatly. They were just as susceptible as the rest of us to that look of disdain she could assume.

Sometimes I found it hard to believe that her children were so daunted. After all, although she called them "the children," they were in their forties and fifties. Eunice Shriver, Pat Lawford, Jean Smith, and Ted Kennedy were fully mature individuals with significant accomplishments and responsibilities of their own. They themselves had almost grown children; they were independently wealthy; they held important positions in government and administered a major charity. A scan of the media proved that they were frequently photographed, looking appropriately cool and self-assured, mingling unselfconsciously with the rich, famous, and powerful.

But back in their mother's house, these world-renowned figures reverted to the status of children, seeking to please the woman who to them symbolized the powerful authority of the adult world. That frail octogenarian, who weighed less than one hundred pounds and stood barely over five feet tall, easily dominated them all.

I first noticed this situation only a few weeks after I began working for Mrs. Kennedy. She and I were up in the attic of the Hyannis Port house, a storehouse of family treasures and trifles where Mrs. Kennedy sometimes spent hours sifting through the past. She had asked Eunice to join us to take a look at something she was considering giving away. (Jackie once astutely observed that "Gramma is never going to be happy until she gets that attic totally cleared out.") Eunice was fidgeting impatiently as her mother and I sorted through a pile of neatly labeled boxes, and her obvious restlessness attracted Mrs. Kennedy's attention. "Be still, Eunice," she snapped, using just the voice in which you might address a rambunctious child. Eunice—then fifty-three years old, the mother of five children, the wife of a former ambassador, the capable and energetic head of the Special Olympics and other successful programs for the retarded—obediently backed into a corner and didn't move again.

Over the next few years, I was to see continual evidence of the combination of respect and awe all Mrs. Kennedy's children had for her. "Don't tell Mother" was for all intents and purposes the motto of the family. For example, once in Palm Beach, Pat Lawford borrowed her mother's almost new Lincoln Continental for a quick trip to the Publix supermarket. In the parking lot, someone backed into her and scraped the side of the car. "Don't tell Mother," she insisted when she got home. "I don't want to upset her. Let's just get the car fixed without telling her." That was easier said than done. Mrs. Kennedy went to mass every morning and often went shopping on Worth Avenue in the afternoons as well. There was no way the absence of the car would go unnoticed. Finally the chauffeur and I worked out an elaborate system by which the car was always parked so that Mrs. Kennedy would get in on the side without the dent. This charade went on for several weeks, until Mrs. Kennedy went to Washington for a few days and the car could finally go into the shop. In the end, she never did find out about that dent.

"Don't tell Mother," said Jean Smith as she asked me to try to get a telephone line installed in the guest bedroom she always used when she visited Hyannis Port. "Don't tell Mother," I was cautioned one hot day when Eunice fainted on the pier and fell into Nantucket Sound. "Don't tell Mother," said Pat on giving me two bottles of wine from the supply of Beaujolais Villages that was her private stock in Palm Beach. The number of things I was not to tell "Mother" multiplied as the months went by.

Unquestionably Mrs. Kennedy loved her children. She once said to me, right out of the blue, "You know, it's funny. You would cut your arm off for your child," and then laid her own arm on the kitchen table. After a thoughtful pause, she added sadly, "But you would do nothing for your mother." To her, this difference was a simple fact. All her life, she had made her children's welfare her first priority, and even in her eighties, she continued to try to watch over them. When she thought it advisable, she didn't hesitate to intervene in their affairs. At an age when many women are content to hand over their responsibilities to the next generation and sit back in their rocking chairs, Mrs. Kennedy remained not just independent, but still fiercely maternal—still, as her son Jack had once expressed it, "the glue that held the family together."

Yet along with her love came what she believed

to be a mother's inalienable right to criticize. Perhaps that was what made her children so anxious about her opinions. In their individual ways, they tried their best to please her.

Teddy Kennedy, her youngest child and only surviving son, seemed to be the most successful in achieving that goal. It was obvious that the bond between mother and son was a very special one. With him, she was always at her sparkling best. When Pat or Jean or Eunice came to visit her, she appeared for the family lunch ready for her nap, in her usual pink pajamas and a dressing gown. But when the Senator (as she always liked to hear him called) was expected, she would dress in one of her vivid suits from Courrèges and even put on a matching wide-brimmed hat to preside over the table. Her manner with her son was almost flirtatious: She assumed a coquettish walk and something of a little-girl voice. She seemed to bask in his warmth, and she often commented that Teddy was the only one of her children to inherit her own father's wonderful sense of humor.

It was true that the Senator could be extremely charming. When I first met him, I was impressed by how much more handsome he looked in person than in photographs. To be perfectly truthful, I thought he was one of the sexiest men I had ever met! I was sure the reports of his career as a ladies' man were not exaggerated; he both looked and behaved the

part. And he could be very funny . . . not so much
by telling jokes as by seeing the humorous side of
everyday life. One morning in Palm Beach, as the
whole group was setting out for mass, the cook was
the last to appear, and she had to squeeze into the
front seat between Teddy and the chauffeur. "I can
tell you're not a ninth child," he teased. "You don't
know how to push your way in." He could even
be funny in writing. In the files, I ran across a
hilarious letter he had written to all the ushers at
his brother Jack's wedding. His cook showed me a
postcard he had sent her from England, showing
the troops at the changing of the guard at Buck-
ingham Palace and on the back the droll message,
"I have invited all these men to lunch when I return."

Yet even Teddy came in for his fair share of
critical comments from his mother. Many of them
were about his weight, since Mrs. Kennedy (herself
a lifelong dieter) considered excess poundage practically a mortal sin. When the Senator came to Palm
Beach, Nellie the cook always made his favorite
dessert, a chocolate roll of rich fudgy cake that was
carefully rolled up with thick whipped cream. When
he showed signs of wanting a second helping, his
mother would scold him like a little boy. His response was equally boyish. He would accept the
reprimand with a blush and then after dinner slip
out to the kitchen to help himself to another slice

of the calorie-laden dessert. "Don't tell Mother," he would warn Nellie as he gobbled down his forbidden treat.

Mrs. Kennedy also corrected her son's grammar when she detected an error. In a speech on the danger of drugs that he made while testing the waters for the 1976 presidential campaign, the Senator began a sentence with "If I was President . . ." His mother promptly fired off a letter dissecting his mistake: Since he was discussing something that was contrary to fact, he should say "If I *were* President . . ." She had me type this up neatly on her best white stationery with the blue border, and then she used one of her favorite ploys for backing a step away from the responsibility of writing the letter. She told me to add in the bottom left corner that the letter had been "dictated but not read," and I signed her name as her secretary. Teddy was so amused by this missive that he had it framed and mounted on the wall of his Senate office.

But not all of her criticisms of her son could be taken so lightly. One day, for some reason, the topic of Chappaquiddick happened to come up. Mrs. Kennedy said quite frankly, "The whole thing was so stupid. I don't blame people for thinking what they did. Mr. Kennedy always told the boys, 'Never go to parties alone. If you want to be in politics, you can't sit in the Stork Club every night with a girl on your arm. Make up your mind.' " In 1980,

she once again criticized her son's public behavior.
"I don't like to see him run against Carter," she
told me when I stopped to visit her in Hyannis Port
(I was no longer working for her at that time). "It
breaks up the party."

It was clear that a major reason for Mrs. Kennedy's underlying favoritism toward Teddy was that
he was a man, in a family that was conditioned (by
Joe Kennedy, I gathered) to accept male dominance.
I remember a speech she made in the ballroom of
Boston's Sheraton Hotel when Teddy was campaigning for re-election to the Senate in 1978. She
first amused her audience by telling them how critical many people were when they learned she was
to have a ninth child, after it seemed the family was
complete. "They warned me I would lose my figure, I would be tied down for years to come, I would
never escape the demands of such a large family."
Then, after a dramatic pause, she shifted the mood
entirely by concluding somberly that if she hadn't
had a ninth child, she would not today have a son.
I looked around and there was not a dry eye in the
audience. Later that year she underscored her views
on the dominance of the male sex in a letter to her
granddaughter Kathleen, saying that she would rather
be known as the mother of a great man than to be
a great woman herself. I wondered how Bobby and
Ethel's daughter, a thoroughly competent young
woman who was thought by some to be the most

gifted Kennedy of her generation, responded to that notion.

I'll never forget the day in Hyannis Port when Mrs. Kennedy's stoic mask slipped for a moment and revealed the depth of her sorrow over losing those great men who were her sons. Mrs. Kennedy and her daughter Jean were talking about dinner that night, and Mrs. Kennedy inquired who was coming to join her. "I'll be here, and Eunice and Pat are coming, and so is Ethel." Her mother's obvious unresponsiveness led Jean to continue. "What more could you want?" she asked teasingly. In a low but carrying voice, Mrs. Kennedy uttered her desire, never before spoken but probably continually in her heart: "I want my sons."

That special feeling about sons expressed itself in many little ways. For example, Mrs. Kennedy, who had been giving away some of her more valuable possessions (both to make sure they were distributed the way she wanted them to be and to avoid heavy inheritance taxes for her children in the future), decided that Teddy should have the complete set of silver from the Palm Beach house. An ornate pattern adorned with a lion's head, it was not only worth a great deal of money (a complete service for twelve plus extra pieces such as a cocktail shaker and an ice bucket) but obviously carried precious memories. She tried to make her decision sound strictly logical; after all, his initial was "K," which was what was engraved on the silver. When someone brought up the fact that Ethel and all of her children had the same initial, Mrs. Kennedy abruptly changed the subject. Mrs. Kennedy later told Eunice that she wanted *her* to have an old English cream and sugar set, but it turned out that she expected her daughter to *buy* it. Eunice handed over a check for four thousand dollars without comment.

I could see why Mrs. Kennedy might take special pleasure in making gifts to Teddy. Whatever his mother gave him—family photos, posters from World War II, a fifty-dollar check for Christmas— the Senator always appeared extremely grateful. Once when he came to lunch with her at Hyannis Port, she told me to run up to the attic and get a set of highball glasses we had found there. The glasses were nothing special, and they came with a plastic tray that would look out of place in any well-decorated home. Yet when I came into the room bearing this dubious gift, Ted showed nothing but happiness. "Maybe I could use this on the boat," he said, thanking her warmly. Perhaps that quality of appreciation on his part was why the tone of her letters to him seemed especially warm and loving. I remember a lovely note she slipped in with his Christmas check one year that mentioned her "heart full of love and appreciation for all you have done throughout the years."

It was impossible to tell whether her daughters

ever resented this special treatment accorded their younger brother. Of all the "girls," Eunice was the one who seemed to be closest to her mother. They shared an interest in helping the retarded, and they were similarly energetic and determined women. Eunice's need to stay active every waking moment of her life struck me as nearly obsessive. I felt she was competing not really with others, but with something inside herself; it seemed as if she was trying to prove something to herself all the time. Perpetually on the go, she was demonstrably less domestic than the other women in the family. Her household simply ran itself, lurching along from one problem to the next. Turnover of staff at the Shrivers was high. Not only was she a very demanding employer, but a difficult one as well. I was told by one of her employees that Eunice had a way of giving everyone unsigned and therefore nonnegotiable paychecks just as she departed for a long trip. In the all-too-frequent periods when Eunice's house was understaffed, she or her daughter, Maria, often called Mrs. Kennedy's cook to ask her how to prepare something. One morning they phoned bright and early to find out how to cook bacon!

It was typical of Eunice that even though she didn't know much about cooking, she undauntedly set about preparing the family meal. Nothing fazed her. I remember the time in Florida when she was late getting dressed and the rest of the family left (in the only car) for mass without her. The unstoppable Eunice simply walked out on North Ocean Boulevard and waved at passing cars until one picked her up. This episode made the local paper, because in exclusive Palm Beach, hitchhikers are about as common as snowballs.

I always thought Eunice cared more for getting things accomplished than she did about the feelings of the people involved. Yet she was certainly an obedient daughter, and she was also a good mother. I did notice, though, that whenever Mrs. Kennedy wanted to discuss what she thought was a problem with one of the Shriver children, she addressed her note to Sarge rather than to Eunice. He was undoubtedly the head of that household.

If Eunice was Mrs. Kennedy's favorite daughter, she could also be the one to cause the most vexation. Mrs. Kennedy was constantly irritated by Eunice's sloppy grooming. "Eunice never did have any flair for clothes and she never cared about her appearance," she once complained. "I used to be ashamed of the way she looked. I was afraid people would think I neglected her." When Mrs. Kennedy went to Washington to attend a benefit for the retarded sponsored by President and Mrs. Ford, she came back shaking her head about the way Eunice had looked: She had lost the belt to her dress and never even noticed it was missing. When Sarge Shriver made his bid for the presidency in 1976,

Mrs. Kennedy decided she had better help Eunice pick out clothes for the campaign. She came back from her shopping trip in the fall of 1975 with practically nothing for herself. "Like a dumb bunny, I spent all my time helping Eunice," she explained. Another time when she was passing through New York, she stopped into Bergdorf Goodman and picked out something she thought would be suitable and had it sent to Eunice. As it turned out, this caused a flap when her other daughters found out about it. In the end, she had to buy them new dresses, too.

Eunice often acted without thinking about the problems she would cause other people. If she passed through Mrs. Kennedy's kitchen and spotted a freshly baked cake, she would simply dig out a handful for an instant snack. If she was having dinner guests at her own house in Hyannis Port, she would drop by her mother's and help herself to the carefully arranged vase of flowers on the dining room table (much to the annoyance of Jeannette, who had done the work of arranging them). She would call to ask Mrs. Kennedy's staff for all sorts of services: searching for a pair of missing earrings (later found in her own house), ordering me to send her a small package by air express, and similar chores.

These requests were usually accompanied by the injunction "Don't tell Mother." But sometimes it was impossible to hide such things from Mrs. Kennedy's vigilant attention. Once, for example,

Eunice called me to ask for the number of the Senator's Washington office, and it just happened that I took the call in Mrs. Kennedy's bedroom, where we were working together. Of course she overheard the conversation, and the result was a reprimand to Eunice. Mrs. Kennedy paid my salary, and she wanted no one else to encroach on my time. The strangest part about this episode was the fact that Eunice got furious at me because she concluded I had "tattled" to her mother. For weeks afterward, whenever I happened to bump into her doing something around Mrs. Kennedy's house, she would say sarcastically, "I suppose you're going to tell Mother all about this."

Pat and Jean seemed to have a more placid relationship with their mother. She did criticize both of them for their drinking, although she didn't realize the extent of it until she began to read hints in the newspapers. Mrs. Kennedy herself never drank, and she was opposed to drinking on principle: "I think it's stupid," she said emphatically. She once told me, "My husband used to say I was terrible because he made a lot of money from liquor and I never drank any." She considered the purchase of liquor an unnecessary expense, and moreover she was convinced that if she kept liquor in the house, the staff would drink it right up. So generally her daughters had to bring their own supply, creating a situation in which drinking took on the character of a secret and solitary vice. Various members of the family would keep their favorite wines in their rooms when they came to visit. Characteristically, an exception was made for Teddy. When he came to Palm Beach, I was always sent out to the liquor store to get some rum so he could mix up his renowned daiquiris. Everyone in the family loved them. So much so that the first time I was sent on that errand, I failed to buy enough rum; the Senator ran out by lunchtime on Sunday and had to ask a favorite restaurant to open up and sell him a bottle.

Pat, the only member of the family without a summer home on the Atlantic coast, was a frequent houseguest in Hyannis Port and in Palm Beach as well. Like Eunice, she was capable of being a demanding guest, deputizing staff members to take care of errands and asking for favors such as picking up a copy of a best-seller and sending it to her air express. Once when I went to meet her at the airport, she arrived with only one bag, but a very heavy one. I offered to get her a porter, but she curtly refused. As she picked up the bag, I said dubiously, "That looks very heavy." She snapped, "It is! I thought you were going to help."

Her personality was a moody one, and she could be very determined about getting her way. On one occasion she and Eunice were planning to go to Boston together, and when her sister was a few minutes late, Pat simply drove off without her, much to Eunice's dismay.

The quietest member of the family was Jean Smith. For the most part, Jean seemed to go her own way. And since the Smiths had sold their summer house in Hyannis Port and bought one in New York, none of the family appeared very frequently. Like everyone else, Jean did come for Mrs. Kennedy's birthday in July and the big get-together over the Labor Day weekend that amounted to an annual family reunion. I happened to overhear an unsettling interchange between Jean and her mother on the subject of Jean's childhood as we were all swimming in the Palm Beach pool. Jean remarked, "I was shuffled off to boarding school at the age of eight," and Mrs. Kennedy replied somewhat defensively, "Well, what was I to do? Your father was always gone, or we were having dinners at the embassy or attending formal affairs. I had no time to spend with you children." Jean ended the conversation almost casually by saying, "That's why I'm still trying to get my head on straight." Her words made Mrs. Kennedy furious. She sputtered and stammered and then got right out of the pool. Even hours later, I could tell she was still nettled by her daughter's remark.

Mrs. Kennedy's maternal sensitivity to the slightest hint that her children had turned out anything but perfect made me understand why the thought of Rosemary, her retarded daughter, still caused her such torment. Rosemary lived under the meticulous care of the nuns at St. Coletta's in Wisconsin. From the time she went there in late 1941 until the summer of 1974, when I started working for Mrs. Kennedy, she had never left the vicinity of the convent. Mrs. Kennedy told me she visited Rosemary every year, and she had always wanted Rosemary to come home for a visit. But the Ambassador disapproved, on the grounds that it would be too upsetting for all concerned. It was not until five years after Joe Kennedy's death that his widow decided to do as *she* thought best. Rosemary came to the Cape in August.

She was the oldest surviving member of her generation—at that time in her fifties, although she looked much younger, with only a few strands of gray in her short curly hair. Tall and somewhat heavy, she was still pretty. Scanning the collection of family photos on display in the sun-room, I always thought the young Rosemary was the prettiest of all the girls, with a smooth, round face and very regular features. She was good-humored, and she generally liked to be around people. She had trouble with my name and ended up calling me "Arbarb," but she invariably greeted me with a smile. So pretty and agreeable—and heart-wrenching.

Rosemary's original mild retardation had been severely complicated by the results of the lobotomy

she had undergone in 1941, when her usually agreeable temperament began to show signs of deterioration. Mrs. Kennedy told me that while she was
away from home, her husband had authorized the
performance of the operation in the belief that it
would calm Rosemary down. The unfortunate results were not only a dramatic increase in her retardation but also a mild paralysis of her right side;
she dragged that foot and had trouble controlling
her hand. Of course the Kennedys had been heart-
sick over this turn of events, and Mrs. Kennedy was
particularly upset by the loss of all the things she
had slowly and painstakingly taught Rosemary to
do. "I was so provoked. After all my work . . .
she was even presented at Court . . . and she was
reading and writing and showing so much improvement." Mrs. Kennedy had even gone to the trouble
of learning to print her own letters instead of using
script so they would be easy for Rosemary to read.
But all that was beyond her reach now. . . . In all
the years I worked for her, I never heard Mrs. Kennedy question her husband's judgment about anything, but I speculated about whether she sometimes
blamed him for Rosemary's condition. Of course
he had done all he could to provide for her financially. There was money in trust to guarantee good
care all her life. At the convent she had her own
house and her own car so she could be taken on

outings. She even had a mink coat, to ward off the chill of the Wisconsin winters.

During Rosemary's visit, Mrs. Kennedy seemed virtually haunted by thoughts of her daughter. If we were working in her bedroom, she would suddenly get up and peer out the window that overlooked the sweeping lawn, hoping (or fearing?) to catch sight of Rosemary. In the middle of dictation, she would get up and walk to the window. "Where is Rosemary now?" she asked herself. After a long pause, she would murmur, "The poor little thing. . . ." One day when Mrs. Kennedy and I were swimming in the pool, the nuns brought Rosemary out, too. But she simply sat in one of the chairs at the side, not even glancing in our direction. Mrs. Kennedy gazed at her daughter for a long time, and for once her sorrow was plainly visible. At last she sighed, "Oh, Rosie, what have we done to you?"

Mrs. Kennedy constantly tried to elicit some sign of affection from her daughter. She spent time with her, and she did her best to make her happy. One day when the two of them were waiting for lunch to be served, Mrs. Kennedy settled Rosemary on the living room sofa and went herself to the piano, sitting on the bench covered by her mother's old needlepoint. She began to play some of her old favorites in the hope of soothing Rosemary. But her daughter reacted restlessly to this form of communication, and Mrs. Kennedy finally had to give up the attempt. Often Rosemary deliberately turned away from her mother, and occasionally she even lashed out at her in anger and hostility. One of the nuns told me that Rosemary couldn't forget how her mother tried to push her to keep up with the others when they were children and that she still felt resentful. I felt so sorry for Mrs. Kennedy, who simply would not stop trying to make some loving contact with her daughter. Perhaps this was especially important to her because of her awareness of some of the costs of her focus on Rosemary. She said in a letter to Ethel and Bobby's daughter Courtney that she felt she had neglected Jack because she was so frustrated and disconcerted by his younger sister Rosemary's insoluble problems.

The visit seemed hard on them both . . . maybe Joe Kennedy had been right after all. Rosemary was obviously bewildered by the change in her normal schedule and at times seemed virtually exhausted by the demands placed on her. One of the nuns said as they left, "Rosemary is very tired. She's not used to all this activity. She lives a very quiet life at the convent." The house itself had an upsetting effect. One day I heard her muttering "Kathleen" over and over; being in Hyannis Port again must have reawakened many memories of the long-dead sister who was closest to her in age.

Mrs. Kennedy's other children did their share

to make Rosemary's visit a good one. The Senator took her and the nuns out on his big boat for the afternoon. And Eunice was wonderful with Rosemary. The way she talked to her was perfectly natural and easy. She never sounded condescending or acted like she was talking to a child. Of course, Eunice had experience with the retarded. She didn't just work for the cause; she became personally involved. And, like her mother, she had been a faithful visitor to the convent in Wisconsin, so the sisters had forged some sort of relationship. Kennedy-like, Eunice tended to plan a full day of activities for Rosemary, including swimming and sailing, but I think Rosemary was often frightened by these experiences, especially since her physical disability made them difficult for her. But Eunice, sure the exercise would be good for her, always insisted.

Over the next few years, Rosemary's visits finally became routine: a winter visit to Palm Beach and a summer visit to Hyannis Port. She was accompanied by two nuns because she required constant attention. She was very likely to wander off, especially if she saw a child. Eunice once tried to take her shopping and lost her in a department store—an event that was quickly picked up by the newspapers. Rosemary was always the subject of media interest. There were constant requests for stories about her, and one journalist even wrote to ask for an interview with Rosemary herself. A photographer in Palm Beach did succeed in getting pictures of Rosemary, and much to Mrs. Kennedy's distress, they were published in the *National Enquirer*.

Each of Rosemary's subsequent visits was just as traumatic for Mrs. Kennedy as the first. Tense and strained while her daughter was there, she nevertheless drove herself to spend as much time with Rosemary as possible, even insisting on going to the airport and sitting with her indifferent daughter in the VIP lounge until her plane began boarding. Mrs. Kennedy invariably became sick for days afterward and often had to stay in bed to regain her strength. She had severe headaches and her stomach was badly upset. The doctor who was called in during one of these inevitable collapses said plainly that he thought Rosemary's visits were simply too much for her and ought to be stopped. I agreed with him, because the toll they took on her was so obvious.

I would have liked to enlist the aid of Mrs. Kennedy's children to do something about the situation, but I had by that time already learned that they were not likely to help. It wasn't, of course, that they didn't care about their mother's welfare. Rather it was that they remained unable to alter the relationship that had existed since they were small children. Their mother was the one who told them what to do, not vice versa.

My first realization that Mrs. Kennedy's children would be of no help in getting her to look after herself came in the affair of the stair railing. In the Palm Beach house, the curving front staircase that rose from the foyer to the second floor was made of stone, with a stone wall as well, and the rather steep stairs had no railing. This worried me for Mrs. Kennedy's sake. She sometimes wandered around the house late at night without adequate illumination, and she often wore floppy slippers and long pajama bottoms (the elastic at the waist kept wearing out) that could trip her up. At her age, even a short fall down those treacherous stone stairs could be a serious matter. My concern doubled when I happened to notice deep grooves in the stone wall by the bend of the staircase—the marks left after years of Mrs. Kennedy's trying to dig her nails into the hard stone for support.

The obvious solution was a railing that she could hang on to while walking down the stairs. I discovered an attractive wrought-iron type, in keeping with the Spanish interior of the house, that could be installed for only a hundred dollars, and the New York office gave me the okay to have it done. But, of course, Mrs. Kennedy would have to be told that we proposed to spend the money. Although many expenditures were made without her knowledge, the whole point of installing a railing was for her to notice—and use—it. As I feared, she agreed in

principle that a railing would be a good idea but
balked at the cost. Since we seemed to be at an
impasse, I decided to appeal to the Senator for help.

He was due to spend a weekend in Palm Beach
soon, I knew. So I telephoned his Washington office
and spoke to his secretary, the ever-reliable Ange-
lique. Would she slip a note to the Senator as he
left for the visit? Just explain the situation and ask
him to try to persuade Mrs. Kennedy to install the
railing. It seemed like a reasonable request, but I
saw when he arrived that he was not planning to
get involved. He had come down for a vacation,
not an argument with his mother. The first time we
were in the same room together, he gave me his
coldest stare, as if daring me to raise the disagreeable subject. Needless to say, the railing was not
discussed . . . and when I left years later, Mrs.
Kennedy was still walking up and down those steep
stone stairs with nothing to hold on to.

Some months later, I tried once again to enlist
the Senator's aid in looking after his mother. This
time it was in regard to Mrs. Kennedy's consump-
tion of sleeping pills. She took them when she had
had an upsetting day or when she hadn't gotten
enough exercise to make her physically tired at night.
The problem was that, like many older people, she
was not careful about how many she took or when
she took them. The result was that sometimes she

didn't wake up as usual the next morning. The maid and I would find her spread-eagle on the bed, and it sometimes took a frighteningly long time to rouse her. Even after she was up, she was only marginally functional for much of the rest of the day, sometimes stumbling when she walked and unable to carry on any extended conversation.

Another aspect of this situation that worried me was the variety of sleeping pills she had and might take. To begin with, she had about nine different doctors (in Boston, New York, Washington, and Florida) and they were all writing prescriptions without knowing what else she might be taking. But she had other sources of sleeping pills as well. Friends and family members picked them up for her whenever they traveled to countries (Switzerland, for example) where they were sold over the counter rather than by prescription. I remember one time when Sarge called to be sure that Mrs. Kennedy had received the fifty sleeping pills he had bought her in Switzerland and sent to the house with thirteen-year-old Anthony Shriver. It seemed to me that at the very least, *one* of Mrs. Kennedy's doctors ought to be aware of all the medication she was taking, so he could check them for side effects or interactions that might be harmful. Such a step seemed rational; after all, she was a frail woman in her eighties who had recently had a stroke. Moreover, it was obvious that someone needed to talk to her about the dangers of these pills and alert her to be more careful with them.

I first attempted this mission myself. One summer morning in Hyannis Port, Jeannette and I once again discovered Mrs. Kennedy unable to get up because of the effects of her pills. Together, we finally managed to get her up and dressed, and then I walked her back and forth on the wide front porch overlooking the ocean for more than an hour. During this period, I screwed up my courage and told her it was dangerous for her to take pills like that. She said challengingly, "How do you know so much about it?" I couldn't help being amused: Here she was, groggy and still disoriented, yet she was just as scrappy as ever! I told her somewhat weakly that I had read a lot about it, but I could see her skepticism about this secondhand expertise. So I switched the ground of my argument and told her to think about what the press would say if something were to happen . . . the headlines would scream that Rose Kennedy took an overdose of sleeping pills. She responded immediately. "Yes, yes, you're right about that." For a time, she was more careful. But eventually she became forgetful again.

I wrote a personal note to the Senator explaining the reasons for my concern. I received a lovely note from him in return saying, "I appreciate your letter and I just wanted you to know that I'm giving it some thought and will be back in touch with you.'' But, in fact, I never heard from him further about the matter.

Instead, not long after, I received a call from Eunice, whom the Senator had apparently gone to about the problem. She said she hoped I would not get discouraged and that the family appreciated all I was trying to do. But she avoided the central question of what to do to help Mrs. Kennedy be more careful about taking sleeping pills. The next link in this chain of events was a conversation with Pat Lawford, who told me that in the future I was not to bother the Senator about Mrs. Kennedy's problems; from now on, she, Pat, would be in charge of the situation. By this time, however, I was not the least bit surprised that Pat had no intention of confronting Mrs. Kennedy on the subject either. When I brought it up, she simply shrugged and said, ''No problem.'' On one occasion, when I pressed her tactlessly, she said, with a note in her voice that sounded virtually helpless, ''There's nothing any- one can do. Once Mother makes up her mind about something, that's it.''

Finally, after another groggy morning, I did get results. Jean Smith called and instructed me to go immediately into Mrs. Kennedy's bathroom, col- lect all the sleeping pills, and flush them down the toilet. ''But don't tell Mother,'' she warned. Of course, I was all in favor of the idea, but I have to

admit that as I crept into Mrs. Kennedy's bathroom
while she ate lunch downstairs, I was just plain
scared. I could all too easily imagine her expression
if she happened to come in and find me at work.
In a way, my pounding heart made me part of the
family, as I, too, was hesitant to incur Mrs. Kennedy's wrath.

After her lunch, Mrs. Kennedy went upstairs
for her nap. A few minutes later, she walked down
the hall to my office and asked if I knew anything
about her missing sleeping pills. I could only lie,
saying, "Oh, no, Mrs. Kennedy." About half an
hour later, she was back. "Are you sure you don't
know anything about my sleeping pills?" she demanded. I saw that as usual it was going to be
impossible to deceive her, so I admitted the truth.
"Everyone was very concerned about you, Mrs.
Kennedy," I explained. She tossed her head angrily. "Hmfph! How can they do this to me, treating
me just like a child!" Even at her age, she was set
on her independence. She went back to her bedroom, and immediately the light on one of the phone
lines went on; it was easy to guess she was calling
the children to give them a piece of her mind. As
it happened, she couldn't reach anyone at that time.
And after a few days, the whole thing blew over.
Later I found out why Mrs. Kennedy forgot the
matter so quickly: She had a secret cache of pills

in her traveling case and was still getting into them. As usual, she had defeated all of us.

She did it again over the issue of her stomach problems. Her stomach was very easily upset. It seemed like all the emotions she managed to refrain from displaying in any other way went right to her digestive system. Then she would be unable to eat even her usual bland diet and suffered discomfort that could keep her in bed for several days. She once told me she was sure she had ruined her stomach by the decades of rigorous dieting it had required to keep her slim, youthful figure. By the time I knew her, she had for years been unable to eat anything but simple dishes such as baked chicken, custard, and pureed vegetables. No salads, no spices, as little fat as possible, lukewarm beverages, meals eaten at precisely the same time every day: She was a slave to her stomach. Her only weakness was dessert, and especially a crisp sugar cookie made from a favorite recipe in *The Fannie Farmer Cookbook*. In both Palm Beach and Hyannis Port, the cook saw to it that there was always a fresh batch in the cookie jar, and Mrs. Kennedy helped herself whenever she walked through the kitchen. During one restless night, she managed to eat every cookie in the jar—all thirty-three of them! This may have been the occasion on which she made the discovery that there were always crumbs at the bottom of the jar that she hated to see going to waste. The next day, she ordered the cook to serve her the crumbs in a little bowl, and I have to confess I couldn't resist the temptation of walking by the dining room to see what she was going to do with them. She neatly solved the problem by pouring them over her usual dish of custard as a sort of crunchy topping.

But such binges were rare. It was more common to find her unable to take any interest in her food and suffering from painful stomach cramps and diarrhea. She had some medicine that she occasionally took at such times, but it had been prescribed many years ago, and her condition seemed to be growing worse. The obvious solution would be to see a doctor about the problem, but apparently that was one of the things Mrs. Kennedy had made up her mind not to do.

So the children resorted to a stratagem that was as comic as it was ineffective. When the Senator came down to Palm Beach one weekend that spring, he and Eunice invited Mrs. Kennedy's New York doctor, also in Palm Beach on a holiday, for cocktails one evening. He was supposed to observe her discreetly and then perhaps engage her in conversation about her ailment. Then, according to their scenario, he would make a diagnosis and prescribe medication that would be more effective. Since I wasn't at the cocktail gathering, I don't know exactly how Mrs. Kennedy managed to elude the doctor's scrutiny: whether she was uncomfortably aware of his interest and gave him a wide berth, or guessed at the plot that had been laid, or simply didn't find the man interesting enough to bother with. Whatever the reason, the doctor failed miserably in his mission and Mrs. Kennedy went along as before, having occasional bad spells with her stomach.

Another failure came when I brought up the problem of Mrs. Kennedy's long walks. She generally went out for an hour or more in the afternoon, but if she couldn't sleep, she might decide to have another stroll at ten or eleven at night. Since both her sight and her hearing were failing, I worried that she might lose her way. And what if she felt ill when she was out alone somewhere? Once she gave us a real fright in Hyannis Port when she went out for a walk on a rainy night that suddenly turned into a classic nor'easter. Jeannette called me at home around ten to say that Mrs. Kennedy had been out for nearly two hours and still hadn't returned. Beginning to imagine the worst, I called the police and rushed over to the house myself. Just as we were all working ourselves up, a vivacious (and thoroughly dry) Mrs. Kennedy appeared—in a car driven by thoughtful neighbors who had seen her sitting on their front porch to take shelter and had invited her in for a cup of hot tea. Needless to say, she was amused to find everyone so worried about her.

After that experience, I enlisted several of Ethel's younger children as a sort of makeshift patrol. Explaining my concern about their grandmother's habit of taking long walks at night, I asked if they could keep an eye on her without letting her know they were watching. Max, then about ten, was especially good about this, perhaps because he was just the right age to love engaging in such conspiracies. When she went out, he would trail her like a spy, lurking out of sight and concealing himself behind the bushes . . . heaven knows what the neighbors thought of it! Of course, it was no real solution to the long-term problem. But once again, Mrs. Kennedy's children, handicapped by their love and respect for their mother and perhaps most of all by their long tradition of obedience to parental command, were literally unable to intervene.

I could see that Mrs. Kennedy must certainly have been maddening at times to her family. About her children's affairs, she could be cool and critical. About her own, she was often headstrong and willful. Yet Mrs. Kennedy remained the center of her children's universe, just as they were hers. No family was ever bound together more tightly than the Kennedys.

4

The Magic Family

The time and energy that other women might spread out over careers and friendships and community service, Rose Kennedy concentrated entirely on her family. Her career *was* her family, and she ran it like the chief executive officer, with a CEO's concern for success. Her family also took the place of friends. Kennedys just naturally did things with other Kennedys, not outsiders. Even her charity work with the mentally retarded was merely an extension of her familial concern over Rosemary.

What journalists like to call "the Kennedy mystique" had become so strong that even the Kennedys themselves couldn't help but begin to believe in it. And much of that mystique emanated from the matriarch, Mrs. Kennedy. Ted might be the head of the family, but Mrs. Kennedy remained its symbol. She was the guardian of the traditions, the link to the past . . . no wonder the other Kennedys were always concerned about her opinion.

Like many people with roots in the nineteenth century, Mrs. Kennedy gave a broad definition to the concept of "family." It didn't mean just her children—although they were of course the first, the inner circle—but the entire web of relationships by blood and by marriage that had been created over three or four generations. All of these connections were important obligations in Mrs. Kennedy's eyes.

She was certainly a formidable mother-in-law. She accepted the husbands and wives of her children into the family, but she expected them to behave like Kennedys. And she always felt free to criticize . . . for someone's own good. For example, she sent Ethel a little note just before the annual RFK tennis tournament suggesting that she try to remember to stand up straight, as her bad posture often spoiled her looks in published photographs. She criticized Eunice's grammar after she was quoted as saying, "with whom I could not live without." Later she told Pat to be sure to use her verbs correctly and went on to give her two pages of examples, some of them rather bizarre: "The girls struck the house." "The lightning struck us."

Mrs. Kennedy delighted in giving both daughters and daughters-in-law "tips" about how to look their best in public. Amusingly, much of this advice she had herself received from England's Queen Elizabeth (the present Queen Mother). She told the girls they should always wear a hat that doesn't conceal the face; they should wear bright colors to stand out in the crowd; and they should remember to pose for photographs with their arms bent and held away from the body to create the illusion of greater slimness. If you look at photos of Mrs. Kennedy in her later years, you'll see she always bent her arms that way, even when she was sitting. Jean Smith once said laughingly that as far as she could see, the pose made you look as if your arm were broken!

Mrs. Kennedy made a special effort to remain close to her sons' widows, Ethel and Jackie. Of course, both of them had summer houses next to hers in the Kennedy compound at Hyannis Port, so it was easy for her to see them frequently. I thought Mrs. Kennedy always seemed particularly eager to please Jackie.

One reason for Mrs. Kennedy's attitude might have been her genuine admiration for the way Jackie had withstood the tragic events of her life. On one of the very rare occasions when the subject of President Kennedy's assassination came up, Mrs. Kennedy said to me, "I don't see how Jackie stood it, being there and witnessing all that." She later ex-

pressed another aspect of her feelings for Jackie in
a letter she wrote to Caroline at the time that Aristotle Onassis was gravely ill. She told Caroline
that she felt so sorry for Jackie, since she had had
so many trials in her life and was still so young. At
the time of Jackie's marriage to Aristotle Onassis,
in 1969, I read rumors that Mrs. Kennedy was very
upset about it. But I discovered that in fact she was
very supportive of Jackie's decision and seemed to
understand some of the reasons behind it. She commented that she thought Onassis was a very charming man, but not at all attractive, and usually rather
badly dressed in ill-fitting clothes, especially baggy
trousers. She compared his physical appeal unfa-
vorably with that of Lord Harlech, one of Jackie's
earlier escorts, but added with wry understanding,
"But then, of course, Lord Harlech didn't own private islands and yachts."

She always enjoyed the glamour of visits from
Jackie and Ari, and she liked to tell the story of the
time Onassis came to visit her in her New York
apartment. When he arrived, he gave her a little
box containing a gold bracelet with a snake's head
outlined in red and white stones. She thanked him
perfunctorily, assuming the bracelet was a piece of
costume jewelry he had picked up in a nearby department store. Some years later, she sent it with
some other pieces to be appraised and was startled
to learn it contained real diamonds and rubies.

I suspect that Mrs. Kennedy was quite impressed by Jackie's good taste and innate elegance. One time when Jackie was sitting in the sun-room of Mrs. Kennedy's Hyannis Port house, she happened to remark on how much she liked the fabric of the curtains (a flowered chintz with a white background) and how appropriate it was for the setting. She casually added that it might look nice to have the sofa and armchairs covered in matching fabric. Her offhand comment generated an absolute frenzy of activity. Mrs. Kennedy summoned Bob Luddington, a decorator from Jordan Marsh in Boston who often helped her with the Hyannis Port house, and told him to buy more fabric and have slipcovers made. The only problem was that the curtains were ten years old and the fabric long since discontinued. It took Bob months, but eventually he tracked down enough of the fabric to carry out Mrs. Kennedy's orders. Then it turned out that the new fabric didn't exactly match the old curtains, since they had yellowed from a decade of hanging in the sun. Still, Jackie proved to be right, and the sun-room did look more cheerful and better coordinated once the new slipcovers were installed.

Mrs. Kennedy's desire to please Jackie was especially evident one evening when she was coming over for dinner. All day long, everyone was running around at top speed, fixing the floral arrangements and digging up some special linen place

mats Mrs. Kennedy wanted to use. There was much
discussion of the menu, and the cook outdid herself
with *boeuf à la mode*, a splendid roast made the
real French way, soaked in red wine, enriched with
a good veal glaze, and finished with flaming brandy.
Dessert was a light but flavorful coffee mousse,
substituting Sanka so Mrs. Kennedy (who rigorously
avoided caffeine because it upset her stomach) could
have some, too. After the meal, Jackie complimented
the cook: "Oh, Nellie, you could go out there and
take a leaf from one of those trees and turn it into
something fabulous!" Such comments made it clear
why everyone tried so hard to please her.

I was always impressed by Jackie's tactful way
of dealing with Mrs. Kennedy. For example, during
the several years that Mrs. Kennedy was virtually
obsessed with cleaning out the attic in Hyannis Port,
she kept pressing on Jackie things she found there.
Some red glass vases, for example, quite obviously
didn't match the cranberry glass that Jackie had
painstakingly collected over the years, but Jackie
graciously accepted them and thanked Mrs. Kennedy with great courtesy. Later Mrs. Kennedy found
a pair of antique tin reflectors, the kind that were
once placed behind candles, and wanted to sell them
to her daughter-in-law. Jackie quietly paid the $170
Mrs. Kennedy asked for, even though with her con-
noisseur's eye she had noticed that the reflectors
were damaged and thus virtually worthless as an-

tiques. "I'm only buying those broken reflectors to make her happy," she explained. Once, when I went to Jackie's house to deliver something else Mrs. Kennedy wanted her to have, I said, "I guess you can put it in *your* attic." Jackie laughed and answered, "Oh, that's all right. I like old attics full of things to go through."

Jackie's gifts to Mrs. Kennedy were always very thoughtfully chosen: a huge white poinsettia to decorate the Palm Beach living room for Christmas, luxurious sheets hand-embroidered to match the color of Mrs. Kennedy's bedroom decor, an ornate silver cross she brought back from one of the Greek islands. In turn, Mrs. Kennedy often spent more time and thought on presents for Jackie than she did for most other members of the family.

Mrs. Kennedy usually dispatched her Christmas shopping quickly and easily by calling Elizabeth Arden's, on exclusive Worth Avenue in Palm Beach, and ordering a sweater sent to each daughter and daughter-in-law. But she was willing to spend more time looking for just the right thing for Jackie. One year she and I browsed in Courrèges, and she was on the verge of buying a simple white pullover to give Jackie for Christmas until she found out it would cost seventy-five dollars. "I'm not spending that much money," she said loudly, and made a quick exit. I was especially surprised by her change of heart because she was so fond of Jackie. But she

clearly felt that particular sweater was overpriced.
In any case, whatever Mrs. Kennedy finally selected, Jackie was always prompt and graceful in
her thanks. She was a good correspondent, and Mrs.
Kennedy liked to save her letters. I found notes
Jackie had written from on board the Onassis yacht,
the *Christina*, on the elegant pale blue stationery
provided for all passengers, and short letters describing a particular event, often addressing Mrs.
Kennedy as Grand-mère rather than Gramma. I even
found a letter that Jackie had written to the Kennedys when she and Jack were on their honeymoon
in Acapulco, full of amusing anecdotes: Jack catching a big sailfish, his efforts to speak Spanish, her
initial difficulty in learning to water-ski. That letter
left no doubt about the fact that Jackie had been
very much in love with her husband.

I thought another reason that Mrs. Kennedy
had a good relationship with Jackie was that she
and her children kept pretty much to themselves.
Despite the fact that Jackie's house in Hyannis Port
bordered Mrs. Kennedy's, they were rarely to be
seen, and Jackie never visited in Palm Beach the
entire time I worked for Mrs. Kennedy. She dutifully put in an appearance at Mrs. Kennedy's birthday party and the big Labor Day family get-together,
and she sometimes formally invited Mrs. Kennedy
to dinner and accepted similarly formal return invitations. But for the most part, Jackie went her

own way, and thus she and her household remained a kind of special treat to Mrs. Kennedy.

Ethel and her family, on the other hand, were constantly visible. Mrs. Kennedy had only to look out her dining room window or step out on her big porch to see everything that was going on next door at Ethel's house in Hyannis Port. Perhaps their relationship had more of the strains common to all close families.

Like most mothers-in-law who come into close contact with their daughters-in-law, Mrs. Kennedy was sometimes disapproving in her comments about Ethel. One of her favorite targets of criticism was what she called ''Ethel's extravagance.'' When I once commented how the smell of Ethel's perfume remained in the house long after she had gone, Mrs. Kennedy remarked drily, ''The rest of us buy French perfume by the ounce; Ethel buys it by the quart.'' (In all seriousness, though, Ethel's heavy scent did seem to bother Mrs. Kennedy because she switched from her long-time favorite by Guerlain when Ethel started using it.)

Ethel was quite knowledgeable about vintage wine and ordered her favorite Pouilly Fuissé by the case. She bought expensive leather belts by the half dozen, and when she liked a designer dress, she often ordered it in two or three colors. The food served at her house was always abundant and usually very luxurious—lobster tails, prime ribs of beef,

and other gourmet goodies, served to even the
youngest children. One night when Mrs. Kennedy
was invited to Ethel's for dinner, she asked me what
the menu was. I told her it would be Alaskan king
crab, rice pilaf, and spinach soufflé. In a tone of
mock awe, she responded, "Oh, my, what it is to
be rich!"

More disturbing to Mrs. Kennedy than Ethel's
extravagance was what seemed like her failure to
discipline her children properly. To be fair, the task
of bringing up eleven fatherless children could over-
whelm anyone. Moreover, the free and easy atmosphere of Ethel's home attracted all the other grandchildren, so disturbances originating in her house
were not necessarily instigated by Ethel's children.
But they did seem to be a noisy bunch, and they
might be found anywhere—playing on Mrs. Kennedy's lawn, running on the beach or frolicking in
the water, crashing around their own front porch,
or even climbing on the roof of their house. It was
just the sort of behavior to worry an elderly lady of
settled habits who had a natural concern for her
grandchildren's safety. Every summer, there would
be a barrage of notes and phone calls to Ethel's
household about problems caused by the children.
Mrs. Kennedy once commented that she thought it
was a shame the way things had turned out, after
they had conceived all those children. But Bobby
and Ethel were so crazy about one another. . . .

It seemed to me that Ethel tried hard to be considerate of Mrs. Kennedy. She was always polite and accepted the rather frequent admonitions from her mother-in-law as gracefully as the circumstances made possible. She understood Mrs. Kennedy's dedication to her regular routine and tried not to upset it. When she was a visitor in Palm Beach, she came prepared to fit right in; understanding that it would be difficult to keep her bathroom cleaned because of the usual shortage of staff, she simply asked for the necessary supplies to do it herself. Unlike most of "the children," she didn't make demands on Mrs. Kennedy's staff, and she was always especially nice to me, so I've always thought of her fondly. And she was considerate of her mother-in-law in small ways. She was the one who noticed (one day in church) that the good costume pearls Mrs. Kennedy usually wore were dirty, and she gave her a new strand; Mrs. Kennedy thanked Ethel in a warm letter that praised her for being wonderfully thoughtful. Ethel frequently invited Mrs. Kennedy over for dinner or sent her famous houseguests over to make a call on her . . . whatever might help make her mother-in-law a little less lonely.

I sometimes wondered if Mrs. Kennedy didn't also share a typical mother-in-law's jealousy of her daughter-in-law's relationship with Bobby. For instance, the one time the supposed affair between Bobby and Marilyn Monroe came up, Mrs. Kennedy said to me, "I don't believe it could have happened . . . Bobby was always so *sanctimonious*." It sounded almost as if she held it against him that he didn't have the roving eye so characteristic of the other men in the family.

For her part, Ethel remained devoted to Bobby's memory. She still wore his engagement ring and wedding band, and even when she traveled, a picture of Bobby in a silver frame was always on the table beside her bed. Yet according to one of the household staff, Ethel had angered Mrs. Kennedy the previous winter when she visited in Palm Beach and had dates with an unidentified "boyfriend," even going so far as kissing him when they were together at the house. I always doubted the gossip, because surely Mrs. Kennedy knew no one could ever take Bobby's place for Ethel. I remember one time when we were discussing Ethel and her children, and I said sympathetically, "She needs a man around, Mrs. Kennedy." She responded, "Don't we all!"

For me, Mrs. Kennedy's attitude toward Ethel was best summed up by a remark I happened to hear her make to herself. She was looking out the window at the scene at the house next door: children running and shouting, toys strewn all over the lawn, no responsible adult in sight. She turned away with a sigh and said almost angrily, "I don't know what

Bobby meant by going away and leaving Ethel with all those children to raise alone.''

Mrs. Kennedy's attitude toward her youngest daughter-in-law, Joan, was more puzzled than censorious. By the mid-1970s, Joan's drinking problem had become obvious, and Mrs. Kennedy was quite aware of it. Once, when Joan turned up in Palm Beach unexpectedly, taking a bus from Cocoa Beach where she had been visiting her mother, Mrs. Kennedy went into her bedroom to greet her. When she came back down the hall, she rolled her eyes, tossed her head, and said disdainfully, "Oh, *baby*!" In fact, Joan, who had been in the house only a few hours, was already packing to return to Washington. Shortly after her arrival, Teddy had telephoned and apparently read her the riot act, for she left as suddenly as she had arrived. On another of Joan's visits, Mrs. Kennedy must have decided to try physical therapy. Before poor Joan could even unpack, she was sent to the library to sort through the dusty volumes looking for signed first editions that might be valuable. She gamely stayed at this dirty and difficult task all afternoon and then shut herself up in her bedroom until the middle of the next day. (She and her husband had separate rooms, a fact I knew Mrs. Kennedy was unhappy about.) On another visit, Joan was assigned the task of checking the condition of all the lampshades in the house, so

Mrs. Kennedy could replace the oldest and shab-
biest of them.

It must have been unpleasant for Joan, the way
people were always watching her. Whenever her
husband saw her, he seemed to be peering at her
intently, as if trying to ascertain her condition. And
the rest of the family acted the same way. She attracted all this attention, even though she wasn't
the only person in the family who ever drank too
much. And she generally behaved herself perfectly
well. Drunk or sober, she was always soft-spoken
and ladylike. In some ways, she seemed more genuinely concerned about Mrs. Kennedy than anyone
else in the family—or at least more observant. On
one of her visits, she made the comment to me that
she saw that Mrs. Kennedy was not really "with
it" much of the time, and she intended to speak to
Ted about it.

At that time in her life, Joan simply seemed
to me like a victim of fate. Perhaps Mrs. Kennedy
had the same feelings, for she didn't really criticize
Joan. Instead, she tried to understand what was
wrong. According to her viewpoint, Joan had everything: good looks, a handsome husband, two lovely
homes, her own secretary, and three attractive children. If the marriage wasn't perfect, and the pres-
sures of fame were sometimes very great . . . well,
those were just things you had to learn to bear. Mrs.
Kennedy herself had borne as much, or more. She

had long ago adopted a philosophy of consciously trying her best to be happy, no matter what the circumstances, and this philosophic commitment was supported by her deep belief in God's goodness and His ultimate purpose. Rose Kennedy refused to consider her own marriage an unhappy one, although (to judge from published reports) there must surely have been periods in its fifty-five-year duration when she felt neglected, even betrayed. But she did her best to focus on only the good things: the beautiful homes, the achievements of the family, the comfort and security of wealth, the opportunity to travel and meet world-famous people. Her own attitude made Mrs. Kennedy literally unable to understand why Joan was suffering. But she tried. She treated her daughter-in-law kindly, spoke of her politely—but never truly could empathize with her, despite her efforts.

Mrs. Kennedy's relationships with her sons-in-law were even more distant. By the time I worked for Mrs. Kennedy, Pat had divorced her actor husband, Peter Lawford, so he never came to Mrs. Kennedy's.

Jean's husband, Steve, also stayed outside Mrs. Kennedy's orbit. Although Steve Smith ran the office in New York that handled the financial affairs of the entire Kennedy family, he had little contact with the matriarch of the clan. I remember that he came once to Palm Beach with Jean and the chil-

dren. He was scheduled to fly to New York for a
few days of business and then return to Florida to
finish out the vacation with his family. But just as
he was leaving for New York, Mrs. Kennedy asked
him—politely but firmly—not to return to Florida,
because the house was already overcrowded. That
was the last we ever saw of Steve Smith.

   I found his absence a little strange, in light of
the fact that he was so important to the family as a
financial manager and general troubleshooter. He
was an influential voice in the family meetings when
the assembled "elders" discussed things like where
the grandchildren should be sent for the summer
and whether Mrs. Kennedy ought to live with one
of the children. He was called in when a child was
in trouble or when legal problems loomed. For example, he made a trip out West to get Ethel out of
a lawsuit brought by a caterer when she refused to
pay his bill for a party she had given. He hired an
attorney and straightened the matter out for her—
and then, when he was ready to return to the East
Coast, Ethel told him there wasn't room for him on
her private plane, so he had to take a commercial
flight. Perhaps it was this sort of experience that
had taught him not to expect much in the way of
gratitude from the Kennedys. I understood he told
someone in the New York office that he was just
waiting for the day when one of the grandchildren
sued him for mismanaging the family funds.

Sarge Shriver was the son-in-law who had the most contact with Mrs. Kennedy. He and Eunice had their own house in Hyannis Port, and he often accompanied his family when they went to visit Mrs. Kennedy in Palm Beach. Sarge came from a well-to-do family and knew how the "old rich" lived, which was emphatically not the way Mrs. Kennedy did things at this period in her life. (Mrs. Kennedy once said of Sarge, "Blue blood, no money.") Mrs. Kennedy's eccentric economies always seemed to pain him. He reminded me of the princess in the fairy tale who was so thoroughly royal that she could feel a single pea through the thickness of a hundred mattresses. Although he knew perfectly well that there was only one domestic in the entire Palm Beach house, he persisted in expecting services possible only from a large staff. For example, one time (after he had just announced himself to be a presidential candidate) he asked me to see that his shoes were polished—as if we had a bootblack hidden away in the back of the house! I ended up taking them to a shoe repair shop to be polished. When Mrs. Kennedy learned that the bill for this service would be $1.50, she was very disapproving of such extravagance.

Sarge certainly could be lavish with other people's money. He was the one who talked Mrs. Kennedy into trading her Chrysler New Yorker in for a more expensive Lincoln Continental. Someone in the New York office commented about that, saying, "Sarge doesn't have two dimes to rub together, but he sure can spend other people's money." And he would casually order hundreds of dollars' worth of food and liquor in Palm Beach, to be charged to Mrs. Kennedy's account. But to give him credit, he wasn't stingy with his own money either. He would spend just as freely when he was the one picking up the tab.

One almost comical afternoon epitomized for me the difference between Sarge's accustomed ways of doing things and the way Mrs. Kennedy liked to run her household. In an outburst of hospitality during the Christmas holidays, Mrs. Kennedy had invited visiting socialite Gloria Guinness to stop in for a cup of tea at the end of her afternoon of shopping on Worth Avenue. She then asked her son-in-law Sarge to take charge of organizing the hospitality for this rare occasion.

Of course, there was as usual no liquor in the house, so Sarge came charging into my office a little before 5:00 P.M. to tell me to arrange to get something to drink. As it happened, I was helping a friend throw a party that night and with Mrs. Kennedy's permission was planning to leave fifteen minutes early. In fact, I was actually in the process of changing my clothes when Sarge burst in. I explained that I was leaving, but gave him the number of a nearby liquor store that always delivered promptly. His initial response was to make a sarcastic query about the hours I was supposed to work. He went on to complain about how the rest of the staff (that meant a total of two people, one of them temporary) were no help either. Then he asked me where to find a tablecloth. I explained that there were none in the house. Since Eunice had earlier asked me to run an errand during my lunch hour and pick up a rental projector to show a film about her brother Jack, I assumed the tablecloth was to be used as a movie screen and suggested Sarge use a sheet instead. He got very huffy with me, but I felt it was hardly my fault that Mrs. Kennedy didn't have any tablecloths.

It was evident that Sarge had riled both the cook and the maid with his spate of demands, and I was afraid there was going to be a domestic explosion before the evening was over. Both servants were perfectly capable of simply walking out if they got too annoyed, so I thought perhaps I should mention the situation to Mrs. Kennedy before I left. I knocked on her bedroom door and she called, "Come in." I did . . . to find my employer wearing a very dressy pinwheel hat and absolutely nothing else! I found conversing with a nude employer rather distracting, so I just quickly explained to Mrs. Kennedy that Sarge seemed to be upsetting the entire staff and the consequences might be disastrous. "Oh, I can't be bothered with that now," she said, as she continued to adjust the hat she planned to wear for Mrs. Guinness's visit. I fled, leaving the entire matter in the hands of fate.

When I came to work the next morning, I discovered a makeshift bar set up at one end of the living room, on a table covered with a white bed sheet. I giggled when I tried to imagine what the coolly elegant Gloria Guinness must have thought about that arrangement! In my office, I found a sixty-five-dollar liquor bill on my desk. And in no time at all, the maid was in my office to tell me how Mrs. Guinness had refused everything except a cup of plain tea.

Later that morning, Sarge appeared in my office and said Mrs. Kennedy had told him he must apologize to me. The effect of the apology was definitely undercut by his next remark, which was to ask me what he had done. I told him he couldn't order Mrs. Kennedy's staff around the way he had been doing. The house was understaffed in the first place, and the pay Mrs. Kennedy offered was so low that I had trouble finding replacements when anyone left. My temper then got the best of me, I'm afraid, and I concluded by telling him that slavery had been abolished one hundred years ago. Actually, when I cooled down, I had to admit that Sarge was only trying to be helpful in his own way. It certainly was true that, with her small staff and tendency to entertain so infrequently, Mrs. Ken-

nedy's hospitality was usually very hit-or-miss. He just never could get used to the limitations of Mrs. Kennedy's household.

I thought Sarge always tried hard to please Mrs. Kennedy. This was vividly demonstrated on an occasion when the Shrivers were visiting in Palm Beach as Mrs. Kennedy was preparing to make a short speech on some occasion on behalf of the retarded. Sarge—a former ambassador to France, running mate of George McGovern on the Democratic ticket in 1972, and presidential hopeful in the upcoming 1976 election—volunteered to help his mother-in-law write her speech. He really worked hard, spending the whole sunny Florida afternoon shut up in the library, diligently writing and rewriting and even calling his sons in to listen to excerpts of his draft. At last, when Mrs. Kennedy woke up from her afternoon nap, he proudly handed her the finished product. She read it over and then asked me to look at it when I came to take dictation in her bedroom. I could tell she was dissatisfied, so when she asked me what I thought, I gave her my honest opinion. "It's a nice speech, Mrs. Kennedy, but it just doesn't sound like you." She nodded her head in agreement and walked over to the open bedroom door. In her most ladylike manner, she caroled out, "Oh, Sarge, dear, I'm afraid it won't do." An ominous silence emanated from the library down the hall, where he had been waiting for the verdict.

I got the impression that Mrs. Kennedy was lukewarm at best about Sarge's career as a politician. She did make a few appearances on his behalf, and she also gave him money to finance his campaign: to my knowledge, about $50,000. But she seemed to regard his political ambitions as a sort of expensive hobby. I remember I once boldly asked her why the Senator didn't come out and endorse his brother-in-law, and she replied airily, ''Oh, he has good reasons.'' It was clear to me from her attitude that she thought her son was doing the right thing by remaining silent. After Sarge dropped out of the presidential race, there were rumors that he might run for governor of Maryland. Mrs. Kennedy said wryly, ''I hope not. I'm getting sick and tired of making contributions to his campaigns.''

Mrs. Kennedy's strong sense of family extended even to the families of her in-laws. When Joan's mother died, Mrs. Kennedy immediately arranged for a mass to be said for the repose of her soul. She also dispatched a warm telegram of condolence to Jackie's sister, Lee, on the death of her ex-husband, Prince Radziwell. She even maintained a little-publicized but quite strong connection with her daughter Kathleen's in-laws. I had read in many books that Mrs. Kennedy had been terribly opposed to her daughter's wartime marriage to the heir of the Duke of Devonshire because he was a staunch Protestant. Kathleen and Billy Cavendish met when

the Kennedy family was in England during Joe's tenure as ambassador. Her father sent the whole family home when World War II broke out, but Kathleen missed her friends in England and soon joined the Red Cross so she could return. She and Billy dated for some time but hesitated to marry because of their religious affinities. Finally, love triumphed and they were married at a registry office during one of his brief leaves from the front. He was killed in action not long afterward. According to some writers, Mrs. Kennedy never forgave her daughter for marrying outside the Catholic Church, and they were still unreconciled when Kathleen was killed in a plane crash in 1948. Of course, I don't know what happened back in the 1940s, but I do know that all the time I was with Mrs. Kennedy she corresponded regularly and affectionately with Kathleen's former mother-in-law, now the Dowager Duchess of Devonshire. She addressed her by her nickname of "Moucher" and kept her up to date with all the Kennedy family news. The dowager duchess responded in the same vein. The connection extended to the next generation as well, for I recall that the present duke (the younger brother of Kathleen's husband) stopped off to see Mrs. Kennedy one time when he was in the States.

Then there was Mrs. Kennedy's own Fitzgerald family. Mrs. Kennedy was one of six children of onetime Boston mayor John F. Fitzgerald, and at the time I started to work for her, all three of her brothers were still living. There were also the nieces and nephews, and the grandnieces and grandnephews, and another generation to come. . . . The Fitzgeralds all seemed to me to be common, ordinary people despite the advantages of John Fitzgerald's political success and Rose's wealthy husband. One of her brothers had been a ticket-taker at the Mystic River Bridge in Boston. Dave Powers, a former aide to President Kennedy, liked to joke about how whenever Jack had to use that bridge, he would slide down in the backseat of the car to avoid notice by his uncle. Another Fitzgerald brother lived in a trailer somewhere in Maine.

It was Joe Kennedy who initiated the practice of providing for the education of the Fitzgerald nieces and nephews, and of course, he did the same for the children of his two younger sisters as well. He had financed the education of fourteen nieces and nephews, and at the time of his death, he was doing the same for the forty-three members of the next generation. According to gossip, Joe Kennedy had never been fond of the Fitzgerald relatives, but he felt an obligation to help them help themselves.

Mrs. Kennedy continued the tradition established by her husband. As the years went by, she grew more and more generous toward the Fitzgeralds. She gave each of her brothers a large annual check—$20,000 to $25,000. Mrs. Kennedy also sent each niece and nephew a Christmas check to put away for their own children's education. Originally, the amount had been $4,000 per child, but by the early 1970s she had, at the urging of the New York office, cut that back to $3,000. By 1976, she had decided to stop sending money after the children reached the age of twenty-one. The last year I worked for her, the New York office insisted on slashing the amount to $500. For families that had as many as seven children and were accustomed to receiving a check for over $20,000 each year, that came as a big surprise.

Part of the reason for the cutbacks was Mrs. Kennedy's concern about the way the relatives were using the money. As someone in the Kennedys' New York office told me, "These people are able to send their children to schools you and I could never afford, Barbara." The problem in Mrs. Kennedy's eyes was that the children were being sent to expensive private schools from the time they entered first grade. She was opposed to that idea, not only because of the expense but also because she thought it was good for children to rub up against all sorts of people. It had been a good learning experience for her own children to attend public school when they were young, and she thought the same principle would apply to the grandnieces and grandnephews. She had been additionally distressed to discover that some of the children were not even going to college, despite all the money she had sent for their tuition.

Mrs. Kennedy once told me she thought she had given away at least $4 million to her relatives. Whatever the actual amount, it was certainly enough to disgruntle her children. One time when we were making the arrangements for one of Mrs. Kennedy's annual visits to Paris, she and I got into a bit of an argument: I wanted to have a limousine meet her at the plane and she said she would just take a cab. I thought it was a foolish economy for a woman her age after such a long trip and said so. Eunice, who had overheard my protestations, later said to me, "Mother's saving all her money for her relatives, so they can ride around in limousines after she's gone." Occasionally, even Mrs. Kennedy began to feel that she might have been too generous. In a letter to one of her Fitzgerald nephews, she commented astringently, "The Kennedy family money is not limitless."

She may have felt compelled to make that observation because the relatives were never reluctant to ask her for money. At the first sign of difficulty, they would turn to Aunt Rose, and although she might initially be irritated by the request, she would usually say yes. One niece, who had for a time been on welfare, received a subsidy of $10,000 to $15,000 a year from Mrs. Kennedy (she asked me dubiously if that was enough to live on). A nephew who had

gotten into some sort of a bind asked Mrs. Kennedy
to tide him over the rough spot, and she arranged
to have the New York office send him $400 a month
as a temporary measure. Then she forgot all about
the matter. Several years later, the New York office
asked me if I could discreetly find out if this fellow
still needed the money. I tried to discuss it with
Mrs. Kennedy, but I could see she didn't remember
anything about it. Since no one wanted to push Mrs.
Kennedy on the subject, the stipend continued—and
for all I know is still being paid to this very day.

   In addition to the outright gifts of money, Mrs.
Kennedy helped in other ways. She lent her sisters-
in-law her fur coats or her designer hats for special
occasions. All the nieces and nephews were invited
either to Palm Beach or Hyannis Port for an annual
vacation. In Hyannis Port, they were generally given
the unused apartment over the garage, formerly the
chauffeur's quarters. But she always saw to it that
the refrigerator was stocked with milk, orange juice,
eggs, bread, sodas, butter, and a cold roast chicken.
I once commented to Mrs. Kennedy that I thought
it was nice of her to do that for her relatives every
year, and she answered, "That's all right, my dear.
My relatives are all nice people and none of them
have any money. This is just a little something I
can do for them." I gathered that not all of them
were completely grateful. One year, a nephew asked
Mrs. Kennedy if she could send him money so he

could take a "real" vacation in Kennebunkport, Maine, instead of going to Hyannis Port. She was hurt by the request, but eventually she did give him the money he asked for.

There was a catch to her generosity, though. Those who accepted it were perennially treated like poor relatives by the Kennedy side of the family. It was very noticeable that Mrs. Kennedy's own children never mixed with "the relatives." Usually the relatives were only invited when the children weren't planning to be around; and if the children did happen to come at the same time, they barely seemed to recognize the visitors. It was really like a caste system, and "the relatives" were definitely at the bottom of the heap.

I noticed this attitude even in the Kennedys' treatment of Joe Gargan. The son of Rose's sister Agnes, Joe had spent most of his summers with the Kennedys after his mother died in 1936. He was especially close to Teddy, but he seemed devoted to all the family. He lived near them in Hyannis Port and looked after Mrs. Kennedy's house in the winter, going out of his way to keep an eye on the whole compound. Yet Joe was still undeniably "second string." When he brought his family to visit in Palm Beach, Mrs. Kennedy told him one night at dinner that his family ate much more than her children did. She suggested that they cut back on chocolate-chip cookies and added she was instructing the cook to cut pompano from the menu to compensate for the cost of their larger helpings.

I couldn't help but feel sorry for some of these guests, especially the ones who had no idea what they were letting themselves in for. I'll never forget the niece of Mr. Kennedy's who came to visit in Palm Beach. It was her first trip down in more than a decade. Her initial surprise came when I was the one to meet her and her daughter at the airport (in my little Plymouth Duster), rather than a chauffeur with a big car. All the way back to the house, she chatted about the good times she had had when she visited Uncle Joe there. She asked if his cabin cruiser was still there (of course, it was long gone) and continued to reminisce about past glories. I knew the poor woman was in for a shock and tried to prepare her for it.

But not even I realized just how awful their visit was going to be until we got back to the house. Naturally the staff the niece remembered was conspicuously absent. The only person available to help them struggle upstairs with their luggage was yours truly. Then when we went back downstairs to the vast and silent kitchen to look for something cold to drink, we discovered there was absolutely nothing in the refrigerator. Apparently the cook-maid had decided to go on strike when faced with the job of cooking and cleaning for these two extra people; she refused even to do the grocery shopping. So

Mrs. Kennedy entertained these bewildered relatives while I rushed out to the store for a few necessities. Later, when the chauffeur got back from
his regular nine-to-five job elsewhere, he went to
the supermarket to stock up.

By the next day, I had managed to get a temporary cook to come in to prepare a few evening
meals that week. The guests had to fix their own
breakfasts; for lunch, I drove them into town to a
restaurant. Sometimes on my way home in the evening, I would drop them off at a shopping mall or
a movie, just to give them the chance to get out of
the house for a few hours (of course, they had to
take a taxi back). It was obvious that they still wer-
en't getting enough to eat, since I kept finding candy
wrappers in their room. The poor niece never got
over her initial shock, and for an entire week she
wore a stunned expression on her face. She wrote
a very nice thank-you letter afterward, but needless
to say, she never came back.

Yet many of the relatives did come back year
after year. Whatever the discomforts, they still wanted
to see Mrs. Kennedy and counted themselves lucky
to be part of the magic. And Mrs. Kennedy, too,
never ceased to value the members of her extended
family, the clan she delighted in serving as matriarch.

5

Palm Beach

The place to observe all of the members of the extended Kennedy family, at their best and their worst, was Palm Beach. Mrs. Kennedy usually arrived at her home there in time for Thanksgiving, and she left shortly after Easter. In the interim, streams of visiting children, grandchildren, in-laws, and other relatives poured across the threshold. But for the life of me, I could never figure out why all those people wanted to go there.

My own first look inside the Palm Beach house was unutterably depressing. I traveled down from Hyannis Port in early October 1974 on the autotrain

that took me and my car to Sanford, Florida, which
was several hours' drive from Palm Beach. My first
problem was merely finding the place. The Kennedy
house is located on North Ocean Boulevard, locally
called Millionaires Row because of the cost of the
lavish oceanfront houses spread along its length.
But as is frequently the case in wealthy neighbor-
hoods, few street addresses were visible on mail-
boxes or front gates; the residents don't want to be
found by the casually curious. After driving back
and forth a few times, I finally stopped a gardener
working on someone's elegantly manicured lawn
and asked if he knew where the Kennedys lived.
He pointed down the road to a curve that was bordered by the rare sight of undeveloped land. "Just
look for the dark red doors," he said.

At first glimpse, the house seemed like a for-
tress. A tall hedge ran the length of the property on
North Ocean Boulevard, punctuated by only a few
openings; a big door painted dark red, with iron
straps and huge circular handles, that presumably
led to the front door; a pair of garage doors; and a
little arched doorway in the hedge. I could see the
Spanish-style house, with its white stucco exterior
and red tile roof, but I couldn't find a way to get
into it. Just as I was about to give up and go look
for a phone, I noticed a driveway at the north side
of the estate that led to a paved parking lot (I later
learned that Joe Kennedy had put this in during his

son's presidency). There the white stucco wall was
pierced by a wooden gate, which turned out to be
unlocked. A short walk led me to a flight of stone
steps that climbed to the kitchen door. It too was
unlocked. I called out "Hello" but got no answer,
so I boldly entered.

I was in a high-ceilinged room that seemed to
be an adjunct to the kitchen. It contained three large
freezers of the type you might find in a restaurant
or hotel and a big metal table. Next to it was the
kitchen proper. It had two stoves and a refrigerator,
with cabinets built in all around. Everything in sight
was dirty and shabby, and at least a generation out-
of-date. I couldn't imagine anyone actually turning
out meals in such a place. Walking on toward what
I hoped was the center of the house, I entered the
butler's pantry, where glass-fronted cupboards held
an array of dishes and glassware. This room alone
was bigger than most people's kitchens. The three
rooms together were obviously designed for the
staging of large banquets for many guests.

Before I could penetrate any further, I was
greeted effusively by an attractive and vivacious
elderly woman with snow-white hair. She gave me
a big hug of welcome and then introduced herself
as "Mam'selle." I later learned that Mam'selle had
been with the Kennedy family for many years. Back
in the 1950s and '60s, she was governess to the
four Lawford children; after Pat and Peter were di-

vorced and the youngest child was school age, she was let go. A few years later, she began to work for Mrs. Kennedy during the winters in Palm Beach. Currently she acted as a combination cook and maid, the same job Jeannette had in the summers in Hyannis Port. Mam'selle was of course French, and despite the fact that she had been in this country for decades, she still retained a thick French accent. When she pronounced my name, it came out "Babella."

Mam'selle whisked me through the house on a quick tour. To my surprise, the dominant effect was of shabbiness—makeshift decor imposed over the fading grandeur of the original building. The house had been designed by famed Florida architect Addison Mizner, back in the mid-1920s, for one of the wealthy Philadelphia Wanamakers. The skeleton of the house was beautiful and clearly designed for lavish living. The most unusual feature was a long passageway, roofed but not enclosed, that led from the door of the hedge past a charming garden area over a stone patio and up to the front door. It was an architectural idea borrowed from a cloister and it conveyed a lovely sense of green peace.

Opening off the entry foyer were an immense dining room to the left and living room to the right, both with windows overlooking the ocean and the front lawn dotted with palms. The floors of those rooms were laid in attractive rosy Cuban tile; the architectural detail was executed in grainy, long-lasting pecky cypress; and the walls of the foyer were rough lava stone, with that lovely but treacherous stone staircase rising in a curve. The house had six large bedrooms facing the sea and four smaller ones for live-in domestics which looked out over the vacant lot to the north, which Joe Kennedy had bought to prevent others from building there. The house had all the amenities expected by the rich: a tennis court, a swimming pool surrounded by pink and gray stone laid in an irregular pattern, a row of dressing rooms complete with showers for the use of swimmers and tennis players, a private entrance to the beach set into the seawall with more dressing rooms for ocean swimmers, and patios on three sides of the house.

But what struck me most forcibly was how run-down and shabby everything was. The house itself was in bad repair, with red tiles falling off the roof and wooden window frames rotting away. Falling coconuts had cracked the glass-topped tables on the patio. Some sort of rust had attacked the stone around the pool and produced ugly stains like dried blood on the elegant pattern. Everything in sight cried out for a good coat of paint. The interior was in even worse shape. Some of the curtains in the bedrooms were so damaged by years of exposure to sunlight that they were hanging in shreds. The old linoleum floors in the kitchen, covered with years of greasy dirt, buckled and crumbled. Upholstered furniture was stained and torn.

Efforts to improve matters had only made them worse. Someone who had painted the walls had simply covered everything in sight: hinges, window pulls, electrical outlets, and even brass locks on the doors. To my horror, this painting was carried to its most extreme point of insensitivity in the dining room. The heavy dark wooden furniture, designed by Addison Mizner in a Spanish colonial style to suit the decor, had been painted white with a flat wall paint, and of course it was already showing the dirt. As I walked from one dingy room to another, it was simply impossible to believe that this was the home of one of the richest families in the United States.

Most depressing of all, from a personal point of view, was the room that would be my office. I nearly burst into tears when I saw it. Situated in what had once been a maid's bedroom, at the opposite end of the back hall from Mrs. Kennedy's room, it still had a rusty old sink in one corner of the room. The window was shaded with a tattered venetian blind, and the room was furnished with a white washstand and a white chest of drawers apparently left over from its previous incarnation as a maid's room. Untrimmed bougainvillea was actually growing inside the walls. The only office furniture was a rusty typewriter table that must have been at least thirty years old, and the pleasant surprise of a lovely dark wood secretary that held some books and a few office supplies. There was no desk at all; a small three-drawer metal file cabinet was hidden away in the closet. Dominating the entire room was a truly hideous overstuffed chair, larger than any other piece of furniture in sight. I couldn't bear the thought of spending hours every day in such dreary surroundings.

Eventually I was able to make that office almost bearable. With the approval of the New York office, I bought a desk and put up some curtains. I even got the hideous chair moved to another room. But all that would happen later. My office turned out to be the least of my immediate worries.

The next morning, after an uneasy sleep that was constantly interrupted by the pounding of the surf, which made the whole house shudder, I began to make a list of the things that should be done before Mrs. Kennedy came back from her annual fall shopping trip to Paris. The tennis court was covered with palm leaves and dead branches, weeds were growing up through its surface, and the net was dangling askew. The pool was empty except for about three inches of water in the bottom, and it looked as if someone had started to paint it and abandoned the job months ago. The grass hadn't been cut for weeks, and the hedges and shrubs all needed trimming. Of course, the house itself required a thorough heavy cleaning. Also, since the previous chauffeur had been fired in the spring, a new one had to be hired. And I quickly discovered that the chauffeur's quarters needed a lot of work just to make them habitable. Not only was the kitchen covered with grime and piled high with dirty dishes, the curtains and bed linens were gone and the mattresses were lumpy and stained: The two bedrooms looked like the inside of a cheap motel. To top it all off, there was a huge swarm of bees buzzing around the bare light bulb in the bathroom, all very active and quite annoyed at the thought of sharing their territory with a human being.

I tried to find out how things had gotten into such a mess. Both Mam'selle and Jim, the Palm Beach policeman who worked nights and weekends for Mrs. Kennedy as a combination security guard and caretaker, made it clear that they had been given no responsibility for making decisions about what needed to be done and who should do it. The gardener worked for a landscaping service that maintained the grounds, so he came only when the service sent him. There was no chauffeur or handyman. No one was in charge . . . with predictable results.

At my wit's end, I called Tom Walsh at the New York office and explained the situation to him. "There's so much to do in this big house," I said in panic, "and so little time to do it in, if we're going to be ready when Mrs. Kennedy arrives."

"That's all right, sweetheart," answered Tom, who was always a tower of strength. "You just do whatever you think is necessary and send me the bills." I thanked him and went right to work. I asked the landscaping service to come in and clean up the yard and clear away the branches and leaves from the tennis court, pool, and patios. A cleaning service sent a team of burly men to do the heavy work of polishing the tile floors, washing all the windows inside and out, scouring the bathrooms, and scrubbing the kitchen floors. When they finished with the house, they even managed to make the garage apartment livable, and the county agricultural agent sent someone around to collect the bees. Meanwhile, professionals were sandblasting and repainting the pool. Since Mrs. Kennedy's daily swim was an important element of her routine, I wanted the pool to be ready and waiting for her. Each of the bills for these services was hundreds of dollars, but there was simply no other way. I approved them all and sent them to New York—to be paid out of Mrs. Kennedy's account. I felt a little nervous about this; I had only worked for Mrs. Kennedy a few months and suddenly I was entrusted with decisions involving what seemed to me to be large sums of money. But, at least, when Mrs. Kennedy finally arrived, the house was ready for her. And I was ready for a long rest!

I really never did understand why the Palm

Beach house was always so shabby. For investment reasons alone, it was silly to let a piece of prime real estate lose its value. And surely it would have been worth spending a little bit of the Kennedy fortune to make the house where Mrs. Kennedy spent half of the year attractive, or at least comfortable. In answer to my tactful (I hope) questions about the situation, Mrs. Kennedy told me the problem was that the house wasn't hers. Joe Kennedy's will left it to the children, with the stipulation that his widow was to remain in it for her lifetime. Mrs. Kennedy thus felt it wasn't her place to go ahead with repairs and renovations. I suppose the children, for their part, were reluctant to act like impatient landlords and begin making improvements right under their mother's feet, even when they could see the need for them. The result of this impasse was that the house simply went a little further downhill every year. Mrs. Kennedy once commented that maintaining a house on the ocean was like keeping up a ship . . . and I thought this ship was in danger of sinking.

But the shabbiness of the house never stopped people from wanting to visit. From Thanksgiving on, the hordes descended. They never came in just twos or threes, it seemed, but in big groups, all at once. Either Mrs. Kennedy was alone or she was swamped with company. During holidays, especially Thanksgiving, New Year's, and Easter, the

house would be jammed, with every bed taken—
and sometimes also a few cots rented to take care
of the overflow. Just watching all the commotion
was enough to make me feel tired at the end of the
day.

Perhaps that was why Mrs. Kennedy always
clung to her accustomed routine, no matter how
many visitors she might have. Her own day started
around eight o'clock, when she got up and dressed
for church. She usually wore a simple cotton dress,
perhaps one of the pretty floral prints she bought at
Lilly Pulitzer on Worth Avenue; generally she also
put on a hat. Dennis, the chauffeur, drove her in to
St. Edward's Church, just a few miles south on the
road to the center of town. Although the front entrance of the church (built in the 1920s) is beautifully designed in the Baroque style, with elaborate
twisted columns flanking each of the three arched
doors, Mrs. Kennedy usually preferred to enter
through the simple side door and slip into her customary pew, near the front on the left-hand side.
As a regular parishioner, Mrs. Kennedy made an
annual gift to the church, usually about five hundred
dollars. Some years earlier, she and her husband
had also donated one of the lovely stained-glass
windows lining the nave. Every morning she put
one dollar in the collection box, never more and
never less. She would have me cash a check every
month and get crisp new singles for this purpose.

When mass was over, she left by the side door and met Dennis, who escorted her across the street to the parking lot (he also attended mass). Dennis was the very same chauffeur who had been let go the previous spring. The only replacement I had been able to find was so young and inexperienced that Mrs. Kennedy was not comfortable with him. So Dennis returned, and things went on as they had before. The main drawback to Dennis was that he had a regular nine-to-five job as a lifeguard at the Sailfish Club, just up the road from the Kennedy house, so he was unavailable during the day. When he did reappear at the end of the day, he was deaf to any requests that he help out by taking out the trash or doing a bit of cleaning. But he was willing to live in the apartment over the garage, and so there was a man on the premises at night. And where Mrs. Kennedy was concerned, he was always willing to do as he was told.

Usually Dennis drove Mrs. Kennedy right back home after mass, stopping only to pick up her morning newspapers. But sometimes she would have errands to do or a function to attend. On those mornings, I would pick her up in the parking lot and do the driving for her, leaving Dennis free to hurry off to his other job. Invariably, when I arrived at the parking lot, the same spectacle met my eyes: Mrs. Kennedy eating her breakfast. She never ate before she left home because she wanted to take communion, so if she planned to go on to other places, she would take her breakfast with her—a thermos of coffee and some slices of toast. The funny part is that she wouldn't eat this breakfast inside her car, because she was afraid she might spill something on the seat. So she stood up in the parking lot, with the cars whizzing by. Dennis handed her a cup for a sip of coffee, took it back and handed her a slice of toast for a bite, took it back and handed her a napkin, then started all over again with the cup of coffee.

But most days, she breakfasted at home. When she got back to the house, she walked in the kitchen door and went directly to the dining room, where she ate alone, sitting at the head of the twenty-foot table surrounded by twelve chairs. The meal consisted of French bread (the only kind of bread that didn't upset her stomach), sliced one inch thick and lightly toasted, served with a little butter and honey. To wash it down, she drank Sanka, in which she dissolved a package of gelatin to make her fingernails strong and her hair glossy. It was her habit to dunk the bread in the coffee, and the general messiness made many guests reluctant to breakfast with her. On very special occasions, she might ask Mam'selle to fix her an egg, too, but normally there was no change from the routine. It seemed like such a shame . . . she had someone in the kitchen who would make anything she asked for. Yet she settled for the same meal every morning of her life.

After breakfast, Mrs. Kennedy took her papers and went upstairs to her room to finish scanning them. She read the *New York Times*, the *Palm Beach Post*, and the *Palm Beach Daily News*, locally known by the nickname of "the shiny sheet" because of the good quality of the paper on which it was printed—it wouldn't do for the society ladies to get ink all over their fingers as they searched the paper for their photographs. She might clip articles of interest about members of the family or people she had met.

When she finished with the papers, Mrs. Kennedy buzzed me (using the intercom button on the telephone) and I walked down the upstairs back hall from my office to her bedroom. The big windows overlooked the bright blue ocean; just sitting on her bed, she had a fabulous view. But I always found the room depressing. The pink-flowered curtains were falling apart at the folds, and their deterioration was hastened by Mrs. Kennedy's attempts to pin them together to prevent the afternoon sunlight from coming in during her naps. The dust ruffle of her bed and the skirt of her vanity were of the same fabric and in little better condition. There was a comfortable chaise, where she usually sat to read, but its faded pink upholstery was dingy and bore ineradicable stains. A bathroom with old-fashioned fixtures stained with rust opened off the bedroom, and there was a roomy walk-in closet, with a safe at the very back for her valuable jewelry.

Usually we went next door to work, in what was called "the massage room" but was probably originally intended as a dressing room for this master bedroom. Here she had installed a massage bed, and a masseuse came in once a week. We used the high bed like a desk top. I sat on one side, in a straight-backed chair, clutching my steno pad, ready to make notes or take dictation. She sat on the other side of the bed and fired away. She would make lists of errands she wanted done, such as ordering a lamp from Burdines or putting flowers in a guest room. She dictated letters declining invitations to dinners and balls, and letters to her children and grandchildren and old friends. Very personal letters she wrote herself, but most of her correspondence I typed on her gray stationery with the simple engraved head that said, "Palm Beach, Florida." More important letters were typed on the ivory stationery with a blue border.

In addition to taking care of her correspondence, Mrs. Kennedy might give me items to enter in one of her three black notebooks. The household book was full of miscellaneous housewifely tips, such as how to clean lampshades or polish stainless steel. It was also used for recording addresses of shops and telephone numbers of workmen. This notebook even contained such information as Rosemary's shoe size and the address of the place from which her special shoes could be ordered. The second notebook was full of Mrs. Kennedy's favorite sayings and quotes, and she added new entries from her reading of newspapers and an occasional book. The idea was that she could look it over before she went to a dinner party and thus be sure of having something interesting to say. The third notebook was for her French expressions and was part of her lifelong study of that language.

By the time we finished going over all these things, it was time for Mrs. Kennedy's daily swim. Unless I was terribly busy or she had lots of company, I usually joined her. If the water was warm and calm, we would go in the sea. Mrs. Kennedy all dressed to go in the water was a sight to behold. She wore not one but two bathing caps. One covered the front of her head and another the back, because, she explained, "I have such a tremendous head." On top of the caps she wore a sun visor to shield her sensitive eyes from the strong outdoor light, and she wore sunglasses as well, to double her protection. Over it all went a big straw hat, which she tied to her head with a chiffon scarf. This getup left her unprepared for sudden emergencies. One day, as we were floating peacefully, a big wave came out of nowhere and simply swallowed her up. I dove under the water, put my arms under hers, and pushed her back up to the surface. The sunglasses stayed under, and the straw hat began to float away, with the pink scarf drifting behind it like a tail. Meanwhile, Mrs. Kennedy was gasping from the sudden shock, and her false teeth came loose. It took quite a while to retrieve everything and get her back up on the beach. She was shaken, but it didn't take long for her to recover her usual aplomb. "Too bad," she joked, "there was no one sitting on the beach to take a picture. It would have been in all the papers that you saved my life."

Most of the time we used the pool, which was heated to the eighty-six degrees that her doctor recommended. The machinery for heating the pool was the bane of my existence. Apparently it had been installed back in the 1960s, after Joe Kennedy had his stroke, and the combination of age and the effects of the salt air made it break down with irritating regularity. The actual heating unit was located a few yards away from the pool, in a sort of pit sunk into the yard. During my first winter in Palm Beach, I swear I must have spent a third of my time crouched down in that pit with a succession of repairmen, trying to get the pool heated properly. After weeks of consultation, the man from the pool maintenance service explained that most of the problems came from the fact that the thermostat was constantly being adjusted. When Mrs. Kennedy got into the pool, she would check the temperature of the water coming into the pool. If it wasn't warm enough, she would ask me to turn up the thermostat immediately.

The repairmen explained that the temperature of the water coming into the pool would vary—sometimes hot and sometimes cold—producing a mix in the pool of eighty-six degrees. But Mrs. Kennedy never accepted this explanation and continued to ask me to move the thermostat up or down, according to the temperature of the water coming into the pool at the moment. I finally developed a technique of bending over and making a big show of adjusting the control without ever actually touching it. Yet still the mechanism malfunctioned frequently.

I concluded that perhaps someone else was playing with the thermostat when I wasn't around. So I had the repairmen install a padlock on the door of the control box, and I kept the key myself. When Mrs. Kennedy and I went swimming, I would take the key and open the door to pretend to make the adjustments she asked for. The rest of the time, the door would be locked and no one else could tamper with the temperamental machinery. Yet we continued to have trouble, and I kept noticing that the thermostat had been changed, and once I even saw on the ground nearby a big stick that had been used to pry open the padlocked door. Mam'selle, Dennis, and Jim all denied doing any such thing. Eventually it dawned on me that our culprit was none other than Mrs. Kennedy herself! She was still determined to make that thing work the way she thought it ought to.

The battle of the thermostat continued for weeks, until the day that she put her hand in front of the place where the water flowed in and it suddenly sucked her arm in the hole, right up to the shoulder. She of course screamed and thrashed around in the pool, so I hurriedly swam to her aid. Mrs. Kennedy seemed to be caught in some powerful suction, and tugging on her arm didn't help. I finally hit on the idea of rotating her arm, and that broke the pressure and she was released at last. I helped her down to the shallow end of the pool and she stood there trembling. Spontaneously I reached out for her hand and held it up to the warmth of my face, in the kind of gesture you might use to comfort a child, and she began to calm down. Once she got over her fright, she snatched her hand away quickly, as if to demonstrate that she was perfectly all right and didn't need any help from anyone. Although I knew she appreciated my aid, she was as determined as ever about her independence.

That incident put an end to her attempts to gauge the warmth of the incoming water, but unfortunately the pool heating system got worse and worse. The maintenance people told me that the only cure was to install a new filter, which would permit the warm water to flow into the pool at a faster rate. When Mrs. Kennedy heard it would cost more than four hundred dollars, she refused to agree, saying she would just give up her swim on cold days.

But I knew how much her daily swim meant to her. It was good for her physical health and perhaps even more important for her mental health. I think she went to the pool to work out her emotions, to fight her way back to her usual calm. I remember one time when she was obviously very distressed by some news about Rosemary, who had started to have convulsions when her medication was changed. We went in swimming that morning, but instead of her usual chatter, Mrs. Kennedy said simply, ''I don't want to talk now. I have something I need to think about.'' Then she paddled furiously back and forth across the pool until she nearly reached the point of exhaustion. Recently I read a book in which the writer mentioned that Rose Kennedy went in swimming as usual on the day of her husband's death and cited the fact as evidence of her coldness toward him. But anyone who knew Mrs. Kennedy would realize that sticking to her daily routine of a swim was simply her way of coping with any overwhelming emotion.

On the increasingly frequent days when the

pool heating system wasn't working right, Mrs. Kennedy would ask me to drive her down to Mary Sanford's house for a swim. Mary, a former starlet who had married wealthy Stephen ("Laddie") Sanford, was one of Mrs. Kennedy's few real friends in Palm Beach. According to the rumors of decades past, Joe Kennedy had been strongly attracted to Mary; if that was true, Mrs. Kennedy's friendship is just another example of her aristocratic ability to ignore the obvious when it was disagreeable. By the mid-1970s, Laddie Sanford had been bedridden for years after a stroke, and Mary, although getting on in years herself, still ruled as the acknowledged leader of Palm Beach society.

I always loved to go there, because the Sanford home was like something out of a 1930s movie. We swam in the indoor pool, small and deep, with a soothing whirlpool. (There was a big outdoor heated pool as well.) Statues lined the pool, and there were complete dressing rooms nearby. One wall was covered with a mural of a mermaid diving down to a large pile of jewelry, and that part of the mural was actually underwater. Mrs. Kennedy told me that the bare-breasted mermaid in the mural was supposed to be Mary, adding that she thought it was "rather obscene." In front of the diving mermaid, there was a casual living room with comfortably upholstered furniture and a glass-topped dining room ta-

ble where meals could be served. To me, it
symbolized the luxurious life I'd always imagined
to be the rule in Palm Beach.

Mary Sanford was always hospitable, but
swimming there was not a long-term solution to the
pool problem. After some discussion with the pool
service people, I came up with a scheme to replace
the filter without letting Mrs. Kennedy know—another one of those ''Don't tell Mrs. Kennedy'' episodes.. With the blessing of the New York office,
I arranged to replace the filter by breaking the job
up into little steps that could be done each afternoon
while Mrs. Kennedy had her nap. The most difficult
aspect of this scheme was that the only way to reach
the pool from the parking lot where the workmen
left their truck was around the ocean front of the
house and thus directly below Mrs. Kennedy's bedroom windows. I held my breath as the workmen
carried the new, heavy metal parts in and the old
ones out; with that sixth sense that told her when
people were trying to put something over on her,
Mrs. Kennedy would surely wake up and catch us
in the act. But luck was with us, and the repairs
were completed in secret. After that, the heating
system worked well, and our daily swim became
much more enjoyable.

After her swim, Mrs. Kennedy would go back
upstairs to her bedroom to change for lunch. Her
usual outfit was a pair of pajamas (usually pink with

a bit of lace around the Peter Pan collar), a belted robe (also in pink or a pink-and-white print) and pale pink Daniel Green slippers with a hard sole. That's the way she would appear in the dining room, promptly at one o'clock, unless she was expecting a special guest. Her lunch was cooked and served by Mam'selle, and it was always a hot meal. She would have a chop or some chicken, rice or more French bread, possibly a pureed vegetable such as carrots, made tasty with the addition of butter and cream. One of her favorite desserts was a gelatin made with fresh Florida orange juice and covered with cream—and, of course, a sugar cookie or two to go with it.

While Mrs. Kennedy was eating, often totally alone in that large dining room, I had my own lunch. I quickly discovered that going into town on my lunch hour was impossible. By the time I drove there and back, I had only about ten minutes left to gulp down a sandwich. But I could never find anything in Mrs. Kennedy's refrigerator that I might use to get my own meal at the house. Luckily Mam'selle solved my problem by offering to fix my lunch when she prepared her own. So she and I fell into the custom of eating our own lunch in the maids' dining room while Mrs. Kennedy ate hers alone in the main dining room. (Mam'selle would have to jump up once or twice to serve Mrs. Kennedy's next course.)

Mam'selle was actually a wonderful cook, although she tried to conceal it from Mrs. Kennedy so she wouldn't take advantage of the fact and expect her to cook for guests. She prepared quite elegant little lunches, and I began often to pick up an accompanying bottle of wine on my way to work. It would have been sheer bliss except for the surroundings. If most of the Kennedy house in Palm Beach was shabby, you can imagine what the rooms guests never saw were like. The maids' dining room had a Formica table, like you would find in a cheap coffee shop, with four kitchen chairs in various states of disrepair. There was a lumpy old daybed covered with a dingy bedspread and an elderly rocker whose stuffing threatened to emerge at any moment.

There was one redeeming feature of the maids' dining room, though. It contained a huge closet known as the "telephone room," which was the control center of the complex phone system Joe Kennedy had installed decades earlier. It enabled calls to be taken anywhere, but once connected, that phone could not be overheard from any other extension. The telephone room proved to be a wonderful hiding place.

What, you may wonder, did we have to hide? For one thing, our lunch. Although Mrs. Kennedy wanted the staff to eat in, we were always uncomfortable (like generations of "downstairs staff" before us) when she actually saw us eating. Whenever we heard her footsteps heading for our little sanctuary, Mam'selle and I quickly shoved our plates in the telephone room and concealed all traces of our luncheon menu. Mrs. Kennedy found us quietly reading the morning paper or watching a game show on television. The same hiding place was used by Mam'selle on her day off when she would leave me a lovely little cold plate for my lunch.

Occasionally, the telephone room was even used to conceal people. For example, Jim, the security guard, sometimes dropped in to chat, a habit Mrs. Kennedy opposed because she expected him to be out guarding the property. So at the sound of her footsteps, Jim would duck into the telephone room and remain there until Mrs. Kennedy left. He did the same thing in my office upstairs, using the clothes closet there, and sometimes relatives or grandchildren also ducked into these hiding places. It was often simpler to disappear than to explain to Mrs. Kennedy what you were up to.

After Mrs. Kennedy finished her lunch, she went upstairs to take a nap, actually getting into bed and closing all the curtains. That was the time I could count on to get my own work done: writing letters and making phone calls to take care of the things we had discussed that morning. But the calm lasted only a few hours. Mrs. Kennedy would be up again by three or three-thirty. If the weather was particularly nice, she might take another swim. Frequently she decided to go shopping on Worth Avenue or to make an appointment at the Elizabeth Arden salon to get her hair done. Since I had to drive her wherever she was going, I often accompanied her on these errands. Mrs. Kennedy loved to shop at Saks Fifth Avenue, the Courrèges boutique, and Kassatly's, a Palm Beach store renowned for its beautiful household linens. The clerks all along Worth Avenue were familiar with her . . . and her sudden changes of mind. She would, for example, select a skirt and even go so far as to have it pinned up for alterations and then decide at the last minute not to take it. Or, more commonly, she would buy a dress one day and return it the next (and then perhaps do the same thing all over again the following week with the same dress). One day, when we were returning a dress at Saks, one of the clerks said to me, "It's getting to the point where these dresses that Mrs. Kennedy buys are just taking a ride, aren't they?" She added tolerantly, "Oh, well, I guess we'll just chalk it up to public relations." The magic of the Kennedy name remained powerful.

The hairdressers at Elizabeth Arden were equally used to Mrs. Kennedy's foibles. She liked to have her hair done every week in Palm Beach, but she didn't have the patience to sit idly under the dryer for very long. She would insist that they take the rollers out while the back of her hair was still wet,

and then she complained about the way it looked.
Finally the hairdressers worked out a system of
sending her home with the rollers still in place, and
then she combed it out herself.

Whatever our errands, we were usually back
at the house a little before five. Then Mrs. Kennedy
changed into slacks and a pullover and her funny-
looking shoes to go out for her daily walk. It was
just two short blocks across to the paved sidewalk
that runs along the shore of Lake Worth, in front
of the big houses there. She walked for about an
hour, sometimes stopping at one of the benches
along the way for a brief rest before she continued.
If the children or grandchildren were visiting, one
of them would go along with her. It was the ideal
time for a quiet and private talk.

Mrs. Kennedy liked to get home to watch the
six o'clock news on television in the comfortable
little den right off the dining room. It was paneled
in warm wood, had built-in bookcases and a door
that opened onto the patio. The walls were hung
with memorabilia, most notably Jack's handwritten
draft of his inaugural address. Houseguests might
join her there, or there might be a cocktail hour in
the living room instead. Teddy might fix his daiquiris for the crowd, or Pat Lawford would make
her favorite bullshots. Then dinner was served
promptly at seven. It was another hot meal, almost
identical to her lunch, although if she had company,

she might plan a more elaborate menu for them. Roast beef was always popular, along with the creamed vegetables Mrs. Kennedy favored. Dessert might be Baskin-Robbins English toffee ice cream topped with butterscotch sauce.

After dinner, Mrs. Kennedy generally retired to her room, where Mam'selle had left a little tray containing a thermos of hot milk and some slices of toasted French bread in case she felt hungry before she went to sleep. She might read for a while. She liked biographies and books about current events, especially when she had met the leading characters. Fiction she read only rarely, and she didn't care for the contemporary style of sexual frankness. I re-member one time she asked me to get her a copy of *Jaws* when she heard the grandchildren talking about it. Apparently she read only as far as the first sex scene, for the next morning she returned the book to me with the terse comment ''Burn this, it's trash.'' Since her eyesight was failing, she couldn't read anything for very long, so she often watched television instead. She liked documentaries and news specials and avoided the shows meant for entertainment only. Her children and grandchildren were very good about calling her in the evenings, just to say hello and bring her up to date on family news, and that helped her pass the time.

Mrs. Kennedy was generally in bed by eleven. Sometimes she remained wakeful and prowled around the house in the wee hours of the night. The next morning, Mam'selle would complain that she hadn't been able to sleep because Mrs. Kennedy had taken a bath at 1:00 A.M. Or I might find illegible notes scribbled on my steno pad, things she had thought of while unable to sleep.

I used to reflect on the difference between Mrs. Kennedy's life-style and that of her neighbors in Palm Beach. She had more money than most of them, more friends in high places, more powerful contacts. She had a closetful of beautiful ball gowns that she had bought in Paris, and even though she had sold some of her jewelry, she still had some fabulous pieces, such as a triple-strand pearl necklace with a diamond clasp, a ten-carat diamond ring, and some elaborate diamond drop earrings. Mrs. Kennedy could have been the queen of Palm Beach society. Yet she rarely went out at all. She attended one or two of the big charity balls of the season— the Heart Ball and the Cancer Ball—and that was about the extent of her social life. She didn't lunch or shop with friends. She didn't dine out at other people's houses, and she rarely invited anyone to hers. "The house is too shabby to entertain" was her excuse. She didn't attend the openings and previews where women wore their designer originals and were photographed for the shiny sheet. When she bought tickets for some benefit, she often gave

them away. Several times Mrs. Kennedy offered
me tickets for some glamorous event, such as an
appearance by Bob Hope at the Royal Poinciana
Theater for the benefit of cancer research; she was
willing to contribute the money to a good cause but
she didn't want to go to the event. Her existence
was solitary, removed from the social whirl that
was going on all around her, barely touched by the
status competition that is so much a part of Palm
Beach life.

Of course, she wasn't always literally alone,
because in Palm Beach, the family was likely to
descend at any moment. Yet even when the house
was full of guests, Mrs. Kennedy remained aloof.
When the relatives or the grandchildren came to
visit, she always greeted them on their arrival, but
then she would retire to the security of her usual
routine, seeing the visitors only at mealtimes. Thus
she tried to remain unbothered by the constant turmoil going on in the house. That, I discovered, was
my responsibility.

The first problem was finding the domestic staff
to cope with the needs of our visitors. Mam'selle
refused to cook for company, so a cook had to be
found whenever we had more than one or two guests.
Some guests brought their own domestics with them
to help out. When the Morton Downeys came to
dinner, bringing Gary Cooper's widow and her husband, Dr. John Converse, they also brought their

own maid to serve the meal. Jean Smith often brought her maid, and both Eunice and Pat occasionally came with a cook. But, of course, it was hard for them to function efficiently in a strange kitchen, and the quality of the meals was often disappointing.

One solution was to try to get a cook from one of the domestic employment services in Palm Beach. Unfortunately, the services knew all about the Kennedys: the low wages, the long hours and hard work in that badly equipped kitchen, the sudden dismissal when the visitors left. So it was all I could do to talk them into sending anyone at all, let alone the cream of the crop. A few good cooks passed through our kitchen, but they were usually available just for a week or so while their regular employers were out of town. Others were either incompetent or nutty —and even those were often unwilling to stay. One of them quit after she tried to get back into the house on her afternoon off. No one heard her shout and knock on the gate, and as I had discovered on my own initial arrival, there was no way in if the door in the side gate wasn't left open. So the poor woman walked down to the beach and then somehow managed to climb up the twelve-foot seawall to get onto the grounds. Mrs. Kennedy and I laughed at this exploit, but the cook was not amused.

The best solution to our staff problem was to hire temporarily a woman who had formerly cooked for the Senator in Washington and was now living in Palm Beach. Nellie was a good soul and an even better cook. Her credentials included stints with Millicent Hearst, Cary Grant, and Gloria Vanderbilt. Of course, she knew how to make all the Kennedy family favorites: the sugar cookies for Mrs. Kennedy, the chocolate roll for the Senator, and her famous chocolate-chip cookies that everybody loved. Nellie was in semiretirement but was willing to come back and work for Mrs. Kennedy during part of the winter. The only problem was Mrs. Kennedy herself: she simply didn't understand the kind of pay appropriate to a good cook in that day and age. Finally, in collusion with the New York office, I came up with a solution. ("Don't tell Mrs. Kennedy," I warned Nellie.) Mrs. Kennedy paid Nellie the thirty-five dollars a day she thought was the top salary any cook could expect, and the New York office paid her the extra fifteen dollars a day that brought the total up to the lowest figure Nellie was willing to consider. So when the house was full of people, Nellie would cook and Mam'selle would clean and sometimes help with the serving of the meals. It was still too small a staff to do everything for six or ten guests, especially when some of them expected breakfast in bed and other special services. But at least there was good food on the table.

Yet every week, a new crisis with the staff would erupt. Mrs. Kennedy would decide, during a lull when she had no guests, that she didn't really need Nellie and tell her to leave. Or during the peak holiday periods when every bed in the house was full, Nellie herself would threaten to leave because she could not go on working eighteen hours every day. She would agree to stay only if we would hire a second maid to take over some of the chores. So then I would be calling the service again, trying to find someone willing to come in temporarily. Of course, since Mrs. Kennedy was not even fully convinced that we needed Nellie, she was even more reluctant to go to the additional expense of a second maid. When I tried to explain to her that we simply couldn't manage with only the one cook-maid when there were guests in the house, she replied that she would just tell everyone not to come. When I pressed her on the subject, she said stubbornly, "I know how I want to live my life and I know how I want everything done."

I was generally caught right in the middle. My job was to please Mrs. Kennedy, and I knew she was upset by the strange faces and the mounting bills. Yet I also sympathized with Nellie and Mam'selle, who worked long and hard under difficult conditions. Nellie, for example, usually ended up fixing three or four different entrées for the same meal. Mrs. Kennedy would set up the dinner menu and Nellie might therefore prepare roast beef, green beans, a salad, and some sort of dessert. Then in the afternoon Eunice would ask what was planned for dinner and respond dubiously, "I don't really feel like eating roast beef, I'd prefer to have lobster." And Pat would march into the kitchen and give brisk instructions: "Of course, I don't eat red meat, so I'll just have broiled pompano." The bills for all this food were astronomical. When I sent them to the New York office after one holiday invasion, I got an immediate call from one of the men there. "What are you people eating down there?" he asked. "Gold nuggets?" In fact, it wasn't like a home at all, but more like cooking in a restaurant.

Or maybe an institution. At times the chaos was unbelievable. I had to post lists on the bulletin board in the kitchen to let people know who was arriving when and where they were staying. Here, from my notes, is one such schedule.

SCHEDULE

WEDNESDAY, MARCH 19, 1975

ARRIVING:
Mrs. Smith   2:45 P.M.
Amanda Smith   National #95
Kym Smith
William Smith
Robin Lawford
Bridie (Smith
  governess)

Jean Bowers
  (Smith maid)
Mary Connelly
  (Lawford cook)

FRIDAY, MARCH 21

ARRIVING:

Mrs. Lawford	5:12 P.M.
Victoria Lawford	Eastern #195

ROOM ARRANGEMENT

Mrs. Smith Amanda Smith	} Lake bedroom
Kym Smith Bridie	} Ocean bedroom
Robin Lawford Victoria Lawford Caroline Kennedy	} Bedroom next to Mrs. Lawford
William Smith	Bedroom next to Mrs. Kennedy
Jean Bowers	Corner bedroom
Mary Connelly	Rear bedroom on north side

I was making and breaking so many plane reservations in and out of Palm Beach that the ticket agent asked me if I was running a hotel! And since

Dennis didn't work between nine and five, I also ended up doing most of the driving back and forth to the airport. The Senator was very good about arranging for his own transportation, but other members of the family expected that to be one of the functions of Mrs. Kennedy's staff. I nearly always drove the grandchildren to and from the airport, and they frequently complained that I drove too slowly. Their parents could be equally demanding. Once I went to meet Pat Lawford and got stuck in the traffic on the bridge from Palm Beach to West Palm Beach, where the airport is located. That made me five minutes late, and when I got there, Pat was nowhere to be seen. Finally I telephoned Mrs. Kennedy and learned Pat had just walked in the door; she had gotten a ride with someone else. The next day I said firmly, "Please don't ask me to go pick up anyone anymore, Mrs. Kennedy." She answered quickly, "I agree."

Easter vacation of 1977 was probably the most frantic time ever. Every bed in the house was taken, and Dennis had even been asked to share his two-bedroom apartment over the garage to hold the overflow. Jean and Pat were there, with most of the Lawford and Smith children. Caroline was there, too (sleeping on a rented cot), and I saw a report in the local paper that Jackie was going to come at the end of the week. We discussed the problem of where she could sleep, and Mrs. Kennedy came up

This picture of Rose Kennedy, one of my favorites, was taken the first summer I worked for her as her private secretary. She is wearing an aqua-colored Courrèges pantsuit that she bought in Paris, along with a matching hat, and standing in front of the beautiful roses that flourished in the sea air at the Hyannis Port house. *(AP/Wide World Photos)*

The Hyannis Port house, with Mrs. Kennedy standing in front of it, bundled up for one of her evening walks. The big window upstairs to the right is Mrs. Kennedy's bedroom. *(From the collection of Barbara Gibson)*

The interior of Mrs. Kennedy's bedroom in Hyannis Port. The room is a lovely mixture of floral prints and white eyelet. Her desk (left), was her favorite working and thinking spot. *(From the collection of Barbara Gibson)*

Barbara, at her desk in her cheery Hyannis Port office. *(From the collection of Barbara Gibson)*

Barbara and Jeannette in front of the Hyannis Port house. *(From the collection of Barbara Gibson)*

An aerial view of the Kennedy house in Palm Beach. The parking lot is on the right of the house, the palm shaded pool on the left. The property is protected from the ocean by a 12-foot seawall. *(AP/Wide World Photos)*

The author, Barbara Gibson. *(Photography by Moya)*

This is Mrs. Kennedy on her way to that Washington benefit on behalf of the retarded that she attended as a guest of President and Mrs. Ford. You would never guess by looking at her that she had been sick all week in Palm Beach before she made the trip. Her gown is a Paris original, and her jewelry includes her famous triple strand of pearls. I shopped for two days to find those shoes. *(AP/Wide World Photos)*

More of Mrs. Kennedy's public duties. Here, she is hostess to a gathering of Irish children at the compound with son Ted. *(UPI/ Bettmann Newsphoto)*

Mrs. Kennedy attending a campaign party with Ted and his younger son, Patrick (applauding). *(UPI/Bettmann Newsphotos)*

The cup in Mrs. Kennedy's hand tells you who her favorite candidate is. *(AP/Wide World Photos)*

Mrs. Kennedy making an appearance in Boston on Ted's behalf. That's her nephew Joe Gargan standing behind her. *(AP/Wide World Photos)*

Mrs. Kennedy and her son, Ted, share a warm moment during a ceremony to dedicate a research institute for the retarded. Mrs. Kennedy's carefully typed speech, and the glasses she needed to read it, are on the table. *(UPI/Bettmann Newsphotos)*

Mrs. Kennedy accompanies the Senator and French President Valery Giscard d'Estaing to lay a wreath at John Kennedy's grave in Arlington, Virginia. *(AP/Wide World Photos)*

Here, a happier occasion —Caroline's graduation from prep school in Concord, Massachusetts. From left to right: John Kennedy, Jacqueline Kennedy Onassis, Caroline Kennedy, Rose Kennedy, Ted Kennedy, and Jackie's mother, Janet Auchincloss. *(UPI/Bettmann Newsphotos)*

Mrs. Kennedy and her grandsons, Christopher Kennedy (left) and Patrick Kennedy (right), share a laugh. *(AP/Wide World Photos)*

One of the clambakes that the Kennedys held every summer to honor the matriarch's birthday. Mrs. Kennedy is standing with her granddaughter Kathleen Kennedy (left) and daughter Eunice Shriver (right). *(AP/Wide World Photos)*

Another clambake at Hyannis Port...notice the huge throng on the lawn. That's Ted to the left of Mrs. Kennedy, granddaughter Kara and daughter Pat Lawford to the right. *(UPI/Bettmann Newsphotos)*

This is the way I always think of Rose Kennedy: her arms full of flowers (including her favorite "infant's breath"), hatted, coiffed, and bejeweled (even on this casual occasion), and her head held high as she meets the public. *(AP/Wide World Photos)*

with the notion of putting her on the massage bed. Somehow I couldn't quite visualize the fastidious Jackie tucked away on that high narrow bed in a little room opening off her mother-in-law's. I wasn't too surprised to learn a few days later that Jackie wasn't coming after all.

As usual, we didn't have enough staff to cope with the demands. The second maid I had hired to help out quit. She said working for the Kennedys was making her blood pressure too high and ruining her health. So the next morning, which was Nellie's day off, I came in and found Jean and Pat standing at the big sink in the kitchen, laboriously doing the breakfast dishes. Later that day I saw Caroline on her hands and knees cleaning a rubber mat, with Mrs. Kennedy standing over her to supervise, wearing her usual big hat. And to think these people came here for a vacation!

Meanwhile, with all that crowd of Kennedys in one place, the media were having a field day. There were reporters waiting outside the front gates, patrolling the beach, trying to conceal themselves behind the bushes on a neighbor's property. They were even hovering overhead in a helicopter, hoping to get photos of the granddaughters in their bikinis (they only succeeded in disturbing Jean and Pat as they were playing tennis). They brandished cameras and communicated with one another over walkie-talkies. Most of these journalists were from the

National Enquirer, and apparently they intended to let nothing stand in the way of getting some sort of scoop. When Mrs. Kennedy went out for her evening walk, they popped up from behind the bushes, whereupon she told them she was just a tourist and it wouldn't be worth taking her picture—but her Boston accent gave her away. Later she asked me to call the Senator's office and see if anything could be done to put a stop to it. An aide reported back, "I talked to our man there and he told me they had gone to considerable expense to get those photographs down there. They won't cancel the operation now."

Although she tried to isolate herself from all the turmoil, Mrs. Kennedy was often badly upset by these periods when so many guests arrived at once. One morning, after a huge Thanksgiving crowd had just left, I found Mrs. Kennedy sitting at the table in the maids' dining room crying uncontrollably. She was distraught because her twelve guests had created such havoc: Lamps had been overturned, towels were left out by the pool and beach, half a turkey disappeared during the night, glasses were broken, possessions left behind that would have to be packed and mailed to the forgetful guest—in other words, the usual aftermath of a Kennedy holiday. I tried to soothe her by assuring her I could get someone in to clean up the mess and set the house back to rights. That calmed her down for a minute, but then she began to cry all over again because she didn't want to hire a strange maid. She just wanted her quiet routine reestablished, with a daily schedule that she felt she could control.

Her distress over these disruptions sometimes led her to cancel visits or ask people not to come. She frequently wrote to her grandchildren to explain that she would be unable to have them visit in Florida or to suggest changing the date of a planned visit to some more convenient time. For example, she wrote Ethel's son David to say that he couldn't come when he wanted to, but added that he might want to reschedule his visit when the Smiths would be there (since they would bring their own staff and the household would thus be more comfortable).

I knew she had really gotten upset when she asked me to call the Senator and tell him not to come down for the weekend as he had planned, since she usually anticipated his visits eagerly. I knew he was not going to like this turn of events, and I dreaded making the call. At first, he merely seemed perplexed: *Why* couldn't he come? I tried to explain how upset she was, how short of staff we were, how difficult it was to look after guests. He listened to all this patiently and then answered, "I'm sure all this is true, but I don't know what to do. I'll speak to my sisters about it." Then he added firmly, "Meanwhile, I would like to come down to Palm Beach." But later he spoke to his mother on the phone and, realizing how distressed she was, canceled his visit.

I was usually very glad to leave that scene of chaos and go home to my own two-bedroom ocean-front apartment in Juno Beach, about a forty-five-minute drive away. Not only was it much more peaceful there, it was also more comfortable. The Kennedy house had neither air conditioning nor central heating. So on those October days when the mercury rose to ninety-five, I sweltered in my small office with inadequate ventilation. And on the not-rare-enough occasions when the temperature dropped into the thirties and forties in the wintertime, everyone in the house had to bundle up against the terrible chill of those stone walls and tile floors. I would go to work wearing heavy tights, lined wool slacks, and two thick sweaters. Poor Mrs. Kennedy felt the cold more than I did. And yet she still went swimming! The air was so cold that steam would come up from the heated pool in billows, and I could only see her head in a bathing cap in the midst of those clouds of steam.

So I would go home at the end of the day, put my feet up, pour myself a glass of wine, and try to relax as I looked out at the ocean. I would think about the funny scene in the kitchen as Nellie stood at the counter making one of her delicious cheese balls, vigorously stirring away and reciting Robert Burns at the top of her voice with her inimitable

Scots burr: "Man's inhumanity to man," she quoted, "makes countless thousands mourn." Meanwhile, Mam'selle would run in and out, her French accent dueling with Nellie's Scottish one. Jim Connors, the guard, might stop in for a cup of coffee and add his Southern drawl to the mélange.

"Barrrrrbara," said Nellie.

"Babella," said Mam'selle.

"Bobra," said Jim.

And then . . . "Baaabara," Mrs. Kennedy would call.

Time for another glass of wine.

Then I would think about the Kennedys, and they began to seem like figures out of a comic opera. There was Teddy, standing in the kitchen wearing nothing but a towel wrapped around his waist, while another one of the girlfriends who looked exactly like Joan waited for him in the President's bedroom, the big room on the ground floor with a separate entrance that permitted people to come and go unobserved by Mrs. Kennedy. Or there was Sarge, a formally announced candidate for president who was being protected by the Secret Service, arriving at the house in pomp and circumstance, only to find no one there to greet him. There was one of the relatives who had stayed for a few days, usually out of sight in his room; when I drove him to the airport, he asked me quite casually, "Could we stop off at the hospital? I don't feel well," and ended up being treated in the emergency room for alcohol withdrawal. (He had no money, so I had to pay for it.) Best of all was the sight of Mrs. Kennedy, concerned because I was having trouble pulling the big Lincoln out of our drive onto North Ocean Boulevard due to a hazardous curve, getting out of the backseat of the car, marching out in the middle of the road in her bright pink Courrèges suit and matching pinwheel hat, and holding up her hand to stop the oncoming cars while she motioned me out onto the road. I'll never forget the looks on the faces of the other drivers!

Yes, there were plenty of amusing moments. And yet the memory that lingered the longest was something Mrs. Kennedy said one afternoon as I told her good-bye on my way home at the end of the day. "You're lucky," she said quite seriously. "You can leave when you want to. I'm stuck here."

6

Hyannis Port

Returning to Hyannis Port in the spring felt like going home. After spending the winter in that big but dreary house in Palm Beach—which struck me as being the perfect setting for a Tennessee Williams play with the theme of pathetic loss and deterioration—it was an absolute pleasure to get back to the lovely white clapboard house overlooking Nantucket Sound. Thanks to the devoted efforts of Mrs. Kennedy's nephew Joe Gargan, the house was always in immaculate condition when Mrs. Kennedy arrived: floors shining with wax, new paint inside and out, freshly washed curtains stiff with starch at the sparkling windows. The rooms were open and airy, attractively decorated in light colors and floral prints, and very, very comfortable.

Mrs. Kennedy, who had spent nearly fifty summers as the mistress of this oceanfront house, had her own little routines that never varied from one year to the next. Her first order of business, as soon as she arrived in May, was the flowers that would be planted around the rambling twelve-bedroom house. This project customarily took hours and hours of planning. Mrs. Kennedy summoned her retired gardener, Wilbert Marsh, for high-level conversations, and she also consulted Alex Johnson, a local landscaper whose men would do much of the work. Finally she settled down to give orders to Arthur, the present gardener (and man of all work).

Mrs. Kennedy was very particular about how she wanted the plantings to look, especially in regard to color. She demanded that the flowers set out in the big wooden window boxes on the porch should match the shade of the curtains in the dining room as well as the paper in the entry hall! And she was always complaining that the reds weren't deep enough, the purples too dark, the pinks not as strong as she expected. She wanted her flowers to look exactly the way they did in the luscious four-color garden catalogs. The beds along the driveway and on the far side of the house, near the tennis court, did look lovely in the summer, ablaze with glorious color, with special emphasis on the brilliant pinks that were her favorites. And every year the pink roses, thriving on sea air, put on a magnificent display against the white fence. She liked to use all the flowers in arrangements for the house, and for that reason always ordered Arthur to plant copious quantities of what she called "infant's breath." I never knew whether she genuinely got the name wrong or just thought it sounded somehow more dignified than talking about baby's breath.

During my first acquaintance with that Hyannis Port house in 1968, while Joe Kennedy was still alive, it was the busy center of Kennedy family life. Even though he spent most of his time in his bedroom, his forceful personality pervaded the atmosphere. He had loved the turmoil of a big family, the continual activity it created, the warmth of family life even when it heated up into a clash—and the house was an extension of his vivid presence. But by 1974 the house had changed, in reflection of the personality of the octogenarian Rose Kennedy. It was dominated by routine, orderly and organized, and was somewhat closed to social activity. During the years I worked for Mrs. Kennedy, she erected more and more barriers between herself and the frenetic flow of family life around her.

One barrier was her edict against other people's use of the tennis court. She sent memos to the other Kennedy houses, warning against losing valuable tennis balls. One day she asked me to tell Maria

Shriver that she should use her own tennis court at home instead of coming to her grandmother's, because she brought friends with her—naturally, you can't play tennis alone—and Mrs. Kennedy didn't like to have "strangers" around the property. She seemed equally resistant to the use of her pool (like the one in Florida, Olympic-size and heated). One morning Rory and Doug Kennedy, Ethel's youngest children, turned up in my office and said they wanted to talk to their grandmother, so I buzzed her on the intercom and put them on the phone. Rory asked if they could swim in her pool, and Mrs. Kennedy answered firmly, "No, dear." She later told me that she didn't want any accidents.

Another barrier was the prohibition Mrs. Kennedy issued against the use of the movie room in the basement of her house. It had been installed by Joe Kennedy back in the late 1920s, when he still had a financial interest in the movie business. It was a scaled-down version of a real theater, complete with projection room and rows of theater seats bolted to the floor. It had for decades been a custom for the family to gather there after dinner to see a current movie. But Mrs. Kennedy was distressed by the fact that soft-drink bottles and junk-food wrappers were sometimes left behind. So she decreed that no more movies would be shown.

Gradually, fewer and fewer members of the family stopped by "Grandma's house." The older

children were away for the summer or wrapped up
in their own lives; the younger children took care
to remain out of sight; even the adults were discouraged by the prohibitions. Mrs. Kennedy was
left in peace to pursue her established daily routine.
Oh, there were slight differences between Palm Beach
and Hyannis Port. She read the *Cape Cod Times*
instead of the shiny sheet; rather than going to St.
Edward's, she attended morning mass at the simple
New England church of St. Xavier's, with the altar
the Kennedys had given in memory of Joe Jr.; her
evening walk might take her over to the local golf
course rather than along the shores of Lake Worth.
But the schedule was the same. The daily menu was
the same. The security of the routine was the same.

Yet Hyannis Port always brought a certain sense
of informality that was missing elsewhere. Mrs.
Kennedy dressed more casually, in old slacks and
her orthopedic shoes. She washed and set her own
hair most of the time, and, in fact, it often didn't
matter what her hair looked like because she covered
it with a big scarf to protect her against the strong
winds of the Cape. No wonder tourists sometimes
stopped her to ask the way to the Kennedy compound. She did indeed look like someone's faithful
servant or impoverished relative when she got bundled up in her usual walking attire of a heavy sweater
and grandmotherly babushka. It never fazed her when
people did approach her, and sometimes she brought

amazed tourists back to the house with her, posing for snapshots on the front lawn and graciously signing autographs. Once she got on a tour bus and rode with the crowd right up to her front door.

For me, it was always such a relief to get back to Hyannis Port. The Palm Beach house was always either too lonely or too crowded. One day Mrs. Kennedy and I were rattling around in that big shabby house by ourselves, and the next there was utter chaos because of the throngs of visiting relatives. In Hyannis Port, there were always people around, but generally they did not disturb Mrs. Kennedy's daily routine. Her health and her spirits were better there, and that made my job much easier.

I also liked Hyannis Port better because my office was so much more comfortable than the one in Palm Beach. It was a sunny room in the hallway of the main floor of the house, just off the foot of the stairs. Nearby, a hall door led outside to the pool and garage, so people were often coming and going. My office had a second door that opened onto the bright and cheery sun-room, and as long as the Kennedys weren't using it, I could keep the door open to give myself more light and space. The furniture in my office was comfortable and practical, and the walls were decorated with interesting paintings and photographs. My favorite item was the painting the Senator had done during his long convalescence from the injuries received when the small plane in which he was campaigning with Senator Birch Bayh crashed in 1964. The painting showed the Hyannis Port waterfront, with all the Kennedy houses charmingly pictured. Its colors were bright, the spirit was cheerful, and the whole effect rather amusing and entertaining. Just being in that office made me feel more relaxed.

I thought Mrs. Kennedy, too, seemed more relaxed when she was on the Cape. Sometimes she sat down at the piano and played just for the fun of it, with particular attention to her specialty, "Sweet Adeline," played with lots of trills. She liked to sing, too. Once, when Bob Luddington, the decorator from Jordan Marsh, came to the house on an errand, he was perplexed by the cacophony coming from the kitchen. "What's *that*?" he asked me curiously. "That's Mrs. Kennedy and the cook singing in the kitchen," I answered. Their favorite was "Danny Boy," with heavy emphasis on the sad parts. The two old women had a high old time together.

Oddly enough, these high spirits were rarely in evidence during the big family get-togethers of the summer season. The Kennedys always convened to celebrate July 22, Rose Kennedy's birthday, and Labor Day, which included a birthday party for the oldest grandson, Ethel's son Joe, born several weeks later on September 24. (Interestingly, at least four other grandchildren, including two of Ethel's girls, had birthdays that were much closer to Labor Day, but the big party over that weekend was always in honor of Joe's birthday.) For the rest of the family, these parties were a time of family solidarity, an eagerly anticipated chance for immersion in a sea of Kennedy faces. For the matriarch of the clan, the events themselves seemed more like royal duties than private fun.

Mrs. Kennedy's children planned her birthday festivities, which usually included a traditional Cape Cod clambake with the whole family in attendance. But for Mrs. Kennedy, the excitement was often just too much, and she would be sick in bed for several days afterward. In 1977, the whole thing got so confused that no one knew what was supposed to happen when. The people who had been hired to cater the clambake drove up late Saturday afternoon in a truck full of lobster pots already on the boil, but none of the family showed up until after ten o'clock that night. Apparently Eunice had made a mistake and told people the affair would be on Sunday rather than Saturday, and so the whole family had merrily gone on with their usual plans until they began to get frantic phone calls about the unattended clambake. The food was long since cold and the fire completely out before most of the guests arrived, and of course Mrs. Kennedy was exhausted. Ted was angry with his sister about this mix-up and its effect on his mother, and Jackie later commented that she thought the family should have their own circus and leave Mrs. Kennedy out of it.

The Labor Day weekend was usually a more successful social event. It really got started the week before, as the grandchildren started coming in from their various summer activities in Europe, South America, Hawaii, and Indian reservations in the western states. As I looked out the windows of Mrs. Kennedy's house, I saw groups of young people walking around the yard, heading down to the beach, going back and forth between the houses, on their way to the tennis court or the swimming pool. Day by day the crowd increased, and every time I looked out I glimpsed another familiar face I hadn't seen since the previous summer. By Labor Day itself, the compound looked like a public park that was hosting a three-day outing. No wonder they don't make friends with outsiders, I thought; there are enough Kennedys to make a good party anytime.

Young Joe's birthday party was masterminded by his mother. Ethel had all the furniture on the ground floor of her house removed and the rugs rolled up to make space for the crowd. There was cold beer on tap, huge pots of chili, grilled hamburgers and hot dogs, maybe some cold boiled lobster. Later, on the tennis court, a six-piece band played for dancing, and the crowd of Kennedys all seemed to enjoy themselves.

But it was Mrs. Kennedy's custom to stay in

her bedroom in her own house for much of the
evening, allowing the grandchildren to pay formal
visits, one at a time, to tell her about their summer
activities. She seemed impressed by the social
awareness of this generation. "When my children
were young," she told me, "they went to far-off
places to learn the culture and meet people in the
government. But these children are really concerned
with the social problems of the people in the countries they visit."

Early in the evening, Mrs. Kennedy would make
her ritual appearance on the arm of her son Ted on
one side and young Joe on the other, looking like
a frail doll between these two large and solid males.
It was never long before she slipped away again,
back to the peace of her own house.

At least in Hyannis Port Mrs. Kennedy had a
lovely bedroom to serve as her retreat. As in Palm
Beach, her room was located on the second floor,
right over the main entry to the house. But there
the similarity ended. In Palm Beach, I couldn't understand how she managed to spend so much time
in a room that was so shabby; but her bedroom in
Hyannis Port was a comfortable and homey refuge.
It was decorated in shades of pink, with accents of
light mint green. The windows were outlined in a
foam of crisp white eyelet through which the summer sun easily penetrated to keep the room bright
and cheerful. The view of the ocean was of course

superb. Mrs. Kennedy could look out the window as she made her daily phone calls relaying instructions to the cook in the kitchen, to me in the office, and to family members in the nearby houses. Often she worked at her desk, an antique lady's secretary with the smooth glow of well-polished old wood. Taped to the top of the desk, facing her at eye level, were mass cards commemorating the lost Kennedys: Joe, Joe Jr., Jack, Bobby, and Kathleen. She had added a few treasured snapshots, such as one of Joe Jr. in his navy uniform and one of Jack visiting his Irish relatives in the early fall of 1963. In Hyannis Port, the memories ran especially deep.

From this airy command post, Mrs. Kennedy's orders flew thick and fast. "Buy a magnifying glass for Eunice. She borrowed mine and never brought it back." "Arrange for Arthur to drive Mrs. Lawford to Boston tomorrow." "Check on the condition of the pillows in the garage apartment." "Write a memo to New York about the young woman Ethel hired to house-sit for the winter. She is apparently escorting friends around the compound, peering in the windows of Jackie's house, and so on. It seems that Ethel found her through a newspaper ad." (Later, everyone had reason to be thankful for the presence of the house-sitter, who spotted and called the Fire Department about a small fire that might well have burned the compound down if it had been unattended.)

When the telephone intercom was inadequate for her communication, Mrs. Kennedy would simply walk to the head of the stairs and call down to my ground-floor office in that carrying voice with her unmistakable Boston accent. Sometimes she also threw down papers she wanted me to take care of: clippings from her newspaper reading, notes for her book of sayings, words she wanted to know the definition of, a handwritten note she wanted me to send. I would scurry around the bottom of the stairs and frantically try to pick up the cascading papers while she stood at the top and issued a steady stream of instructions.

As in Palm Beach, however, many of Mrs. Kennedy's instructions were not followed by the household staff. Jeannette, the maid of all work, had managed to issue her own set of instructions that her employer was forced to follow. For example, it was an accepted rule that Jeannette could never be disturbed in the afternoons when she was watching her favorite soap operas. As I had learned, it was also a rule that she would never wait on other staff members, and it was a rule that she wouldn't cook for anyone but Mrs. Kennedy. One day I learned of another rule when I overheard Mrs. Kennedy, passing through the kitchen on her way to her late-afternoon walk, say apologetically to Jeannette, "I didn't have time to straighten my room yet, I'll do it when I return." It made me wonder about the conversations the two of them had at night when everyone else was gone. Jeannette was obviously more successful in issuing ultimatums than was Mrs. Kennedy.

One of Jeannette's most faithfully observed rules was that she would not stay in the house when any of the Lawfords were there. For reasons she never made entirely clear to me, she disliked the entire family so much that she arranged to go on vacation the minute the Lawfords entered the house, and she wouldn't return to work until she was sure they were gone. Since the Lawford family didn't have a house of their own on the Cape but always stayed with Mrs. Kennedy, this rule created an ongoing problem. Some summers I managed to get Nellie to come up from Florida and do the cooking. Or Pat Lawford would bring her own cook (who otherwise was expected to take an unpaid vacation whenever her employer was away). Jean Smith was always very good about bringing a maid with her, and if her own didn't come, she would hire and pay for the extra household help herself. She said cheerfully, "I know Mother doesn't like to spend money, but I do!" At least in Hyannis Port, the servant problem was never such a crisis as it was in Palm Beach. If there was no one to cook at Mrs. Kennedy's house, guests could simply go eat with Ethel or Eunice or Teddy or Jackie.

But there were times when the lack of a maid

was really felt. One of the funniest was when Governor Brendan Byrne of New Jersey came to visit Mrs. Kennedy. He was attending a meeting in Hyannis and had arranged to pay a courtesy call one Friday afternoon at four o'clock. No one heard the car drive in, so one of the governor's assistants came in the back way to tell me they had arrived. I zipped round to the front door, introduced myself as Mrs. Kennedy's secretary, Barbara, and settled the governor and his two aides in the sun-room while I tried to get things organized. It turned out that Mrs. Kennedy was still getting dressed, and Jeannette was nowhere to be found . . . until I had the idea of looking in her bedroom, where I found her peacefully napping. I woke her and told her about the situation, but she refused to get up; her uniform was dirty, she said, and she wasn't going to serve. I went back downstairs to do it myself.

Mrs. Kennedy had meanwhile made her entrance, dressed to the nines in an outfit that included a matching hat. When I asked if anyone would like something to drink, Mrs. Kennedy responded by calling me ''Janet'' (her version of Jeannette)—as if that would turn me into a proper maid! When I was in the kitchen making iced tea and pouring some glasses of cola, Jeannette finally came out to help. She was worried that all we had was sugar-free cola, so she took matters into her own hands and added saccharine tablets to the soft drinks. ''This will make

it taste like real Coke,'' she said happily. As I passed
the cold drinks, I noticed the governor looking at
me with an odd expression, no doubt trying to figure
out whether I was Barbara the secretary or Jeannette
the maid. But his expression was nothing compared
to the looks on the faces of his two aides drinking
the saccharine-spiked colas.

As they left, I noticed one of them staring at
Ethel's house. She had a group of college students
doing some painting, and curtains were flying out
the window and furniture was strewn all over the
yard. I would love to know what those men said
about their visit to the Kennedy compound as they
drove away.

Experiences like this virtually guaranteed that
Mrs. Kennedy received fewer and fewer guests as
time went by. It was Ethel's house, not Grandma's,
that was the real center of activity in Hyannis Port.
Ethel entertained constantly. Even though there were
nine bedrooms in the house, she never had enough
space. Her garage had been converted into a two-
bedroom apartment, and then she expanded into the
little building at the rear of Jackie's yard that had
formerly been used by the Secret Service. One Saturday morning I even saw guests coming out of the
little dollhouse built for Ethel's children to play in;
I discovered that it held a pair of twin beds for the
overflow!

Later that morning I told Mrs. Kennedy about

the amusing sight and she giggled, then she was silent for a moment and sighed, "The poor child." Mrs. Kennedy attributed Ethel's desire to surround herself with people to her attempt to deal with the loss of Bobby, and she never ceased to feel sympathetic about the cause of Ethel's actions, even if she was sometimes inconvenienced by their results.

If you went into Ethel's home by the front entrance, you had to contend with the sagging and rotted porch floor and the Kennedy children climbing on the porch roof and occasionally dropping water bombs on passersby. If you went in the back entrance, you stumbled over huge boxes of groceries just delivered from the market, giant piles of laundry waiting to be washed, and a bunch of children telling the cook what they wanted to eat. There were no set hours for daytime meals; people just turned up when they were hungry and told the cook what they wanted. Following the custom established long ago by Bobby, at night everyone ate together at the dining room table: children, governesses, secretaries, visiting relatives, and famous guests.

And the famous guests were, more often than not, on hand. Ethel's houseguests included athletes like Rafer Johnson, Bruce Jenner, Rosie Grier; columnist Art Buchwald and TV journalist Barbara Walters; singer Andy Williams and comic Buddy Hackett; the beautiful Farrah Fawcett and the folksy David Hartman. These famous faces drifted around the compound, playing tennis on Mrs. Kennedy's court, walking across her lawn to get to the beach, sometimes stopping in to pay their respects to the matriarch of the family. Art Buchwald created a bit of a stir by taking the Kennedy kids to a nude beach. (Ted's younger son, Patrick, later reported he had been too embarrassed to look.) Buddy Hackett didn't like boats, but preferred to stay inside and cook (especially chili). Rafer was an enthusiastic sailor. It was fun to watch the comings and goings of these glamorous visitors.

The doings at Ethel's house could be counted on to provide entertainment. I always got a kick out of watching Ethel handle her large volume of correspondence. She would lie on a comfortable chaise in her front yard, redolent of suntan oil, stretched out in her bathing suit to get the full benefit of the sun. Her secretary would be sitting next to her, fully dressed, bolt upright on a chair, feverishly scribbling away.

Most of Ethel's employees didn't last long; the demands of that large and lively household simply ground them down. There was at least one new cook every summer—sometimes two or three. She hired many of them fresh out of a cooking school in Virginia, but their newly learned skills were rarely adequate to the demands of working for Ethel Kennedy. The cook literally fixed meals all day long, from early morning until late at night. One of these young men told my son, "Every night I go home and change my clothes and go out to the nearest bar and stay until they close. The next morning, when I wake up, I sit in the shower for about forty-five minutes. It takes all that time to get me in here to face this every morning." Jackie once painted a picture as a present for Ethel, depicting the house with children running in and out, hanging out of the upstairs windows, playing on the roof. One cook is trudging out the back door, clothes askew and hair untidy, head down and hastily packed suitcase in hand. Simultaneously, through the front door strides the new cook, neatly dressed and looking hopeful and confident. One thing I always liked about Ethel is that she thought the picture was as funny as everyone else did.

Perhaps it was that aspect of Ethel's personality that made people congregate at her house. You could often find the Shriver children there, having a snack or an extra meal. Jackie's children, Caroline and John, headed there as soon as they got to Hyannis Port, to see their cousins and catch up on all the news. There was always something going on at Ethel's because she liked to keep herself busy. She played a lot of tennis and she loved to sail. Every day Ethel had the cook of the moment prepare huge lunch hampers, filled with sandwiches, deviled eggs, roast chicken, lobster, cheese, fruit, cookies, cold soft drinks, and beer and wine; Mrs. Kennedy called this Ethel's "movable feast." Around noon, she would sweep up everyone in sight—children, houseguests, miscellaneous friends, my son Kevin when he was with me for the summer—and they would go off on one of her sailboats for a few hours. If by chance she happened to forget the dogs (a pair of spaniels that seemed to enjoy sailing), she would stop the boat and they would jump in the water and swim out, where someone would haul them onto the boat.

One memorable day the movable feast came to grief. It was not long before Labor Day, and an unusually large crowd had turned up at the pier at noon to go out on the boat with Ethel. Arthur happened to be outside as they were embarking and he later told me at least twenty-five had boarded the sloop. "They'll never make it," he predicted. As it turned out, he was right. Luckily they weren't too far from shore when the boat capsized; several people spotted the mishap and all on board were quickly picked up. The boat, hampers and all, sank right down to the bottom, like a toy in a bathtub—only this was a $65,000 toy. (The boat was eventually refloated.) Afterward, houseguest Buddy Hackett congratulated himself on his foresight in having decided to stay behind in Ethel's kitchen to whip up a batch of chili.

Part of the chaos at Ethel's house was due to the large canine population. I remember that in the summer of 1977, Ethel had eight dogs: the spaniels, a whippet, some little dogs that looked like animated dust mops, and a pair of big black dogs that loved to bark and jump up on people. One night that summer, one of the big dogs attacked Mrs. Kennedy. She told me about the incident the next morning. "My dear, he had me on the ground." Her dress was all dirty and her hip was bruised; the cook told me that when she came in afterward, her teeth were chattering from the fright it had given her. I don't think the dog meant to harm her, but it was big and enthusiastic, and she was small and frail, and the outcome was inevitable. Really, I was surprised that it happened only once. Everyone in the neighborhood complained about those dogs, and I always felt that they were one of the riskier aspects of going to Ethel's house.

The contrast between Ethel's household and Jackie's, located just a few hundred yards away, was enormous. At Jackie's house, things always seemed to be peaceful and well organized. Whenever I had occasion to go there, I usually found the same scene: a house so quiet I thought perhaps no one was home, Jackie enjoying the sun on her very private deck or stretched out on the porch sofa with a good book in her hand and a cold drink by her side. She came to Hyannis Port for a vacation, and unlike the rest of the Kennedy family, she actually seemed to be able to relax.

Another way Jackie was different was her thoughtfulness about the people who worked for her. She arranged summer schedules so that each of her domestic staff would have a chance to be in Hyannis Port for a few weeks of sun and ocean air. They were even urged to bring along their children. One day I found the maid's baby gurgling happily in a playpen that had been set up in the kitchen. And Jackie was always careful to tip all the local people who helped her out. For example, she gave Arthur a generous tip at the end of the season for tending her lawn and garden. Although he also did yard work for Ethel, as well as Ted and Eunice when he had the time, none of them ever thought of offering him something extra for his trouble.

Several times Jackie asked me to help her out with some typing. The first time, I assumed it would be like the work I did for the other members of the family, for which I usually received only a "thank you." But when I finished the work for Jackie—typing up some pages of Russian translation for a book she was working on at Doubleday—I was surprised to receive in return a handwritten note of thanks along with a check for a generous sum, hand-delivered immediately by her butler. No wonder everyone knocked themselves out for Jackie.

It was impossible to ignore the glamour that surrounded Jacqueline Kennedy Onassis, and yet she herself never gave any sign that she was aware

of it. I remember the first fall I worked for Mrs.
Kennedy, when Jackie called me one day. She always stayed on the Cape longer than the rest of the
family, taking particular pleasure in the quiet autumn days. She had called to check on whether Mrs.
Kennedy had gotten off to Paris on schedule the
day before, and I described the rather frenzied departure. Then we got to talking about the strain of
these long trips on Mrs. Kennedy's health, and her
admirable desire to keep up her usual activities as
long as she was able. Jackie said with affectionate
amusement, "You wouldn't believe what Gramma
goes through with the saleswomen and fitters when
she buys her clothes from a French couturier." Apparently Mrs. Kennedy was an absolute perfectionist about fit, outdoing the standards of even the most
meticulous employees. Suddenly I realized we had
been on the phone for nearly half an hour, just
chatting in a casual way. I found Jackie to be a very
private person, who preferred to remain uninvolved
with all the daily crises of life in the Kennedy compound. But she was never aloof, never unfriendly.
She was either absent altogether, or she was totally
present: open, interested, responsive.

As I thought about Jackie, Ethel, and Rose
Kennedy, it struck me that the famous Kennedy
compound had turned into a matriarchal society. In
the 1950s and '60s, the presiding spirit of the place
had been relentlessly masculine, created by the highly

competitive Joe Kennedy and his equally competitive sons Jack and Bobby. Those were the days of
the much-chronicled football games, played with a
cutthroat determination to win; of the sailboat races
that also had to be won rather than merely enjoyed;
of dinner conversation that was as competitive as
any sport; of guests who were powerful figures in
the world of international affairs. But now the ethos
of the compound was created by the three widows
whose houses seemed to cluster together for support. Kennedys were no longer winning races but
sinking their sailboats offshore. Guests, however
charming, were merely famous, never powerful,
and often no longer even active in the careers that
had brought them into the public eye. The glories
of the past were obviously fading.

It was then that I realized how formidable the
loss of Rose's husband had been. With Ted rarely
present, the Kennedy compound was desperate for
a masculine presence. Someone to demand that the
domestic staff stay on its toes and to let loose a few
colorful curses when that didn't happen. Someone
to make the children and the dogs behave by occasionally throwing a little fear into them. And all
the husbands were missed. Those three lonely women
needed someone to bring them out from behind the
defenses they had spent years constructing.

I remember that one day a neighbor called to
complain about the problems caused by the steady

stream of curious tourists who wanted to see the
Kennedy compound. The influx posed a security
threat to the neighborhood, she said, and she thought
something ought to be done about it. She demanded
to speak to whoever was "in charge." Ruefully, I
realized that her request summed up the problem of
the compound: There was no one in charge. Life
went on, children dashed around the place, adults
entertained guests, repairs to the property eventually
got made, the big Labor Day party was held one
more time. But as I watched all this going on around
me, I always thought it was like the good ship *Lol-
lipop* without a captain: Even though it looked like
a good time was being had by all, they were only
going around and around in circles.

Ted Kennedy tried to fill the vacuum. He would
scoop up everyone in sight and take them out on
his yawl for an afternoon of real sailing. Or he
would stop by to see his mother and inject much-
needed warmth and laughter into her otherwise rather
cloistered existence. He would take the boys out
fishing and proudly return with a big one to cook
for dinner. He loved children (Mrs. Kennedy told
me he had always wanted a big family like Bobby's)
and he enjoyed playing uncle. Once he drove gaily
into the compound driveway in a Winnebago camper
he had rented for a week and, like the Pied Piper,
gathered all the children he could find to take them
on a trip to Maine. (Subsequent reports from some

of the children indicated that he had also stopped in Boston to pick up a girlfriend to go along on the trip.)

But there was more than any one man could do. He had inherited his brothers' weighty political legacy as well as the position of head of the family and father figure to seventeen nieces and nephews made fatherless by death or divorce. And all this was on top of his own concerns with his career, his presidential aspirations, his marriage in crisis, his three children to care for—Ted Jr. with his leg lost to bone cancer, Patrick with such severe asthma that oxygen tanks were kept in the house, and Kara in her teens with the usual problems about her own identity. It was too much to expect of any one man that he could handle all of those roles and fill all those needs by himself.

So we drifted on. It was easy to see why Mrs. Kennedy chose to remain isolated within her own home: The surrounding confusion and chaos were too much for her. Sometimes they were too much for me! There was the day I had to go to the Hyannis airport to meet Ethel's private plane. It turned out that I was one of a sizable convoy. It took several vehicles to load up the children, the dogs, the luggage, the sports equipment, the maids, a coffeepot, flower arrangements from a dinner party the night before, all of which came out of the plane like clowns out of a circus car. Ethel never believed in traveling light; even when she came to Florida for a visit of a week or so, she arrived with mounds of luggage. The turmoil involved in getting that family from the airport to their house was unbelievable.

Perhaps even more unbelievable was the problem involved in getting the Shrivers *to* the airport. Eunice called one morning and asked if I could drive her and her sons Mark and Anthony to the airport in Mrs. Kennedy's car. I explained that she would be using it to go to mass at noon, so Eunice suggested that I drive to their house in my own car and then use their old 1960 Lincoln to transport them all. "Can we leave here at twelve-twenty?" she pressed. I agreed.

I arrived at the Shrivers at twelve-ten only to find that Eunice was just getting into the shower. She told me to wait in the living room, but the house was so dirty I didn't want to sit down. When she finally appeared, I handed her a pile of copies of *Times to Remember*, the book of Mrs. Kennedy's memoirs published in 1974, which Maria had left for her grandmother to autograph. "Do you want to pack these with your things?" I asked.

"Can't you mail these yourself?" she replied. "I have a million things to do and I can't take care of everything. Just call my secretary in Washington and get the addresses," she ordered. Then she added, "Do you think you can do this without bothering

Mother?'' I smiled ruefully at her version of ''Don't tell Mother.''

We all got into the car and set out, but hadn't traveled more than a few blocks when the car had a flat tire. It was obvious that the question of what to do next was up to me; Eunice seemed to be waiting for me to solve the problem single-handedly. I could have walked back to get my car, but it was too small to hold all the people and luggage crowded into the big Lincoln. So I boldly approached a woman I could see pulling out of her driveway and asked her to take everyone to the airport. She was surprised, but she eventually agreed. I walked back to Mrs. Kennedy's and called a garage to fix the tire. They later reported that it was in shreds and that the spare was also unusable, so I told them to put on a retread and send the Shrivers the bill. After work, I walked back to the house to pick up my own car and to check that the garage had returned Eunice's car, as promised. I found all the doors and windows open, just as if the residents had only gone next door for a few minutes. They had left the house until the following spring and not even bothered to close the front door.

Experiences like this made life at Mrs. Kennedy's house seem positively normal. Well, almost. . . . By now I took it in my stride when Mrs. Kennedy announced that we were going to straighten up the attic. It no longer bothered me that we had been doing this afternoon after afternoon for four years in a row. At first it had simply seemed silly, because the attic was perfectly neat. But I finally realized it was Mrs. Kennedy's way of revisiting the past and perhaps also coming to terms with it, and it was more important to her than answering letters from strangers. So I stopped worrying about the correspondence and spent the time the way it mattered to my employer.

And, of course, poking around the attic was always fascinating. There were pieces of antique furniture and collections of old china. There were two large cedar-lined closets that Mr. and Mrs. Kennedy had used for storage of evening clothes, hats and shoes, things like the soft velvet hat the Ambassador had worn when he got an honorary degree from President Eamon De Valera of Ireland. Trophies and awards and commendations that were not important enough to hang in the house but too meaningful to throw away were neatly stored in the attic. One day we found several forgotten treasures: one of Toscanini's batons in a glass case, and a frame that held a plate that had been used by George Washington, along with a lock of his hair. (We got that out and hung it in the dining room: it was later appraised at $3,000.)

Best of all were the old letters, postcards, scrapbooks. It seemed that Kathleen especially had been a great one for keeping memorabilia, and the attic contained her old dance programs, albums of snapshots, newspaper clippings about her friends, even letters that she had written her family in the sadly brief period between the time of her marriage and the battlefront death of her husband during World War II. There were also letters from Jack Kennedy to his parents that dated back to his wartime service in the South Pacific. I was afraid these might be upsetting to Mrs. Kennedy, but when she read them, she began to laugh in appreciation of Jack's wit and quite enjoyed these messages from the past, many of which he had jokingly signed with the pseudonym "Betty Blitch."

The attic even contained scrapbooks that dated back to the time Rose Fitzgerald was a high school girl and her father was the mayor of Boston. The distant past was vividly alive for her, and she was careful to keep up with the few friends from that period who were still living.

One of them, Marie Greene, came for lunch one day. The two women had been estranged for several years after biographer Gail Cameron interviewed Mrs. Greene for her book *Rose*, and Mrs. Greene said of Mrs. Kennedy's mother, "Josie, of course, was a bitch." But somehow the old friends had reconciled, and Mrs. Kennedy was in high spirits as she waited to greet her guest. She looked wonderful, dressed in one of her designer outfits

complete with big hat. As soon as Mrs. Greene
arrived, they went into the bright and cheerful sun-
room, with its alcove decorated with hundreds of
family photos. I figured the flow of reminiscence
would be fast and furious, but when I went in to
tell them lunch was ready, I found Mrs. Greene
working very slowly on finishing an interminable
sentence, while Mrs. Kennedy was looking as if she
were about to fall asleep. I waited for Mrs. Greene
to grind to a halt, but she gave no sign of doing so
in my lifetime. Eventually I decided I had no choice
but to interrupt. Mrs. Greene gave no sign she had
heard me and simply continued talking. Mrs. Kennedy, wearing a rather martyred expression, was
staring fixedly at the ceiling. The cook later told
me that the lunch went on in the same way, and
that she had spent twenty minutes waiting for Mrs.
Greene to answer the question of whether she wanted
coffee, tea, or Sanka. When Mrs. Greene finally
left, Mrs. Kennedy came into my office and sighed.
"I thought I was in a bad way . . . she really is
stupid!" We laughed together, but I could tell Mrs.
Kennedy was proud that she was more vigorous and
attractive than most other women her age.

   She also maintained a busier public schedule
than her contemporaries. She was frequently interviewed by the local press. She appeared, with other
members of the family, at the dedication ceremonies
at the Kennedy Library. Richard Avedon took her

photograph for *Rolling Stone*—unfortunately on a day that she was in a bad mood. She had asked me to stay with her to help, to be sure her dress was properly arranged and to remind her to keep her hands out of sight, since she thought they were the one feature that really betrayed her age. But during the shooting session, she changed her mind and suddenly announced, "Barbara, please leave the room. You're distracting me." The picture that appeared in the magazine was shot almost immediately afterward. Everything is there in her face for the world to see: her anger, her desire to be the eternal center of attention, and all the pain she has suffered.

Part of Mrs. Kennedy's public schedule was campaigning for her son in her native state of Massachusetts. During Ted's 1976 campaign for reelection to the Senate, she made several appearances on his behalf. One was a reception on Cape Cod, in nearby Falmouth. As she was dressing, she asked me to call Eunice, who was supposed to accompany her, to see whether or not she was ready. I admitted that I had just seen Eunice and Ethel walk by on their way to the tennis court. Mrs. Kennedy was obviously worried, and when Eunice bounded upstairs ten minutes later, I had the feeling the discussion was far from pleasant. A few minutes later, Mrs. Kennedy came downstairs, looking smashing in a floor-length blue chiffon dress embroidered with silver medallions. She stood in the entry hall and suddenly hiked up her dress to adjust her underwear. "Those two ninnies," she said, "are out on the tennis court when they should be doing this. After all, I'm eighty-six years old!" Just then Ethel turned up, miraculously dressed in that short time and also looking very nice. I heard later that Mrs. Kennedy was the hit of the reception. She told the audience, "It's all right to go campaigning when you are sixty-six, or even seventy-six. But when you get to be eighty-six it is a little too much. Don't let your children do that to you!" Everyone laughed and applauded.

Despite—or perhaps because of—her heavier public schedule in Hyannis Port, Mrs. Kennedy usually seemed happier when we were on the Cape. I felt much the same way. Since the house was in good repair and we had few houseguests, household crises were at a minimum. And when problems did arise, there were members of the family around to intervene. Compared to Palm Beach, Hyannis Port was practically a vacation, and I was always sorry when it was time to leave in the fall.

I never could decide whether to laugh or cry over Mrs. Kennedy's departure. The moment itself was the picture of propriety. While the car waited in the driveway to take her to the Boston airport, the staff assembled on the wide front porch to tell her good-bye. Jeannette, Arthur, myself, and perhaps Joe Gargan and one or two other people lined

up to kiss her good-bye and wave to her as she
disappeared down the driveway; this was the staff
ritual, so her children never participated. Then the
minute she was out of sight, everyone rushed away
with unseemly haste. (Their pay stopped as soon as
their employer left.) Jeannette was so anxious to
leave that while she was standing on the porch waving good-bye, she had her car idling in the back
driveway and the door on the driver's side standing
open so she wouldn't waste a precious second before
she zoomed away.

It was just one more example of the difference
between the storybook appearance of life with the
Kennedys and the reality.

7

A Matter of Money

W hen it came to matters of money, I always felt Mrs. Kennedy's attitude could only be described as eccentric.

There was no question that the Kennedy family was indeed very wealthy. Recent estimates put the total family holdings at somewhere close to half a billion dollars. In the recently published *The Very Rich Book*, Jacqueline Thompson says there are only ten families in the entire country whose amalgamated net worth exceeds the Kennedys'.

But, while Mrs. Kennedy could at times behave like the woman of great wealth that she was, at other times she was more like an ordinary housewife on a restricted budget. Her respect for thrift probably stemmed from her relatively less affluent childhood and was compounded by her simple inexperience with matters of money. Like many widows of her generation, she had an Old World sense of economy that had never been relaxed because her husband had always handled all expenditures. She had no experience in making money or in deciding how to spend it, and so her inclination was to save it when she could. Like many wealthy people, Mrs. Kennedy would spend appropriately for what she considered "necessary luxuries," but would be more careful with nonessential expenditures. But, unlike others of her class, Mrs. Kennedy had what I felt was a very peculiar and severe idea of what was necessary and what was not.

For instance, every year she sent all her distant relatives large checks for Christmas, and she was unfailingly generous whenever one of them was in need. But when it came to her own grandchildren, she could certainly never be accused of being the one who spoiled them. Each of the twenty-nine grandchildren, even the ones who were then in their teens, got just fifteen dollars on their birthday. Exceptions to this rule were rare. One year Pat Lawford suggested that it would be nice for Mrs. Kennedy to give her godchild Victoria Lawford a portable electric typewriter for her birthday. Mrs. Kennedy responded to this suggestion with a very funny letter

about the impossibility of spending such a large
amount as $125. She explained that she was already
going to have to spend extra money on her godchild
Maria Shriver that year because it was her twenty-
first birthday. She went on to remind Pat that Joe
Kennedy had already given all the grandchildren a
great deal of money and so she herself was not in
the least concerned about them. She closed sweetly,
"Much love and affection."

The mention of her children's independent
wealth was just one of the ways Mrs. Kennedy
honored the memory of Joe Kennedy. Years after
his death, she remained devoted. She liked to talk
about the days of their courtship, and she once said
emphatically, "I fell in love when I was only seventeen and I never fell out!" She often spoke ad-
miringly of his talent for making money, which she
regarded with a kind of mystical awe. "He was
really wonderful," she told me one day. "Why, he
could make even you rich!"

But, without her husband there to guide her,
Mrs. Kennedy often ended up worrying most about
the smallest expenses. She would become obsessed
with the idea that she was spending too much money
for phone service and decide to take out some of
the extensions—a convenience that cost only $6.50
a month in a house worth millions. Or she would
get all fired up about making a donation to the local
thrift shop, and she and I would spend hours sorting

through old clothes and household goods. Then Dennis or Arthur would spend more time delivering the things to the shop. Many of the things she donated weren't even salable. The funniest example I remember was when she gave the Hyannis thrift shop *one* of Teddy's old sneakers.

One day I heard Mrs. Kennedy telling the cook not to fix her a baked potato for lunch because it would cost too much to turn on the oven to cook (this in a house where the bill for the outdoor pool was over six hundred dollars a month). Another time, when Jeannette was away and I volunteered to prepare her dinner she told me she wanted to have the baked potato left over from the day before. I was distressed because that very morning I had cleaned out the refrigerator and thrown away the wizened potato I found lying at the back of the shelf. "I've never warmed up a baked potato before," I temporized. "It's very simple," explained Pat, who was visiting at the time. "Just scoop it out and put it in a double boiler with butter, salt and pepper." So I rushed downstairs calling Arthur to come help me retrieve the potato, which I luckily found I could easily wash off and still use. Later, when I asked her how the meal had been, she answered, "Well, the lamb chop was so-so, but the potato was delicious."

When the family was visiting, Mrs. Kennedy set a bountiful table. When the Shrivers and Lawfords stayed with Mrs. Kennedy in Palm Beach over Christmas one year, the grocery bill for their eight-day stay was more than $1,700, and on top of that, there were additional large bills from the liquor store, the fish market, and the gourmet specialty store. A typical dinner menu (often planned by Sarge Shriver) might be:

> *Cold Vichyssoise*
> *Shrimp Cocktail*
> *Crown Roast of Lamb (2)*
> *Tiny New Potatoes*
> *Two Vegetables*
> *Baked Alaska*

Yet when the guests left after the holidays, Mrs. Kennedy decided to turn off the water cooler to save electricity. And when the water man came one time to pick up the empty ten-gallon bottles, she chided him for taking one that still had a tiny bit left. Would he please empty it into a glass so it could be drunk?

Another incident that emphasized the contrasts in spending and saving in Mrs. Kennedy's household occurred in Hyannis Port. We were paddling around in the pool, talking about this and that, and she asked me if I had remembered to order the lobster for dinner that night. She had invited some of the family over for the delightful treat of fresh boiled Maine lobster served with lots of melted butter—a luxury that cost more than fifty dollars to feed that many people. "Yes, they'll be delivered this afternoon," I said, "and I thought you might like potato chips, too, so I ordered a bag of those." She replied thoughtfully, "I believe we already have a bag in the kitchen." "Oh, well," I replied, "you can always use them." But the thought of those unneeded potato chips clearly worried Mrs. Kennedy, and a few minutes later she asked me to leave the pool and call the shop back and cancel the order for one 59-cent bag.

In fact, for some reason it was most often food that brought out Mrs. Kennedy's economical streak. I'll never forget the affair of the missing pieces of chicken. The day after chicken had been served to dinner guests in Hyannis Port, Mrs. Kennedy went into the kitchen and counted the leftover pieces in the refrigerator. She discovered she was missing two, and the fact caused an uproar. Jeannette, put on the spot because she was unable to account for the loss, suggested maybe I had eaten the missing pieces. So Mrs. Kennedy stormed into my office and exclaimed, "You took my chicken!" I had to laugh, but to satisfy my own curiosity, I did a little detective work later that day and established that the chicken in question had been appropriated as a snack by Bobby Shriver. That fact became one more of the "Don't tell Mrs. Kennedy" conspiracies.

Sometimes she would say to me, "I'd like to

see the food bills . . . why don't I ever see them?''
The answer, of course, was that I had been instructed by the New York office to show Mrs. Kennedy only small bills, then approve the rest and
send them on to New York. And those food bills
were definitely not small! So I would just answer
that I didn't know. "I ought to see them," she
would insist. "I don't know what that cook is doing.
She could be ordering strawberries out of season
for all I know.''

One reason the New York office kept those
larger bills from Mrs. Kennedy was so that necessary repairs and maintenance could be done. Her
reluctance to spend for that purpose had allowed
the Palm Beach house to deteriorate to the point
where the value of that very valuable oceanfront
property was declining. Things got in such a state
that in the fall of 1976, several people from the New
York office went to Florida to assess the situation,
decide what repairs were needed, and then hire
someone to do them all. When I got to the house
in early October, I found the front door missing,
plaster all over the dining room, and a huge hole
in the back of the garage apartment. Plumbers, electricians, sandblasters, and painters were scurrying
around all corners of the house and grounds. The
people who set this chaos in motion had wisely
retreated to New York.

In the middle of all this uproar, Mrs. Kennedy

called to say she was ready to come down—a few weeks earlier than expected—despite Jean Smith's efforts to delay her with dinner parties and luncheon guests. Of course, she knew nothing about the extensive renovations in progress. In order to finish the work before she arrived, we had to ask the various contractors to come in and work double-time over the weekend—thus unfortunately spending more money to keep her from finding out she was spending money. By the time Mrs. Kennedy arrived, everything was finished except the garage apartment, which looked like a bomb site. For the next week, Dennis, Mam'selle, and I had to make sure Mrs. Kennedy went in and out through the formal front entrance rather than the back way, which would take her right by the garage. She never noticed the repairs to the rest of the house, except to comment that everything looked very clean and fresh.

Sometimes all our subterfuge failed. For example, the big old-fashioned freezer in the Palm Beach house broke down that same fall, and I hired a man to fix it. Mrs. Kennedy walked into the back kitchen while he was at work. I had to confess what was going on and tell her the repair was going to cost a hundred dollars. I pointed out that we needed a working freezer, especially since the house would soon be full of company. "What will we do when everyone comes for Thanksgiving and Christmas?" I asked.

"We can make do with the freezer compartment of the refrigerator," she replied triumphantly.

"But there's not nearly enough space," I explained. "And this is the only place for all the ice cream that everyone eats for dessert."

"They don't need ice cream," Mrs. Kennedy shot back. "They can eat milk and cookies for dessert." I looked at her out of the corner of my eye and said, "Now, Mrs. Kennedy . . ." and she finally laughed and said, "Oh, all right," and went back upstairs to her room.

We had the same sort of problem about carpeting for the attic steps in the Hyannis Port house. They were very steep and a bit slippery and I was afraid someone would fall, perhaps Mrs. Kennedy herself. But I knew I would have to clear it with her, since she would see the carpeting. I told her I was worried about the safety hazard and added that I had even slipped on those stairs myself. Sears could carpet them for about fifty dollars, I explained. There was a silence, then, "It must be you," she said briskly. "After all, we've been here for forty years and no one else has ever fallen on those steps." No more was ever said about the carpeting.

The whole episode reminded me of a story I had heard from someone in the New York office about the time years before when Mrs. Kennedy had instructed the maid to put a low-wattage bulb in the hallway lamp to save on the electric bill. Joe Kennedy took one look at the gloomy hallway and said indignantly, "Christ, Rose, you might save a few cents a month on that light bulb, but it will cost thousands of dollars if I have to go to the hospital with a broken leg from falling in the dark."

Mrs. Kennedy's inexperienced concept of spending and saving didn't improve after her husband's death because of the peculiar role of the New York office in the family finances. The office, on the thirtieth floor of the Pan Am Building, had been set up by Joe Kennedy to manage the privately held real estate and oil companies he owned, to administer the trusts he had established for the children and grandchildren, and to operate charitable and memorial activities he had set in motion. There were about a half dozen employees in the New York office. The ever-helpful Tom Walsh was one of the key figures there, and Steve Smith was more or less at the helm. Most of the people who worked there had been hired by Joe Kennedy, and he had indoctrinated them with his policies. He had spent his life building up a fortune so that none of his children or grandchildren would ever even have to think about money. Instead, the employees of that office were the only ones who understood his tangled financial empire. The family was not to be bothered with such mundane concerns.

The New York office handled all financial

transactions for Mrs. Kennedy—and for everyone
else in the family, too. Fixed expenses such as taxes,
mortgage and maintenance payments, insurance, and
so on were automatically paid by the office when
due. For other expenses, the family just had the
bills sent to New York. If a Kennedy wanted to buy
filet mignon or rent a car or splurge at Cartier,
paying the bill was simply a matter of having it sent
to the New York office. If someone in the family
wanted to buy another house, they called the New
York office for approval. If Mrs. Kennedy wanted
to leave her brother $25,000 in her will, she called
the New York office to see if she had it to leave.
Kennedys who overspent eventually had the matter
forcibly brought to their attention. Those like Mrs.
Kennedy who underspent on maintenance had the
money put out for them behind their backs.

I could understand how easy it was for all the
family to leave things to the New York office, because I often did the same thing. The people who
worked there were always very nice to me, particularly Tom Walsh, a fatherly sort of man who called
me "darling" and did all he could to make my life
easier. The first winter I went to Palm Beach with
Mrs. Kennedy, I talked to Tom about finding myself
an apartment to rent, since I had definitely decided
I would never "live in" at Mrs. Kennedy's. "Just
look around for something you like, darling," Tom
advised me. "How much rent will you pay?" I

asked. "Just find a place you like and let me know about it," Tom responded genially.

The same thing happened when I talked to him about leasing a car for me. Even though I was getting mileage for the driving I did in my own car, I felt that my little Duster was depreciating far too rapidly because of the number of miles I was putting on it, driving back and forth between Massachusetts and Florida and rushing around on errands like going to the airport to pick up visitors or into town on my lunch hour to buy something Mrs. Kennedy needed urgently. So I suggested to Tom that they might lease a car for me. "Of course, darling," said Tom. "How much will you pay a month?" I asked. "You just shop around and see what kind of a price you can get," answered Tom. I really didn't know whether he expected me to look at Pintos or Cadillacs, but I ended up with a wonderful little Mustang with an all-white interior and a tape deck that was the envy of all the Kennedy grandchildren. "God, Barbara, what a nice car," said Caroline after she had borrowed it one afternoon to slip past reporters. In such circumstances, it is easy to lose touch with financial realities. The New York office could take care of those for everyone.

The system was set up to protect the entire family from financial worries. The result was that none of them—Steve Smith excepted—really knew anything about how to manage money. They didn't even know how much they had. Mrs. Kennedy, who was certainly worth millions, had no idea what she could afford and what she couldn't. For example, acting in what they believed to be her best interest, the people in the New York office would tell her she couldn't afford to give so much money to relatives. Then, behind her back, the same people would authorize significant expenditures to reroof the Hyannis Port house or buy new appliances or, in my case, to pay for the services of a personal secretary to make Mrs. Kennedy's life easier. No doubt their budget decisions were correct, but the point is that these were New York's budget decisions, not Mrs. Kennedy's. More than once, she became exasperated and telephoned the New York office to demand to know how much money she had. They always said they would let her know . . . but no one ever returned the call.

This way of handling money—which I have learned is not at all uncommon in families of great wealth—tends to make people behave like children. Lacking both full knowledge and real responsibility, they are naturally unable to make sensible judgments about how much they should spend. If they spend too much or too little, indulge all their appetites or fail to buy enough food to stay alive, someone else will have to deal with the consequences.

I am sure this was partly the cause of Mrs.

Kennedy's erratic spending behavior. And the more frequently that decisions about paying for necessities such as a new clothes dryer or maintenance of the pool were made behind her back, the more it must have seemed to her that she was right in taking the attitude she did. For example, in Palm Beach she had flatly refused to spend any money to fix the pool heating system. So the New York office and I conspired to have it taken care of without her knowledge. The necessary repairs were made (and her account was charged for the cost), so the heating system functioned perfectly from then on. But from Mrs. Kennedy's point of view, it must have appeared that the heating system just stopped giving trouble. Naturally, she would conclude that she was right in refusing to spend any money to have it fixed, since the problem seemed to have fixed itself. So the next time I asked her to spend money on some kind of repair or maintenance, she would be even more likely to refuse.

The contradictions that grew out of this situation continually boggled my mind. Take the matter of Mrs. Kennedy's annual trip to Paris. She always stayed in the elegant and luxurious Plaza Athenée, where she was such a dependably regular guest that the hotel even kept her belongings in storage for her from one year to the next, so she didn't have to travel back and forth with her pajamas, dressing gown, cosmetics, alarm clock, and so on. She would shop at the couturier salons, spending more than $1,000 for a dress from Jean-Louis Sherrer, $450 at Dior for blouses, $250 on a new hat. Yet in order to travel to Paris, she insisted on getting the lowest possible fare, even though that meant she would have to leave at an inconvenient time and stay away for three weeks. Of course, she flew tourist instead of first-class, and because she found the food inedible she had the cook pack her a little lunch of chicken sandwiches, her favorite cookies, and milk in a thermos to tide her over. And she wouldn't let me hire a limo to meet her; she always said she'd just take a taxi. In fact, not only did she take a taxi, she usually tried to save a little more money by sharing it with someone else waiting in the taxi line. She did that once on her arrival back in New York, and the woman was so flustered to find herself riding in a yellow cab with Rose Kennedy that she actually fainted! The driver had to stop and revive her.

One of Mrs. Kennedy's favorite economies was particularly frustrating to friends and relatives who wanted to give her presents for birthdays and Christmas. Mrs. Kennedy invariably returned presents for credit. She would deny herself, and instead use the credit to give others gifts. Teddy gave her a pretty and stylish beach coat for her birthday (or, to be more accurate, he had me pick it out and put it on his account), and she returned it for credit. Jackie gave her a lovely pair of hand-embroidered sheets from Porthault for her bedroom in Hyannis Port; her mother-in-law first asked her to exchange them for green rather than pink embroidery and then eventually returned the green ones for a credit. When Ted noticed how old her record player was (Mrs. Kennedy said merrily, "It's an antique, like everything else around here, including me!") and gave her a fancy new one, she made him return it for credit. When people sent flowers for her birthday, she asked the florist to stop delivery and give her a credit instead. This led to embarrassing situations. More than once, someone who had sent flowers dropped by to see how they looked. This called for quick thinking on my part: Since good manners forbade a vistor's invasion of Mrs. Kennedy's bedroom, I would usually claim that she had decided to put the flowers there.

I used to amuse myself by working out the complicated trail that led from one present to another. For example, Mrs. Kennedy had received a handsome picture frame from Barbara Walters as a thank-you after she visited Hyannis Port; the frame was promptly returned to Cartier for credit. A few months later, Mrs. Kennedy bought Jackie a sweet little gold pillbox for Christmas with that credit. . . . There were many similarly tangled trails.

It was a real feat of ingenuity when someone came up with a present that Mrs. Kennedy would actually keep. Jackie managed it one time by bringing back from Greece a beautiful silver crucifix to which she had tied a bright strand of ribbon so it could be hung on Mrs. Kennedy's bed; not even Mrs. Kennedy could resist such a gift. One year the children arranged to have the books written by various members of the family bound in matching leather for the bookshelves in the living room of the Hyannis Port house. Mrs. Kennedy appreciated the thought but noted that the leather didn't really match the colors of the living room. Color-coordinated or not, she kept the specially bound and stamped volumes. The grandchildren often got around the problem by asking her what she wanted for Christmas or a birthday and then simply buying whatever it was. Her requests were for such exotic items as white ankle socks (which had to be purchased in the children's department) or a new rosary or a pair of binoculars so she could keep an eye on "you people" at the pier or far corners of the yard. Of course, having asked for these gifts, Mrs. Kennedy couldn't return them, and it was most frequently in this way that the family outsmarted her and made her accept something nice for herself.

Mrs. Kennedy also frequently returned things she had bought herself, when she got home and decided she didn't really need them. Since most of the places she shopped were used to her foibles, they generally took things back without a fuss. But one day she gave me a lipstick and a bottle of nail polish remover to take back to the drugstore for credit. The clerk took a look and then protested, "But these have been used." Embarrassed, I mumbled something about Mrs. Kennedy not liking them. "Oh, really," said the clerk, "this sort of thing has been going on for years with her account." The next time she gave me used cosmetics to return, I simply threw them away and never mentioned the subject again.

Having learned my lesson from that experience, I was more cautious when one day on Worth Avenue she asked me to return a straw hat to Saks, since she just remembered she could get the same thing at Buttner's in Hyannis for less than half the price. But I explained that hats were a nonreturnable item and stood fast in my refusal to do the errand. "Oh, all right," she said, "I'll do it myself." So she gathered up her purse and sauntered back into Saks. A few minutes later, she returned empty-handed. "They didn't want to do it," she said triumphantly, "but I talked them into it."

Many of Mrs. Kennedy's economies were amusing. For example, she always had me get old desk calendars on sale at the end of the year when they cost next to nothing. She would use them for making notes and then refer to the current calendar hanging on the wall (which was given to her every year by the church) to confirm the actual date. She never tipped bellboys, porters, taxi drivers, or hotel maids. Instead, she carried with her a supply of specially printed cards, about the size of a postcard, that had a picture of President Kennedy on the front and some of his favorite passages of Scripture on the back, along with the famous line from his inaugural address, "Ask not what your country can do for you; ask what you can do for your country." She autographed these cards and handed them out in lieu of tips, saying blithely, "Save this, someday it will be worth money."

I tried to handle her requests to economize tactfully, but sometimes the two of us ended up in a fight. This happened annually about the telephones in the Palm Beach house. Every fall when I arrived, I had the phones in the house turned on. Then Mrs. Kennedy would arrive and tell me to have them all—except hers and mine—disconnected until the guests began to arrive for the holidays. Every year I explained to her that it actually cost more to have them turned off and then back on again than it did just to leave them alone. But every year she was convinced her method of economy was more effective.

Our funniest argument was probably about the security guard. At one point she decided (wisely, I thought) that we needed a security guard on the premises. So we hired one from an agency, and they explained that we could get one without a uniform or, for an extra daily fee, a man in full uniform.

After a lot of thought, Mrs. Kennedy concluded that she wanted the deterrent effect of the uniform, and so we agreed to pay the extra fee. But once the guard reported for duty, it fretted Mrs. Kennedy that he did nothing but watch, which seemed to her very much like idleness. So she came up with the idea that she could get more for her money by asking the guard to do some painting around the house while he was keeping an eye out for intruders. The guard was not particularly enthusiastic about the idea, but he finally agreed—on one condition. He wouldn't do it while he was wearing his uniform because it was expensive and he was likely to splash paint on it. I pointed out to Mrs. Kennedy that we were paying extra for the uniform and that it seemed silly to ask the guard to take it off. If we wanted a painter, we could just hire one—at a much lower hourly wage. She seemed to agree with me at that time, but later she went out and told the guard to start painting. I saw that it was useless to continue discussing the matter.

Mrs. Kennedy also found time to worry about the way other people in the family spent their money. When her grandson Christopher Lawford thoughtfully called her from school at Harvard, she reprimanded him, like a typical grandmother. "Next time, call at night because it's cheaper." When Ethel sent everyone her funny Valentine that showed her sitting on Rosie Grier's lap (he was dressed in a red costume with a silly-looking hat), Mrs. Kennedy went to the trouble of sending Ethel a handwritten note about how silly it was to waste Kennedy money mailing things like that around. When the children got together to give her a new Jacuzzi for the pool after her old one broke down, she refused to accept it on the grounds that it was too expensive. The Whirlpool dealer wouldn't take it back, so it ended up in the Smiths' summer house; Mrs. Kennedy, of course, thought it had been returned.

While Mrs. Kennedy so habitually denied herself things, she could be on the other hand a very generous gift-giver. Her friends received lovely Christmas presents: orchid plants or a bottle of Joy perfume. And she was always very sweet about remembering me at Christmas and on birthdays. The first year I was with her, she walked into the maids' dining room one afternoon when Mam'selle, Dennis, and Jim were observing my birthday with a little cake and a few gifts. Minutes later, she buzzed for me to come to her bedroom. "How much does a bottle of champagne cost?" she asked curiously. "I'd like to give you one for your birthday." And it didn't have to be a special occasion for her to do some nice little thing for me. She found out that I used the same Elizabeth Arden moisturizer that she bought in large bottles, so she told me to bring my little bottle to work with me and she would refill it from her big one. And when she realized how tiring it could be to make the long drive back and forth from the Cape to Florida (the only way to get my car back and forth), she arranged to have me take the autotrain.

But sometimes Mrs. Kennedy's sense of thrift led her to offer things that were just plain inappropriate. She meant well, but I could only smile when she gave me an old nail pencil that had obviously been used many times. It was also difficult to find the right response when she gave me a bag of her old cotton balls that she thought I might be able to get one more use out of. Perhaps the most questionable of all these gifts was one of her old worn-out bras, after she discovered that we wore the same size.

In some ways, Mrs. Kennedy just never adjusted to the idea that she was wealthy. When she first married Joe Kennedy, they lived like many other struggling young couples, watching their budget as their family grew rapidly. Despite her money and worldly position, she could often behave like any ordinary housewife. Sometimes, on the cook's day off, I would walk out to the kitchen and find Mrs. Kennedy there, in an old calico apron, merrily stirring something in a little pan that she was fixing for her lunch. (It used to worry me because her eyesight was so bad, and she would lean right over the flame in her pink nylon robe that could catch fire in a second.) You would never guess you were seeing the glamorous Rose Kennedy if you caught her in the middle of her homemaking activities. Those close to her were used to such behavior, but it sometimes surprised people who didn't know her well. For example, in 1976, she went to visit Jackie's mother, Janet Auchincloss, at Hammersmith Farms, a lovely Newport estate right on the water that afforded a wonderful view of the tall ships sailing by in that bicentennial year. When she came home, she told me that she got up in the middle of the night and went downstairs to the kitchen to fix herself a little snack. I always wondered what the staff thought when they came to work in the morning and saw her pots carefully soaking in the sink. Mrs. Kennedy had not grown up with servants and still didn't expect to have them do everything she was used to doing for herself.

Perhaps part of Mrs. Kennedy's uneasy accommodation to the family's great wealth was due to her knowledge that many people considered the Kennedy family to be nothing more than nouveau riche. That accusation had been hurled against Joe Kennedy by blue-blooded Bostonians from the moment he made his first million. Throughout the rest of his life, he retained an edge of bitterness over the snubs and exclusions the family had borne. Rose had certainly come in for her share, and they may have affected her even more deeply. Her husband at least had the satisfaction of knowing that he was outwitting most of the world, including his patrician critics, as he amassed one of the largest fortunes in the country. But Rose Kennedy had no such sense of achievement to fall back on as a consolation (except for her determination to be the mother of great men). Besides, people are usually cattier about the social failings of a wife than a husband. Women are expected to know the social proprieties and are frequently criticized when they fail to understand them. For example, I read in one of Stephen Birmingham's books that acquaintances had criticized Rose Kennedy for going out to a weekend on Long Island in a chauffeur-driven limousine, rather than driving herself in a station wagon (a real "woody" would be best) as was the accepted upper-class custom. That limo gave away that fact that she was new to monied society.

By the time I knew Mrs. Kennedy, she had had decades to learn how to blend in. She was always very observant of details such as how a table was set, how a letter was addressed, how a thank-you note was phrased, and she was careful to do all of these things "the right way" once she had learned what it was. I learned that much of her knowledge of the correct way to do things dated back to the period when she was the wife of the

American ambassador to England and had a staff to explain to her all the fine points of protocol.

How she loved to remember those days! Scattered throughout both her houses were framed portraits of herself taken during that period, usually wearing a dress with a long train and a jeweled coronet in her hair. One day we were both looking at one of these photographs hanging on the sunroom wall and I said, "You were so beautiful then, Mrs. Kennedy," and she answered soberly, "Yes, yes, I was, wasn't I?" She often reminisced about the people she had met in those years in England, with special emphasis on her conversations with the King and Queen. On one visit to Windsor, she and the Queen had a good chat about the problems presented by their children. She told me that the Queen said she never had any trouble with Elizabeth (the present Queen), who was always obedient, but that her younger sister, Margaret, could be very willful and sometimes created discipline problems.

But I don't think Mrs. Kennedy was ever truly comfortable in such exalted circumstances. She was afraid she wouldn't be accepted, and I believe that fear lingered on and kept her from trying to become a part of society in Palm Beach, or Washington, or New York. She preferred to live quietly by herself, seeing few people other than family, and at least part of the reason was that such a life protected her from even having to be aware of the social barriers between herself and the old-money upper class.

I was interested to notice how many of her real friends were also women who had through marriage reached a position higher than the one they were born into. Mary Sanford, for example, was simply a Hollywood starlet before she married Laddie and eventually became one of society's *grande dames*. The Duchess of Windsor, of course, was the most famous Cinderella story of this century. C. Z. Guest had been a chorus girl before she married socially prominent Winston Guest. These were the women who put Mrs. Kennedy at her ease.

It was an ease that was difficult for her to achieve with women whose upper-class social position went back for generations. I think this was why she was always a bit in awe of her daughter-in-law, the former Jacqueline Bouvier.

It always seemed such a pity that Mrs. Kennedy could not let herself spend the money that could make her truly comfortable. The biggest problem was always the household staff, which was always too small. Her cook was also the cleaning lady, often able to do neither job well. Her chauffeur was also the gardener, or worked elsewhere during the day, with the result that she had to ask me, or one of her children, or anyone who happened to be around, to drive her where she wanted to go. One day in Hyannis Port, decorator Bob Luddington came in the back way, escorting Mrs. Kennedy. Later I asked him where they had been. "She got me to take her to church," he said in mild surprise, "and I'm not even Catholic!"

Because Mrs. Kennedy asked her household staff to do so many different jobs at one time, she was really very badly served. It was not the fault of the employees in question, who had such taxing jobs that they had to refuse to take on extra work, such as cooking for guests. As it was they would often be unable to keep up with the demands of the household when guests were in residence.

It always appalled me that so much of Mrs. Kennedy's existence was dictated by what the staff would or wouldn't do. Family visits turned into an emotional strain; in fact, guests of any sort created a big flurry—remember what happened when Gloria Guinness merely came to tea. This made Mrs. Kennedy even more socially isolated. It kept her from inviting friends and family for meals or visits. Unquestionably, it limited the possibilities of her life. The sad thing was that all it would have taken was a few thousand more dollars a year to provide enough competent staff. It was ridiculous that the entire burden of cooking, cleaning, and serving in two large houses should fall on the shoulders of three elderly women: Mam'selle, Nellie, and Jeannette, and Nellie had kidney trouble that now requires twice-a-week dialysis. Yet she is *still* holding down the fort for the Kennedy family, baking Ted's favorite chocolate roll and her bourbon-laced cheese balls.

Poor Mrs. Kennedy. All that money and she still couldn't live comfortably.

8

Public Life

Not long after I started working for Mrs. Kennedy, she advised me to start keeping a diary of my activities as her secretary. "It will be nice for your children and grandchildren to read about your days here," she urged. "You should take advantage of these things while you have the chance. You will probably never have another job like this one," she added with a wry laugh.

As her comment indicated, Mrs. Kennedy had a very strong sense of history, and she knew her family had a secure place in the historical record of the United States. Much of her time and energy was spent in keeping the image bright. When I worked for her in the 1970s, Mrs. Kennedy was still very much in demand for personal appearances, interviews, and photographs. She was the member of the family who most seemed to symbolize its virtues for an admiring public. Old scandals might crop up to embarrass the Kennedy men, but Rose Kennedy's fame remained untarnished.

Ten years after JFK's assassination, Mrs. Kennedy continued to receive a heavy volume of mail. Strangers wrote letters of sympathy and affection. They asked for favors or jobs or financial aid. People who didn't know her personally would send flowers or handmade gifts, such as afghans, doilies, and hankies embroidered with a rose. They would send their own treasured mementos, snapshots, and beautiful cards that Mrs. Kennedy sometimes pasted up on her desk. Sometimes a letter would be prompted by a dream or a psychic vision, giving the writer an important message about the past or future to deliver to Mrs. Kennedy. Occasionally, the letters were desperate, such as the one from a man in New Delhi who said he would drink poison if he didn't receive $3,000 from Mrs. Kennedy by a certain date. (The date had already passed by the time we received the letter.) There was very little hate mail, and when such a letter did come, it was sure to be unsigned and minus any return address. Sending a hate letter to Mrs. Kennedy must have seemed as shameful as spitting on the flag.

I worked out ways of handling most of this mail without bothering Mrs. Kennedy. The volume of little gifts that came in made it impossible to accept them, so I refused all packages at the post office unless I recognized the return address. That was much simpler than taking them home, opening them up, and then repacking them to return to the sender. One time when I was away from Hyannis Port for several weeks on my own vacation, Arthur made the mistake of accepting all the packages that arrived. When I returned, I found a huge pile. Dreading the work of sending all those gifts back, I came up with the bright idea of calling Dave Powers at the Kennedy Library in Boston. That kind man was not only willing to take them off my hands, he even sent a truck to collect them. They are no doubt still neatly stored in one of the several warehouses around the Boston area that contain material the library has no room to display.

For the most part, answering the mail was a time-consuming but not difficult task. I had the engraved cards devised by a former secretary that thanked people for their letters and explained that Mrs. Kennedy was unable to answer personally. I also sent out some of the cards that Mrs. Kennedy used for tips, the ones with President Kennedy's picture on the front and some verses from the Bible on the back. Mrs. Kennedy's failing eyesight and arthritic wrists made it difficult for her to autograph these cards herself, so she asked me to learn to imitate her signature and do it for her. I sent these out in response to particularly sweet or touching letters. Another of our printed responses was a card that gave Mrs. Kennedy's recipe for Boston cream pie. It was mentioned in her book as her family's favorite dessert, and for some reason, that detail was widely publicized, so we had hundreds of requests for the recipe.

The mail also brought in many requests for interviews and appearances, especially at charity events, and Mrs. Kennedy and I had worked out some form letters to cover these situations. Usually such letters of refusal went out over my signature and said something like, ''Mrs. Kennedy asks me to thank you for your letter. It has been the policy of Mr. and Mrs. Kennedy not to accept such invitations except for charities with which the family is connected. I hope you understand why she cannot make an exception in this case.'' I was amazed at the number of such requests.

Interestingly, the volume of mail did drop off not long after I began to work for Mrs. Kennedy. It happened about the time that reports of Judith Exner's alleged affair with Jack Kennedy in the White House hit the news media, and I suppose the drop represented some degree of disillusionment with the Kennedys. Since I didn't show Mrs. Kennedy most of the mail anyway, she had no knowledge of the change. But she did get on to the Judith Exner story, despite my efforts to keep it from her. She read about it one day in the shiny sheet, which ran a picture on the front page to accompany the story. Later that morning, Mrs. Kennedy said casually, "I saw the Exner woman's picture on the front page this morning with her large breasts. I just don't see how all that could have been going on in the White House with all the staff and other people around."

Mrs. Kennedy always handled a few pieces of mail herself, dictating replies for nearly an hour to the two or three pieces I showed her. Usually she would get tired and cross before she finished and tell me to handle the rest. She wrote regularly to a few old friends and of course to members of the family. She also corresponded with the Duchess of Windsor and sent her packages of Wrinkies, skin-colored tapes Mrs. Kennedy wore on her face to prevent wrinkles. (I think the duchess preferred the more effective remedy of plastic surgery.) The last time Mrs. Kennedy saw the Duchess in Paris, she couldn't stop talking about how old she looked. She tried to imitate the way the Duchess tottered around and nearly fell over herself. The Duchess, by the way, was ten years younger than Mrs. Kennedy.

Mrs. Kennedy was steadfast in her refusal to become involved in anything that might seem political. She was upset when Boston College announced they had named her Catholic Woman of the Year, because she never accepted such honors. She was also upset when Jackie wrote and asked her to come out in favor of the ERA. Mrs. Kennedy wrote her daughter-in-law immediately, saying she did not want to become involved in such an issue, adding that "Grandpa and I decided years ago it would be best this way."

The media often wrote or called to ask Mrs. Kennedy for interviews. A woman who was writing an article about Eunice wanted an interview to discuss her childhood. A Dutch magazine wanted to take pictures (they snapped the two of us emerging from our daily swim in the ocean). One of the networks wanted to do a program with Mrs. Kennedy and Lillian Carter (or as Mrs. Kennedy called her when she reported the offer, "Old Lady Carter"). I'm sorry that event never came off.

Mrs. Kennedy told me to refuse most of these requests, but sometimes that refusal didn't stick. I remember a big flap in the summer of 1975, when Frank Falacci of the *Cape Cod News* called to ask for a birthday interview with Mrs. Kennedy. I refused, as per policy, but afterward I mentioned it to Mrs. Kennedy because I thought it would boost her morale to know she was still in demand. "No, no," she said, "you were right, I don't want to do it." But after I left the house, she called Frank herself. During their conversation, she let slip that

her son was going to run for President in 1976—
the story made the front page of the *Boston Herald*.

Mrs. Kennedy also turned down most invitations. But when she did decide to attend a function,
she took her duties as an ambassador for the Kennedy family very seriously. Most of her attention
went into carefully planning her appearance. Even
in her eighties, she was interested in fashion and
proud of her looks. I always admired the spirit that
kept her looking like a fashion plate at her age.

Over the years, Mrs. Kennedy had adopted
certain principles to guide her in choosing her outfits. She loved hats and liked to wear large ones
even though she was a small woman; she said it
was all right as long as the brim didn't extend past
her shoulders. She thought women should always
wear something white near the face, to set off their
complexions. It might be a scarf, or a piece of lace,
or simply some pearls. She also thought older women
ought to be sure to put something soft around the
neck, to camouflage the signs of age. She favored
ruffled collars or collars trimmed with lace. She
tried to buy her suits and coats in neutral colors,
such as black and white, on the grounds that they
never went out of style and could be worn frequently
witout reminding people that they had just seen that
outfit. But she loved cheerful colors and had a particular weakness for vibrant shades of pink. Some-

how she often ended up purchasing something in
the bright shades that made her feel "up" rather
than the neutral shades she considered more practical.

Mrs. Kennedy had some truly beautiful clothes
to wear to formal functions. One of my favorites
was a black evening gown she bought in Paris in
1975, with a velvet bodice embroidered in gold and
covered with a filmy chiffon overblouse. When she
modeled it for me on her return, I said, "Mrs.
Kennedy, you look like you're thirty-eight in that
dress." She shot back quickly, "You mean twenty-
eight, don't you?" That same year she also bought
a lovely red dress as well as the aqua chiffon in
which she was photographed by Richard Avedon.
She always willingly spent whatever it cost to buy
these dresses. She once told me that Mr. Kennedy
could always tell the difference between designer
originals and off-the-rack clothes, no matter how
carefully copied; he wanted her to wear the originals
and look her best. ("And," she added thoughtfully,
"he was meeting a lot of beautiful women.") So
she continued to follow his preferences when it came
to the wardrobe she needed for her public appearances. The only time her husband asked her not to
follow fashion was when "tent" dresses were in
style. He complained that he had already seen her
in maternity clothes for too many years.

Mrs. Kennedy had some marvelous jewelry to

wear with those gowns, too. Some of it was kept in the bank and the rest in her bedroom safe. One day she took out a pair of fabulous diamond drop earrings and asked me to take them to a jeweler's on Worth Avenue to have the clips tightened. She was afraid, she said, she might lose one when she was dancing. I loved it—I just hope that when I get into my eighties, I have to worry about losing my earrings during a bout of madcap dancing.

When she got all dressed up, Mrs. Kennedy did look wonderful. She had dark hair with only a few strands of gray; she never had to dye it. She remarked once, "My mother always had black hair, too. And she lived to be ninety-three, still really not very gray." She was willing, however, to help nature when she saw the need for it. She had had her eyes lifted several times, and her neck had been done also. But I don't believe she ever had an ordinary face-lift, because I didn't see any telltale scars.

Mrs. Kennedy also loved all the artifice of cosmetics when she was making her public appearances. She wore false eyelashes, which she put on herself—shaky hands and poor vision notwithstanding. And we often talked about such important items as the best mascara to wear and the way to apply eye shadow and our belief in the advertising claims made for various skin creams. She used Elizabeth Arden skin-care products (although she urged her granddaughter Maria to invest in some of the more expensive Laszlo line). She was always very conscientious about sticking to her beauty routines, believing in good skin care, lots of water and fresh air, moderate exercise, and a weekly massage.

For years, Mrs. Kennedy had worried about her weight and dieted rigorously to stay svelte. But by this time of her life, she no longer had a tendency to gain, and in fact she even began to drink liquid Sustagen to keep her weight up. I noticed that when she wore slacks, she had become so thin they didn't even bend when she walked. Despite her short stature, she wore clothes well because of her excellent posture and her lovely long neck, which reminded me of Audrey Hepburn's. She tried to look like Audrey Hepburn in the bust also. She thought a heavy bustline was aging to a woman, and so she had a special bra arrangement made for her in Paris. A kind of flannel was stitched over the outside of a long-line bra, which hooked onto an old-fashioned corset with stays. It gave a smoother, flatter line under her designer clothes.

Mrs. Kennedy's dedication to the job of looking her best for public appearances was really nothing short of valiant. I was especially struck by this in the fall of 1977, when her health seemed to be deteriorating. She had been in New England Baptist Hospital for nearly a week, but then she seemed to get some of her strength back. So her children decided to carry on with plans for her fall visit to Washington and New York. A few days after she arrived in New York, she called me at home in the evening to say she had done something to her knee and was unable to walk. "All that walking around Hyannis Port, up hills and over bad roads, and then I go to New York and hurt my knee," she complained. "You're just not a city girl," I teased her. Yet it was only a few days later that she called again and asked me to send her a pair of gold shoes to go with a shimmering orange dress she planned to wear to a ball. With a bad stomach and an even worse knee, she was not only going to a ball, she was determined to wear the shoes that would look best with her dress, whatever their degree of discomfort! A truly amazing woman.

But not all of her appearances were that formal. Often they were daytime activities that only called for a suit and one of her trademark big hats. For example, she attended the Palm Beach area Special Olympics for the retarded and the handicapped and made a little speech to the participants and supporters. Afterward, she gave a prize to a first-place winner, a retarded boy about thirteen years old. As she handed him the award, she enveloped him in a big bear hug and invited him to sit with her during the rest of the ceremony. That was the Rose Kennedy I especially like to remember.

One of her funnier daytime appearances came

one time in Florida when she was asked to speak to a workshop on retardation that was being held at the Colonnades Hotel on Singer Island. One of the other guests at this function was John D. MacArthur, the somewhat eccentric billionaire who had established the MacArthur Foundation. MacArthur was at that time just recovering from a serious stroke, and when Mrs. Kennedy was introduced to him, she took it into her head that he was one of the retarded. On the way home, I tried to set her straight, but she never did understand who he was.

Perhaps the most unexpected public appearance was her attendance at a Republican campaign breakfast starring Nancy Reagan. This was in 1976, when Nancy's husband was making what would be an unsuccessful bid for the Republican nomination and Mrs. Kennedy's son-in-law Sarge was making what would be an unsuccessful bid for the Democratic nomination. Mrs. Kennedy read about the gathering in her morning paper and asked me if I would drive her to Junior's Restaurant in the Palm Beach Mall so she could check it out. I had assumed it would just be a big milling crowd, but it turned out to be a sit-down affair that was fully covered by the media. The moment we were escorted to our seats, the reporters showed up (Nancy had not yet made her entrance) to interview Mrs. Kennedy. She explained why she had come: "I always traveled with my father when he campaigned, and he ha-

bitually made it a point to find out what the oppo-
sition was saying and what its campaign strategy
seemed to be. I'm very interested in what Mrs.
Reagan has to say."

Just at that moment, Nancy Reagan entered the
room and came straight over to Mrs. Kennedy to
shake her hand. "It's good to see you here," Nancy
said graciously, showing not a trace of the surprise
she must have felt. After the speech, Mrs. Kennedy
wanted to leave without going through the receiving
line to shake Mrs. Reagan's hand. So she took off
at full speed, wandering around hallways and back
doors, looking for a way to make an unobtrusive
exit; I was trotting along behind her trying to catch
my breath. Suddenly we went through a doorway
and found ourselves emerging onto the stage *behind*
Nancy Reagan, as the receiving line crept by in
front. Mrs. Kennedy squared her shoulders, stepped
to the head of the line, and positively exuded charm
as she shook Nancy's hand one more time. As we
left the room by the official exit, she said to me,
"Well, what were we to do? It was the only way
out."

That night as I watched the eleven o'clock news
on Channel 5, the first thing I saw was a giant close-
up of my face. The entire coverage of the campaign
breakfast focused on the fact that Mrs. Kennedy
was there, and the interview with her was played
in full. I was sure Nancy Reagan must be annoyed

at being so badly upstaged. Sarge and Eunice were also annoyed, it turned out, because Mrs. Kennedy had drawn attention to the campaign of a conservative Republican at the very time she was declining to make any campaign appearances on Sarge's behalf. But despite their scowling, the next morning Mrs. Kennedy was beaming in triumph.

Mrs. Kennedy's stamina could be amazing. In the spring of 1975, she was invited to sit in the President's box at the televised premiere of a Barbra Streisand movie. The event was going to benefit the retarded, a cause in which Streisand also took a personal interest, so Mrs. Kennedy agreed to attend. When word got out that she was going to be in Washington, she was also invited to a lavish dinner at the Iranian embassy, along with Pat, Jean, Eunice, and Ted.

Several weeks before she was to leave for Washington, Mrs. Kennedy began having terrible headaches that virtually knocked her out. To cope with the pain, she relied heavily on sleeping pills, and the combination of the pain and the pills brought on another bout of stomach trouble. Her condition worried everyone. Most visits from the family were canceled and the few who did come brought their own domestics and did their best to avoid disturbing Mrs. Kennedy.

I thought it might be the better part of wisdom to cancel the visit to Washington, but Mrs. Kennedy was determined to go. We packed a beautiful Christian Dior gown for the premiere, and a few other Paris creations for the rest of the visit, and off she went. The next evening, I watched the televised coverage, and she looked absolutely radiant. It seemed hard to believe that the stylish self-possessed regal woman I saw on television was the same person who had been unable to leave her room for days before her trip. Her ability to summon hidden reserves of energy always amazed me.

An appearance that did not go so well was the ground-breaking ceremony for the Kennedy Library. Mrs. Kennedy had just been through a serious bout of her stomach trouble and seemed both physically and mentally weak when she got in the car with Joe Gargan to drive to the ceremony. She was in a bad state when she arrived and had to be taken to the bathroom immediately; since there was a long line in front of the ladies' room, they took her into the men's. When it came time for her to take the silver-handled shovel for a ritual dig, she was so confused she didn't know which end of the shovel to use. For several days after the event, she had to stay in bed. At her age, these appearances took a lot out of her.

Yet as long as she had the strength, she tried to conceal the effects of age and illness. Many times when I drove her to some little local event in Palm Beach, such as a luncheon to benefit the retarded, she would be so weak and tired that she would lie down in the backseat during the drive. But when we arrived at our destination, she sat up, adjusted her hat, and got out of the car with her shoulders back, her chin held high, and all the poise in the world. She knew what the public expected, and as long as she was physically able, she gave it to them.

Her physical condition made it necessary for her to turn down most requests for media appearances. She said no to an idea for a bicentennial television special that would have her and her grandchildren walking the Freedom Trail in historic Boston. She turned down the invitation to appear on a talk show hosted by Kathryn and Bing Crosby. She turned down an offer of a TV special on Rosemary to help draw attention to the plight of the retarded. She simply did not have the strength to do all the things she might have liked to do.

The one person she always said yes to was Teddy, her only remaining son. Whatever she could do to help his political career, she was willing. She would give interviews, attend receptions, make speeches. She was his secret weapon, a veteran campaigner who never failed to move audiences. Of course, that's not to say these appearances were ever easy.

I remember in particular one she made in the fall of 1976, only weeks before election day, on behalf of Ted's reelection to the Senate. His staff had arranged a reception in her honor in the ball-room of Boston's Sheraton Hotel, and sent out four thousand handwritten invitations. Mrs. Kennedy spent the morning dressing and doing her makeup, and she was looking her best when we left Hyannis Port at noon. But when we got into the suite reserved for Mrs. Kennedy at the hotel, she announced that she was tired and intended to take a nap. So she took off her clothes, ran a bath, put on her pajamas, and retired for a snooze. About the time she got up again, the suite began to fill up with people. The Senator arrived with three aides, wanting to talk about the details of Mrs. Kennedy's appearance. Joan turned up, saying she wanted to talk to Gramma, and her husband was watching her warily. Joan went into the bedroom with the announced intention of helping Gramma with her makeup, but Mrs. Kennedy refused all assistance. This led to a comic spectacle: Joan chasing Mrs. Kennedy around the room, makeup in hand, trying to catch her to apply it. On television later, it was obvious that Joan was wearing too much makeup, while Mrs. Kennedy was not wearing enough.

Finally it was time to go downstairs. As we rode the elevator down to the ballroom, Mrs. Kennedy suddenly asked me, "Barbara, did you clean up the cosmetics in my bathroom?" I said yes, although in truth I had not had the time; but I knew she shouldn't be upset or worried before she made her appearance. She was satisfied, but Ted, who knew perfectly well I had not told the truth, cocked a bold eyebrow as if to say, "Aha, I caught you!" Just one more "Don't tell Mrs. Kennedy" conspiracy.

There were thousands of people in the ballroom waiting to meet Mrs. Kennedy, and I saw her begin to shake. She was introduced to the audience by the Senator's older son, Teddy; her grandsons Christopher Lawford and David, Joe and Patrick Kennedy were also on the stage with her, as were Ted and Joan. Although she mixed up the order of her speech, it went over very well. This was the time that she told the audience how glad she was she had had that ninth child: "If I hadn't had the ninth, I would now have no sons." Some members of the audience were openly weeping, and afterward, they all wanted to crowd up on stage and shake her hand.

I saw that she was completely worn out, so I went up beside her and asked if she would like to leave. Although Ted was pressing her to stay, we went back to her room, where she changed into ordinary street clothes and wrapped a scarf around her head. Seeing her slip out the door of the hotel afterward, you would never guess that this woman had just held an audience of thousands in the palm of her hand. When we got into the car, she lay down in the backseat and closed her eyes. "It's not like it used to be," she mused, "when candidates handed out cigars with dollar bills wrapped around them at the polls on election day.'' Then she said to me, "You see, Barbara, if we campaign, this is what we will do. Except we'll go from town to town." I didn't reply. I knew her son hoped she would be able to do that, but it seemed out of the question at her age. Indeed, the next day, she had to be admitted to New England Baptist Hospital, for painful stomach cramps and severe diarrhea.

Another part of Mrs. Kennedy's public life was her career as a writer. Her book, *Times to Remember*, had come out in hardcover just about the time I began working for her, and she spent a lot of time autographing copies and sending them to people as disparate as Bishop Fulton J. Sheen and Al Smith's son. She had written the book with the aid of diaries she had kept for years, which I was able to take a look at. They were wonderfully detailed, telling where she went, who was there, what they said, starting from the time Joe Kennedy was appointed ambassador to England and Rose began her real public life; they also contained little swatches of the fabric of her evening gowns as well as engraved invitations and dance cards.

Her publishers, Doubleday, aware of this wealth of material, had suggested that she might like to write another book. She was tempted, I know; she refused some requests for interviews with the comment that she planned to write another book herself and didn't want to give away her material. But the truth of the matter was that she really didn't have the strength any longer for the sustained work of writing another book.

Still, she loved being an author. In an amusingly jaunty letter to Caroline, written in the winter of 1975 (about the time the paperback edition of her book came out), she talked about having more books to autograph all the time and concluded that she didn't know how many ''mills'' she had made but couldn't spend it anyway because it is all for the retarded children.

That was the cause that still had her total commitment. It was her own family tragedy that drew her to work on behalf of the retarded, but it was genuine personal involvement that kept her at it as her health began to fail and her vitality to run low. She made public appearances whenever she could to speak about the problem. She even did a TV spot to promote the Special Olympics in Palm Beach County. That turned into a circus. At the very last minute, Mrs. Kennedy decided to change all our thorough plans, with the result that the media people came at different times, tramped in and out through the kitchen, and parked in front of the garage instead of in the parking lot. While Mrs. Kennedy was being made up, she thought she had lost the diamond clip (shaped like a little safety pin) that she used to adjust the length of her pearls, and she went into a tizzy and got everyone else upset. (The shortener was found elsewhere, of course.) The confusion caused the makeup girl to make a mistake: Mrs. Kennedy's makeup looked much too harsh on the screen. After the taping, chaos continued to prevail as Mrs. Kennedy, on the spur of the moment, invited everyone to stay for a drink. Nellie and I had our hands full, since she wanted to serve not merely drinks but also sandwiches and coffee. In Mrs. Kennedy's hands, the simple business of taping a short public affairs spot turned into a day-long problem for all concerned. Still, except for the makeup, the finished announcement looked very good.

On another occasion, the *Ladies' Home Journal* shrewdly offered Mrs. Kennedy a contribution of $10,000 for the retarded if she would write an article about the way Christmas was celebrated in the Kennedy family. She decided that she couldn't write the article herself, but she really wanted the retarded to get that check. So she had a little talk with her son, Teddy, who then "volunteered" to write the article himself . . . for the same fee, of course. Once she talked him into taking on the job, she began to supervise him mercilessly, constantly asking him about his progress and demanding to see a draft so she could make corrections. When the article was finally finished, the magazine sent a photographer to take a picture of the author and his mother that would be run with the article. This was in Hyannis Port, and they decided to take the pictures at the point where the front lawn turns into a beach. When she was dressing, Mrs. Kennedy wanted to wear one of her Paris couturier suits and a hat, but I suggested that it seemed unsuitably formal for a family picture on the beach. So she changed to a wonderful bright red sweater and a pair of white pants, and she looked absolutely perfect. Every one of those pictures turned out well, and the one that was eventually printed made her look twenty years younger, and quite beautiful. And, of course, the best reward came later, when Teddy handed over the check he had earned for the retarded.

Mrs. Kennedy knew from firsthand experience just how expensive the care and training of a retarded child could be, so she knew that more money was always needed. She also worried about the plight of the older retarded, like Rosemary. What happened to those whose parents had died, leaving no one to take care of them anymore and no financial resources to provide substitute care? She knew of one home for older retarded people through her friends, the Morton Downeys, who had a retarded daughter there. She began to think of establishing another, and to that end she wanted to make some changes in her will, so that she could leave money for that purpose. In all Mrs. Kennedy's activities for the retarded, Eunice was her faithful lieutenant. She, too, was committed to the cause of the retarded, and she helped her mother grapple with the practical aspects of providing help.

If Eunice handled the practical side, it was Mrs. Kennedy who felt the emotional side of the problem. One day she and I were talking about the number of celebrities who were willing to work for the retarded because someone in their own family was afflicted. Mrs. Kennedy said sadly, "That's what I mean. You can have all these worldly things, but still, something like that can happen to you."

With her activities for the retarded and her position as matriarch of the Kennedy clan, Rose Kennedy was constantly in the public eye. In fact, I don't believe she ever really had a private life outside the four walls of her bedroom. Even in her own home, the curious followed her. In both Palm Beach and Hyannis Port, we more than once had the nasty surprise of finding strangers in the house, who had just walked boldly in. Sometimes the intention was simply to get a close-up glimpse of Mrs. Kennedy; sometimes I feared the possibility of darker ideas. One summer in Hyannis Port, there was a death threat against her that the FBI took seriously. Mrs. Kennedy was never told about it, but I was asked to get her out of the house so they could check it. They instructed me to whisk her off to church, where agents could keep an eye on her. She was willing to attend an afternoon mass, but somewhat perplexed by my insistence on the matter because she knew I wasn't Catholic. "Oh, well," I said, "we're all trying to get to the same place." She answered thoughtfully, "Yes, yes, you're right," but still seemed a bit puzzled. Eventually an agent who was lurking around the church told me it was all right to take her home again. Apparently, they had established that the threat was not serious.

Most people were content to stare from a distance, but even so, they were always *there*. If Mrs. Kennedy went for a walk on the beach, someone in a boat would begin to gawk. If she went into town to shop, tourists would nudge one another as she passed. I guessed that one reason she went back to Palm Beach year after year was that the town took Mrs. Kennedy in its stride. There were so many rich and frequently photographed faces in Palm Beach that nobody made a big fuss over the appearance of Mrs. Kennedy.

Of course, in Hyannis Port there were always summer tourists standing at the end of the street trying to peer down and sight a Kennedy. And there was always some entrepreneur ready to take advantage of the desire to Kennedy-watch. One year I noticed a truck coming into the compound several times a week. Arthur told me it was the dry cleaner picking up and delivering at Ethel's house. But I couldn't understand why, after backing out of Ethel's drive, the truck proceeded on down to the circular driveway in front of Mrs. Kennedy's house and sometimes even went around to the parking lot in the rear. Then one day I noticed that there were people in the rear of the truck. I spoke to the guard at the end of the street about this, and he found out that the delivery man was taking people into the compound in his truck and charging them for a tour.

Being so highly visible, Mrs. Kennedy couldn't even make mistakes in private; they soon became public knowledge. I remember one time when I met Mrs. Kennedy at the airport after one of her little jaunts to Washington. The whole thing started out in a funny way, when I found Mrs. Kennedy trying to walk down the up escalator, crossly pushing the rising stairs with her foot as if to say, "You *will* go down." When we finally emerged, we got into the Lincoln, which I had parked near the exit door. But when I tried to put my key in the ignition, it wouldn't fit. Puzzled, I tried again several times. Then I noticed a pair of leather gloves on the front seat, which were certainly not mine. I looked in the rearview mirror and saw an identical Lincoln—same model, same year, same color—parked behind us. It dawned on me that we were in someone else's car! As we got out, I noticed the guard grinning. He came over and told me he had noticed the second car pull up in front of me and had feared there would be a mix-up. The point of the story is that the anecdote was all over the airport before nightfall. When Ted came in the next day to stay with his mother, several people told him about it immediately. He thought it was a great story and teased us about it for days. But it made me realize that a public figure has to expect that even little gaffes like that will become public knowledge.

I'm sure that her constant celebrity was in some ways a trial to Mrs. Kennedy. And yet she obviously enjoyed being in the limelight. When she encountered tourists looking for her after mass, she would walk right up to them and say, "Hello, I'm the President's mother. That's his pew right over there." She loved to have her picture taken with any member of the family, at any time of day, by either professional or amateur photographers. She always studied published photographs carefully to see how she looked, and would decide accordingly to wear more or less makeup, adjust the angle of her hat, retire one outfit or wear another more frequently. She didn't like it when pictures made her look old, though. There is a famous photo of the Kennedy family taken in 1960, the morning after election day, when the close race was finally called and all the world knew John F. Kennedy would be the next president. The photographer in charge had arranged it so that Mrs. Kennedy was seated next to Jackie, whose youthful glow does indeed make Mrs. Kennedy look like the "older generation." That particular photo was nowhere to be seen in either of Mrs. Kennedy's houses.

Mrs. Kennedy always seemed very conscious of her place in history. She once remarked, as we were peacefully swimming in the ocean, "Mr. Kennedy was so lucky to have me for a wife. I had gone to college and was well educated, whereas the other girls from East Boston were just high school graduates. I had traveled abroad, met Sir Thomas Lipton, spoke French and German." What she meant was that she was prepared to play a part in the Kennedy dynastic history. As daughter of a mayor, wife of an ambassador, mother of a president and two senators, she knew she would be read about by generations to come.

Naturally she always took a great interest in books, magazine articles, and television shows about the Kennedy family. One of my first tasks when I started to work for her was to go through her copy of *The Founding Father*, a biography of Joe Kennedy, and transcribe the comments she had made in the margins about what she felt were inaccuracies. She wrote to an old friend in England to tell her not to be tempted to read Lord Longford's book on the Kennedys because he had called Joe Kennedy "predatory towards women." She watched the tape of the TV special called *Rose Kennedy: Good Times, Bad Times* without any comment . . . and then watched it again. Together, she and I watched a special Mike Douglas show that focused on her book, with a long personal interview and film clips and photographs as well. I found it rather odd to see on the flickering screen those photographs that now seemed so familiar in their spots on the wall or in their silver frames on top of a table. Mrs. Kennedy kept up a running commentary. She worried about the way her makeup looked in the interview. She wondered aloud why they didn't mention the fact that proceeds from the book were going to help the retarded. When they showed pictures of the inauguration, she remembered how cold Jack had been with no coat, and how Jackie was also freezing because there had been no time for the tailor to put a lining in her coat. "They put the parents at the end of the podium where we couldn't really see what was happening," she remarked crossly.

When the show was over, there was a long silence. Then she said slowly, "How could that happen? Two boys in one family assassinated. . . ." To break the growing feeling of sorrow, I said quickly, "Mrs. Kennedy, I thought the program was done very well. And you looked fantastic in your interview." She answered, "Of course, dear, it's only natural you feel that way, since you are here now and know the family." Then she walked to her bed to straighten out the spread and I went to help her. It was a gesture we were to repeat many times in years to come, a silent signal that an emotional moment was over and done with.

Another program she watched with interest was

Young Joe Kennedy, the Forgotten Prince. I mentioned having seen the previews, which appeared to contain some love scenes. She commented, "I don't remember him being in love with anyone in particular. It was always Jack who had some girl. He was so much in love with the Finklestein girl up the street. She married a boy she fell in love with in high school. She was very unsophisticated and rather tomboyish, but Jack was wild about her."

But it was not just the Kennedy family that she found fascinating to follow in the media. I remember with amusement when she watched *Eleanor and Franklin* on television. Her chief comment? "Sarah Roosevelt [FDR's mother] died when she was eighty-seven, didn't she?" When she read a report that Amy Carter had sat down at the piano after some White House dinner, she exclaimed, "How absurd! To get all dressed up and attend a dinner party and afterwards have to sit and listen to some nine-year-old play the piano." When she read about how the Fords entertained Queen Elizabeth and Prince Philip, she criticized their choice of a menu. They had served a veal roast, which she pointed out was not particularly American. "When I gave a dinner for the King and Queen at the embassy," she recalled, "I thought it should be a regular American dinner with corn on the cob, turkey, sweet potatoes, ice cream, and strawberry shortcake."

When Rose Kennedy thought history was in

danger of making a mistake about a member of the family, she was capable of vigorous action. For example, she was quite distressed to read in one of James Reston's columns his statement that President Kennedy was not a religious man. She fired off a letter in return, stating, "Like his brothers and sisters, my son Jack was reared in a home with a deep and abiding faith. He practiced that faith constantly until his death."

Sometimes it was her own family she had to set straight. One day at a family lunch in Hyannis Port she and Ted were talking about *Camelot*, the musical he had taken her to see the night before. She commented that people had referred to President Kennedy's administration as "Camelot" because it strove for certain ideals. Ted said he would like to get away from that label. "It implies royalty, or a dynasty," he commented, obviously understanding the political liabilities of such a connotation. In fact, he concluded, it was really the opposite with the Kennedys, who were just plain people who liked things like hominy and grits. Mrs. Kennedy looked at her son in amazement and then said spiritedly, "We do not!" The whole family laughed in acknowledgment of the truth of her protest. Not even Ted Kennedy could be allowed to rewrite what Mrs. Kennedy knew to be the truth behind the Kennedy legend.

In a broad sense, you could say that most of

Mrs. Kennedy's time was spent in arranging the way the Kennedy family would go down in history. That was why she was so concerned about the disposition of all those things in the attic: They were part of a historical record. She made arrangements to give the desk on which President Kennedy signed the Nuclear Test Ban Treaty to Caroline and John, but most of the papers, photos, and memorabilia went to the Kennedy Library or the Kennedy Birthplace. She rather hoped, in fact, that the Hyannis Port house might also become a museum, open to the public: "After all," she remarked, "it's where the President spent most of his time growing up." She thought carefully over the disposition of each and every scrap of family history. One dress was donated to the Smithsonian, another to the library. These papers were put away in the bank vault, those given to the library. One day, young Christopher Kennedy was in my office and happened to see a pile of things that were being sent off to the library as per Mrs. Kennedy's instructions. "Why does Gramma give everything to the library?" he asked plaintively. "I'd like to have something that belonged to Uncle Jack."

But for Mrs. Kennedy, this was a matter that transcended personal sentiment. Her most important mission, in the years left to her, was safeguarding the memory of her husband and her sons.

9

The Grandchildren

An important part of the Kennedy legacy was the next generation. Mrs. Kennedy had twenty-nine grandchildren . . . twenty-nine chances for another president, senator, or attorney general. Yet the grandchildren also provided Mrs. Kennedy with twenty-nine reasons to worry.

Mrs. Kennedy's ideas about bringing up children had crystalized when her own were young, more than fifty years earlier. She had been a good disciplinarian, a patient developer of their abilities, a moral guide, and a continual good example. She sent her children to church regularly, she checked their homework every night, she dutifully recorded their heights and weights several times a year, she made sure they visited the dentist. She kept track of each child's shoe size, food preference, and serious illnesses; she also gave special attention to the ones who needed to be encouraged to speak up and the ones who needed a good dose of discipline. Her success as a mother was one of her proudest accomplishments, and she knew it was the reason she would go down in history.

But when Mrs. Kennedy tried to apply her old-fashioned notions to the raising of her grandchildren, they often seemed hopelessly out-of-date. For example, she sent them all a memo (formally headed from "Mrs. Joseph P. Kennedy") telling them to drink more milk to make their teeth nice and white—and she really believed this was true. Her son Jack had done it, she said, with excellent results. She sent other memos urging them to watch their grammar or to see certain programs on television that she thought would be educational. She instructed her children to subscribe to Catholic family magazines so the grandchildren would absorb their wholesome point of view.

I think she was dimly aware that her prescriptions for the Kennedy grandchildren's upbringing were hopelessly inadequate. For these were no ordinary children. They were kids who had played hide-and-go-seek in the White House, concealing themselves under the President's desk. Senators and congressmen were regular dinner guests; so were famous actresses and Pulitzer Prize winners. During the crisis surrounding the integration of the University of Alabama, top-ranking officials of the Justice Department who called the attorney general with updated reports often chatted with one of Bobby's kids before they got down to business, and young children frequently sat in their fathers' laps as world affairs were debated and decided. The grandchildren had been constantly photographed from their earliest youth and were resigned to the fact that all of their actions would be reported in the news media. And, of course, in one way or another, all of the children were victims of the violence and tragedy that had struck the Kennedy family. Small wonder that they had some problems as they were growing up.

Many of these problems were concealed from Mrs. Kennedy. She worried about the fact that they might be drinking Coke and thus harming their teeth; it never occurred to her that they might be using it. When David Kennedy was first hospitalized for his drug problem, his grandmother was told that he had a bad case of the flu that turned into pneumonia, a story she apparently accepted without question. When Christopher Lawford was later treated for the same problem, she had no more inkling of the truth of the matter. In fact, I shared much of her innocence. Although I was working there at the time and spending all day in the compound, I too had no idea of the extent or the severity of the problem. We knew nothing about it until it began to be covered in the news media. The adults in the family were skilled at covering the problem up—which had, of course, been another part of the problem.

Yet I certainly was aware that many of the grandchildren seemed spoiled and willful. When any of them were around, they frequently made my already difficult job just a little bit harder. For example, stationery, pens, and pencils steadily disappeared from my desk whenever they were around and sometimes I couldn't find paper to write a letter on. Once in Hyannis Port, Bobby Shriver was bold enough to take the typewriter right off my desk, carrying it home to his house where he was working on an overdue paper for school. I was unable to handle any of Mrs. Kennedy's correspondence until he was persuaded to return it. (Mrs. Kennedy wrote him a letter telling him in the future he should rent a typewriter when he needed one.) I was advised by the maids and former secretaries alike that I should keep the petty cash locked up or the grandchildren would take it as well. Many of them had the habit of borrowing small sums—five or ten dollars—from a maid or chauffeur and never paying it back.

One issue that caused continual trouble the whole time I worked there was the use of Mrs. Kennedy's car. With the number of teenage kids in the family, there were never enough cars around for them all. In Palm Beach, where everyone flew down to visit, the shortage could be especially acute. The grandchildren all loved to borrow their grandmother's Lincoln Continental, but they were usually irresponsible about caring for it or returning it. Several of them borrowed it for a day in Hyannis Port when it was practically brand-new and returned it covered with scratches from driving it through the heavily wooded acres of undeveloped land Joe Kennedy had bought some years before near Osterville. Bobby Shriver borrowed it once for the afternoon and took off with a bunch of friends (five in all) and a German shepherd; I winced to think of the effect on the upholstery. Then it turned out that he wanted to keep the car for two weeks and use it to go back to Yale. Since Mrs. Kennedy was in Europe at the time, I felt I couldn't take the responsibility for making that decision. Once the car got as far away as New Haven, who knew if I would ever get it back in time to go to Palm Beach? As I hesitated, Bobby told me firmly that I had nothing to worry about. "I called Mummy and she said I could. And after all, Mummy is her *daughter*," he added, making it plain that the status of a secretary was vastly inferior. I made several calls to both Sarge and Eunice about the matter, but neither of them really wanted to take the responsibility for telling me to give Bobby the Lincoln. In the end, Sarge decided that Bobby should rent a car to take back to school. Since Bobby had already spent his allowance for the next two months, he couldn't pay for the car himself, and he didn't have a valid credit card. So I drove him to the car rental place at the Hyannis airport and used my own card, sending the slip on to the New York office for reimbursement. Some weeks later, they called back to inquire why I had rented a car for Ethel's son Joe. It turned out that Bobby had playfully signed Joe's name to the bill so his cousin's account would be charged instead of his own.

That winter I had a rerun of the same argument with Bobby's sister, Maria. She was staying in Palm Beach for a few days while her grandmother was away, and she wanted to take Mrs. Kennedy's car to drive to a party in Miami. This time I was sure the answer should be no, especially since Mrs. Kennedy had recently been having trouble with the car and wanted me to take it to a garage to be fixed. But Maria didn't like to take no for an answer, and she, too, assured me that her mother had said it was perfectly all right. I called Eunice to discuss the situation, and Maria was very angry when she found out. "You shouldn't have bothered Mummy. She has enough on her mind right now." (This was the year that Sarge was making a run for the presidency.) Eunice suggested that we should settle the problem as we had done before, by renting Maria a car. But before I could get that done, Eunice called back to say that on second thought she didn't want her daughter to go to that party in Miami anyway.

Eventually, it was decided in a family council that none of the grandchildren would be allowed to borrow Mrs. Kennedy's car again. If they genuinely needed one, I would get them a rental. One of the first victims of this new policy was Christopher Lawford, visiting his grandmother in Palm Beach. Of course, he needed a car to get around and see friends, so Mrs. Kennedy told me to rent one for the duration of the trip. Always mindful of unnecessary expenses, she added that I should get an economy rental. I ended up with a Gremlin, and poor Christopher was mortified at having to drive that low-budget model around snobby Palm Beach, meeting friends who were driving expensive imports.

Occasionally I let some of the grandchildren use my own car to run errands or go to lunch nearby. Caroline was always very responsible about getting my car back at the time she promised, and appreciative of the favor. In many ways, she seemed more adult than the rest of her generation. Unlike most of them, she always made an effort to carry on a conversation when I drove her—to the airport or to the doctor for allergy shots—and I found her generally interesting to talk to.

It was Caroline who pointed out to me how

much getting together for the holidays—Christmas and Easter in Palm Beach, Fourth of July and Labor Day in Hyannis Port—meant to all the grandchildren. It was their only real family continuity, she explained, in lives that were full of change and travel. Many of the grandchildren were away in boarding school for much of the year, and frequently their holidays were spent elsewhere. This peripatetic life-style made it hard for them to maintain friendships . . . as did the very fact of being a Kennedy. So the cousins looked forward to being together at those big holiday gatherings. It's what made it worth it to Caroline to sleep on a rented cot in the Palm Beach house, scrub the front door mat on her hands and knees, and confront photographers every time she tried to swim. Even today, I notice, when Jackie has more or less abandoned the compound in favor of her house on Martha's Vineyard, Caroline continues to use the Hyannis Port house whenever she can get away in the summer. It allows her to stay in touch with her Kennedy relatives, many of whom she rarely sees the rest of the year.

By the mid-1970s, the grandchildren especially treasured those holiday get-togethers because they were separated most of the time. It was about that time that Ethel and Bobby's son Joe had the accident while driving the Jeep on Nantucket that injured his brother David and left David's girlfriend paralyzed. Various of the teenage male Kennedys were buying and using drugs and getting into scrapes with the law because of it. Arthur even discovered marijuana plants growing in unsuspecting Jackie's garden! The result of all this was apparently a family council that resolved to send the older children away for the summers; the combination of the free time in Hyannis Port and the encouragement of cousins was thought to be pernicious. So every summer thereafter, the teenage grandchildren were dispersed. Some went to Indian reservations to work, others interned in congressional offices, others traveled.

So it was only on the holidays that they saw one another again. Perhaps one reason those holidays always seemed so frantic was that the kids were trying to make up for lost time together. They played tennis, went sailing or fishing, walked around the compound together. Since I saw many of them only once a year, it was sometimes difficult to tell them apart. You could always pick out Ethel's son Bobby Kennedy, though, because he would stroll around with an exotic bird on his shoulder or an unusual pet of some sort following behind.

I have to admit that my own relationship with many of the grandchildren was not very good. I was in the awkward position of having to enforce Mrs. Kennedy's commands or take responsibility for her property, so I constantly had to oppose their wishes. For example, Maria Shriver called me in Hyannis Port one day in the fall, after Mrs. Kennedy had left for Paris, and said she would like to bring some friends over one evening to see a movie. This, of course, was exactly what Mrs. Kennedy had strictly prohibited, and I had to tell Maria so. She persisted in her request, so finally I called Mrs. Kennedy's nephew Joe Gargan for advice. He agreed that I should not take the responsibility for going against Mrs. Kennedy's command, but he called his cousin Eunice to get her explicit permission, which she gave. Although Maria and her friends promised to clean up after themselves, I found trash in the theater the next morning, and all the mirrors upstairs had lipstick prints on them. Since Jeannette was never employed when Mrs. Kennedy was away from Hyannis Port, there was no one to clean up the mess except me.

Mrs. Kennedy took a special interest in Maria, who was her godchild. She wrote Maria letters recommending operas and ballets that she ought to see to improve her cultural awareness. She also advised her that by the age of twenty-one she should get into the habit of taking good care of her skin. Maria was one of the most attractive of the granddaughters, and Mrs. Kennedy always liked to see her dressed formally and looking her best. She lent Maria that fabulous triple-strand pearl necklace (which Maria will one day inherit) to wear to meet Prince Charles, and Maria did indeed look lovely on that occasion.

Of course, Mrs. Kennedy also felt free to criticize Maria when she didn't live up to Kennedy expectations. An example was the summer that Maria appeared at the compound in a halter top. It was not especially revealing by present-day standards, but Mrs. Kennedy was horrified. She immediately fired off a letter to Maria's father asking him why he permitted Maria to "show her breasts" that way. In the future, whenever Maria was around the compound, she was more decorously dressed.

Mrs. Kennedy was never hesitant about expressing her disapproval of any aspect of the grandchildren's behavior. She got mad at Willie Smith because he consumed so many soft drinks, which she was sure was bad for his teeth. Christopher Lawford came in for his share of criticism because he asked for breakfast in bed when he was visiting Palm Beach; Mrs. Kennedy thought that was an unnecessary luxury that kept Nellie from attending to more important work. She was taken aback when she discovered that Ethel's children didn't tip the servants when they were visiting someone but mistakenly tipped the hostess instead, so she immediately wrote Ethel instructing her to correct their mistake. She was extremely irate when she heard that the grandchildren complained about having to use plastic glasses at the pool in Palm Beach. "I will not take that sort of gas!" she exclaimed. "They either drink out of plastic glasses or go thirsty. There is no reason to take good glasses to the swimming pool or tennis court.''

Looking back at my notes, it is sad to see how many of Mrs. Kennedy's letters to her grandchildren contained complaints about their behavior or refusals of their requests. She wrote to David Kennedy to tell him he couldn't come for Easter because there wasn't enough room, and added that he might try to come later when ''we could probably squeeze you in''—not exactly an open-arms welcome. David's sister Kathleen and her husband were also disinvited for the same reason. She wrote a querulous letter to Anthony Shriver telling him she thought of him as she walked on the lawn in Palm Beach, because ''the holes that you people made playing ball during Christmas'' were finally almost green again.

Sometimes, instead of writing directly to the grandchild, she wrote to a parent. She told the Senator that he ought to encourage Kara to speak up more at home so she would overcome her shyness and learn to take part in discussions.

Yet Mrs. Kennedy could also be a loving and supportive grandparent. When Ethel's daughter Courtney went to college at Stanford and found that she had trouble adjusting to California life and living so far away from the rest of the family, Mrs. Kennedy wrote her a warm letter, encouraging her to strive to adapt to her new surroundings and telling her that she had felt just the same when she had gone away to school in Germany. She concluded by telling Courtney to have faith in herself, faith in her program, and faith in God, and "to decide this year is going to be one of the best years of your life." She was proud of Bobby Kennedy's television special about the wild animals of Africa and impressed by the fact that he was paid several hundred thousand dollars for it. She wrote to him after another public appearance to tell him she thought his speech was excellent. (She closed by coquettishly telling him to "come down any time with a pal, preferably male!") After young Teddy lost his leg, she wrote proudly that he was a wonderful example to everyone and urged him to keep up the good work, even though she understood that it was not always easy.

She was careful to remember every grandchild's birthday, and she communicated with most of them frequently. Once she found some funny postcards at the local drugstore to send to Ethel's children, and she was crestfallen when I said I was afraid they might be stolen in the mail for the value of her signature. I suggested putting them in an envelope, but she said crossly, "What fun is that?" A few hours later, she came back with her solution to the problem: She had written the message upside down.

Of all her grandchildren, Mrs. Kennedy was perhaps closest to Caroline. She worried about the effect of the problems Caroline had already encountered in her young life, and she wrote to her granddaughter whenever she saw her name in the news. She wrote to say how sorry she was when Aristotle Onassis was ill; and when Teddy went to the Onassis funeral, his overseas call to Mrs. Kennedy was chiefly to tell her how Caroline and John were handling the crisis. She was concerned when the house where Caroline was staying in England was bombed by a terrorist group, and she was sympathetic about the problems Caroline had in being followed constantly by the press. Her letters to Caroline were both affectionate and supportive; she said that she often thought of Caroline's father and how proud he would have been of her and how delighted with her progress. She made special arrangements to be sure that Caroline and her brother, John, would get things that had belonged to their father. In her will she arranged to leave them not only the President's valuable desk but a painting that had been one of his favorites.

Mrs. Kennedy was also very concerned about Ethel's son David, although she didn't know all the details of his problems. He often looked pale and unwell, and that worried her greatly. Later she read in the papers that David had been arrested on drug charges, and, of course, that upset her, too. We discussed it when I went back to visit her in Hyannis Port in the fall of 1979. She thought it was a tragedy for Ethel's sons that their father wasn't around to guide them. She added, "Mr. Kennedy was so wonderful in that respect." Perhaps that was why she always put a lot of faith in a father's influence. I remember she used to sympathize with the problems I had in bringing up two children alone and worried about how hard it must be for me as a single parent.

Several years later Nellie gave me an account of Mrs. Kennedy's last visit with her grandson David. Actually, I saw her just a few days before he died, during that Easter vacation of 1984. It was a distressing visit, because she was very feeble and confused. Her eyes were so bad that she was sitting only a foot or two away from her huge television set, and she didn't know me until I began to talk. She was not able to feed herself, and I hated watching the nurse spoon food into her mouth. Our conversation was pitifully brief. I asked her if she was getting ready to go to the Cape; she looked at me in perplexity and asked, "Where am I now?" I told her she was in Palm Beach, and she said, "Then it must be too cold to go to the Cape." Nellie told me this was the most she had said in days; I think she instinctively associated my presence with working or answering questions.

David saw Mrs. Kennedy one or two days later, and only a day or two before he died. Apparently he and his younger brother Doug turned up at the Brazilian Court Hotel without any advance notice. Even if his grandmother had known he was coming, David couldn't possibly have stayed at the house, because it was extremely crowded. The Senator and his son Teddy were there, as were Pat Lawford, Steve and Jean Smith, and Eunice. It was so crowded that Sydney Lawford and Ted's younger son, Patrick, were sharing a room, and Sarge had decided to go stay at the Breakers, Palm Beach's exclusive hotel, rather than fight the mob scene at the house. Apparently Doug called the house several times asking for Patrick, but always missed him. Finally Doug called again to say he and David wanted to come visit their grandmother. Nellie showed them up to Mrs. Kennedy's room, and she told me David later came out crying. It had been a long time since he had seen her, and he was upset by the deterioration in her physical and mental condition.

That's an indication of what Mrs. Kennedy meant to her grandchildren . . . the indomitable matriarch was at the heart of the family unity and continuity. Yet for the sake of her own health, it was necessary to keep many of the family problems hidden from her. She was certainly unaware of the swirl of family controversy over David's situation in the late 1970s. On the advice of Steve Smith, David had been sent to a hospital in California for treatment of his drug problem. Steve was angry because David's mother refused to sign the papers taking full responsibility for this step. In the end, it was Kathleen Kennedy who put herself on the line to help her brother.

The fact that David had not seen his grandmother for several years was not particularly unusual. Although Mrs. Kennedy kept in touch with all the grandchildren by letter, she frequently seemed to discourage their actual presence. Part of the reason was the usual one that she didn't have a domestic staff that could handle guests without disruption. Her age also had something to do with it. In her eighties, she was understandably set in her ways and no longer open to many new experiences. The pleasures of the young completely mystified her. She once wrote to Caroline about the way "the younger crowd" behaved in Palm Beach, explaining that the schedule was to start out at 1:00 A.M. and wander from one nightclub to another. The result, which Mrs. Kennedy deplored, was that the grandchildren were sleeping through "the best part" of the Florida day. In another letter to "Moucher," the Dowager Duchess of Devonshire, she made the same complaint and added that she heartily disapproved of the system. "It is really awful," she said, but comforted herself with the thought that the grandchildren were there only a few weeks a year during their school vacations.

It's easy to see why the grandchildren were

somewhat uncomfortable about their visits to Gramma. She kept careful track of their comings and goings and tried to inform herself of the time at which each guest came home at night. Since her bedroom was right over the front porch in both her houses, it was hard to sneak in without her knowing it. This was why all the grandchildren wanted to stay in what was called the President's Bedroom when they came to visit. In both Hyannis Port and Palm Beach, the President's Bedroom was a comfortably furnished room on the ground floor, rather than upstairs with the rest of the bedrooms, and it had a private entrance, which had been very convenient when President Kennedy was visiting his parents and trying to conduct the business of state at the same time. The grandchildren wanted to stay there not because of the historical association, but because of the freedom offered by that private entrance. Of course, Ted liked to stay in the President's Bedroom for the same reason, and you can be certain he always got first choice. But if he wasn't around, the boys all tried to get to stay there.

Occasionally, Mrs. Kennedy put a spike in their advance planning by tell Mam'selle or Jeannette to lock up the entire house at night, including the separate entrance to the President's Bedroom. In Palm Beach, this left the grandchildren with no choice but to wake someone up in order to get back home after a long night of fun. In Hyannis Port, one grand-

son found an alternative. Since the house there was
built up off the ground, there was a short staircase
to the private entrance, and he simply stood on the
staircase and jimmied the lock on the nearby window, then crawled in. It was worrisome to discover
how simple it was for him to break in.

Visits to Gramma had other difficult moments.
Many of them came in the dining room. What with
her lifelong commitment to dieting, her bad stomach, and her usual fare of plain things plainly cooked,
Mrs. Kennedy had by this stage of her life virtually
lost all interest in food. And it seemed that she didn't
understand why others didn't feel exactly the same
way. For example, at mealtimes you were supposed
to discuss world affairs, not the food you were eating; there was no enthusiastic gourmet talk about
the perfect little young lettuce leaves or an exquis-
itely ripe piece of cheese, no comparison of dress-
ings made with walnut or extra-extra-virgin olive
oil from Greece, no rhapsodizing over a light piece
of pastry or an unctuously smooth sauce. Mrs. Kennedy's etiquette seemed to require that you ate with
as little attention to your food as possible.

It also required that you *ate* as little food as
possible. Mrs. Kennedy had settled on a rather odd
form of service at her table. When the meal began,
bowls and platters were served to each person, in
the formal European style; it was usually Mam'selle
in Palm Beach and Jeannette in Hyannis Port who

performed this ceremony. But then, instead of passing the food around again a little later, they simply put all the dishes on the sideboard and left the room. So anyone who wanted a second helping had to get up from the table, walk over to the sideboard, and serve himself. I suppose, in a relaxed atmosphere, this might have encouraged some people to help themselves to a generous encore, but in Mrs. Kennedy's dining room, she was sure to be watching you intently. You could practically hear her counting the peas going onto the plate, estimating the size of a piece of meat—and looking critically at the person who proposed to eat all those calories to calculate the damage to figure or complexion. Only the hungriest and skinniest of her teenage grandsons ever dared help themselves to seconds.

The granddaughters were especially careful to watch what they ate in Mrs. Kennedy's presence, because she could be quite harsh about any tendency toward plumpness. Ted's daughter, Kara, went through a period of overweight in her early teens, and Mrs. Kennedy worried about it constantly. She felt most of her granddaughters suffered from a figure flaw anyway: She thought they tended toward heavy thighs. Whenever she pointed that out, as she did about Caroline, Maria, Kara, and the three Lawford girls, she was always quick to add that the problem came from the *Kennedy* side of the family. Once the *Star* ran a picture story that she just loved, putting forth the thesis that Rose Kennedy had a better figure than any of her granddaughters and demonstrating it through carefully selected photos. You had better believe that she clipped that article to save! I would love to know what the granddaughters thought—after all, it's not a very flattering kind of publicity.

In view of all this, it was not really surprising that the older grandchildren preferred to visit when their grandmother wasn't at home. For example, Ethel's son Joe stayed in the apartment over Mrs. Kennedy's garage one winter, working on a fishing boat and hanging out with local friends. Unfortunately, he left the place looking like a disaster area, and Mrs. Kennedy was very angry about it. Later Joe's brother Bobby, then in his early twenties, stayed alone in the Palm Beach house one summer, working on his book about Alabama judge Frank Johnson; I don't believe Mrs. Kennedy ever learned of his extended stay. I do remember discussing the issue of Bobby's book with Jean Smith, who told me she had pulled strings with friends in the New York publishing community to help get the book published. I commented on the fact that a book was nevertheless quite an achievement for a young man his age and added, ''I hear Bobby is going to be good political meat for the future.'' Jean looked right at me, cocked an eyebrow quizzically, and said flatly, ''I doubt that very much.''

One reason the grandchildren preferred to use Mrs. Kennedy's homes only when she herself was absent was that they frequently brought companions of the opposite sex. I remember the time Maria Shriver came to stay for a few days in Palm Beach. I assumed she had come alone and was surprised when I walked through the dining room the next morning and found her having breakfast with a young man. On another occasion, Christopher Lawford brought a girlfriend to Palm Beach, at the same time Ted was there with a semiregular local girlfriend much younger than himself. The two "dates" became very chummy, chatting about makeup and putting on rock music and dancing together as the two Kennedys watched. It was a bizarre scene that could have come right out of a decadent Italian movie.

It seemed that where the grandchildren were concerned, it was one "Don't tell Mrs. Kennedy" situation after another. There was the discovery that Sydney Lawford, after asking her grandmother for money to put gas in the car, charged the gas on Mrs. Kennedy's account at the local station and used the money for personal spending. There was the time that a perplexed tow-truck operator called and asked what to do with Stevie Smith's BMW, which he had left in Lynn, Massachusetts, with only the vague instruction to tow it to New York—no address given. There was the time Christopher Lawford left the door to the beach dressing rooms open at the Palm Beach house and some stranger simply wandered into the house. Whenever possible, there was a conspiracy of silence about such events so they wouldn't upset Mrs. Kennedy.

But sometimes the grandchildren's misdeeds could not be kept from her. She had a real instinct for uncovering things we were trying to hide. For example, once Victoria Lawford and Jackie's son, John, made brownies in the Hyannis Port kitchen and then tracked the sticky chocolate batter all over the white rug in the living room. Before anyone could clean it up, Mrs. Kennedy arrived on the scene. She got that look—with the cold eyes and the dilated nostrils—that was enough to make anyone feel ashamed and embarrassed. She got that same look when she found me in the office writing a check to the airlines for fifteen dollars to pay for the cost of a little dog that Victoria and Robin Lawford brought with them on the plane. When they arrived at the airport, carrying the dog in a satchel, they were told they would have to pay extra for the dog. They called me (at home in the evening) in tears because they didn't have the money. I called the airline manager (also at home in the evening) and asked him if he would let them on the plane with the dog if I would promise to send a check the next morning, and he

finally agreed. But Mrs. Kennedy caught me in
the act of writing the check, and the whole story
came out. She made sure that the fifteen dollars
was billed to Sydney and Robin by the New York
office, and fumed about how they ought to be old
enough to learn to check into things like that the
next time.

Yet Mrs. Kennedy never let any momentary
irritations stand in the way of her efforts to teach
the grandchildren the Kennedy way of doing things.
She constantly urged them all to try to do their
very best. She suggested that Kathleen should start
typing her correspondence because her handwriting was not legible. In a memo to all the family
about an episode of Alistair Cooke's *America*
dealing with Irish immigration, she reminded them
that they lived in a great country: "when you think
of someone coming over in 1864 with no education but a lot of guts," whose descendant became not just an eloquent speaker but also the
President of the United States. She had me send
copies of Longfellow's poem on the ride of Paul
Revere to every Kennedy household so the grandchildren could memorize the poem and recite it
at a family picnic on the Fourth of July. She also
sent them facsimile copies of the Declaration of
Independence and pointed out how many of the
signers had attended Boston Latin School, the rigorous private academy where both Joe Kennedy

and John F. Fitzgerald had been students. When it seemed that Bobby's son Joe might run for office, Mrs. Kennedy wrote his sister Kathleen an enthusiastic letter. She mentioned once again that she had always preferred being the mother of a great man to being a great woman herself, and added that it might be even more of a thrill to be the grandmother of a great man. And she seemed sincerely disappointed when Caroline obeyed Jackie's wishes and bowed out of accompanying her grandmother to a political tea. Everyone in the family knew that Jackie didn't care for the hustle of "press-the-flesh" campaigning. Mrs. Kennedy still believed politics was a noble profession and hoped to see more of her grandchildren involved in it.

When the grandchildren visited, she tried to imitate the kind of conversation that Joe had insisted on when his children were growing up. At the dinner table, she asked them various questions, such as, "What is the meaning of Passover?" or "Why does Lent last forty days?" "What is a sheik?" or "Why is the Middle East different from the Far East?" Other times, she asked questions she herself was curious about, but it sometimes developed that no one else knew the answer, either, so such discussions ended up being of little educational value. But she never stopped trying to make the grandchildren interested in world affairs and curious about the things they read or saw. One year when we were talking about what we needed to take to Palm Beach, Mrs. Kennedy told me to go out and buy a map of Africa so everyone would be able to follow the political change there.

She liked to listen to her grandchildren talking, to get an idea of what kinds of things interested the younger generation. The pool was a great place for this kind of information-gathering. As she dog-paddled back and forth to get her daily exercise, she could hear what the grandchildren, lounging around the pool with cold drinks, were saying. One day she told me, "These children are so advanced. The other day I heard them talking about pregnancy and the fetus . . . the fetus! Why, I hardly knew what the fetus was myself until about two years ago!"

It amused me to hear her use words she had picked up from listening to the grandchildren. One was "gas," which she used when she was complaining about their refusal to drink out of plastic glasses. Another day I heard her say, "Excuse me, I have to go to the john." Startled, I exclaimed, "What?!" She answered defensively, "Well, that's what everyone else calls it nowadays." It was all part of her determined effort to keep up, like looking up new words—"trendy," for example—and copying down her expressions for dinner conversation. Her grandchildren provided Mrs. Kennedy with a window on the world of the younger generation.

Children evoked in Mrs. Kennedy a tenderness that nothing else could by this time of her life. She would always say hello to the children or grandchildren of neighbors. She responded with great warmth to the retarded children she met in the course of her charitable activities. And she was invariably kind to me whenever my duties as a mother conflicted with my responsibilities as her secretary. When my son, Kevin, had hepatitis, she not only sent him leftover roast beef and extra blankets—well-meaning gestures even if somewhat inappropriate—but she also was careful to send me home on the dot of five or even earlier every evening, saying, "Your son needs you, Barbara."

She also went out of her way to help my daughter, Kathleen . . . although I was not especially pleased at the result. Kathleen had been living with her father in Holland and had fallen in love with a Dutch boy. She was seventeen, and I wanted her to come back to this country; she wanted to live on her own in Holland so she could be near her boyfriend. I explained this whole situation to Mrs. Kennedy, who had always taken an interest in my children. She sent them postcards when she was in Europe, made sure they were invited out on the boat in Hyannis Port, and listened sympathetically when I had problems with them. When I told her about this one, she volunteered to talk to Kathleen, who was with me for the summer.

So one sunny morning, I sent Kathleen up to Mrs. Kennedy's bedroom, where she stayed for a long time. When she finally came back down, I heard Mrs. Kennedy calling down the stairs after her, "Remember you are not alone. You have someone of importance on your side." It seemed that when Kathleen began to talk about the situation herself, Mrs. Kennedy came down firmly on the side of young love and urged Kathleen to go back to her boyfriend! The story made her think of her own life, the boy she had fallen in love with when she was seventeen, the years she had loved Joe Kennedy but had to keep it a secret, seeing him only when their joint ingenuity could invent a way. She had a bit of a glow as she explained to me, "Like Kathleen, I was only seventeen, and Mr. Kennedy and I were not supposed to have dates. He was a manager of the tennis team at Boston Latin School, so he arranged for the team to play at Concord, where my uncle lived. So he went there with the tennis team, and I visited my uncle that weekend, and no one was the wiser." Even in her eighties, Mrs. Kennedy had a very romantic heart.

Perhaps the only valid conclusion about Mrs. Kennedy's behavior was that she was in many ways a typical elderly grandmother. She loved her grandchildren, often without understanding them . . . and sometimes even without liking them.

She enjoyed seeing them all together, and she

liked to hear about their achievements and accomplishments. She always made a special effort to send gifts and cards when one of them graduated from high school or college. She congratulated Ted's children Kara and Teddy on their progress in learning French. She was pleased and amused when Bobby Shriver became an entrepreneur and had his own clambake business in Hyannis Port; she was also impressed when he went to work for a Baltimore newspaper, and wrote him jokingly to say her only objection to his job was that he would now know more about the news than she did. She wrote Ethel's daughter Kathleen, the first of her generation to marry, a lovely letter saying how much pleasure she took in knowing that Kathleen had a happy marriage.

I'll always remember a conversation we had one day when Mrs. Kennedy was not feeling well. Her eyes were bothering her so that she couldn't even read the papers, and she was also suffering from a bad stomach upset. When I went up to her room, she was lying on her faded chaise, facing away from the bright light reflected from the ocean, staring at the walls of her shabby Palm Beach bedroom. After a long silence, she said, "Why do people go on living and living when they get so old and don't feel well and can't enjoy anything?" More silence. Then she asked wearily, "Do you see anything for me to live for?"

I answered, "I don't know, Mrs. Kennedy; I think it would be nice to see how your grandchildren turn out."

After another long pause, she retorted, "Oh, I don't care about them."

The sad truth was that she had been so fully invested in her children that there was little left over for the next generation. All of her hopes and dreams had been wrapped up in her nine children, and now in her old age, many of those dreams were lost forever. Through the fates of her nine children— four now dead and one permanently institutionalized—she had suffered so much pain and loss, been through so many highs and lows, that she simply didn't have the emotional energy to start all over again with her twenty-nine grandchildren.

10

Rose Kennedy . . .
Alone

Rose Kennedy was a familiar figure to millions
of people the world over. She was the matriarch of a large family; just a gathering of her
grandchildren could fill up an ordinary living room.
She was one of the wealthiest women in the United
States, able to surround herself comfortably with
servants and the usual entourage of the rich, had
she chosen to do so. Yet the way I remember seeing
her most often was all alone.

When I first went to work for Mrs. Kennedy,
I was amazed by her solitude. In Palm Beach, even
when the house was full of visitors, Mrs. Kennedy
kept to her own schedule, and neither her children

nor her grandchildren were allowed to disrupt it. In Hyannis Port, the compound was full of people all summer long, but few of them ever entered Mrs. Kennedy's carefully ordered world.

I believe Mrs. Kennedy's lonely life evolved out of a combination of her habits and preferences, and the fears of her family and friends about upsetting or distressing her. Over the years, people simply stopped making the effort to include her in their activities or to join her in hers. She, too, clearly lost the desire to join them. In many ways, her life was that of a recluse.

Of course, when I knew Mrs. Kennedy, she was old and in precarious health, which may have caused her to become more isolated. But I suspect that she had always preferred her independence. For example, she liked to reminisce about her trips with Joe Kennedy and how they always went their separate ways. In New York, he would stay at the Waldorf-Astoria Towers and she would stay at the Plaza; in Paris, he would stay somewhere convenient to a golf course and she would stay near the couture houses. She said they would meet for dinner or an evening at the theater and talk about what they had done that day. She attributed the fact that they always got along so well together to their frequent separations and independent existences. Her daughter Jean said her mother's independence was her own first introduction to the ideals of the women's movement. It might perhaps be the case that Mrs. Kennedy's attitudes were shaped by the necessity of adjusting to a husband who was often away from home for long periods and who was rumored to be involved with numerous other women. If so, she had long since made a virtue of necessity and had in reality come to prefer being alone most of the time.

It was easy to see that most of her pleasures came from things she did alone. Her daily swim, which had started out as a therapeutic measure, had turned into one of her greatest sources of comfort and well-being. But she preferred to swim alone, or with me, because with me she could completely drop her guard. Her newspaper reading was another solitary pleasure. She read several papers every day, went through them carefully, and clipped some articles to save. But she never discussed what she had read with anyone else and never consulted the files of articles she had clipped. She simply liked the feeling that she was still keeping up, even though she rarely shared the results.

In fact, Mrs. Kennedy at the time I knew her was one of the most inner-directed people I had ever met. Occasionally, in matters of etiquette, she might be concerned with what other people thought. But mostly she did things for her own reasons and paid little heed to the opinions of others. Even her efforts to stay abreast of the latest slang, or her questions to "Moucher" about the correct way to address her son, the Duke of Devonshire, were not induced by any worry about what other people would say if she didn't know. It was important to *her*, for her own image of herself, that she know these things.

Her desire to keep up with the world and to keep improving herself was totally remarkable for someone her age. When I first began to type quotations to go in her "expressions" book, a fat black three-ring notebook, I assumed that the book represented a species of busywork—something that made her feel like she was still a part of the world of the famous and powerful—and would never be used. I was dead wrong. She studied those pages of expressions frequently, sometimes pinning them to a towel or the front of her bathrobe so she would readily see them and work on memorizing them. Once I remember driving home at the end of the day and catching sight of her sitting under a tree with a large scarf covering most of her face, studiously poring over a sheet of expressions like a schoolgirl cramming for an exam.

She didn't just work on her expressions in English, mind you. She also studied them in French so she would be prepared for social events during her European trips or when she met foreigners in Washington. She worked hard at keeping up her French. Each week, while she had her hour-long massage, she put French-language records on the phonograph and listened to such things as excerpts from *Madame Bovary* or a historical account of the reign of Louis XV, to improve her French vocabulary and practice her comprehension skills. She liked to practice speaking French, too. Once she wrote a very funny letter to her grandson Teddy about her attempts to speak French to some distinguished visitor she met at a cocktail party Pat Lawford gave in New York. Intimidated by the man's perfect English, Mrs. Kennedy claimed she hardly dared to say "Bon soir" to him, but she did pluck up her courage to ask him what she needed to practice before her next trip to Paris. She concluded humorously that he kept going on in perfect English, and "I was very mad." It's easy to smile at the imagined scene—we all know how haughty the French can be about attempts to speak their language. But how many eighty-five-year-olds do you know who would have been so determined to try to improve themselves and their accent?

Mrs. Kennedy lived by a stoic philosophy. She never complained, and she genuinely did her best to accept whatever life brought her, including the trials of old age. Perhaps there was a bit of the New England Puritan about her, too. She thought it was unnecessary to spend money on the staff or the other conveniences that could make her life more comfortable . . . it seemed to me that she believed life was not meant to be a comfortable journey. In fact, she never did anything just because she enjoyed it. She really did like to travel, but she always needed an excuse to do it: She needed to buy clothes in Paris to uphold the standards set for her by her husband, or she had to see the eye doctor in Washington, or a European trip would give her the opportunity to polish her French. She had the same attitudes toward going to a play or concert or museum. In actual fact, she enjoyed it greatly, but she rationalized it to herself as a duty to keep up with cultural events. I remember that she encouraged me to go to New York and see a play, not because it would be fun, but because it would be a good experience for my daughter. According to her philosophy, it was all right to do anything for your children (including let them have fun), but that principle didn't apply to one's self. Mrs. Kennedy's satisfaction—perhaps even her happiness—came from the knowledge of having done her duty.

Of course, in this rather demanding view of life, she was supported by her deep religious beliefs. In many ways, the Catholic religion was the organizing principle of Mrs. Kennedy's life. It helped her organize her time; she created a schedule that revolved around her daily attendance at mass. It organized her beliefs and gave her a coherent outlook on life. Most deeply, it organized her expectations of the future.

Mrs. Kennedy was one of the few people I've

ever known who seemed absolutely unafraid of death. Unlike many people her age, she rarely spoke about it—didn't talk about "when I am gone" or refuse to plan for the future on the grounds that she might not live to see it. But when the subject of death came up, she seemed perfectly comfortable with it. I remember once in Palm Beach, Mrs. Kennedy and I went to the pool for our daily swim when it started to storm, with thunder and lightning. I was apprehensive about getting in the water, but Mrs. Kennedy got right in and called to me, "Come on in! Don't be a ninny!" I saw another bolt of lightning and must have looked like I was about to depart (I probably was) because she added gaily, "Don't you want to stick around and hear my last words?" Another time she wanted to swim in the ocean during a shark scare. "I'm not afraid of the sharks," she said firmly. "I've been swimming here for years." "Well," I answered, "I am! And with my luck, the shark would go for me and you'd swim in to shore." She laughed and said, "Where do you want me to send your check?"

Once Mrs. Kennedy thought there might be something wrong with her heart. She was taking her afternoon nap, and suddenly she called me to come to her. "My heart is making funny noises," she said without the slightest trace of anxiety or self-pity. "Please come listen to it." I put my ear over her chest but didn't notice anything unusual.

Within ten or fifteen minutes, she called me again to say her heart was thumping wildly. This time I telephoned her doctor, and he told me to bring her right in to his office. I helped her get ready, and she insisted on getting dressed up as if she were going to a social event. She got all excited about the whole thing; it seemed that she relished the drama of having something really wrong with her, without having the slightest fear of the consequences. As it turned out, the doctor could find nothing wrong at all. I thought she seemed just a tiny bit disappointed that the drama was all over.

This blitheness about her health and safety was the result of her deep religious beliefs rather than a conviction of her invulnerability. In 1975 and '76, she spent quite a bit of time planning for the eventuality of her death. She was not morbid, and in fact she never even mentioned the word. But many of her activities revolved around getting things in order for the next generation. That was part of the reason for the obsessive visits to the attic and continual inventory of all her possessions. She was giving many of the most valuable of her things to the next generation. Jean Smith was given a lovely vermeil tea set that Joe Kennedy had purchased in London at a Red Cross auction during World War II. He later discovered it had been donated by the King and Queen, and in appreciation of his generous bid, they added a vermeil tray to go with the tea set. Ethel was given an expensive painting of pink flowers that had always hung in Mrs. Kennedy's bedroom. Ted got the silver, and Jean was given an antique table. Mrs. Kennedy sold some of the jewelry she no longer had occasion to wear, and she decided to put other valuables in the bank vault, out of harm's way. That was what she did with President Kennedy's handwritten draft of his inaugural address that used to hang in the den at the Palm Beach House.

She also spent countless hours tinkering with the provisions of her will. The outlines were generally clear and stable; she left some of her estate to benefit the retarded, and the rest was divided up, more or less equally, among the family. It was the minor provisions that gave her the most trouble. For example, she debated for days about whether she should leave her old and not very well-to-do friend Mrs. Marie Greene $5,000 in her will or not, in light of the fact that Joe Kennedy, always the thoughtful provider, had arranged an annual payment of $5,000 for her lifetime. Did that mean Marie had already been given enough, or did it mean Mrs. Kennedy ought to be sure to make her this one last gift? And what about the nephew who was a priest? Should he get less than the other nieces and nephews, since he had no children to provide for? And since she was leaving Caroline and John their father's desk, shouldn't she deduct a sum equivalent to its value from the amount she was leaving Jackie? Was her estate big enough to afford a $25,000 legacy to her one living brother? These questions went round and round in her head, and she was constantly sending notes and making calls to the New York office about such matters. She asked them to handle drawing up the changes and sometimes also to explain them to those most concerned. As she put it, it was "quite an emotional experience" for her to do it. Her will was continually redrafted. I remember when a new will was brought to the house in the summer of 1976, and Mrs. Kennedy asked Jeannette to witness it; Jeannette said it was the fifth time she had been a witness.

This activity bespoke a concern about the future of her family, not a fear of her own death, which she faced serenely. Her faith in an afterlife was rock-solid, as indeed was her faith in all the beliefs of her church. She observed all its rituals and respected its demands. She regularly had mass said for all of her dear departed, and her own prayers were frequent and heartfelt. To me, her relationship with the Church was epitomized by her letters to members of the Catholic clergy; her invariable closing was "Your respectful child."

Interestingly, the fact that Mrs. Kennedy was alone so much of the time didn't mean that she had forgotten how to have fun. She had a lively sense of humor, which always made our conversations enjoyable. She giggled a lot, and she was a gratifying audience for funny stories. I remember telling her about my trip back from picking Joan up at the airport, when the alarm on the Lincoln started up and couldn't be turned off. My description of how we went through sedate Palm Beach with the alarm wailing and attracting the attention of every passerby really tickled her, and she laughed a long time at the conclusion of the story, in which Joan and I were driven back to North Ocean Boulevard in a pickup truck by one of the men who worked at the garage where we took the car to be fixed. She had a keen sense of the ridiculous, which must have been a help on more than one occasion in the life she led.

She could also "play," in the sense psychologists mean when they describe emotionally healthy human beings. Music was a particularly good outlet for this, as her duets in the kitchen with Nellie or her own renditions of "Sweet Adeline" on the piano attested. I especially remember one time, that last summer I worked for her, when she confounded everyone by her high spirits. Teddy was around that weekend, and Doris Kearns, the esteemed biographer, and her husband, Richard Goodwin (once a Kennedy staffer), were in town. Somehow, the whole group, including Nellie, the cook, ended up going on Saturday night to the Irish Pub, a quaint spot in Hyannis with old wooden tables and live Irish music. Mrs. Kennedy threw herself into the spirit of the evening and began singing along with all the old Irish ballads she loved so well. She enjoyed herself so much that she didn't get home until the early hours of Sunday morning. Her doctor couldn't get over it. Only a few days before that, she had been quite sick, and he was thinking of sending her back to New England Baptist Hospital for observation and tests. Then the next thing he knew, she was out carousing until two o'clock in the morning! Surprisingly the outing didn't seem to do her a bit of harm . . . probably because she was having so much fun all the time. She once told me, "Never pass up an opportunity to have some fun. You never know what's around the corner."

Despite her inner reserves, there were times when it was obvious to me that Mrs. Kennedy was not just alone but also lonely. I remember particularly one Christmas in Palm Beach when none of the family was there with her. She had hoped that some of the children and grandchildren might decide to come, so she bought a tree as usual several days before the holiday and set the staff to work decorating it. "I've never done it myself," she explained to me. "The men always did it." I never knew who she meant by "the men," an expression I had often heard her use. For example, once when I went to pick her up at the airport, she said as we were leaving, "Shall we get the luggage ourselves or shall we send the men for it?'' I often wished that there *were* some helpful men around to do the heavy jobs, but in fact, Dennis was rarely on the premises, and not particularly helpful when he was, and Jim Connors, the guard, worked only a few nights a week. So most of the work fell on me and the elderly women, like Mam'selle and Nellie, who worked for Mrs. Kennedy.

Once we had the tree up and the house decorated, it did look lovely. The lights lining the long entryway had colored bulbs, and the small trees around the front patio were also covered with bright twinkling lights. Large red poinsettias lined the front entrance hall, and in the living room there was not only a tree but a number of plants that had been sent as gifts, including a beautiful huge white poinsettia from Jackie. At night especially, the house had quite a festive look.

But no one ever came to spend that Christmas with Mrs. Kennedy. On Christmas Eve, she ordered Dennis to take down the tree and take it to the local Catholic school where it could be enjoyed by all the children. Since she had the habit of opening any present she received the moment it came, there were no packages left behind . . . nothing for Mrs. Kennedy to look forward to opening on Christmas morning. I had a small surprise for her. I had asked a friend who made hats from palm leaves to whip one up for Mrs. Kennedy to wear in swimming on sunny days. I put it, before I left that night, by her plate in the big dining room, set for just one person to have breakfast on Christmas morning. I felt sad as I·walked out the door and home to my own family, where our Christmas Eve celebration was waiting. I called her the next day to wish her a Merry Christmas and was relieved to hear that she was going out to the Wrightsmans for Christmas dinner.

I couldn't really blame Mrs. Kennedy's children and grandchildren for this state of affairs. I knew she had turned down their invitations to visit with monotonous regularity. She returned their Christmas gifts, and she often scolded their extravagance whenever they attempted to do something for her. If someone brought her flowers or sent her a plant, she would tell them they ought to save their money, since they never knew when it might be needed. When family members telephoned, they were admonished to call at a different time so it wouldn't cost so much money.

Still, I thought it was a shame that she had nobody around her who really understood her and her habits. Even her domestic staff was of fairly recent origin. Nellie had previously worked for Ted, and Mam'selle had worked for Pat, but neither of them had worked for Mrs. Kennedy for very long when I arrived on the scene. Jeannette, too, had only been there a few years longer than I had. In fact, of all the people I met when I first worked in the Kennedy house in 1969, not a single one was there when I returned in 1974. Mrs. Kennedy had none of those long-term associations that can make daily life at once more comfortable and more comforting.

It bothered me to realize that I was one of the most stable elements of Mrs. Kennedy's existence. Dave Powers, whose sense of humor had made him one of Jack Kennedy's most valued aides, once kiddingly told me I ought to be in the *Guinness Book of World Records* for staying in the job longer than anyone else ever did. Previously the turnover in the position had been notorious. I remember telling my predecessor, Jay Sanderson, over a friendly lunch several years after I started to work for Mrs. Kennedy that she was thinking about writing another book. "What's she going to call it," asked Jay pointedly, "*Secretaries I Have Known*?"

Certainly Mrs. Kennedy could be difficult to work for, sometimes demanding and imperious, often stubborn and irrational. But I always knew I received at least as much as I gave. I was warmed by her charm, enjoyed her company, and took satisfaction in knowing I was really able to help her. And I felt she was always a positive influence. I remember the times that she commented on my bad posture as I stood in her bedroom or sat at my desk; although her remarks could make me feel like a child, they also made me aware of my posture and helped me improve it. She encouraged me to watch my weight and to be careful about what I ate. She subjected me to the same scrutiny she used on herself, commenting favorably on my long curly eyelashes but explaining that I was using a foundation that was too light for the color of my skin. She gave me a little bottle of her own darker shade, so I could see for myself the improvement it made. She noticed what I wore to work and gave me compliments on outfits she thought were particularly becoming. She tried to break me of the habit of saying "okay," which she thought was too informal. She was a perfectionist herself, and she applied those same high standards to those around her. It's one of the reasons I knew she cared about me, too.

More effective than any of her specific comments was the example she set for me. Here was an eighty-five-year-old woman listening to recordings of Proust's works in order to improve her French vocabulary and accent; carefully eating a ripe banana every day for the potassium to improve her health; buying the latest makeup so she could stay in style; going out to campaign in front of thousands of people even when she was half-sick, just because she thought her son needed her. She was so interested, so vital, so determined to keep improving herself. Those traits are rare at any age, but particularly unusual for a woman in her eighties. When you thought about the sorrow she had borne, and saw how free she was from self-pity or constant recrimination against fate, how determined to be cheerful and happy in her daily life—well, Mrs. Kennedy was a constant inspiration to me.

Unfortunately it was gradually becoming clear, both to me and to Mrs. Kennedy, that she didn't need a secretary. As her health deteriorated, she could take on fewer and fewer engagements of any sort. And she didn't really handle her own affairs any longer. The New York office already took care of most of her bills and her business. When I first went to work for her, Mrs. Kennedy made several spirited efforts to get things back in her own hands, writing to Tom Walsh in New York about how she could take a load off his staff by paying her own bills. But within a few years, she had lost the energy and the interest to try to find out about her own financial position, and she was quite content to let New York take care of it all. I realized it would be just as easy for them to take care of her mail, too, since very little of it was personal. Mrs. Kennedy had got to the point where she couldn't even manage the two or three letters a day I would show her. A simple note from a friend would throw her into high anxiety, bringing on headaches and stomach upsets. And most of the time, her eyes were so bad that she couldn't read her own correspondence, her hands so shaky she couldn't write her own replies, or even her familiar notes in my shorthand book to tell me what ought to be done the next morning.

What Mrs. Kennedy needed was not a secretary, but a combination nurse and companion. That would meet her needs better, and I knew it. Eventually, she knew it, too. That was a hard thing for her to acknowledge, partly (I like to think) because she and I had developed a supportive and even devoted relationship, and she hated to see me go. Partly, it was also that giving up a secretary was symbolic of the end of her genuine independence. Henceforth, the New York office and the family would make all the important decisions about her life.

Another woman might have kept quiet about the situation, letting it drift on as long as possible. But that was not Mrs. Kennedy's way. As soon as she faced the fact herself that I had very few secretarial duties left, she was determined to act on her realization. She was never a person to sweep things under the carpet.

One day that last summer I was with her in Hyannis Port, she walked into my office at a particularly frantic moment. It was not long before the big annual Labor Day bash, and Ethel's secretary had just called to say their outdoor man had quit: Did I know of someone who could get their lawn in shape? While I was trying to make calls about that, I was also coping with the arrangements for the arrival of the Smith family and their maid, and taking a call from the governess hired by the Senator. She was with the Senator and the two older children on the boat at a Nantucket dock, and she wanted me to check on Joan and Patrick, who had been left behind in the house. I promised I would find the time to jump in the car and drive out to the house to see how they were getting along.

Mrs. Kennedy watched and listened without comment for a few minutes as I struggled to deal with the complications of the Kennedy family. Finally she said in her clear, carrying voice, "One consolation in all this . . . I'm leaving this very soon!" I couldn't think of a tactful reply to her almost cheerful view of her own death, and the moments ticked by. Finally she concluded, "If you're smart, you'll leave, too."

With that clue to what was going on in her mind, I was not surprised when she began to ask me a few days later about how much mail there was to handle, whether I was sending it to the New York office, and other questions about my work. I felt I owed it to her to answer honestly, to let her confirm the fact that most of my time was spent coping with the family and in acting as a companion to her. "You'd probably be better off with a second maid or a nurse, Mrs. Kennedy," I explained. After a pause, she agreed. From then on, we shared the tacit assumption that I was leaving sometime in the near future, and it was just a matter of weeks before I made my plans and told Mrs. Kennedy I would quit when she left Hyannis Port that fall.

The remaining weeks were hard for us both. Sometimes I felt so sad for her that I was on the verge of volunteering to stay on and look after her as a nurse, even though it was not the right kind of work for me and certainly the wrong career path for me to take. Then some incident between us would remind me that Rose Kennedy was not a woman who would accept other people's pity; she didn't want it and, in the end, didn't need it. Ultimately we both accepted that my departure was inevitable.

I finally gave notice, and it was arranged that I would stay on a few weeks after Mrs. Kennedy left Hyannis Port in the fall to catch up with the correspondence and close the house, and that would be the end of my tenure as secretary. In those last days we had together, Mrs. Kennedy was invariably kind and thoughtful. She told me that I was always welcome to stay in either house or the New York apartment whenever I wanted to, and she frequently asked about my plans for my son's education for that last year of high school. Once she simply said, "You're always in my prayers, dear."

Then it was time for Mrs. Kennedy to leave and for us to say good-bye. True to style, she refused to enter into any emotional scene. I lined up on the front veranda with the others: Arthur, Jeannette, and Nellie, who had come north that summer to help with the cooking. Everything was just the same as it was every fall . . . with one exception. This time, Mrs. Kennedy didn't kiss me good-bye. I knew it was just her way of maintaining her self-control.

We all chatted with Mrs. Kennedy for a few minutes, and Nellie said to her, in her bluff Scots burr, "You've had the best of everything, haven't you, Mrs. Kennedy?"

"Yes, yes," she answered, "I've had the best of everything, and I've also had the worst of everything."

Nellie and I looked at one another then, as if to say, "And so she has."

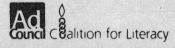

THE MURDERER NEXT DOOR

To his neighbors, Jerry Brudos was a gentle, quiet man whose mild manner sharply contrasted with his awesome physical strength.

To his employers, Jerry was an expert electrician, the kind of skilled worker you just don't find anymore.

To his wife, Darcie, Jerry was a good husband, and a loving father to their children, despite his increasingly bizarre sexual demands on her, and his violent insistence that she never venture into his garage workroom and the giant food freezer there.

To the Oregon police, Jerry Brudos was the most hideously twisted killer they had ever unmasked. And they brought to light what he had done to four young women—and perhaps many more—in the nightmare darkness of his sexual hunger and rage. First, Jerry Brudos was brought to trial . . . and then, in a shattering aftermath, his wife was accused as well. . . .

LUST KILLER

Ann Rule

(writing as Andy Stack)

UPDATED EDITION

A SIGNET BOOK

SIGNET
Published by New American Library, a division of
Penguin Putnam Inc., 375 Hudson Street,
New York, New York 10014, U.S.A.
Penguin Books Ltd, 27 Wrights Lane,
London W8 5TZ, England
Penguin Books Australia Ltd, Ringwood,
Victoria, Australia
Penguin Books Canada Ltd, 10 Alcorn Avenue,
Toronto, Ontario, Canada M4V 3B2
Penguin Books (N.Z.) Ltd, 182–190 Wairau Road,
Auckland 10, New Zealand

Penguin Books Ltd, Registered Offices:
Harmondsworth, Middlesex, England

First published by Signet, an imprint of New American Library, a division of Penguin
Putnam Inc.

First Printing, June 1983
Fourth Signet Printing (First Printing, Updated Edition), August 1988
25

This book is dedicated to the late Albert Govoni, editor of *True Detective*, with gratitude for fourteen years of friendship and superior editing in crime writing.

Acknowledgements

I wish to thank a number of people and organizations who have helped with the research on this book, and who have shared their memories, reliving the emotions they felt. Although the subject matter is horrific, the book is presented in the hope that it may add to the psychiatric research that may one day find a way to treat aberrant minds before they explode into violence. Barring that, *Lust Killer* is written in the belief that the more we learn about the serial killers who rove America, the more quickly we will stop them from ever killing again.

My gratitude goes to: Lieutenant James Stovall, Salem, Oregon Police Department; Detective Jerry Frazier, Salem Police Department; Lieutenant Gene Daugherty, Oregon State Police Criminal Investigation Unit; Sergeant Rod Englert, Multnomah County, Oregon Department of Public Safety; Detectives B.J. Miller and "Frenchie" De Lamere, Corvallis, Oregon Police Department; Archives Department of the Oregon State Supreme Court; Special Agents John Henry Campbell, R. Roy Hazelwood, John Douglas, and Robert Ressler, of the Federal Bureau of Investigation's Behavioral Science Unit, Quantico, Virginia.

Special thanks to Sharon Wood, who survived to relate a terrifying encounter. Most of all, it is my profound hope that some intelligence gained herein will mean that Linda Slawson, Jan Whitney, Karen Sprinker, and Linda Salee did not die in vain, and that understanding their tragedies may save young women old enough to be the daughters they never had.

Prologue

She bent her head against the blast of rain-drenched wind and shifted the heavy case she carried to her other hand. It was January 26, 1968. She was nineteen years old, pretty, slender, and . . . discouraged. Selling encyclopedias door-to-door was not the glorious career her area instructor had promised. It was difficult and scarcely rewarding. Every morning she left her home in Aloha, Oregon—a suburb of Portland—full of enthusiasm, and every evening she returned with her sales book empty. She knew that if she could sell just one set with the yearbooks and the atlas and all the frills that went with it, she would be able to pay rent for a month, buy groceries, and maybe even a few new clothes. That was what kept her going—thinking that each day would be the day. She had listened to the enthusiastic teachers who gave the indoctrination, and she'd memorized all their suggested spiels. She'd even practiced in front of her bedroom mirror, but her prospective customers hadn't reacted the way the role-playing "customers" had in class.

When she knocked on doors, people listened impatiently and then shook their heads and shut the door in her face. When she was given a lead, she usually found that the customer wasn't nearly as interested as she'd been led to believe. Most of them didn't have one book of any kind displayed in their homes, and she couldn't believe they were going to shell out several hundred dollars for a whole set of genuine leather-bound encyclopedias. The best pitch was supposed to be that encyclopedias would make their children succeed in school and grow up to be doctors and lawyers and professors, but it always bothered her to stress the

9

"guilt" approach. "Don't you want your children to have all the advantages you never had? Concerned parents *all* buy encyclopedias for their families, you know."

It bothered her to sit on couches so worn that their bare spots were covered with quilts or towels and suggest that the answer to being poor was to buy her product. She could see the people felt bad enough as it was. She knew if they signed up, they'd be stuck with payments for her fancy books for years. Well, nobody bought anyway, but she always left thinking she'd made them feel worse about being low on money.

The well-to-do homes she approached already had encyclopedias. And those people made *her* feel bad.

Linda Slawson had come from Rochester, Minnesota, to live in Aloha. She had somehow expected warm, balmy weather in Aloha. She had thought of Hawaii and California when she pictured the West Coast and Oregon. Boy, had she been wrong. It rained so much in Portland that it seemed like she never got dry. Sometimes it just drizzled and sometimes it poured and sometimes it blew in soppy gusts—but it always rained. Locals said it got better in the summer, and she should really go into Portland for the Rose Festival in June, but . . .

Her feet hurt. She never should have worn high heels, but she had figured she wouldn't have far to walk from the bus to the address the company had given her near Forty-seventh and Hawthorne. She liked to dress nicely; it made a better impression on customers. But high heels on a darkening rainy night had been a really dumb choice.

Her hands felt numb from carrying the satchel full of heavy books, and she thought the weight of it was what was bothering her neck. When she finally got back to her apartment in Aloha, she was going to have a good hot bath and just forget all about encyclopedias.

She paused under the streetlight, set her gear down, and reached into her purse for the slip of paper with the address on it. The ink smeared instantly in the rain and she couldn't tell if she was supposed to go to 1541 or 1551—or maybe it was 1451. She was tempted to just pack it in, wait for the next bus, and go home.

Indecisive, she started walking again. And then she saw a man in the yard of a house a little way up the block. Maybe she was in luck. He was looking at her, and he waved as if he was expecting someone.

She smiled at him. "I had an appointment to show some encyclopedias to someone. Could this be the house?"

He smiled back and beckoned her in. He was a big man, pudgy but not fat, and he had a moon face. "Come on in."

"Oh, that's good. I thought I was really lost." She moved toward the front steps, but the man took her elbow and pulled her with him, heading to the back.

"There's some company upstairs. We can talk without being interrupted downstairs. My workshop is down there. I'm really interested in buying encyclopedias. You don't mind?"

She looked at him and debated. He was big, but he looked harmless. Kind of dumb, almost—but he seemed serious about buying, and that hadn't happened in a long time. "Well . . ."

"My mother and my little girl are upstairs, and they have visitors. It would be so noisy. And I want to hear what you have to say."

"Okay. Sure."

She followed him into the basement through a rear door and sat on the stool he pulled up for her. She could hear footsteps overhead, the floor above her creaking.

"So," he said. "Tell me about your encyclopedias. Could I buy them tonight?"

"You could order them. I could get the whole set out to you in . . . say, a week. If you have a little girl, I think you'll be interested in our children's books, too. How old is she?"

He seemed distracted, impatient now. "Oh . . . she's only six—but she's very smart. She's starting to read."

"Good. Here, let me show you . . ." She bent to open the case with her brochures and the sample books.

"Let me turn that light on." He moved behind her. She heard him fumbling with something, and half-turned. The last thing Linda Slawson felt was a crash against her head. She fell heavily from the stool, brilliant lights exploding behind her eyes, her ears ringing, and then black velvet covered everything.

He was breathing heavily, although it had taken so little effort to swing the length of two-by-four against her head and feel the satisfying "thunk" when it hit. She had dropped like a stone.

He knelt beside her and checked to see if she was still breathing. He thought he detected a slight movement in her ribs. And then he placed both his hands around her neck and squeezed for a long time. Her neck was so frail; he could feel little bones inside crushing under his hands. When he was sure she was really dead, he let go and stared down at her.

He felt such exhilaration. He had planned and fantasized about doing this for so long. He had come close so many times. Now he had done it, and she belonged to him to do with what he wanted.

He didn't like her hair. It was short—so short that she almost looked like a little boy. He would have preferred a woman with long, flowing hair. Someone who looked like the pictures he'd collected. No matter, really, though, because she had a nice body and she was wearing high heels—the kind he liked.

Footsteps sounded overhead, and he jumped, startled. He wouldn't be able to do all the things he wanted to do if his stupid mother decided to come down and interrupt him. *Damn her.* He'd always hated his mother, and now she had to be here when everything else was going so well.

He worked at quieting his breathing, pulled himself together, and walked upstairs. His mother was there, playing with his daughter. She'd never taken very good care of him, but now she was sure happy to come over and baby-sit. And his wife was always wanting to get away from him, so she just welcomed the old bat every time she showed up.

"I'm starved," he said. "Don't bother with dinner, though. Why don't you take the kid and go get some hamburgers?"

"It's raining. It's nasty out there. Why don't I just fix some—"

He peeled a five-dollar bill out of his wallet, ignoring her dithering. "I want a double-cheeseburger. You get what you want for you two. Stay there and eat yours, and then order mine when you're ready to come home. No hurry. Knock on the floor when you get back."

When they were finally gone, he hurried back to the basement. The girl was still there, still lying just as he had left her. He was so excited, he hardly knew where to start.

But just as he bent over her, he heard someone upstairs again. *Damn!* The steps were heavy male footsteps, and he heard someone shouting his name. Hurriedly he grabbed the body under the arms and dragged it to the shadowy place under the steps. He kicked the satchel full of books into a corner. Then he went out the back door and around the house to the front door. His friend Ned Rawls was there. All happy and glad to see him and walking in like he owned the place. He never should have let Rawls have a key to the place.

He had to make small talk with Ned, and be careful not to show impatience. There was so little time before his mother came home with the kid, or his wife and the new baby came back. He laughed at some joke Ned told him. He explained he had a project in his workshop he had to finish, and promised to call Ned later. It took ten minutes to ease the guy off the porch and back into his car.

When he got back downstairs, he was trembling with anticipation. He pulled the girl out from under the steps. She looked so pale. Normal, as if she was still alive—and that was good—but so pale. Like a big doll. His to play with.

Her skirt and blouse weren't very interesting. He liked pretty clothes, and hers didn't do anything at all for him.

But he had a pleasant surprise when he undressed her. Despite her boy's haircut and plain clothing, she was wearing wonderful underwear. A blue bra and slip

and girdle, and beneath the girdle, bright red panties.
They were perfect; he couldn't have picked better
himself.

He looked at the underclothing and touched it, and
removed the garments one by one, especially pleased
with the red panties. He redressed her in her fancy bra
and slip and girdle, carefully hooking all the hooks.
He was good at that. He'd practiced so many times.

He had a long time to play with her before his
mother came home with the hamburger for him—but
he was frustrated when she rapped on the floor. He
had to go up and get the damned thing, thank her, and
sit there and eat it as if he was hungry. And all the
time, *she* was waiting patiently for him in the basement. He smiled to himself. At least *she* wouldn't go
away and leave him, not until he chose to let her go.

When he went back to her, she sat where he'd
propped her. He thought about having sex with her,
and decided that wasn't necessary. He berated himself
because he had no film for his camera. That was an
important thing that he'd neglected to do. But he'd
had no idea he would meet a door-to-door saleslady
and it would be so easy to lie to her and coax her
inside.

But he did have all his other precious things. All the
filmy, lacy panties and bras that he'd stolen over a
long time. He could never decide which was the best—
sneaking into dark apartments and stealing the underwear while he could hear the women sighing in their
sleep only a few feet away from him, or playing with
his collection of satin and silk that still smelled faintly
of their perfume and skin after the garments belonged
to him.

He'd never had anyone he could use as a model
before. He couldn't show all that stuff to his wife,
because she might get suspicious. Now he chose bras
and panties and slips with inches of lace edging the
satin, and spent hours dressing and undressing the girl.
He liked the red panties best of all. They were just
right for her.

He had worked through the scenarios in his head for
years, and never told anyone what he thought of,

always dreaming of captive women. And he wasn't disappointed at all now that he had pulled it off. He knew he couldn't keep her with him forever, but he could remember the way it was now. Next time, he would take pictures too.

His wife came home, and he went upstairs and talked to her briefly, and told her to go to bed—he'd be along when he finished his project. He loved his wife. He really did love her, because she was sweet most of the time, and quiet, and because she didn't nag him. But things just weren't the same since the baby boy was born. He'd wanted to be with her when that happened, right there in the delivery room, and she'd chosen to share that experience with another man. With the doctor—not with him. It just tore hell out of him that she'd choose another man like that.

When they were all asleep, he went back to the basement. He played dress-up with the dead girl some more, reveling in the quiet that was marred only by the soft whisper of the rain against the windows. He would have to get rid of her before the sun came up. Too bad, but that's the way it was. He needed to have something that belonged to her, though. Not her bra and panties; he already had so many of those from so many women who didn't even know what he looked like or who had stolen from them.

He had a freezer, but it wasn't big enough to keep her in, and all the women roaming through the house would find her anyway. His mind was working well. He understood certain things clearly. He was right-handed, so it seemed proper that he should cut off her left foot . . ..

He did that, cutting cleanly through her ankle. The foot didn't look right without a shoe, so he slipped the shoe on it before he put the foot into his freezer.

He was pleased with himself. He had convinced Ned Rawls that he was brewing nitroglycerin in the basement, and scared him off easily enough. He'd gotten his fool mother and his wife to go to bed, and now all he had to do was to slip the dead girl into the Willamette River, where no one would ever find her. He already had an engine head to use as a weight, and he was so strong he could handle it easily.

There were many bridges crisscrossing the Willamette River in Portland. In the daytime, cars choked them. But not at two A.M. He chose the St. John Bridge, and just to be on the safe side, he pretended that he had a flat tire. The stupid cops never showed up to help when you really needed them, and he counted on that now. He pulled a jack out of the trunk, nudging her body aside, and set it up under the rear bumper.

It worked like a charm. Nobody in the few cars that passed by even looked twice at him. When there were no cars in sight at all, he lifted the girl from the trunk, along with the engine head, and carried her to the bridge rail. She fell free, and an instant later the deep waters of the Willamette pulled her in and covered her over. The splash itself had been surprisingly gentle, too soft to draw attention.

After he couldn't see her any longer, he undid the car jack, stowed it in the trunk, and drove away. The only thing that bothered him was that he remembered too late the ring she'd worn. Some kind of bulky class ring that said "St. Somebody" on it, and "1967."

He didn't even know her name. It didn't matter. He was sure no one would ever find her.

No one did.

Back at the encyclopedia sales office, they figured that Linda K. Slawson had just decided to quit. Nobody remembered the place where she was supposed to go on the night of January 26. Salespeople came and went. It was to be expected.

Her family worried, and then grew frantic, and made a Missing Persons report to the Portland Police Department. But all efforts of the Missing Persons detectives led nowhere. Linda K. Slawson remained on the missing rolls, certainly not forgotten by either the investigators or by her family. There simply was no place left to look for her. The earth might as well have opened up and swallowed her.

The big man with the moon face kept her foot for a while. He used it as a model to try shoes on. When he grew tired of that game, he put a weight on it and tossed it too into the Willamette.

And then he planned and fantasized and wondered what he could do next. What he'd done to the girl in the red panties had been so exciting and so fulfilling that he had no intention of stopping.

—— 1 ——

He was a monster. He was not born a monster, but evolved grotesquely over the twenty-eight years, eleven months, and twenty-seven days that passed before Linda K. Slawson had the great misfortune to cross his path.

Jerome Henry Brudos was born in Webster, South Dakota, on January 31, 1939. His parents seem to have been a hopelessly mismatched couple. They already had one son a few years older than Jerome, and they apparently did not particularly want another; the older brother, Larry, was intelligent and placid and gave them little trouble. A girl would have been preferable. Instead, Eileen Brudos gave birth to a red-haired, blue-eyed second son whom she would never really like. As all babies do, he must have sensed that. When he was old enough to form his feelings into words, he would call her a "stubborn, selfish egotist." If she did not like him, he grew to *despise* her.

Eileen Brudos was a stolid woman who dressed neatly and plainly, and "never, never wore high heels," according to Jerome.

Henry Brudos was a small man—only five feet, four inches tall. He moved his family a dozen times during his sons' growing-up years. They usually lived on a farm, farms that gave so grudgingly of their produce and livestock that the elder Brudos had to work a full-time job in town to support them. Like most small men, Jerry Brudos' father was easily offended and hostile if he thought someone was taking advantage of him, and was quick to react with verbal abuse. Whatever his father's faults, Jerome Brudos vastly preferred him to Eileen Brudos.

The Brudoses lived in Portland during the Second

World War. Employment was easy then, and their
financial picture was fairly stable.

Five-year-old Jerry Brudos was allowed to roam
freely, and on one occasion he was pawing through a
junkyard when he found something that fascinated
him. Shoes. Women's high-heeled shoes, but nothing
at all like anything his mother had ever worn. These
were constructed of shiny patent leather with open
toes and open heels and thin straps to encircle the
ankles of the woman who wore them. They were a
little worn, of course, and one rhinestone-studded dec-
orative clip was missing. Still, they pleased him, and
he carried them home.

More for comic effect than anything else, he slipped
his stocking feet into the shiny black shoes and paraded around. Eileen Brudos caught him at it and was
outraged. She scolded him severely, her voice rising in
a shriek as she went on and on about how wicked he
was. She ordered him to take the shoes back to the
dump and leave them there. He did not understand
why she was so angry, or just what it was that he had
done wrong—since obviously no one wanted the old
shoes anyway. He didn't take the shoes back; instead
he hid them. When he was discovered still sashaying
around in his forbidden high heels, there was hell to
pay. His mother burned the shoes and made him stay
in his room for a long time.

When he was finally let out, he ran to a neighbor
woman who was very pretty and soft and kind to him.
He liked to pretend that she was his real mother and
that he had no connection to Eileen. He already hated
Eileen.

Little Jerry Brudos had another friend when he was
five—a girl his own age. She was often pale and tired
and couldn't play; he did not know that she was dying
of tuberculosis. Her death was the most terrible thing
that had ever happened to him, and he grieved for her
for a long time.

The neighbor woman who was kind to him was
sickly too, and suffered from diabetes. Years later, in
his own mind, the episode with the stolen shoes, his
girlfriend's death at the age of five, and the kind

neighbor woman were intertwined in his mind, and he
could not speak of one without the others.

By the time Jerry Brudos was in the first grade, the
family had moved to Riverton, California. He had a
pretty teacher who invariably wore high-heeled shoes
to class. She always had two pairs on hand, one to
switch to if her feet got tired or if she planned to go
out on a date when school was over. Stealthily now,
because he had learned that high-heeled shoes were
not to be noticed overtly, he stared at his teacher's
footwear, entranced by the slim heels. When he could
stand the temptation no longer, he stole the shoes she
kept in her desk and hid them under blocks in the play
area so he could take them home with him. But somebody found them and took them back to the teacher.
Days later, he confessed that he had taken them.

She was more puzzled than angry. "Why on earth
would you want my shoes, Jerome?"

He turned red and ran from the room.

Jerry Brudos failed the second grade. He was a
sickly child. He had measles and recurring sore throats,
accompanied by swollen glands and laryngitis. As an
adult he remembered having a number of "toe and
finger operations," probably to treat fungus infections
around the nails. He had two operations on his legs.
What the defect was is obscure; Jerry Brudos himself
recalls only that there was something wrong with the
veins in his legs: "The veins were ballooning and I had
to have the operations because they were not doing
their job."

He often had migraine headaches that blinded him
with pain and made him vomit. Because of the headaches and because he seemed not to comprehend the
basics of reading and writing, school authorities thought
he might need glasses. His brother had sailed through
school with As, and Jerry's I.Q. tested normal or
above, but he sometimes seemed vague and slow.

Glasses were prescribed but they were hardly more
than window glass, a placebo. He still had headaches,
an ailment that would plague Jerry Brudos to greater
and lesser degree for much of his life.

He must have spent some time in bed recovering,

locked in with the mother he avoided whenever possible, but that part of his life is blanked out in his memory.

He got along all right with his brother, despite the fact that Larry excelled in school and was always deferred to by Eileen. Jerry seldom saw his father because he was always working—on the farm or on his town job.

Jerry's fixation with women's shoes was solidly entrenched. On one occasion his parents entertained visitors who brought their teenage daughter with them. The girl wanted to take a nap, and lay down on Jerry's bed. He crept in and was transfixed to see that she still wore her high-heeled shoes. As she slept, one of the heels poked through the loose weave of the blanket. The sight was tremendously erotic to Jerry. He wanted her shoes. He worked to pry them off her feet, but she woke up and told him to stop it and get out of the room.

It should be pointed out that Jerry Brudos was still a small boy when his shoe-stealing episodes took place, well under the age of puberty. Sex, of course, was a subject forbidden in his home. Like all farm-raised youngsters, he observed sexual behavior among animals. He knew what bulls did to cows, and he knew that boars quite literally "screwed" female pigs with their peculiar but functional penises. He had seen dogs and cats mate. But he would never dare to ask how intercourse between humans was accomplished. Touching and hugging, any demonstration of affection, was discouraged in the Brudos home. He heard jokes at school, and laughed with the other boys—remembering particularly a joke about a girl sliding down a banister—but he never admitted he didn't understand the punch line or the point of the joke. And he was completely unable to make the connection between the strange excitement he had when he was around women's shoes and his own sexual drives.

It was just something that was peculiar to himself. But he sensed that it had to be a secret thing. Why else would his mother have been so enraged over his shoe theft when he was only five? Why else would the teenage visitor have been so angry with him? And his very need for subterfuge and secrecy made his obsession all the more thrilling.

Looking at the fair, bland-faced Jerry, the child who seemed dull in school, no one ever detected the fires burning in him. That there was danger there, however incipient, would have seemed laughable.

For all of his life, women held the reins of power over Jerry Brudos—in one way or another. Eileen, his mother, was strong, rigid, and intractable. He could not please her; he had never been able to please her, and she clearly ran the household. She railed at him for the most minor lapses, and it seemed to Jerry that his brother got away with everything. Larry avoided chores just as much as Jerry did, but their mother always had an excuse for Larry. Larry was "exceptional" and "gifted" and needed the time to study. Their father and Larry both knew that Eileen had it in for Jerry, but there was nothing they could do about it. She ruled with a firm hand, and all three males in the family chose evasive tactics rather than confrontation.

The other females who had been important to Jerry Brudos deserted him; his little girlfriend died and left him, the neighbor lady became too ill to have time for him, and his teacher never quite trusted him after he admitted the theft of her shoes. He learned early that women could not be counted on.

He wavered constantly between depression and frustration and the rage that is born of impotence.

Heading into puberty, he was an accident looking for a place to happen.

The family moved to Grants Pass, Oregon. Their new neighbors had a house full of daughters, and Jerry and one of their brothers often sneaked into the girls' bedrooms to play with their clothing. His fetish expanded to include female undergarments. Secret woman things. Brassieres and panties and girdles and the complicated harnesses that they used to hold up their silky nylons. He now loved the feel of the soft cloth, almost as much as the shoes that were so different from men's.

The Brudoses moved again before Jerry was thirteen, and lived on Wallace Pond near Salem, the state capital. Jerry's father made another lackluster attempt at farming there in 1952.

Larry was sixteen and had the normal pubescent male's interest in the nude female body. He collected pinup pictures and sometimes drew pictures of Superman's girlfriend, Lois Lane—portraying Lois nude and wearing high heels. Given the puritanical views of Eileen Brudos, Larry prudently kept his cache of pictures locked up in a box.

Jerry found the box, picked the lock, and pored over the pictures. And it was Jerry—not Larry—who was caught in the act. He didn't tell on his brother, but accepted the punishment. Nobody would have believed that it was Larry's collection anyway, because Larry was the good son and Jerry was the bad son.

At the age of sixteen, Jerry had his first wet dream. Eileen, who steadfastly denied all sexual matters, found his stained sheets and scolded him severely. The nocturnal ejaculation had startled him, too, and he wondered if it was something people should be able to control. His mother made him wash his sheets by hand, and he had to sleep without sheets the next night because he had only one set and the offending sheets were still hanging damp on the line.

Jerry began to create bizarre fantasies of revenge. He worked for days digging a hidden tunnel in the side of a hill on the farm. His plan was to get a girl and put her into the tunnel. Once he had her, he would make her do anything he wanted. He could picture it all clearly, but he ran into a problem when he tried to think what it was he wanted the captive girl to do. He still didn't know enough about sex to focus on what intercourse was, and he certainly didn't understand rape. He only knew that the thought of a captive woman begging for mercy excited him.

At the same time, Jerry began to steal shoes and undergarments from neighbors' houses and clotheslines. He had quite a little stash that he studied and touched and kept carefully away from Eileen Brudos.

Interestingly, Jerry never stole his mother's clothing or was tempted to try her things on.

If anyone suspected that it was Jerry who was making off with the neighborhood underwear on Wallace Pond, he was never accused. And then the peripatetic Brudoses moved again—this time to Corvallis. Corvallis is the site of Oregon State University and lies twenty-five miles west of what is today the I-5 freeway that runs from Canada to Mexico. It is a fertile region, as is the entire Willamette Valley. The Long Tom River flows just east of Corvallis, and the Pacific Ocean is fifty miles to the west.

By the time the family moved onto yet another farm, Larry was in college—doing well in his study of electronics. Jerry was skilled in the same field, but his accomplishments paled in comparison to his brother's.

Jerry was almost seventeen, and he had learned the basic facts of life. Still, he had never *seen* a naked woman, and he was determined that he would. His hostility toward and distrust of women in no way mitigated his lusting after them.

Jerry continued to steal women's clothing. At home, in the privacy of his own room, he would take his treasures from their hiding spot and fondle them. He would later tell psychiatrists that touching female garments gave him "a funny feeling." He used the clothing for masturbation, but he failed to achieve an orgasm. The only ejaculation he had experienced to date had come from "wet dreams."

In the late summer of 1955, Jerry Brudos crept into a neighbor's house and stole undergarments belonging to an eighteen-year-old girl who lived there. The stolen clothing by itself soon began to pall, and Jerry thought that it would be so much better if he could have pictures of a real girl, mementos he could keep. He formulated a complicated scheme.

He approached the girl whose lingerie he'd stolen and told her that he could help her get her things back. He bragged to her about a secret; he had been working with the police on the case. He had inside information. She was a little doubtful, but Jerry was persuasive. Since he lived in the neighborhood where the thefts had occurred, he said the police found him the perfect undercover man—no one would suspect he was working with the cops.

The girl debated. She wanted her things back; she'd worked hard to buy them. And Jerry was a kid—only sixteen; he looked like a big clown. She wasn't afraid of him, and maybe he *did* know something.

Jerry Brudos invited her to his home on a night when he knew everyone else in his family would be gone. When he heard her knock on the door, he called to her from upstairs, "Up here! Come on up—"

She edged up the shadowy staircase of the old farmhouse, following the sound of his voice. His room was dim and she couldn't see Jerry. Suddenly, a tall figure wearing a mask jumped out at her and waved a large knife.

"Take off your clothes—or I'll cut you," the voice behind the mask said. "Do it!"

He pressed the knife against her throat, and she could feel its sharp edge cutting. Her heart convulsed as she realized she had made a terrible mistake in judgment.

Trembling, the girl removed her clothing. She wasn't stupid; she knew who it was behind the mask—but she didn't know what he was going to do to her. She didn't have a chance to fight, she'd have to go along with him.

Her captor produced a cheap camera with a flash attachment, and she realized that he wasn't going to rape her; he wanted to take pictures of her!

He directed her how to pose, and took some shots when she was totally naked, and then some when she was partially clothed. She did what he asked, terrified that he might still have more in mind than photographs. He moved quickly, giving her orders to move this way, to bend, to turn.

When the roll of film was finished, the masked figure walked out of Jerry Brudos' bedroom. His victim threw on the rest of her clothes frantically and was just heading toward the stairs when Jerry, without a mask, walked into his bedroom. He was breathing heavily.

"Hey, are you OK?" he asked. "I was out in the barn, and somebody came along—I couldn't see who it was—and locked me in. I just managed to break out! Did you see anyone around here?"

She shook her head, and edged past him, running for home the minute she made it to the front door.

Jerry Brudos actually believed he'd fooled his victim into believing it was a stranger who had forced her to pose nude. He figured he'd pulled it off when nobody came around accusing him.

He developed the pictures and *really* saw what a naked woman looked like for the first time. He'd been so intent on taking the pictures before somebody came home and caught him that he hadn't stopped to savor his subject. He'd been in such a hurry that he hadn't even become sexually excited. But then Jerry Brudos' fantasies had never included *interaction* with a female; in his fantasies, women acted only on his bidding. He was the Master and they were only slaves.

His first impression of a nude female was that "she looked awful funny." But he soon took great pleasure in looking at his photographs while he handled his subject's stolen panties and bras, incorporating her, his prisoner, into his fantasy.

Later, his victim told police, "I knew who it was all the time; I wasn't fooled by that mask and his phony story about being locked in the barn, but I was afraid of him. I was scared if I told he would find out and he would kill me. . . ."

Eight months passed after the episode of forced picture-taking; Jerry wasn't worried about being discovered because nothing had come of it. But he had looked at those same pictures so often that they no longer produced the effect they once had. Besides that, they were smudged and tattered.

He needed a new captive.

Jerry Brudos couldn't find a girl who would date him. He was big and clumsy and suffered from teenage acne—"acne vulgaris," the doctors called it. His pimples were even more obvious when he blushed scarlet. When he was nervous, he ducked his head and his voice became a croak.

But it was more than his appearance and his awkwardness; there was something about Jerry Brudos that turned girls off, something scary that triggered an almost visceral reaction warning them to stay away from him.

Nevertheless, on a warm April evening in 1956, Jerry Brudos managed to lure a seventeen-year-old girl into his car on a ruse. He began to talk as if they were on a date together and she stared at him, baffled. She had only accepted a short ride.

Her bewilderment turned to panic when he stared straight ahead and drove faster, farther and farther away from the main roads. Finally, he pulled into an overgrown driveway and parked at a deserted farmhouse, its siding grayed from the weather, the wind blowing through its glassless windows.

She looked around and saw that they were miles from other houses, from anyone who might come to help her if she screamed.

Without a word, Jerry Brudos dragged the girl from his car and began to beat her. His fists rained down on her face and breasts, and she tasted her own blood warm and salty in her mouth. Fearing it would do no good, she screamed anyway as the huge, strange boy continued to pummel her. He pulled at her clothing, ordering her to strip for him. He wanted to see her naked, he said gasping. She twisted and kicked and tried to get away.

The sun would be setting soon, and she knew if she didn't get help, she would be dead by the time the sun rose again. She screamed with all her might, and his fist crunched sickeningly into her nose.

Fortunately, a couple from a farm down the road happened to be driving by just at that moment. The husband wrenched his steering wheel and turned quickly into the weed-choked yard. They saw the old car parked there, and the tall, heavy young man bent over someone on the ground beside it.

"She fell out of the car," he explained, reaching out to help the sobbing girl up. "She's just hysterical because it scared her."

The girl shook her head violently, trying to speak through her swollen mouth.

The couple looked on doubtfully, and the boy shrugged his shoulders. "Well, actually, what happened was that some weirdo attacked her. I came driving by and I stopped to help. She was fighting him off when I came up, and he took off through the fields over there."

This version didn't make any more impression on the couple than the first one, and they insisted on taking the girl—and Jerry Brudos, who went along quite meekly—back to their house, where they called the Oregon State Police.

Faced with the police, Jerry Brudos admitted that he had beaten the girl himself. He said he'd wanted to frighten her enough to make her take off her clothes so he could take pictures of her. He denied ever doing such a thing before. He seemed baffled by the incident himself; he felt his temper had just gotten the best of him. But police found his camera equipment in the trunk of his car, and recognized premeditation before the attack.

Jerry Brudos' victim was treated in a local Emergency Room and found to have extensive bruises and a badly broken nose.

Investigators searching Jerry's room on the farm in Dallas, Oregon, came upon his cache of women's clothing and shoes. And they found photographs. Pictures of women's undergarments and shoes, and photos of a nude girl. Jerry had an excuse for this, too. He insisted the pictures had been taken by another boy, and that he had only developed them.

"I had to . . .he said he'd beat me up if I didn't. . . ."

Jerry Brudos was arrested for assault and battery. He was referred to Polk County Juvenile Department which began a background investigation.

Eileen Brudos was outraged, and Henry was stunned. There had never been anyone on either side of the family who showed signs of mental illness or violence. *What in the world could be the matter with Jerry?*

A review of the case for which he was arrested, the presence of fetish items in his room, and a talk with the eighteen-year-old neighbor girl who now felt safe to come forward, convinced authorities that Jerry

Brudos had deeper problems than the average juvenile delinquent.

He was committed to Oregon State Hospital for evaluation and treatment in the spring of 1956.

Jerry Brudos seemed humbled and meek as he talked to a procession of psychiatrists. He said he was a sophomore in high school. He liked sports but he didn't like rough competition. "I don't like to fight or to push people around, or be pushed around—so I don't go out for any of the teams."

He gave his hobbies as working with radios, electronics, mechanics, and . . . photography. He had belonged to 4–H, Boy Scouts, the Farmer's Union.

The Jerry Brudos who sat in Oregon State Hospital seemed impossibly remote from a sadistic sex criminal. He blushed crimson when asked about his sex life—or rather his lack of sexual experience. He said he "suffered" from nocturnal emissions—"wet dreams"—about every two months. He tried to lead a clean life; he didn't drink. He didn't smoke.

No, he had never had a sexual relationship with a girl. He had never even been out alone with a girl; sometimes, he had been in large groups where girls were present. Yes, he had taken the pictures of the neighbor girl and she had been the first naked woman he had ever seen.

Doctors were a little puzzled, searching for a diagnosis. One psychiatrist wrote on April 16, 1956:

"The boy does not appear to be grossly mentally ill. He comes shyly into the interview situation and sits down in dejected fashion to talk with great embarrassment about his difficulty. It is difficult for him to form any relationship with the examining physician although he does warm up slightly through the course of the interview. He is precisely oriented in all spheres; speech rate, thought rate, and psychomotor activities are within normal limits. Flow of thinking is relevant, logical, and coherent. He tends to be evasive on a basis of his acute embarrassment and is somewhat rambling and verbose in trying to tell his story. He appears to be somewhat depressed at the present time and his predominant mood would appear to be of depressed, dejected embarrassment. His affect is appropriate to thought content. *There is no evidence of suicide, homicide, or destructive urges.* He feels that he sometimes has trouble controlling his temper but that it has never got him into trouble except on this last occasion when he maintains that he cannot remember too clearly exactly what he did but was told that the girl received a broken nose. There is no evidence of hallucinations, delusions, or illusions. He denies any sense of fear except over what is going to happen to him, and he says he has some sense of guilt over having got into trouble but does not feel particularly guilty over having taken the photographs. . . . Intellectually, he is functioning well within the limits of his educational background. His insight and judgment are questionable; he feels that there must be something the matter with him and he hopes that he will be able to find out and have it cured here. . . .

The provisional diagnosis of Jerry Brudos' problem was: "Adjustment reaction of adolescence with sexual deviation, fetishism."

Jerry was not a full-time patient at the mental hospital. During the day, he was allowed to attend high school at North Salem High School. He moved among the other students as a nonentity, a tall, pudgy youth with raging acne.

He was smart, probably brilliant, in mathematics and science, and yet no one remembers him. None of his teachers. None of his fellow students. Years later, one of his defense attorneys would realize with a start that he and Jerry had been in the same homeroom at North Salem High. But the lawyer could remember no more about Jerry Brudos in high school than anyone else could.

When he became infamous, teachers and peers *tried* to remember Jerry. They still couldn't. He had moved through North Salem High and left no ripple behind.

He was a loner. The odd duck, hurrying through the halls with his head bent. His after-school residence at the state hospital was kept secret. All anyone at North Salem High knew was that he never came to the football and basketball games and never showed up at the dances, where Elvis Presley's records of "Blue Suede Shoes" and "Heartbreak Hotel" played over and over.

He belonged to another world.

Jerry Brudos' fantasies, as black and horrific as they were, remained his own. When he stared at the pretty high school girls, at their clothing, and especially at their wonderful shoes, he did it covertly.

At the mental hospital, Jerry talked often with the doctors. A second diagnosis was "borderline schizophrenic reaction" a handy catch-all diagnosis of the era.

Jerry remained at the hospital for eight or nine months. Henry and Eileen Brudos were adamant that they didn't want him home until he was cured of whatever ailed him.

But before a year had passed, he *did* come home to the family farm in Dallas. Jerry had not been missed much. Eileen had been working at a wool mill, and Henry worked the farm and had a job in town. Larry was doing well in college. Jerry was the only problem they had.

In the end, the staff at Oregon State Hospital had determined that Jerry Brudos was not that far removed from normal. A bit immature, certainly, overly shy, and given to tall stories, but not particularly dangerous. When he left the hospital, he was advised to "grow up."

Back in Corvallis, Jerry returned to high school. There was 202 students in his graduating class. He enrolled in audiovisual and stagecraft courses for his electives. It is somewhat ironic that this noncommunicative youth should pick courses that dealt principally *with* communication, with reaching out and touching others through the radio or from the stage. What he could not seem to do in a face-to-face encounter, he apparently sought to do through the media. His goal was to obtain an FCC license so that he could be employed at a radio or television station.

He was quite adept at electronics; he has been described by some who knew him as "brilliant" in that field, and, in the same breath, "lazy." He was skilled at electrical wiring, too, and he was a fair backyard mechanic.

Jerry Brudos graduated 142nd in the class of 202, with a grade-point average of 2.1, just above a C. He attended Oregon State University for a short time, Salem Technical Vocational School for a while, and dabbled at a few other advanced schools.

On March 9, 1959, Jerry joined the U.S. Army and was sent to Fort Ord, California, and subsequently to Fort Gordon, Georgia, for basic and advanced training in the Signal Corps. He eventually achieved the rank of E-2. With his skill and interest in communication and electronics, the Army might have been the perfect choice for him.

But his obsessions had never left him.

He became convinced that a Korean girl had come into the barracks one night and crawled into his bunk and tried to seduce him. "I didn't want her and I came up fighting and beat her badly."

The dream woman returned on several occasions, and Jerry wondered that none of his barracks mates teased him about it. At length he decided that there was no real woman—that she was only a dream. No one complained of the noise that accompanied his beating of the woman. No one even noticed when she came in the night to tease and fondle him.

Jerry worried that he hated the woman so much he wanted to beat her and kill her. He went to the Army chaplain, who referred him to Captain Theodore J. Barry, the staff psychiatrist. Dr. Barry determined that Jerry was not fit for the service because of his bizarre obsessions and recommended discharge for him under AR 635-208. On October 15, 1959, Jerry was discharged—disappointed and wondering why the Army should let him go for such a minor thing.

Jerry Brudos, twenty years old now, returned to Corvallis, Oregon, after his discharge and moved into the two-bedroom house where his parents lived. He was allowed to live in the second bedroom; but then

Larry came home from college. As always, Larry came first. He was given the extra bedroom, and Jerry was relegated to a shed on the property. He covered the windows so no one could peer in at him and "because I wanted to keep out the light."

His old anger at his mother surged back. Larry had the good room; he had the shed.

Both Mr. Brudos and Larry came to Jerry and advised him to give up trying to find favor in his mother's eyes. "She will never treat you well. She never has and she never will." They seemed sympathetic to him—but as impotent as he was in trying to change things.

He stayed away from home as much as possible, and when he was on the Brudos property he sequestered himself in his darkened shack and tried to shut out the knowledge that his mother still seemed to be in control of his life.

One evening, Jerry went over to Salem on an errand. He spotted a pretty young woman walking near the telephone office. She wore a bright red outfit, and he could not take his eyes off her. He followed her, excited by the scarlet clothing. She did not realize he was just behind her as she turned into the doorway of an apartment house. Only when she was in the dim, deserted foyer did she hear the soft footfall right behind her. She turned, frightened. She opened her mouth to speak, but before she could utter a sound, Jerry simply closed his hands around her neck and choked her until she fell to the floor, semiconscious. Jerry looked down at her, lying helpless there, and debated what he should do to her.

She was lucky: he only stole her shoes.

It happened again in Portland. The stalking of a woman who wore sexy shoes. Again, he choked his quarry, but this time the woman fought back and he managed to make off with only one shoe.

Back in his shack, he slept with the shoes, remembering the power he'd had over their owners—if only for a short time. Somehow, this made him feel stronger now when he had to deal with his mother.

— 2 —

Despite his disfavor at home, Jerry Brudos was functioning effectively in his chosen career goal. He obtained his FCC license and, with it, a job as an operating engineer at a Corvallis radio station. It gave him a modicum of self-esteem, and he seemed, at least outwardly, to be less of a loner. He had a skilled job—something that few men could qualify for. He bull-shitted with the station employees, and they accepted him.

He was a big man. At six feet and 180 pounds, he had far outstripped his father's five feet, four inches.

He was still a virgin.

Jerry Brudos had an old car that he had fixed up, and he was eager to have a steady girl of his own. Although he distrusted women generally, he thought he might find a woman who would be perfect—someone who would be totally committed to him—and someone who would welcome him sexually whenever he wanted. Once he found her, he would keep her away from the rest of the world. She would belong to him alone.

Jerry met his woman when he was almost twenty-three, met her through an unusual channel. Since he was not adept socially, he found it hard to meet women. There was a young boy who came into the station to watch Jerry work at his control panel, a kid who "bugged" Jerry with questions and with his constant visits.

But the kid brought Darcie to him. One day Jerry asked the boy if he knew any girls that Jerry could date, and the boy, eager to please, introduced him to Darcie Metzler.

Darcie would pay dearly in years to come for the

romance that began as if it had come right out of a
popular love song.

Darcie was seventeen, a pretty, big-eyed young
woman with thick dark hair, when she met Jerry
Brudos. She was very quiet and shy, but not unpopu-
lar with boys. She dated frequently and went out with
boys she describes as "good-looking." She had grown
up in a family that was strictly dominated by her
father, a man of Germanic extraction, and she was
chafing to get out and be on her own. She was too
submissive to rebel—she had never been the type to
question authority, and she loved her parents. But she
dreamed of having her own home, where she could
make her own decisions.

She was exactly the type of woman Jerry had been
looking for.

When the little boy brought Jerry to her house and
introduced him for the first time, she wasn't very
impressed. In fact, she didn't like him at all. His
clothes were neither neat nor stylish. Her first view of
him was of an average-looking man in rumpled, paint-
spattered pants. She thought he could have dressed up
a little when he was meeting her for the first time. He
had thinning blond-red hair and a bit of a double chin;
he certainly wasn't as attractive as the guys she usually
dated.

"I probably wouldn't have accepted a date with him
at all—except that he asked me to go swimming, and I
love to swim."

For some reason—perhaps because she was so shy
herself—Darcie didn't threaten Jerry or make him feel
angry. She laughed at his jokes and made him feel
good.

"He was full of fun and full of jokes," she recalls. "I
was so shy that I couldn't even get up in school to
recite or answer questions, and he seemed so confident."

It is quite possible that Jerry Brudos could not have
impressed a woman of his own age so much, but
Darcie Metzler was six years younger than he. She was
impressed with his job and with him. She gave him the
attention and admiration he'd never found before.

He was very tender with her, demonstrating niceties of courtship that the teenage boys she knew didn't understand. He pulled out her chair for her, opened doors, bought small gifts and flowers. He put her "on a pedestal," and she liked that.

And to ensure that she would be absolutely dazzled by Jerry, there was the fact that her parents didn't like him and said so. Nothing drives a girl quicker into a lover's arms than parental disapproval.

Brudos didn't like his mother-in-law-to-be much better than he liked his own mother—which was not at all. He found her "stubborn and independent—like me." He didn't like Darcie's father, either. "He felt because he was older that he could decide what we would do, where we would go—all of that."

Jerry was very jealous of Darcie. Fiercely jealous. She was flattered by that in the beginning, considering jealousy to be part of true love. Since she was spending all of her time with Jerry anyway and had no interest in any other man, she felt protected by his possessiveness.

In retrospect, after all the horror had been acted out and had almost destroyed her, Darcie believes that she never really loved Jerry Brudos. In 1962, she thought she did. "While my home life was a good one, there was this feeling that 'getting married' would be much better than listening to your parents."

Brudos recalled their betrothal more pragmatically. "I wanted someone to sleep with, and she wanted out of her home."

He had never had intercourse with a woman when he met Darcie, despite all of his erotic fantasies. That lack was remedied soon after they began dating. Apparently Darcie found him normal sexually—or perhaps she had nothing to compare his performance to. She did not know about his background of mental illness.

She certainly did not know of his fetishism or of his rage toward women.

Because her parents were so adamantly opposed to Jerry, the two lovers decided that if she were to become pregnant, they would be allowed to marry. Darcie proved to be instantly fertile, and they were married within six weeks.

Darcie was thrilled with the event. She did not consider that theirs had been a "shotgun" wedding, because she had planned the pregnancy and because she felt she had a sensitive, successful husband.

Jerry was relieved. He had been terrified that Darcie would meet his brother and would leave him in favor of Larry. Since Larry had usurped all good things from him so far, he was sure that he would take Darcie away too.

A daughter, Megan, was born to the couple in 1962, and the marriage seemed to be a happy one for the first three years. Jerry found jobs easily enough, although he couldn't seem to hold on to them. It was no great concern to Darcie because he could always find another. He spent a great deal of money on presents for her on holidays and anniversaries, and he continued to be kind and considerate. She was so busy with the baby that she didn't tumble to the fact that she was virtually a prisoner in her own home.

She didn't know that when she said or did something that made her husband "depressed," he prowled and stole underwear and shoes to make him feel better. She had not seen the flashes of temper that "scared the hell out of" people who knew him.

Jerry's choice for their intimate behavior was her guideline too. When they were home together, they were nude. They continued to "run around the house without clothes" until Megan grew from an infant to a toddler and Darcie balked at being naked in front of the child.

And Jerry, always an avid—if sometimes secret—photographer, insisted on taking nude pictures of Darcie. He had taken a few shots before their marriage, and more on their wedding night. She didn't feel comfortable with it, but he assured her that she was his wife and it was all right. She didn't mind the black-and-white snaps because he could develop them in his own darkroom, but she objected to color slides. They had to be processed commercially. Jerry had an answer for that, too. He explained that if he took the

first and the last slides in a series of pleasant scenery
or something else innocuous, nobody would ever look
at them. Big labs process too much film to look at
every single picture.

"Darcie," he explained, "they look at the first or
the last—and that's all."

She relented, but she never felt good about it.

Jerry's suggested poses were so strange. He directed
the naked Darcie to ride on Megan's tricycle, toward
him, away from him. Darcie's buttocks bulged over
the tiny seat, her breasts were draped over the handle-
bars. When she saw the finished print, she winced.
She begged him to rip the pictures up, and he promised he would.

But he didn't.

Some of her husband's requests were bizarre.
Jerry had Darcie pose, sitting on the floor, with
a nylon pulled over her face so that her features were
distorted into a grotesque mask. And, as always,
she was nude. Some of the pictures featured Darcie
wearing nothing but spike-heeled black patent-leather
shoes.

One day, those pictures, along with so many others,
would become police exhibits. Darcie Brudos, who
had been embarrassed that someone in an anonymous
photo lab might see her naked image, could never
have imagined that her nakedness would be seen by
scores of strangers, that she would be questioned
in court about why she would pose for such kinky
pictures.

Nor could she have possibly foreseen why her private sex-life with Jerry would be such a subject of
speculation.

Even when they weren't taking pictures, Jerry wanted
Darcie to wear high heels all the time—not just when
they went out, but when she did housework. They
made her back hurt, and aggravated her bad knee.
She tried to explain that to Jerry, but her arguments
seemed to depress him.

In a way—a way she could not possibly know at the
time—Darcie Metzler Brudos had become the fantasy
girl that the sixteen-year-old Jerry Brudos had wanted

to place in a secret tunnel, someone his own to do with what he wanted.

She usually went along with him. She was not an assertive woman. Her father had been dominant; now her husband was dominant. She was a little afraid of him, yet could not say why. She compromised again and again with her hulking husband in a marriage that she has described as "very good" at first, and then, as three or four years passed, "stranger and stranger." The shy, soft little woman wanted only a happy home—but achieving that became increasingly difficult.

Darcie was hurt to see that Jerry was so removed and disinterested in their daughter. "He was very distant with Megan." If the toddler tried to crawl in Brudos' lap or to kiss him, he invariably pushed her away. He avoided any physical contact with his own child, and Megan sensed that she somehow displeased her father. On one atypical occasion, Brudos took Megan on an outing to feed ducks, and the child was overjoyed at receiving attention from him, but it was only an isolated incident and Brudos returned behind the invisible wall he'd built between himself and Megan.

Darcie wondered if he resented Megan because she took so much of her own time. That may have been a partial explanation for Brudos' behavior. It may have been that he did not trust himself with the girl-child, that he felt an incestuous attraction. If the latter was true, Megan was saved from something far worse than neglect.

In Brudos' eyes, Darcie was perfect. He had such a tenuous lid on his underlying violence, but if she had managed to remain completely docile, submissive, and obedient, he might have maintained the status quo longer than he did.

She could not. Such small things depressed Jerry. Small mistakes grew into gargantuan betrayals in his mind.

The Brudoses moved from one rented home to another—twenty houses or more in their seven years together. From Corvallis to Portland, and back again, and then for a while to Salem. Darcie got used to packing everything and moving on, but she always dreaded the news that they would have to move again. She knew Jerry was smart and clever with anything electrical, and she wondered why he couldn't hold a job. She wanted to have her own home, someplace permanent where she could put up curtains and plant bulbs and know she would be around to see them come up. But she never was; they were always living someplace else when spring came. And she began to worry for Megan, who would be starting school soon. What would it do to the child to have to adjust continually to new schools?

Jerry had done the same thing already, of course—moving constantly up and down the West Coast when he was a child. If he had done it, he didn't see why Megan couldn't.

In 1965 Jerry had a job at an electronics firm in West Salem, working as a technician. His employer found him a "Casper Milquetoast kind of guy." But he also recalls him as "the most brilliant electronically oriented mind I've ever seen. There wasn't anything he didn't know about electricity and circuitry."

The boss liked him well enough, although he seemed a sissy and totally nonaggressive. Brudos worked in the company for months, went fishing with the boss, and never, never showed any signs of temper. He was placid and amenable to suggestion. He just didn't apply himself, and that was the only explanation his employer could give for his being stuck in a technician's job. "With his First Class FCC license, he could have run any television or radio station in the country. But his only ambition was to read—read and study— and that was the end for him. He always carried a bound portfolio with him, filled with letters of recommendation. Each letter was encased in plastic, and he was really proud of those things. They were from college professors and electronics experts—character references. He must have shown them to me four or five times; he wanted people to think he was important."

One thing Jerry Brudos never discussed with the

men at the plant. That was women. He presented himself as a solid family man, and he never participated in the sometimes ribald conversations of his fellow workers. He didn't drink, and he didn't smoke, and his employer was sorry to lose him when he left.

He came back to visit after a year or so. He still wasn't running a television or radio station, not even a small one.

Brudos had an explanation for that, a story that was a total fabrication. He said he'd enlisted in the Navy and had been injured in the explosion of a shell aboard ship. He recalled that the accident had killed two of his buddies, and that he had spent a year in a naval hospital himself, his injuries so severe that he had become eligible for a service pension. It was a patent lie—all of it. Since he had been released from the Army for psychiatric reasons, the Navy would never have accepted him. His former boss didn't know that, of course, but the story sounded fishy.

And yet even with Brudos' transparent attempt to make himself a hero, his ex-employer couldn't help liking the guy. He was pitiable, sitting there with his usual hangdog expression, his shoulders sloped forward as if he expected rejection. So, what the hell— he'd tried to make himself sound macho with some fairy tale. His old boss took Jerry home to meet the family, and didn't question him about what he'd *really* been up to while he was gone.

Two events occurred in Jerry Brudos' life in 1967 that seemed to unleash the perverted obsessions that had lain smoldering inside him for so long. Given the extent of his aberration, some thing at some time would have triggered him. The monster within was growing restless. His migraines were accelerating both in number and in magnitude and he was experiencing what he called "blackouts."

He had managed to alleviate his depressions—the terrible black, hopeless feelings that swept over him when he thought Darcie did not love him enough— with his nocturnal prowls to steal underwear and shoes. Each time, for a while, his stolen garments made him feel better. But his spells of feeling good lasted such a short time.

When Darcie became pregnant again, Jerry was enthusiastic—far more than he had been over her pregnancy with Megan. It was almost as if he was going through the gestation right along with her. He wanted to do it all; he wanted to be right there in the delivery room when his son was born. He had no doubt at all that it would be a son.

His own father had not been very easy to reach, closed up, really, when he'd needed to talk, or just plain not there. But, given the choice between his parents, he thought his father at least had tried the best he could. Jerry, though, would be a good father to his son—right from the beginning.

In a way, and on an unconscious level, Jerry foresaw his son's birth as a rebirth for himself too. When he saw that baby emerge into the world, he would be released from the bad things he had been doing.

He thought Darcie understood how important it was that he should be in the delivery room with her. He believed he could trust her to send for him when it was time.

She didn't. He tried to follow her into the delivery room, and found his way blocked. The doctor had left firm orders that he was not to be allowed in! Even the announcement that he had a son didn't mitigate his anguish, and he could hardly bear to look at the infant at first.

He was plunged into despair when Darcie came home and told him that *she* had asked the doctor to keep him out.

"*Why?*" he asked her, bewildered. "You told me I could be there."

"I didn't want you to watch another man play with me," she said. "I didn't think it was right."

It was such an odd way to describe a physician's part in the birth of a baby. But, considering how he had always told Darcie he could not bear to have "another man touch you," she may have thought that *any* touching would disturb her husband.

Tears sprang to Jerry's eyes, and he could not be

consoled. Instead, he went out into the night and stole another pair of shoes. This time, it wasn't enough. He was still full of rage and hurt.

A short while later, he was in downtown Portland and saw a girl wearing a pretty pair of shoes. Rather than knocking her down and stealing her shoes, he decided that he would follow her until she went home and take the shoes from her there. He watched her for hours, staying just behind her while she shopped for groceries, following her onto the bus and jumping out the doors behind her just as they began to close. He watched her go into an apartment building, followed, and noted which window was hers.

He waited until he was sure she was asleep, and then he crept into her apartment. It was exciting to have varied his procedure this way, to know what the woman looked like who slept so close to where he fumbled in her closet. He told himself that he didn't want her; he had only come for her shoes.

But she woke up and saw the dark shadowy figure kneeling on her bedroom floor. Before she could cry out, he was beside her on the bed. He had to choke her then because she might be able to tell someone what he looked like. He would make her unconscious before she could turn on the lamp beside her bed. Her throat was so soft, and he applied just enough pressure with his big hands. She sighed and went limp.

He had not thought of raping her, but having her so helpless stimulated him. He moved his hands over her body. For that moment, she belonged to him, and he felt a powerful erection, the strongest he had ever had.

He raped her there in the dark, and when he was finished with her, he took the shoes and left.

They were the best shoes he'd ever stolen.

The birth of his son—without him—had been the worst thing that had ever happened to him. He had erased the disappointment of being robbed of that experience by having the woman.

The second event of 1967 almost killed Jerry. He had made his living as an electrician since he'd left the radio station in Corvallis. He was very cautious, and certainly knowledgeable about safety precautions, yet he came very close to electrocuting himself.

He was working at one bench and reached across to connect a live wire in his hand to terminals on another bench. Instantly his body became rigid as a jolt of power ran through him, 480 volts raced from his right arm through his chest and down his left arm, and the force of it picked him up and threw him across his bench and onto the floor.

He was not rendered unconscious, but he was dazed and burned. And his neck was injured, cervical damage resulting that would stay with him.

A weaker man would have been killed, but Brudos survived. Indeed, he was never even hospitalized.

And so he was quite well and strong enough to lift heavy objects—even the deadweight of a body or an automobile engine—by January 26, 1968. He had beaten women, and stolen their lingerie and shoes, and choked them, and, finally, raped one. But he had never killed a woman.

Not until Linda Slawson came to his door hoping to sell him a set of encyclopedias. . . .

3

Ironically, even as her husband's mental problems had progressed into homicidal rage, Darcie Brudos thought that maybe their marriage was getting better. He had been so unhappy about the events surrounding Jason's birth, but he seemed to have forgiven her once she had explained her motivations to him. He became enthralled with Jason, showing the youngster so much more attention than he'd ever shown their first child. He took Jason with him when he went on errands, and he talked about teaching Jason how to use the tools in his workshop—when he grew up a little. It hurt Darcie that he still ignored Megan, but it was nice that he seemed to accept Jason.

He let Darcie herself have a little more freedom, allowing her to visit girlfriends or to bowl. She knew he wasn't crazy about having his mother baby-sit for Megan while she was away, but he didn't really put his foot down. He was always downstairs in his workshop anyway, fiddling with some electrical project or other, or out with his friends buying engine parts in junkyards.

His headaches, however, had grown worse. She had to keep the children quiet so much of the time because any sound seemed to cause him excruciating pain when he had one of his migraines. It was easier just to take them both with her and go spend the days with girlfriends where the kids could be themselves. She thought maybe the electrical accident had caused the headache problems to be so bad now. But she couldn't persuade Jerry to go to a doctor about it.

The brief spate of calm after Jason's birth didn't last very long. Darcie blamed herself for part of the trouble. She no longer enjoyed sex with her husband. She

45

wasn't even sure why, but when he accused her of being uninterested in him, or disgusted by his touch, she had to agree with him—even though she would not admit it out loud. They weren't kids on a honeymoon any longer; she couldn't go dashing around the house naked now. She *hated* posing for nude photos, obeying his instructions to pose this way and that.

He wanted her to dress up "fancy" all the time, saying that other women looked good and she didn't. But you couldn't wear sexy clothes while you were doing dishes and washing diapers.

He wanted to go out dancing. Well, that hurt her bad knee, and wearing spike heels all the time made her back hurt. When she told him so, he looked offended and drove off somewhere. She had no idea where he went or what he did.

She knew he was very sensitive, and she sensed that she should not argue with him or disobey him, but she was no longer the pliable girl she had been when they were married. She wanted something beyond the cloistered life in which only the two of them existed.

Jerry lost his job in Portland and in the spring of 1968 they decided to leave the house at Forty-seventh and Hawthorne and move to Salem. In a way, Darcie was glad to go—especially when they found the nice little house on Center Street. It was not a lavish house, but it was kind of cute and cozy. Gray shake and close to the ground. It had a big yard full of evergreens, roses, and flowering trees. There was a fence around the yard, just white chicken wire, but sturdy enough to prevent the children from running out into Center Street, a main thoroughfare in Salem. There was an attic for storage, and the garage had a workshop portion where Jerry could set up all the gear he'd accumulated. The garage wasn't hooked onto the house itself, but connected by a breezeway. Jerry looked at the place and deemed it perfect for them.

Darcie had friends in Salem, and she liked living in a smaller city than Portland.

For Jerry Brudos, coming back to Salem was the completion of a circle. The Oregon State Mental Hospital where he had been incarcerated a dozen years earlier after beating his teenage date was only a few blocks down Center Street from the gray house. Its proximity didn't seem to bother him; he never spoke of it at all.

Salem, Oregon, is one of the lovelier cities on the West Coast, and the capitol city of Oregon. The Capitol Building itself is gleaming white and topped with an immense statue of a pioneer, a golden figure that can be seen for miles. The parking strips of Salem are planted with roses that bloom from May through December. There are carefully preserved mansions alongside modern homes, and the land outside Salem is verdant and productive. Green beans, corn, peas, hops, and strawberries grow abundantly in the Willamette Valley, and Salem has processing plants where the crops are canned and frozen.

There are paper mills in Salem too, and when the wind is right, their acrid smell laces the air, assaults the nose, and leaves a metallic taste on the tongue.

The brightest high-school students in Oregon are drawn to Willamette University in Salem, and the politicians come to the legislature. Others, as Jerry Brudos once had been, are locked up in the state's institutions—all located in Marion County (except for the boys' reformatory in Woodburn, a few miles north). The Oregon State Prison, the Hillcrest School for Girls, the Oregon State Mental Hospital, and the Fairview School for the Developmentally Disabled surround Salem. Some of the inmates escape, but most are only paroled or furloughed or dismissed from custody. Many of them remain in the Salem area to live in halfway houses or blend, however roughly, into the mainstream.

Salem police and Marion County sheriff's personnel expect a little more trouble than most lawmen—the percentage of the population that is a little strange exceeds that of most areas.

Jerry Brudos did not stand out as "strange"; he was too covert for that, and he seldom left the little house on Center Street. Despite the job opportunities offered through the food and paper-mill industries, he was not able to find work. Maybe he didn't look that hard; his headaches were bad, and his neck hurt.

And he had so much on his mind.

He moped around the house or puttered in his shop out in the garage, and Jerry packed on pounds. There were new rolls of fat around his waist and under his chin. One day, Darcie mentioned to him that he seemed to be gaining weight, and he grunted and disappeared into another room in the house. He was gone for a short time. When he returned, his wife was shocked to see Jerry standing before her, dressed in a woman's bra—stuffed with something to look like breasts—a girdle, stockings with garters, and the biggest pair of black pointy-toed high-heeled shoes she'd ever seen. Somehow, he'd managed to tuck his genitals inside the girdle so that he almost looked like a woman, turning and posing for her. All he needed was a wig. . . .

Jerry looked so peculiar, a great big freckled man standing there in women's underwear—funny, really . . . but not funny. Darcie laughed nervously, but she was frightened and embarrassed. It seemed a little sick.

Darcie was naive. She didn't know what a fetish was. She didn't know about transvestites or sexual psychopaths. She knew that some men were gay, but Jerry had always been entirely masculine. Their own sex life had always been straight when it came to intercourse. He'd never asked her to do anything that was kinky or repulsive. Nothing beyond posing for nude pictures.

He seemed a little disappointed at her reaction. There was an awkward silence, and then he left the room. When he came back, he looked like himself again.

She wondered where he'd gotten the girdle and bra, but she didn't ask him. She didn't want to make him angry or upset. Because it made her worry when she thought about her husband dressing up like a girl, she put it out of her mind. She had enough to worry about: money for bills, and keeping the children quiet, and trying not to irritate Jerry.

She could not have known, could never have visualized in her worst nightmares, just how bad things were going to get.

— 4 —

As the Brudoses settled into their Center Street home in Salem in the summer of 1968, a detective worked in his offices in Salem's hundred-year-old city hall, perhaps a dozen blocks northwest of them. Though he was a twenty-year police veteran, and though fifteen years of that time had been spent in the detective unit, where he'd seen his share of violent crimes, Jim Stovall could not foresee how bad things would get either. And when it was over, he would deem the Brudos case the most shocking of his long career.

Every heinous criminal has his nemesis, his alter ego—the one detective out of dozens whose whole existence is taken up for a time with catching his quarry. Jerry Brudos—for all of his macabre fantasies—was a most intelligent man, a planner and a schemer. He would not be caught easily, and, once caught, he would be difficult to break.

If there is a working detective in America who could be the model for the brilliant investigators portrayed in fiction, it would be Jim Stovall. That he happened to be living and working in Salem, Oregon, in the black period of killings in 1968 and 1969 was one of the few bright spots in a terrible story.

In the summer of 1968, Brudos and Stovall did not know each other, although it is very possible that they passed each other on the streets of Salem, that Brudos drove past the looming old city hall, that Stovall drove past the gray house on Center Street. And, oddly but not mystically, long before he ever confronted Jerry Brudos, Stovall would draw up a psychological profile of the killer he sought that was as clear and detailed as if he were psychic.

But that was later, much later than the sunny, rose-filled days of mid-1968—because, at that time, Brudos had not yet begun to carry out the rest of his killing plans. He still waited, basking in the afterglow of the perfection of Linda Slawson's murder.

Jim Stovall and Jerry Brudos had a few things in common. They each had a wife and a son and a daughter. Both of them had been in the armed services at one time. And both of them were planners and given to attention to detail. That was all. One of them worked to save lives. The other . . .

Some good cops are cerebral and some work with gut feelings—the "seat-of-the-pants" cop who knows what he knows but cannot tell you why. Stovall is that rare cop who is both, and woe to the criminal who wanders into his line of vision.

Jim Stovall is a tall, handsome man with clear gray eyes, waving iron-gray hair, and the physique of the athlete he is. He looks like a bank president, or a TV newsman, or—yes—the glorified image of a slick detective. He looks a great deal like the actor Rory Calhoun, but would be embarrassed if someone should mention it to him.

In the Second World War, Stovall served in both the U.S. Army and the U.S. Marine Corps, where he was a rifle-range coach. When the armistice was declared, it seemed a natural progression that he should sign up with the Salem Police Department.

Like most veteran cops, Stovall has lived through hairy incidents. As a rookie with less than a year on the force, he responded to the most dangerous radio squawk an officer can get: "Family fight." An enraged husband had left the family home after threatening to come back and kill his wife. Since a fair percentage of angry husbands do just that, there was a "want" on the suspect's vehicle. Stovall spotted the car, signaled it to move over to the side of the road, and approached the driver's door from the rear, stopping just behind the driver. Instead of the driver's license he'd requested, the man came up with a Luger—pointed at Stovall's heart.

Stovall could see that the man was wild-eyed and

shaky, likely to shoot. He kept his voice and his eyes steady as he spoke. "Look . . . you don't know me too well—so I'll give you a chance to point that in another direction. . . ."

The driver's finger tightened on the trigger, and Stovall could almost hear his mind deciding what to do. They stared at each other for five . . . ten . . . fifteen seconds, and then the gunman laid his weapon down on the seat beside him and surrendered.

Had things gone badly, the Salem Police Department would have lost one hell of a cop.

Stovall was the top marksman in the department for eighteen years, and still shoots an occasional 98 or 99 on the FBI's PPC course. One night, he was staked out in the hallway of a building where a rash of burglaries had occurred. After a boring night, he heard the tinkle of broken glass somewhere in the building. The would-be burglar met Stovall in the hall, where the officer flashed his light into the man's face and challenged him. The suspect broke and ran into a room, locking the door behind him. Stovall aimed at the shadow behind the glass door and fired his .38. He then heard a crash, followed by the sound of running feet.

Stovall thought he had missed the man, until a doctor in a Salem hospital's emergency room reported that a man had come in for treatment of a "nail wound." Stovall went to the hospital and recognized the man he'd seen for a split second in the rays of his flashlight. The burglaries stopped, and the thief recovered at leisure in prison.

Promoted into the detective unit after only five years on the force, Stovall availed himself of all training opportunities. He has a certificate in legal medicine from the Harvard University Medical School, has had many hours of study at Willamette University's Law School, and studied police business administration at the International City Managers' Association Institute of Training in Chicago. He has attended the Southern Police Institute in Louisville, Kentucky, and schools on visual-investigation analysis and link-analysis-charting techniques given by the California Department of Justice. He has also studied advanced psychology and hypnosis. And he is an expert photographer and a licensed pilot.

A dog-eared square of paper is always tacked where Stovall can see it above his desk: "THE ELEMENTS OF SCIENTIFIC PROOF MUST BE PRESENT TO ESTABLISH AND SUBSTANTIATE A SCIENTIFIC CONCLUSION."

And Jim Stovall has solved some homicide cases that defied solution, by meticulous attention to detail, by seeking and eventually finding that minuscule bit of physical evidence that starts the first ravel in a case that seems impenetrable.

When a lovely twenty-three-year-old woman was beaten and stabbed to death in her bedroom in Salem, Stovall determined that the bludgeon weapon was a broken soft-drink bottle, its green fragments glittering in the sheets that covered her.

Every man the girl had ever known or dated was located and questioned, amd all of them were cleared. Then the victim's mother remembered a seventeen-year-old boy she had encountered on the street. "He said he'd been away for a year, and he mentioned to me that he would like to call my daughter and come over to see her sometime—but I don't think he ever called or came around, because she never mentioned him."

Jim Stovall recognized the youth's name—he'd been arrested for minor juvenile offenses and there was a warrant out for him on a burglary charge. When he was taken into custody, he grudgingly let the detective have his clothing and shoes for lab examination.

There were a few specks of dark red on the suspect's clothes—too little to classify as to type. But in the heel of the youth's shoes, Stovall saw a tiny sliver of green glass.

At the Oregon State Crime Lab the shard of glass was compared with the bottle fragments found at the death scene under a scanning electron microscope and then in an electrospectrometer with a laser attachment for elements and light refraction. *The samples were identical.* They could only have come from the same batch of bottles, a circumstance that indicated it was highly probable that they had come from the *same* bottle.

Faced with that information, the killer confessed that he had killed the victim when she refused his sexual advances.

One of the strangest cases Jim Stovall ever solved was a classic "man found shot dead in a locked room with no weapon in sight."

Investigating a report on a man who had disappeared from his usual haunts, Stovall and his partner, Sergeant John Kelly, checked the doors of the man's home and found them all locked. The front door was open, but a locked screen door prevented entry. The windows were all locked from the inside. Stovall broke the screen-door lock and stepped inside. The occupant lay facedown several feet from the front door. His right hand still clutched a nutcracker, and his mouth was full of nut meats. Until the dead man was turned over, it looked as if he had succumbed to a heart attack. But, faceup, there was a small red hole in the front of his shirt, over his heart.

Stovall and Kelly looked for the gun that had to be there. An odd suicide, but then, suicides are not normal under any circumstances. Since all the doors and windows had been locked from the inside, and since the dead man was alone in the house, the only answer had to be suicide—unless one believed that a killer had arrived and left via the chimney like Santa Claus. But there was no gun anywhere on the premises, so how could a suicide be explained?

Neighbors were quick to offer a motive for murder. The dead man had been seeing another man's wife, and the other man was insanely jealous. It was not at all surprising that the victim was dead. What was curious was *how*.

Stovall, who takes as many as one hundred photographs at homicide scenes, shuffled through his developed pictures and stopped when he came to a shot of the screen door. He enlarged it, and enlarged it again, and again.

And there it was. A slight gap in the screen. The bullet had been a .25-caliber, quite small. When it passed through the wire mesh of the screen, it had made a hole, all right—and then the metal strands had snapped back almost as good as new. Unable to be seen by the naked eye, the piercing of the screen showed up in the photo lab. Stovall had weighed the variables, and figured that was the only way. Even if he couldn't see it, he expected to find a tear there.

Jim Stovall's main goal is to find the truth—not to put people behind bars. If the truth sets a "good" suspect free, those are the breaks; it only means that the answer has not yet been ferreted out.

One Salem husband came very close to going to jail for the murder of his wife because a pathologist skimped on the autopsy.

"Failure to perform a complete autopsy or to save material for toxicological analysis is a dangerous practice—even if you have a suitable answer at the time," Stovall says.

In murder, of all human phenomena, things *are* seldom what they seem. In the mysterious death of the forty-year-old victim, it looked clearly as if her architect husband had killed her because he was tired of dealing with her emotional problems. Men have shuffled their wives off for far less.

Stovall and his crew found the woman dead one summer afternoon, lying in her kitchen in a welter of blood with a wound on the top of her head. The medical examiner ruled it a homicide—probably by beating and strangling. Her throat had the hemorrhages peculiar to strangulation, and the state of rigor was well advanced when she was found. Time of death was pegged at ten A.M. because of the rigor mortis.

"There was something not quite right," Stovall recalls. "Her hands were flexed in such a way that I was suspicious."

The husband stated that he'd been home for lunch at noon and that his wife had been fine then. "I took two containers of raspberries out of the freezer for her because she was going to make a pie."

The postmortem examination had included only a cursory look at the head and throat, and the time of death stipulated marked the husband's statement as a lie. He could not have seen his wife alive and well at noon.

Hardly popular with the M.E., Stovall insisted on further tests, and the contents of the victim's stomach were found to be laced with strychnine poison. That made the case a whole new ball game.

Stovall searched the kitchen shelves above where the woman had fallen, and found an old container of poison on the top shelf. A check of sales on strychnine in the Salem area showed that four and a half pounds of the stuff had been sold in the previous twelve months—all in minute amounts sold from a dozen different outlets.

The husband, more bewildered than ever, was given a polygraph test and passed it cleanly. He did remember buying some rat poison many years before, but had forgotten it was even in the house.

"That poor woman killed herself," Stovall says. "Witnesses said she'd been slipping back into her old depression. She had time enough to take the poison, rinse out the glass, and replace the container on the high shelf. Then convulsions seized her and she fell, striking her head on the sharp kitchen counter. Strychnine kills from sheer exhaustion from the constant convulsions. The throat hemorrhages were caused by convulsive spasms, not from strangulation. And when death is caused by a convulsive disorder, rigor is accelerated. She *was* alive at noon—just as her husband said."

A grand jury overturned the murder charge and ruled the woman's death a suicide.

Jim Stovall keeps a constant reminder of the need for attention to forensic detail in solving crimes above his desk, but *beneath* his desk he keeps a pair of ski boots. That is his avocation and his passion away from the police department. A skier for thirty-five years, he is a member of the Professional Ski Instructors of America—teaching skiing in Oregon and also in Colorado during his vacations. His whole family skis. Today his daughter is a ski instructor, and his son is a skier and a lawyer.

In 1970 Jim Stovall was named *Master Detective*'s

National Police Officer of the Month, and singled out by *Parade* magazine for an honorable mention in their annual salute to the ten most outstanding police officers in America.

He would never have a case more challenging than the one that began in earnest on November 26, 1968—exactly ten months after the disappearance of Linda Slawson. The second case was part of a pattern, but a pattern with too few variables yet known to be apparent. But the serial killer is never satiated. He kills and moves on to kill again and again, until something stops him. He choreographs his killing so carefully, remembering which of his deadly steps succeed and incorporating them into his pattern.

And in so doing, he leaves, for the men who know what to look for, a path as plain as a trail of bread crumbs.

5

By the fall of 1968 Jerry Brudos had found a job, again as an electrician, for a firm south of Salem. Not a great job—but a job. His marriage was still intact, but it was strained. Darcie had cooled to his sexual advances; she did not often refuse him, but he sensed she found him disgusting. She was away from their home so much now, spending four days a week with two sisters who were her good friends.

He still ruled the home with an iron hand, however. He told Darcie that the shop area was his and that he didn't want her going out to the garage without his permission. He got a strong padlock and put it on the door to assure that he would have privacy. She complained some because the freezer was out there, and he said flatly, "Just tell me what you want for supper and I'll get it out of the freezer for you. I don't want you butting into my darkroom when I'm working—you'll ruin everything if you do."

He didn't worry so much about her poking around in the attic. He told her that he'd seen mice and rats up there, and that scared her. He had his treasures up there, boxes of shoes and bras and slips, all sizes. Some were even large enough for him to slip into himself to spend hours enjoying the feel of the soft cloth against his bare skin. The things were his, and he didn't want Darcie touching them or asking him questions about where he'd got them.

He didn't even like to have her come home unexpectedly from her silly visits to her friends. "You call me before you come home," he told her. "I like to have some warning who's going to pop in on me."

"But I'm your *wife*," she protested.

"You just call, like I told you."

There was no point in arguing with him. She did call, but that didn't seem to be enough. Jerry flooded her friends with calls of his own whenever she was away from home. "He wanted to know where I was, what I was doing, when I was coming home. He was terribly jealous of me, wondering who I was with— and I never was with anyone but my girlfriends. Once I asked him why he was always checking on me, why I couldn't come back to my own house without calling first. He made a joke of it. He said he wanted to be sure he got the blond out of the house before I got there."

He had never cheated on her, not as far as she knew. It was a dumb joke. She was a little afraid of him now, because he seemed so strange. He had never harmed her physically, but he was so big, and even his friends said he was the strongest human they'd ever seen. He could carry a refrigerator all by himself and never even show the strain.

Jerry Brudos had begun his fantasy about capturing women when he was seventeen. By the time he was twenty-nine, he had refined it and polished it until it had grown to something right out of Krafft-Ebing, a nightmare of sadism.

He wanted to find someplace where he could set up an underground "butcher shop." It would have cells where he could keep his captives, and a huge freezer room. When he had it all ready, he would take a bus and go out and round up pretty girls and bring them back to his torture complex. He would choose which ones he wanted for his pleasure. He would shoot them and stab them and beat them and play with them sexually, and no one would be able to find out. When he had them, he would take pictures of them for his collection. When he was finally done with them, he would take them into his freezer room and freeze them in the positions he wanted so that he could keep them forever.

He acknowledged that there were problems with his plan. For one thing, it would take thousands and thousands of dollars to finance such a complex. He had barely enough money to pay rent and buy food. He still had to borrow money from his bitch of a mother and play up to her so he could use her car when he needed it. He was smart enough to earn a lot of money, but he just had bad luck: everybody took advantage of him, and so he worked for peanuts.

Practically, too, he figured that if so many girls turned up missing, somebody would catch on and the cops would start sniffing around.

But it was a plan that always stayed in his mind.

It made him dizzy thinking about it. Sometimes he woke up in the middle of the night feeling dizzy, and he knew it was because of his sexual fantasies. He could end them only by rolling over and having sex with his wife. Now when he made love to her, he felt that he was making love to someone else—to one of his captive women. He knew that it was Darcie, but he had an uncanny sensation that it was not.

He didn't hurt her, and she never knew.

At work, the men kept on with their filthy jokes about women, They thought hc was some kind of prude because he no longer bothered to laugh. They treated him like he was nobody; it gave Jerry pleasure to realize what fools most men were.

6

Autumn came to Oregon and all the flowers turned black with frost, everything but the roses. The oak leaves turned yellow and covered the red earth, their branches hung with moss that wafted in the wind like an old woman's hair. And the rains came, weeks on end of steady gray rain that dripped from eaves and trees and pushed the rivers up over their banks. From time to time a violent storm swept in from the Pacific Ocean, and the rain pounded incessantly then against the windows of the gray shake house on Center Street and drummed on the thin roof of the garage workshop.

Thanksgiving was just around the corner, and that meant that Jerry would be spending time with people he detested: his own mother—who would complain that she missed her husband, now long buried, and her favorite son, working a thousand miles away, and Darcie's parents, just as bossy and opinionated as they'd ever been.

The constant rain and the dull job and the holidays coming up made him restless. His headaches were like a hammer pounding in his head, demanding that he leave the crowded house and the whining kids and his wife who didn't seem to respect him the way she once had.

It was hard to find trophies in the winter. Nobody hung wash out on lines because it would never get dry. He had to prowl and watch and go inside to steal underwear.

He had to do something to stop the headaches and the dizziness.

At twenty-three, Jan Susan Whitney was well along in preparing for her future goals. She was almost finished with her degree at the University of Oregon in Eugene, some sixty miles south of Salem. No longer attending college full-time, she now lived in McMinnville, southwest of Portland. She had her own car, an older model Rambler, and a job and friends in both McMinnville and Eugene.

Jan Susan Whitney was a pretty girl with short, thick brown hair and blue eyes. She was five feet, seven inches tall and weighed 130 pounds.

She was, perhaps, more trusting than most—or only naive; she occasionally picked up hitchhikers on her trips between Eugene and McMinnville.

On November 26, 1968, Jan concluded a visit to friends in Eugene and headed north on the I-5 freeway toward her apartment in McMinnville. She was dressed in black bell-bottom slacks and a green jacket when she said good-bye to her friends. She planned to be home that evening; it was only a short drive, two hours at most.

Thanksgiving was two days away, and Jan had plans to be with friends and relatives. She was happy, and dependable, and intelligent. There was no reason at all—no predictable reason—for her to completely disappear.

And yet, she did vanish that night.

Since she had been in transit, it was almost impossible for investigators to pin down just where she might have vanished, or if she had been taken away against her will. A check of her apartment indicated that she had not returned from her trip to Eugene; mail and papers had stacked up, and dust lay heavy in the small rooms.

Jan Whitney had not called any of her friends or family. She had simply disappeared somewhere along the I-5 corridor.

A description of her car was sent out on the teletypes in Oregon and adjoining states.

The car was found parked in a rest area on the road leading up to the Santiam Pass just north of Albany, Oregon, and slightly east of the I-5. The red-and-white Rambler had no external damage, and it was locked.

The Oregon state police ordered that the vehicle be

towed into the garages of the Identification Bureau for processing. It was found to have a minor mechanical problem that would preclude its being driven, but there was absolutely no evidence that the driver had been injured in the car.

No blood. No sign of struggle. There were a few personal items belonging to Jan Whitney. There were no keys.

In processing the Rambler, state police I.D. technicians lifted a good latent print from one of its hubcaps. With the technology available in 1968, a single latent print was worthless to detectives unless they had a suspect's print to compare it to. (FBI fingerprint files had single-print information only on the ten most-wanted criminals.)

The discovery of her car in the lonely parking lot made things look ominous for Jan Whitney. She would have no reason to be there on a foggy, dank November evening. If she had left her inoperable car and attempted to walk along the freeway for help, she had not been seen. Since pedestrians along I-5 are quite noticeable because they are so few and far between, it would seem that *someone* reading news stories of her disappearance would have come forward if she had been seen that night. A search of ditches and the land bordering the freeway netted nothing. Not one sign of the missing woman. If she had fallen and been injured, or even killed after being struck by a passing car, she would have been found by the men and dogs that searched.

There seemed to be no ready explanation for the fact that her car was found in the parking lot at the foot of the Santiam Pass. Jan Whitney had been headed for McMinnville, and a detour toward the pass made no sense. Yet her car was there. Why?

Jan Whitney was gone, just as inexplicably as Linda Slawson had disappeared in Portland ten months to the day earlier.

Thanksgiving came two days after Jan Whitney vanished. Jerry Brudos took his family away for the holidays to visit friends and family. While they were gone, there was an accident. A car went out of control on Center Street, sliding on rain-slick streets and crashing into Brudos' garage workshop, damaging the structure and punching a hole in the exterior wall. The Salem police investigated the accident, but they could not get into the garage to estimate the damage because the doors were all locked.

When the family returned, Jerry was agitated to see that there was a hole in the wall of his private workshop. He told Darcie he would take care of some things and then call the police.

A few hours later, he contacted the Salem police accident investigator who had left a card and unlocked the garage so that the officer could check the damage from the inside. When this was accomplished, Jerry nailed boards over the splintered wood and the workshop was completely closed off again.

Jerry was away from home that night for some time, but Darcie didn't think much of it; he was often gone for hours, and he never explained where he had been when he returned.

The Oregon State Police continued their probe into the mysterious disappearance of Jan Whitney, but all the man-hours of work netted exactly nothing.

Oregon State Police Lieutenant Robert White attempted to trace the anonymous correspondent who had mailed a letter from Albany. Sent in a plain envelope, and tediously printed as if the writer wished to disguise his handwriting, the letter said the writer had been at the Santiam rest stop where Miss Whitney's Rambler was abandoned, and, more startling, indicated that he had been present when Jan Whitney disappeared.

Lieutenant White appealed to the public, asking the informant to come forward. But that was the end of it. If the writer was telling the truth, he chose for his own reasons to remain silent. He might have gleaned his information from newspaper accounts of the missing woman, or he might have had actual knowledge, either as a witness or as a perpetrator. There was no way of telling.

Jerry Brudos continued to commute to his job at

Lebanon, Oregon—a tiny hamlet just east of the I-5 freeway—beyond the Albany exit.

Christmas came, and the new year, and Jerry Brudos celebrated his thirtieth birthday. His headaches had improved for a while, but then he felt nervous again and they returned worse than before.

Darcie thought about leaving him. But she had no skills to get a job, and there was no money, and she did not believe in divorce.

7

Jan Whitney had been missing for four months when spring came again to the Willamette Valley. Linda Slawson had been gone for fourteen months. They had disappeared fifty miles apart, and there were not enough similarities between the two cases to allow law officers to connect them. The girls were both young and slender, and attractive—but one apparently had vanished from the streets of Portland, and the other from the freeway south of Salem. At any given time, there is always a handful of women who have disappeared in a metropolitan area. Most have chosen to leave for their own reasons, and eventually return or at least contact their families.

Some do not. Stephanie Vilcko, sixteen, had left her Portland-area home to go swimming in July 1968—and never returned. Stephanie's disappearance came to a tragic denouement on March 18, 1969. A Forest Grove high-school teacher discovered her skeletonized body along the banks of Gales Creek five miles northwest of Forest Grove. By the time she was found, the ravages of time and weather had obliterated tissue that might have told forensic pathologists how she had died. Wind, ice, and water had also carried away any shred of physical evidence left by a killer—if, indeed, there was a killer.

Stephanie, Linda, and Jan were only three among a dozen or more such cases. There had been headlines when the women first vanished, and then column-long articles on back pages of area papers, and finally, small items from time to time. In police departments, the files on the missing and dead women were growing thicker. Cases which detectives wryly refer to as "losers" are always thicker and more complex than the "winners"; they may slip from the public's mind—but they are never, never forgotten by the men who work through one frustrating false lead after another.

Thursday, March 27, 1969, was a typical example of spring in Salem, Oregon; the daffodils around the courthouse were in bloom, along with the earliest rhododendrons and azaleas, but they were alternately buffeted by rainy winds and warmed by a pale sun washing down through the cool air.

Karen Sprinker, nineteen years old and a freshman at Oregon State University in Corvallis, was enjoying a short vacation between terms and had come home to Salem to visit her parents. Her father was a prominent veterinarian in Salem, and Karen had elected to follow him into the field of medicine, although she planned to treat human patients. She was carrying a heavy premed schedule at Oregon State, and earning top grades.

Karen was beautiful, but not in a sultry way; she embodied the sweetness and warmth of an innocent young woman. In an age when chastity was becoming old-fashioned, Karen Sprinker was a virgin, confident in her own principles. She had thick, almost black hair that fell below her shoulders and tumbled across her high forehead in waving bangs. Her eyes were dark brown, and her smile was wide and trusting.

She had never had a reason not to trust.

Karen had graduated from Sacred Heart Academy in Salem in the class of 1968. She was class salutatorian, a member of the National Honor Society, a National Merit Scholarship finalist, winner of the Salem Elks' Leadership Award, and a member of the Marion County Youth Council. With her intelligence and concern for people, she was a natural as a future doctor. All things being equal, she would be practicing by 1979, a full-fledged M.D. before she was thirty.

Shortly before noon on March 27, Karen Sprinker headed for the Meier and Frank Department Store in Salem. She was to meet her mother for lunch in the store's restaurant, and then the two of them were going to shop for spring clothes that Karen could take back to school.

Meier and Frank's is the biggest department store in Salem, located in the downtown area. It is a block and a half east of what were the Salem Police Department's offices in 1969; it is a block and a half north of the Marion County sheriff's offices in the basement of the courthouse. The store complex contains its own many-tiered inside parking garage, a nicety for shoppers, who can avoid walking through the rain that is a definite possibility from November until June.

Mrs. Sprinker waited in the luncheon room for Karen, who was driving her own car. Their lunch date was set for twelve, and Karen was unfailingly prompt. At twelve-fifteen Karen's mother looked at her watch, puzzled. She waved the menu away and asked for a cup of coffee, trying to concentrate on the models wending their way through the crowded room while they showed the store's new outfits.

At twelve-thirty she began to watch the door for sight of her daughter. People nearby finished their meals, and new groups sat down. And still Karen didn't appear. Her mother wondered if there had been some mistake about the time. No, she was sure Karen had understood.

Mrs. Sprinker left the restaurant and found a pay phone nearby. She called the family home, but no one answered. She went back to the lunchroom, but Karen still hadn't arrived. At length she left a message with the hostess, asking her to tell Karen that her mother had gone home—and would be there waiting for a call.

Karen wasn't at home. Everything there was just as Mrs. Sprinker had left it. Karen wasn't at her father's clinic, nor had she called there.

Karen Sprinker's parents went through all the steps that worried parents take when a dependable, thoughtful child cannot be found. If Karen had been an unpredictable girl, or a rebellious girl, it would have been much less frightening. But Karen had always been the kind of daughter who called home if she was going to be even fifteen minutes late. She was happy with her life and with her family. She loved college, and she'd been looking forward to the shopping trip, to the chance for some girl talk with her mother.

The Sprinkers called all of Karen's friends—and none of them had seen or heard from her. All of them were as puzzled as the Sprinkers, stressing that Karen had no problems that her parents might not have been aware of.

Her mother was aware that Karen had been in her menstrual period, and wondered if perhaps she had suddenly been seized with severe cramps, or even if she might have fainted. She had never had unusually severe periods, but there was always the possibility that she had become ill. Her parents called Salem hospitals to see if she might have been admitted.

None of the hospital admitting records listed Karen Sprinker. No illness. No accident.

Reluctantly going to the police—because that step seemed to mark Karen's disappearance as something so much more ominous—the Sprinkers reported Karen as missing.

The Salem police tried to reassure Karen's parents; they had seen so many "missing" people come back with reasonable explanations of why they were gone. Teenagers, particularly, tend to walk away of their own accord. They often have secrets their parents do not suspect, or romances that they think their parents won't approve of. Because they have never been parents, they cannot understand the worry that results when they are late getting home.

The officer taking the complaint urged the Sprinkers to try to remember something that Karen might have said, some hint she might have given about something she planned to do or someplace she wanted to go.

"Could she have gone back to her dorm at Oregon State?"

"No," her mother said impatiently. "I've already called. She hasn't been back since the term ended. Her room is locked."

As the Sprinkers painted a picture of their daughter's habits and her consideration for others, the officer felt a chill. *This* girl didn't sound at all like a runaway. She didn't sound like a girl who might suddenly decide to get married or take off with a boyfriend.

In almost any police department in America, the policy is not to take a formal complaint on a missing adult for twenty-four hours—simply because most of the missing come back within that period. If there are signs of foul play, then of course the search is begun immediately. The reason for the twenty-four-hour delay is pragmatic. There is not enough manpower even in a big police department to look for everyone; there would be no time for other police business. Missing-persons detectives can concentrate only on cases that deal with true vanishings. If a child is missing or if there are indications that the missing person has come to harm, the twenty-four-hour limit is forgotten.

A preliminary report was taken, listing "Karen Elena Sprinker—missing since 12:30 hours, March 27, 1969. Meier and Frank (?)" Then the Sprinkers went home to sit by the phone, to listen for the sound of Karen coming through the front door.

They waited all night long, without any word from Karen.

Salem police went to the parking garage at Meier and Frank, on the off-chance that Karen had come to the store but for some reason had not appeared for her date at the restaurant. They searched through the levels of the parking garage and found no sign of the missing girl, nor signs of anything unusual in the shadows of the looming concrete ramp that wound around and up.

Not until they reached the roof. And there they found Karen Sprinker's car, parked neatly between the diagonal lines of a parking slot, and locked. There was no way to tell how long it had been there; Meier and Frank puts no time limit on shoppers' parking.

Like Jan Whitney's car, there was nothing about it that was out of the ordinary. Some of Karen's books were on the seat, but otherwise it contained nothing. When it was hauled in for processing, technicians at the lab found no blood and no semen on the seat covers or the door panels. There were no cigarettes in the ashtray, and the latent prints lifted from the steering wheel, dashboard, and other surfaces were only those of the Sprinker family.

Whatever had happened to Karen Sprinker had not happened in the car itself.

Scores of shoppers parked on the roof floor every day, and they had only to walk down a flight of concrete stairs to reach a door into the store itself. A matter of a few minutes. Karen had come to the store in broad daylight. That figured, because she was to meet her mother at noon. It would seem to be one of the safest spots in the city of Salem.

But the investigators, led by Jim Stovall, hunkered down and checked the floor from the missing girl's car, down the steps, and all the way to the door for signs of something, anything she might have dropped—even drops of blood.

The parking garage was empty of shoppers now, and while they worked, their own voices echoed as they bounced off the gray walls, making what had been a normal, secure place seem somehow eerie.

"You know," one of the detectives said slowly, "as close as these stairs are to the store entrance, they could be a lonely spot if a young woman happened to be the only one at a given moment who was leaving the parking area. That door into the store is heavy—it would take a little muscle, a little concentration to open it. For those few moments, a woman would be terribly vulnerable."

"Yeah," another responded. "It wouldn't do much good to scream. The traffic noises below, and the hubbub of the store inside—nobody could hear through the door, and nobody could hear on the street. If there wasn't anyone else on the roof to help . . ."

Their musings produced terrible pictures in their minds—remembering the photograph of the slender, smiling girl.

Karen Sprinker's disappearance became the prime case for Jim Stovall and his fellow detectives. Stovall's own daughter was only two years older than Karen, and he knew too well what her family was going through.

The Salem *Capital Journal* and the Salem *Statesman*

carried Karen Sprinker's picture with the question "Have you seen this girl?" under it, and the public responded. There were the usual crank letters and the usual informants who really knew nothing but wanted to espouse theories that sounded good to them. Most of the tips were totally useless, but all leads had to be followed, because one of them might have been vital.

One early lead seemed promising. A Southern Pacific Railroad ticket agent called Salem police to say that he'd seen a girl who looked "just like Karen Sprinker" leave Salem by train for San Francisco. "There were two men with her, and she didn't act like she was afraid of them, but you never can tell. She might have been afraid to ask for help."

The Salem papers printed the information the agent had called in, and almost immediately a Mount Angel man called police to say that the girl on the train had been *his* daughter, who was also a brunette with pretty brown eyes. "She's okay. She's safe in California, and she was traveling with family friends."

A service-station owner who had lived on the Oregon coast contacted Stovall's office to say he was sure he'd sold gas to Karen Sprinker. "She gave me a credit card to pay for the gas, and I'm almost positive the name was Sprinker.

Stovall and Lieutenant "Hap" Hewett left at once for the Oregon coast, but when they got to the station, the owner said he had sent the credit-card slip routinely into the company's home office in Tulsa, Oklahoma. He had mailed it off before he'd read about Karen Sprinker in the newspaper.

The detectives contacted the home office of the oil company, and the personnel there were most cooperative. They went through thousands of credit slips, looking for the one allegedly signed by Karen Sprinker in Oregon. "They finally found one from that station," Stovall recalls. "But the name was Spiker, not Sprinker."

A motorcyclist notified Hewett and Stovall that he had picked up a hitchhiker near Tigard, Oregon, and given her a ride on his Harley. "She had long black hair, and she said she was from Salem."

"Where'd you take her?" Stovall asked.

"She wanted to go to some hippie place in Portland—that commune out by Portland State U. So I took her."

Stovall pulled out a picture of Karen Sprinker. "Is this the girl?"

The biker studied the photograph, and then handed it back with a shrug. "Maybe . . . maybe not. It looks kinda like the chick I picked up. I meet a lotta chicks, and it's kind of hard to tell, you know?"

That Karen Sprinker would have been hitchhiking or that she had any aspirations toward living in a hippie commune seemed unfathomable—but then, the fact that she was still missing was just as hard to understand. Anything was possible.

Karen's boyfriend was anxious to pursue any avenue that might help him find the young woman. He went to Portland, dressed in jeans and a batik shirt, his beard deliberately unshaven. He wanted to look like a hippie, and he succeeded. For several days he loitered around hippie hangouts, blending into the rough crowd until people there got used to him. He asked carefully casual questions, and mentioned he was looking for his "old lady who split on me."

Sitting in dark rooms that smelled of marijuana, eating sprouts and brown rice, and listening to babies cry in counterpoint to rock music, Karen's friend knew she wouldn't be comfortable in this counterculture, but he wanted so badly to find her and take her home safe to her family.

In the end, he gave it up. Karen was gone, and no one knew where—or, if someone knew, no one was telling.

Salem detectives gave the young college student credit for trying and empathized with his frustration: their own efforts weren't producing any solid leads either.

One story reached the Salem Police Department circuitously, and was so bizarre that it might have been dismissed . . . and yet . . .

Two high-school girls in Salem went to a woman they trusted and described a peculiar person they had seen while they were shopping at Meier and Frank a few weeks before Karen Sprinker vanished.

"There was a person in the parking garage," one girl began.

"A *person*?" the woman asked.

"Well, it looked like a woman. I mean, we thought it was a woman at first, but . . ."

"But what?"

"We saw this tall, heavy person. All dressed up with high heels and a dress. 'She' was just standing there in the garage, as if she was waiting for someone. She was tugging at her girdle and fixing her nylons."

"But you don't think it was a woman at all—is that it?"

"Yes!" the other girl said. "The person looked so strange that we drove on up the ramp and came around again. And now we're sure it wasn't a woman at all. It was a man dressed up like a woman!"

The housewife who listened to the girls' story urged them to go to the police.

Men in drag are not terribly unusual; it is sometimes a harmless aberration, but given the circumstances surrounding Karen Sprinker's disappearance, the presence of a huge man in women's clothing in the Meier and Frank parking garage in early March signaled a possible connection.

"Suppose there was a man there, dressed up like a woman," one investigator offered. "Suppose he pretended to be ill, or even called Karen over to ask her a question? She wouldn't be as cautious if she thought it was a woman. She would have walked up to him, never expecting trouble. She was the kind of young woman who would have been eager to help."

"And he could have grabbed her?"

"Yes."

Perhaps that was the way it had happened. Perhaps not. The transvestite incident could have been a random thing, some alumnus of one of the state institutions in Marion County, some frightened and completely nonviolent man who acted out his kinkiness by waltzing around Meier and Frank in a dress and spike heels. Store employees did not remember ever seeing such a creature.

Whatever had happened, Karen Sprinker never came

home. Good Friday passed, and then Easter, and classes began again at Oregon State University, but Karen wasn't there to join her friends. Sadly her family cleared out her room in Callahan Hall in Corvallis. Everything Karen had owned—her books, records, treasured photos, clothes—everything had been left behind except for the green skirt and sweater she'd worn on March 27, and her purse.

By the third week in April, there was so little to hope for. Karen's body had not been found, so there was still the faintest of chances that she might have suffered an injury or illness that had brought on amnesia. Not knowing was the worst of all; there was the possibility that she was being held captive somewhere, unable to call home.

Karen Sprinker's picture was tacked over Jim Stovall's desk—a reminder in front of him always that she waited, somewhere, for someone to come and find her. He had never known Karen, but it almost seemed that he had; he had learned so much about her, admired all the accomplishments and ambitions in a girl so young, that she was far more to him than a picture on a wall.

It is always that way with good detectives. They come to know the victims of the crimes they investigate as well as their own families. And knowing, they are driven to avenge them.

8

Darcie Brudos read about the disappearance of Karen Sprinker; there was no way to avoid it unless you didn't read the papers and never watched television. She found it quite frightening, and she discussed it with her women friends. She didn't worry about herself so much, but she was concerned about Megan, and she watched her little girl carefully while she played in the yard. She took her to school and picked her up each day. Meier and Frank's store was less than a mile from their house, just west down Center Street several blocks and then a few blocks north.

The papers were hinting that there was a maniac loose, suggesting that whatever had happened to Karen Sprinker might happen to someone else if the person wasn't caught. Darcie wouldn't go out at night by herself any longer, and she kept the doors and windows tightly locked when Jerry was gone.

He was gone a lot. Working in Lebanon during the day, except for when his headaches were too bad. And then he had so many errands to run, and auto parts to buy—the ones he found by rummaging through junkyards in Portland and Salem. Sometimes he went to Corvallis; he occasionally did yard work for a friend over there. She had no idea where Jerry went most of the time, and it annoyed him when she asked.

He was getting even more obsessed with privacy in his workshop. If she rapped on the door to try to get in to check what was in the freezer, it seemed to make him angrier than ever. He always said he would get what she wanted, but that was inconvenient because she wasn't always sure what food was left. Sometimes she just wanted to have the chance to stand there and

see what was in the freezer and hope it would give her
an idea for supper.

Jerry had been upset when she'd found the door to
his darkroom open one day and walked in after checking to be sure the light was on. She'd gone out to the
garage to do the laundry and thought she'd just peek
in at Jerry and say "Hi."

There were trays of developing solution on the
counter, and she looked idly at the pictures he was
printing. And then she gasped with surprise when she
saw that the pictures were of women. Nude women.

"Jerry? What are these?" she blurted.

He smiled and moved quickly in front of the counter
so that her view was blocked. "Those? Nothing. Just
some film a kid from the college asked me to develop
for him. I didn't know what they were until they
turned out. Just kid stuff. I'll tell him not to bring that
kind of pictures around anymore."

She didn't know whether to believe him or not, but
then she thought about the way Jerry was. He was
pretty bashful around any woman but herself, and she
couldn't imagine him taking nude pictures himself—
not of anyone but her.

"Okay. But don't let Megan see those pictures. Get
them back to the guy."

Jerry promised that he would, and she promised
that she wouldn't barge into his workshop again.

"Use the intercom, Darcie. That's easier. Just tell
me what you want, and I'll get it for you."

Darcie sighed. It was easier not to argue with him.
He had always been different, a little out of step with
the rest of the people she knew—but all her friends
had complaints about their husbands too. It seemed to
be a matter of accepting the things you didn't like
about your mate and trying to work around them. She
knew he was unhappy with her own growing independence. Independence. She had to smile at that.
She had so little freedom, really. With the kids to look
after, and having to report to Jerry all the time, every
minute of her days and nights was accounted for.

There were other things that Darcie Brudos tried
not to think about. She hadn't seen Jerry in women's

clothing since he'd put on the bra and girdle, but she'd found some pictures that upset her. Jerry had left them lying around—either carelessly or deliberately.

She recognized that it was Jerry in the pictures, but it was the Jerry who liked to dress up in women's underclothes. In one he lay on his back on their bed, holding a pillow over his face in a clumsy attempt to hide his features. He wore a white bra—it had to be a 48 C at least—and a long-line panty girdle, also white, stockings, and those same black highheels. Where on earth could he have found them? He wore size 13 shoes.

Another picture was almost the same, only Jerry was lying flat on his stomach, with his left arm draped over the edge of the bed, his right arm tucked beneath his "breasts," and his head turned to the right. Then there was one where he wore a black slip, trimmed with black lace, and those same shoes. She wondered who might have taken them, and then realized that he'd probably photographed himself. He had a thirty-five-millimeter camera that had a remote-control attachment. Once, when they were traveling, he had posed all four of them in front of a sign that said "You Are Now Leaving the State of California" and clicked the shutter in his hand. That picture had turned out just fine, so she knew he had the equipment to take pictures that way.

She had shoved the pictures away someplace; she sure didn't want anyone else to see them. He was still always after her for sex, even when she let him know she wasn't interested. If he was a homosexual, she was sure he wouldn't want intercourse with a woman. Men were either gay or they weren't, according to what she knew. It wasn't something she could discuss with her girlfriends; that would be a betrayal of Jerry, and anyway, it made her ashamed.

Whenever Darcie managed to put her worries out of her mind, it seemed that something else happened to bring them all back. Sometime after she'd found the pictures, she found a "thing"—she couldn't quite figure out what it was. It was round and heavy, a few inches in diameter, and it seemed to be made of some kind of plastic. She had held it and turned it over, and then realized that it looked just like a woman's breast— not as large, but almost a perfect replica.

"What is this, Jerry?" she'd asked.

"That? That's just an idea I had to make a paperweight."

"A *breast*?"

"For a novelty item. Kind of a joke."

"It looks so real."

"Yeah." He took the mold from her. "Well, it didn't work. I put too much hardener in the plastic."

She had to go way back in their relationship to remember when Jerry had told jokes that were really funny. All of his "jokes" now had a sexual or a hostile tone. He seemed either angry with her or disappointed in her. She vowed that she would try to be nicer to him, dress up more in the fancy clothes he liked on her, and try to be more loving.

If she only tried harder, she thought their marriage might get better.

—— **9** ——

On Wednesday, April 23, 1969, Karen Sprinker had been missing for three weeks and six days, and the Salem police had virtually run out of new leads. Forty-seven miles north of Salem, in Portland, the news of the Sprinker disappearance had never been headlined, and it is doubtful that Linda Salee of that city had ever heard of Karen Sprinker.

And yet Linda Salee was about to become part of a dread sisterhood.

Linda Dawn Salee was twenty-two years old, a tiny woman who stood only five feet, one inch tall. But she was one of those feisty, bouncy little women who excel at athletics. She was really quite strong and wonderfully coordinated; she had a shelf full of bowling trophies to prove it.

Linda Salee was also exceptionally pretty. She had ash-blond hair which she wore in the teased pompadour style so popular in the late sixties. Her eyes were blue and fringed with improbably long lashes, and her smile revealed perfect teeth. Indeed, Linda's smile was so outstanding that she had won a "Miss Smile" contest a few years back.

Like Linda Slawson, Jan Whitney, and Karen Sprinker, Linda Salee was so attractive that she always drew appreciative male stares. She had a boyfriend whom she loved and she wasn't interested in other men at all.

Linda worked days in the offices of Consolidated Freightways in Portland, and she left work at four-thirty P.M. on April 23. She planned to drive to the huge shopping mall at Lloyd Center and shop for presents for her boyfriend's birthday. Then she was going to go to the Eastside YMCA for a swim in the pool there, where her boyfriend was a lifeguard. They were both interested in sports and in physical fitness, just one of the many things they shared in common. Since she worked days and he worked evenings, the only way they could see each other during the week was for Linda to come to the pool and swim.

Linda drove her own car, her pride and joy—a bright red Volkswagen Bug—to Lloyd Center and parked it carefully on the sixth floor of the parking garage. She wore a beige coat against the cold that belied the fact that spring had begun officially more than a month earlier.

Because she was in love and because she was a young woman of generous spirit, Linda spent a lot of money on presents for her boyfriend. Her original plan had been to get him a leather watchband. She went to a jewelry shop first and the clerk there remembered her well. It was a slow period in the day, and she took a long time making up her mind. She finally made a selection, and headed for a men's clothing store.

Again, the clerk who waited on her remembered her. She was so pretty, and so careful about her shopping. She bought her friend a blue suedecloth jacket and a pair of walking shorts. As she left the men's store, the clerk glanced at the clock on the wall and noted that it was five-fifteen P.M.

She sat on one of the benches provided for tired shoppers and opened the small sack that held the watchband. Seeing it in the bright lights overhead, she decided it wasn't the right color after all. She walked back to the jewelry shop and apologized to the clerk. "I'm sorry. It's not what he wanted. Could I return it?"

Her money was refunded, and Linda smiled at the clerk and left the shop, headed for the parking garage.

At the YMCA pool, Linda Salee's boyfriend watched over the shouting, leaping kids in the water. He had to keep a close eye on them. The adult swimmers were content to do their laps doggedly, get it over with, and head for the showers. The kids were another story altogether; if you didn't watch them, they'd run on the decks, cannonball off the board without looking for swimmers below, or attempt to venture into the deep end of the pool when they couldn't swim well enough to manage it. He sat on his perch high above the pool and scanned the water constantly, his nose itching from the chlorine fumes that permeated the air. Sometimes Linda could emerge from the women's locker room and sneak up on him before he noticed her. Her light touch on his toes always made him jump—and made him happy too. She was a dynamite-looking girl, and he was proud to see her swimming in the pool and know that she was *his* girl.

It was cold outside, and rainy, and the temperature outside, combined with the fumes in the pool, steamed up the glass face of the wall clock. The young lifeguard looked at it and realized it was after seven o'clock. He looked at the clock again to be sure it was that late, and it was. Almost seven-thirty.

Linda should have arrived an hour ago. Where was she?

The kids' swim session was over, and an "Adults Only" session began. With a spate of time when he didn't have to guard so closely, Linda's boyfriend watched the door of the women's locker room. There were more men than women always, and on this Wednesday night, only a few women drifted out, tucking their hair under their caps. A couple of overweight gals over forty who were determined to slim down. The tall woman who came every night, rain or shine, and swam as if she'd once been a champion. A few teenagers who giggled and paddled around the shallow end.

Linda never showed up.

Her friend changed into his street clothes when the last swimmer was out of the pool, and drove to her apartment. His knocking went unanswered and he was a little angry with her—but only for a few minutes. He knew her too well to think she would have stood him up. She had been excited about his birthday and had teased him about all the presents he was going to get. Even now, standing in the empty hall outside her apartment, he half-expected to see her jump out and yell, "Surprise!"

When Linda Salee didn't arrive at her job at Consolidated Freightways the next morning, her friends and family grew frantic for her safety. There was simply no explanation but that she was someplace from which she was unable to come home.

Oregon state police investigators, aware of the other cases involving missing young women, treated Linda Salee's disappearance very seriously. With the information that she had intended to go shopping in Lloyd Center, they joined detectives from Portland in a search of the grounds and parking garage.

It was like a replay of Karen Sprinker's case. Linda Salee's car was located in the parking garage. It too was locked and there were no indications that a struggle had taken place in or around the vehicle.

There was no conclusion to be drawn other than that someone had taken Linda away against her will.

Comparing the cases of the missing women, detectives in Oregon saw similarities again and again. Four pretty young women had disappeared from the mainstream of life within sixteen months, leaving no clues at all behind. All the girls had vanished within a fifty-mile area. None of them had anything in her background that would have made her a likely candidate to run away. There were no witnesses. There were no bits of physical evidence—not a piece of clothing, a dropped purse, a shoe. Not even a brush of blood or a hair. Not one of them had reported to friends or police that she had reason to be afraid because of an insistent suitor or an obscene phone call.

That meant that the Oregon investigators were looking for the most elusive kind of suspect, someone who snatched victims by random choice. Someone had apparently watched until he saw women who appealed to whatever obsession drove him. And then he had stalked them until he found them in places where they could not call for help. Whatever ruse or device he had used to get them, he had done it quickly and silently.

They were gone.

It almost seemed as if the person who had taken them away had deliberately chosen victims from areas patrolled by different police agencies. Linda Slawson from the jurisdiction of the Portland city police, Jan Whitney from the I-5 freeway, policed by the Oregon State Police and Linn County Sheriff's officers, Karen Sprinker from the city of Salem, and Linda Salee from the city of Portland again.

Whoever had taken them—and it had to be assumed that it was a male, and not a woman responsible—he was devious and clever.

But not clever enough. Communication between law-enforcement agencies is essential, and when a major case occurs, every agency within a prescribed area becomes aware of it. Something terrible was happening in northern Oregon, something that posed a threat to pretty young women, and bulletins and teletypes flooded every law-enforcement agency in the region. Descriptions of the missing girls and the circumstances of their disappearances were sent to the thirteen western states via teletype.

Lane County detectives in Eugene, Oregon, forty-four miles south of Salem, watched the developments of the missing girls' cases closely. They had an unsolved homicide case whose victim resembled the other women. Mrs. Janet Shanahan, twenty-two, had been found strangled in the trunk of her car, the vehicle abandoned on a Eugene street only a day after Linda Salee vanished.

Janet Shanahan fit the victim profile quite closely; the M.O. was different, however, in that her body had been found. But in trying to figure a phantom killer's M.O., this was a significant break in the pattern. Further, the other women had disappeared in time periods that were at least a month apart. That, too, stamped the Shanahan case as outside the pattern.

Whatever the answer was, lawmen moved with speed. They did not want to think that, when the end of May approached, there would be another abduction—that still another young woman would fall prey to the faceless marauder who seemed to rove at will through their territory, picking off one beautiful victim after another.

—— 10 ——

The Long Tom River is a narrow tributary that branches off the powerful Willamette River some twelve miles south of Corvallis. It wends its way south for twenty-four miles and finally empties into the Fern Ridge Reservoir just west of Eugene. Rushing between banks choked with thick underbrush, the Long Tom is an excellent river to fish—for those who know the prime spots. Except for the hamlets of Monroe and Cheshire, there are no towns close to the Long Tom; it is a country river, and hardly known to those who don't live in the area where it flows. In places it is grand and picturesque, but in other spots the Long Tom is as lonely and bleak as a ghost river.

Until 1961 the Irish Bend Road crossed the Long Tom through an ancient covered bridge, one of the few still standing in the Northwest. The weathered structure is reminiscent of the covered bridges in Pennsylvania and New England. By 1961 modern vehicles found the passage through the old bridge far too tight a squeeze, and a new concrete bridge was built parallel to the old—but preservationists insisted that the old Bundy Bridge be saved. And so it remained in 1969, a relic of the past whose foundations nudged the new bridge crossing—no longer functional for anything but to give shelter to fishermen when the wind wailed along the river and rain dripped down the brims of their hats.

The Bundy Bridge site is one of the busiest along the river, but in comparison to city rivers, it is still a quiet spot. In winter and early spring the Long Tom creeps high up on the pillars that support the new bridge, full of rain and melted-snow runoff from mountains and foothills.

By May 10 the river had fallen back, and lapped listlessly at the double quintet of concrete pillars. A man could stand close to shore now and the water would reach only his waist. Old timbers caught on naked saplings and choked the shallows, looking like sea creatures drawn from the bottom. But the bank vegetation had begun to green, and there were a few spring daisies and wild irises brightening the weeds there.

A lone fisherman parked his truck on the Irish Bend Road that Saturday and gathered his gear for an afternoon of fishing. The sky was leaden and full of clouds that lowered overhead and threatened to burst and spill their substance at any moment. No matter; neither fish nor fishermen mind rain.

The angler walked onto the Bundy Bridge and peered down into the muddied water. He shivered involuntarily as a sudden gust of wind pulled at his jacket. He watched a flight of water birds lift off the far shore and wing downstream, and thought how deserted the Long Tom seemed. An occasional car had swept by on the road, but when the traffic disappeared, it seemed as if he could hear every crackle in the brush along the bank.

He hunched his shoulders and turned back to the river, looking for a good spot to drop his line. He didn't want to get it caught on one of the tree snags and spend a half-hour getting disentangled.

The current caught his lure and tugged it downstream. He cast again, farther out.

And then he saw something.

A large bulky object floated just beneath the surface of the Long Tom, twisting lazily in the drift, but caught by something that held it fast. It wasn't a log; it seemed too soft for that, and yet too solid to be only a bundle of cloth. He watched it idly, and felt an odd prickling at the back of his neck.

The fisherman laid his pole carefully on the bank and sidestepped down, placing his feet tentatively in the damp weeds. He caught onto a maple sapling and hung out over the river to get a closer look.

He saw, but could not compute what he saw for a moment or two—and then he reeled back in horror, almost losing his footing and plunging into the Long Tom himself. The object in the river was a human being. He could see fine light hair fan out and undulate in the river's flow, and caught a glimpse of pale flesh.

He did not wait to see if it was a man or a woman caught in the river, or even to wonder how the body had come to be there. He was up the bank in three leaps, and headed for his truck.

The call came in to the Benton County sheriff's office, and Sheriff Charles E. Reams dispatched deputies to the Long Tom River. The deputies radioed back that the presence of a body in the Long Tom had been confirmed. It was that of a young woman.

"She's been in the river some time," the officer reported. "And she didn't just fall in. The body's weighted down with a car transmission."

The news that a young woman's body had been found was electrifying to detectives in northern Oregon, and investigators in Salem and Portland waited anxiously to hear who she was and how she had died. Since the body had been found in Benton County, the case was technically and legally under the jurisdiction of Sheriff Reams's department, but Reams and Benton County District Attorney Frank Knight were fully aware of the wider ramifications. If this woman proved to be one of the missing women, it would be the first break—however tragic—in the baffling cases.

District Attorney Frank Knight is what lawmen call a "policemen's D.A.," an indefatigable worker who stays with a case from the very beginning. Stovall would voice his admiration for Knight many times over the weeks that followed. "He's the kind of D.A. we most admire—he's with us all the way, always available. If we need legal input in a hurry, he's there. From the moment that first body was found in the Long Tom, Knight was part of the team. He never got in the way of our scene investigations, but he put in as many twenty-four-hour days as the rest of us did."

The road leading to the Bundy Bridge was cordoned off, and only lawmen and officials from the Oregon State Medical Examiner's Office were allowed to cross the barriers. Reams and Knight stood by as the girl's body was lifted from the Long Tom and carried up the bank.

It was not an easy task; the deputies who had gone into the river were strong, husky men, but the girl, when weighted down by the transmission, weighed almost two-hundred pounds.

She was a short woman, and quite fair. She had ash-blond hair and blue eyes. They had somehow expected that it would be Karen Sprinker, but it was not. Karen had been taller and was a brunette.

This girl was young too, and the waters of the Long Tom had been cold, preserving her body with the heedless tenderness of nature. A beige coat still clung to the body, but many of her garments were gone—either torn away by the current or deliberately removed by the killer who had put her into the river.

William Brady, Chief Medical Examiner for the State of Oregon, was on his way from Portland, and the body would not be moved until he arrived. In the meantime, Reams sent deputies to canvass the countryside to see if anyone might have seen something or someone dumping a heavy burden into the Long Tom.

It was a fruitless task. The closest farmhouse was a good half-mile from the Bundy Bridge. No nearby resident had seen anything suspicious. It was likely that the disposal of the body had taken place under cover of darkness.

Throughout the day, into the night, and for days following, the bridge over the Long Tom would be the site of intense police investigation.

Dr. William Brady arrived to make a preliminary examination of the dead girl. Brady is one of the foremost forensic pathologists in America, a tall, dapper man who dresses more like a visiting ambassador than a working medical examiner. He eschews the coveralls worn by most investigators at a grisly crime scene, and yet he does his work so deftly that he emerges as immaculate as when he arrives.

Brady came to Oregon from New York City. He was a forensic pathologist in the Manhattan office of the New York City Medical Examiner's Office before he set up the most sophisticated state medical examiner's system in the country. Oregon abolished the coroner system in 1956, and today its medical examiner's system is a model for other states.

Because Oregon is essentially a rural state with the bulk of its population in Portland, Salem, and Eugene, Brady feels that law-enforcement agencies in small communities should have the benefit of the expertise of a state medical examiner. No body may be removed in a suspicious death until removal has been authorized by a deputy medical examiner, and thereafter it is not to be undressed, washed, or otherwise prepared before autopsy.

Too many wrongful deaths go undetected in areas without a medical examiner's system, because once vital physical evidence is lost, it can never be recovered. Too many victims of wrongful death are buried without autopsy, and the killers' secrets are buried with them.

Oregon has never had more than 150 murders in a given year, and only one-third of those merit intense investigation. When that murder rate is compared with statistics of cities like Houston, Miami, and Detroit, Oregon seems a safe place to live.

But not for everyone. Not for the young woman who was transported to Dr. Brady's offices to await autopsy.

The girl was Linda Salee. Detectives had suspected that it was she right from the beginning. Decomposition was moderate; it could not have been Linda Slawson or Jan Whitney. They had been gone too long for visual identification. Someone had taken Linda Salee more than seventy miles away from the Lloyd Center shopping mall, killed her, and then had thrown her away in the Long Tom.

Her killer had made a tactical error. He had either misjudged the depth of the lonely river or had been unable to carry the weighted body out into the center of the river, where the depth was so much greater.

Or perhaps he'd been so cocky that he didn't care if her body was found. Perhaps something in him made him seek discovery of his terrible handiwork.

Linda Salee's body had been bound to the auto transmission with nylon cord and copper wire. A reddish fabric resembling a mechanic's industrial cloth was caught in her bonds. That might prove to be a valuable clue. A mass-produced item certainly, but something that must be saved along with the cord and wire.

The cause of death? Dr. Brady found the classic signs of traumatic asphyxiation. There were the petechial hemorrhages (pinpoint hemorrhages) of the strap muscles of the neck, the lungs, the heart, the eyes, that occur when the lungs cannot take in air. The hyoid bone at the back of the tongue, that fragile u-shaped bone, was fractured. There was the broad, flat mark of some kind of ligature around the slender neck.

And, with these signs, there would be a faint bit of comfort for Linda Salee's family. Death by traumatic asphyxiation, by strangling, is quick. Loss of consciousness occurs very rapidly, and death itself follows quietly.

Had Linda Salee been raped? That was impossible to determine. Long immersion in water dilutes any semen that may be present, so that no absolute tests can be made.

There was something else found during the postmortem on Linda Salee, something that would be kept from the media because it was so bizarre and unexplainable at the moment.

Dr. Brady found two needle marks in the victim's rib cage, one on each side, three or four inches below the armpit. The skin surrounding the needle punctures was marked by postmortem burns. Dr. Brady had never seen anything quite like it before.

There were some bruises, some contusions and abrasions. Linda Salee, the spunky little bowler, had fought her killer ferociously. But she had been too tiny and he had won.

*　　*　　*

The activity at the Long Tom River continued throughout the weekend. Reserve sheriff's officers— skilled scuba divers—combed the river from shore to shore and north and south of the Bundy Bridge. A half-dozen of the black-rubber-suited swimmers dived again and again into the muddy river to find . . . what? Perhaps the clothing that was missing when Linda Salee was found. Perhaps her purse. Possibly even something left behind by her killer.

They came up with old tires, junk, and tangled clots of weeds that had felt like cloth in the depths of the water. They grew chilled and exhausted, and still they dived, carefully working the river in a grid pattern, covering every inch of it. It was dangerous, macabre work. Sometimes the divers surfaced and felt the tree snags clutching at them. Sometimes they worked in rat's nests of debris, feeling claustrophobic.

But none of them quit.

What had happened to Linda Salee enraged normal men. Especially police officers. If they could not have saved her, they would now find her killer and hand him over to the judicial system.

On Monday the horror accelerated into nightmare. Fifty feet from where Linda Salee's body had been found, a diver discovered another figure floating beneath the surface. A figure bound to something that held it down.

He headed for the pale light above him and surfaced with a shout, signaling his fellow divers to join him.

There was indeed a second body in the river.

The news was flashed immediately to Salem police headquarters, and Jim Stovall and Salem Detective Jerry Frazier ran for their car and sped toward the Long Tom. They were there when the divers brought up Karen Sprinker.

Karen had been missing for forty-six days. Forty-six days of agony for her parents. Forty-six days of hoping against hope that she might come back to them. With the latest discovery, that hope was gone.

When the divers carried Karen to the banks of the Long Tom, there was no doubt that her death had been similar to Linda Salee's. Her body was weighted down with the head of a six-cylinder engine. It had been lashed to her body with nylon cord and copper wiring like that used to tie the other body to the auto transmission. There was also a red mechanic's cloth tied to the engine head.

The Oregon investigators, working their individual cases—but conferring with one another—had begun to think that the girls' disappearances might be part of a common plan, and had approached their probe that way. But the knowledge that they had been right was more alarming than reassuring; they did, clearly, have a maniac loose in the state, a lust killer, moving undetected, the worst kind of killer because he does not stop killing until either he is apprehended or is himself dead.

Karen Sprinker's body was autopsied by Dr. William Brady, and on preliminary examination the cause of death seemed the same as Linda Salee's: traumatic asphyxiation.

The term "autopsy," loosely defined, means "to find out for oneself." Homicide detectives and forensic pathologists must set their minds on two levels. Their job—and their duty—is to consider their cases scientifically, to maintain a kind of objectivity into which none of their own emotions intrude. If they are not able to suspend feelings, they cannot do their jobs. What they have to cope with is too tragic. Later, when the killer has been caught, they can afford the luxury of rage and tears. While the search for clues is going on, they must be clinical and detached.

It was extremely difficult to be detached about Karen Sprinker, the innocent young woman whose dreams of becoming a doctor had been wiped out by the killer who left her body floating in the Long Tom.

Lieutenant Jim Stovall and Lieutenant Gene Daugherty of the Oregon State Police—who would work closely together in the intense probe that lay ahead—were present at the postmortem examination of Karen Sprinker.

From this point on, Jim Stovall and Gene Daugherty would be the two investigators at the head of the

probe into the search for the killer of Linda Salee and
Karen Sprinker—and perhaps of other young women
still missing. Daugherty, stationed at the Oregon State
Police headquarters in Salem, is a big man, well over
six feet, muscular, with the sandy hair and ruddy complexion of a true Irishman. Like Stovall, he was one of
the best detectives in the state of Oregon. They would
work exceptionally well together, sharing a belief in
the power of physical evidence and the necessity to
find some common denominator that would link a
suspect to the crimes. Neither of them would see much
of their wives and families for a long time to come.
Nor would Jerry Frazier, the dark-haired, compactly
built Salem police detective who had been assigned to
work with Stovall. Other detectives in many Oregon
jurisdictions would be drawn into the probe as it moved
inexorably forward, but Daugherty, Stovall, and Frazier
would continue to be at its center until the end.

Any reputable pathologist insists that reverence for
the dead be maintained during autopsy; although the
body must be examined to determine cause of death
and to search for possible vital physical evidence, those
in attendance never forget that the deceased deserves
respect. Dr. Brady is a stickler about this, and Stovall
and Daugherty agree with him. The men were silent as
Brady began.

Although Karen Sprinker had also succumbed to
asphyxiation, the ligature marks left on her neck were
somewhat different from those on Linda Salee's throat.
In Karen's case, the ligature had been a narrow band—
probably a rope. Again, it had been a rapid death;
young women do not have the throat musculature to
stave off strangulation. And, again, it was small comfort.

Karen Sprinker had been fully clothed when she was
discovered in the Long Tom. She wore the green skirt
and sweater that her mother had described on the
missing-persons report. She wore cotton panties, but,
surprisingly, the simple cotton bra she usually wore
had been replaced by a waist-length black bra that was
far too big for her.

Odd.

The bra could not have been Karen Sprinker's; her

mother had inventoried all of her clothing to see what was missing when Karen had vanished, and she owned no underwear such as this. Further, Karen's bra size was 34 A or B, and this long-line black bra had to be at least a 38 D.

As Brady removed the brassiere, sodden lumps of brown paper toweling dropped out.

Karen had no breasts; her killer had removed them after death.

And then he had fashioned the illusion of breasts by stuffing the cups of the black brassiere with wadded paper towels.

There were indications that Karen Sprinker had been sexually assaulted by her killer, but, again, it was impossible to tell absolutely because of her long immersion in the river. There were no other obvious wounds on her body.

The results of the autopsy on Karen Sprinker were withheld from the press. Again, only the terse "death by traumatic asphyxiation" was given to the media.

Karen Sprinker and Linda Salee had been stalked and abducted by a lust killer. Stovall and Daugherty had little hope that Linda Slawson and Jan Whitney would ever be found alive. They stood by while the divers continued their combing of the depths of the Long Tom, half-expecting a shout of discovery that meant those girls too were hidden there.

After days, however, the search was suspended. The river was empty of bodies now, and would give up nothing more to aid in the investigation.

11

Jerry Brudos read about the discovery of the bodies in the Long Tom River. He was not particularly concerned. The cops didn't know anything, really. The papers weren't telling everything; the cops had to know a few more details than the paper was giving—but not that much more. He had been very careful. He had planned it all well. Actually, he figured the cops had to be pretty stupid. They'd been right there with their noses poking through the hole in his garage, and they hadn't seen anything at all. They'd only thanked him for his time and signed the forms for the insurance claims. He had to smile when he heard Darcie dithering about the dead girls and how frightened she was. Darcie didn't know anything either.

He felt quite magical, and full of power. Well, he'd waited long enough to exert his power, and now, nobody was going to stop him. Not his mother, or his wife, or the police. Not anyone.

Even Darcie was being nicer to him, beginning to do the things that he'd begged her to do for years. He thought she must sense his new confidence, and he loved her more than ever, if possible. She was really the only woman he had ever loved.

Darcie had started taking dancing lessons! Now they would be able to get dressed up and go out dancing together and she would wear high heels and pretty clothes and every man on the dance floor would be jealous because she would dance with no one but him.

All the shrinks over the years had insisted that his thinking wasn't normal, that he needed therapy. He had the last laugh now; his thought processes were as smooth as tumblers in a lock. He could plan and carry out whatever he wanted to do, and it all worked. He didn't need a shrink to tell his troubles to. He didn't need to "grow up," and he didn't have to bow down to anyone.

The thing was that, once he started on one of his prowling plans, and once he had a woman, he was seized with a feeling that what he was doing was right, that there was no need for him to consider if he should stop or go ahead. He just let the fantasy take him over.

He reveled in having control. He could move about at his own whim. The one thing he could not bear was to have someone else decide what he should do and where he should be at any given time. He was in charge of his own destiny. That was important.

Sometimes he still had his dizzy spells and sometimes he still got depressed, an overwhelming black depression that settled over him and made him too sad for words. Then he would begin to wonder why Darcie had waited so long to take dancing lessons. He had asked her to dance with him for years, and she wouldn't. He wondered if it was too late now.

And he couldn't enjoy sex with her the way he once had. It left him feeling empty, and she didn't seem very enthusiastic or satisfied with him. If she knew how strong and important he was, she might be more sensual. But he couldn't tell her; she might not understand.

Damn. That forced him to remember his failures. Before the short little girl at Lloyd Center, he had struck out twice. It made him feel bad to think about it.

He had to think about his few failures; he needed to evaluate what had gone wrong and correct it. There was that blonde bitch in Portland. He was still furious with her.

On the twenty-first of April, Jerry had gone to the parking garage at Portland State University to look for a girl. He had his toy pistol and he'd thought that would make a girl frightened enough to go with him.

He'd found himself a prime lookout point, watched women crossing the street far below his perch in the parking lot, and finally chose the one he wanted—a slender woman with long red-gold hair and very full breasts. She wore a bright red linen dress, the hemline stopping at mid thigh, and tantalizing high-heeled pumps.

He didn't know it, nor would it have mattered to him, but her name was Sharon Wood and she was twenty-four years old. She was, on that gloriously warm April day, a perfect target for Jerry Brudos. Actually a gutsy, intelligent young woman, Sharon was having a bad day on April 21. The last thing on her mind was caution. She had far too many other things to worry about. Her abduction should have gone smoothly.

Jerry Brudos, like the majority of serial killers, could pick up on that temporary vulnerability almost as a wolf catches the scent of fear in his prey. The distracted victim is the ideal victim for a predator.

It was three-thirty that afternoon when Sharon left the Portland State history department where she worked as a secretary. She had been married for seven years, had two little children, and her marriage was about to blow all to smithereens. On this afternoon, her about-to-be-ex-husband had agreed to meet with her, and her mind was on that meeting.

She was feeling lousy physically, too, suffering with a middle-ear infection and using antibiotics; her hearing, at best, was not acute. Now sounds came to her muffled and indistinct. She was near-sighted, and adjusting to newly prescribed contact lenses. The senses she needed most were blurred that afternoon.

It wasn't surprising that Sharon was distracted and depressed. She couldn't even find her damned car keys, and she'd had to dump out the contents of her purse on her desk before she left her office. She hoped she could find the extra key she'd hidden in a magnetic box under the car frame.

Sharon tapped her foot impatiently as she waited for the "Walk" sign to flash at the corner of Broadway and Harrison in downtown Portland. She hadn't the vaguest awareness of the big man watching her from his perch high up in the parking garage across the street. Eight stories high with open sides, packed with cars belonging to some of the 9,000 Portland State students and faculty, the parking garage had always seemed safe enough to Sharon.

And it *was* broad daylight. People streamed by her on either side as she waited.

As Sharon Wood headed across the street, she hoped that she could find the spare key, and then she realized she wasn't even sure on which level she'd parked that morning. She was going to be late meeting her estranged husband.

Sharon would recall years later that she had never before in her life encountered any manner of sexual violence. . . .

"As I sped down the steps into the basement level, my high heels clicked on the concrete," she recalled. "The heavy doors shut automatically behind me, cutting me off from daylight and the campus population. I walked about fifteen feet forward and looked around for my car, and realized I was on the wrong level."

Sharon turned to go back up the dead-space area between the parking levels, and sensed—if only obliquely—that someone was behind her. She recalls it was only an awareness of someone in back of her, not a distinct impression of a man or a woman.

"Instinct told me not to return to the more isolated stair area, so I pivoted and started for the daylight entrance on the far side of the building," she said.

Sharon still had not looked around, but she walked rapidly, giving into that "gut feeling" that warns of nameless, faceless danger. But she had walked only a few steps when she felt a light tap on her shoulder.

She turned her head and looked directly into Jerry Brudos' pale blue eyes.

"I could sense the evil and I *knew* I was going to die. . . ."

And then she saw the pistol. The big, freckled man promised her, "If you don't scream, I won't shoot you."

Almost unconsciously, Sharon Wood made a choice. "No!" she screamed at the top of her lungs, at the same time backing away from the man with the gun. Undeterred, Jerry Brudos stepped quickly behind her

again and grabbed her in an arm-lock around her
neck. She was five feet four inches tall, and weighed
118 pounds. The man who held her in a "half nelson"
was over six feet tall and weighed 210 pounds.

Kicking and screaming, Sharon continued to shout
"No!" She tried to grab for the gun that was right in
front of her face, twisting and pulling at the fat fingers
that held it.

The man's huge hand passed close to her mouth,
and she bit into the fleshy thickness of his thumb as
hard as she could. She tasted blood, *his* blood, and she
tried to let go. But, in her terror, her jaw had locked.
She *could* not release his hand, and they danced a
kind of crazy dance in the dimness of the parking
garage as Jerry Brudos tried to free himself of the
kicking, biting blonde who had seemed such an easy
target.

In desperation, he wound his free hand around and
around in Sharon Wood's long strawberry blonde hair
and pulled her head toward the concrete, forcing her
body to the ground.

"Oh, God," she thought. "Now, he's going to rape
me right here."

Brudos still had a grip on Sharon's hair, and began
to beat her head against the floor. Hazily, she saw a
Volkswagen "Bug" driving toward them as she began
to lose consciousness. Only then did her jaw relax
from its muscle spasm and her attacker pull his thumb
free. Through bleared eyes she saw him pick up his
gun and run. How odd, she thought hazily: Once *he*
became the captive, he acted scared to death . . . he
was fighting to get away from *me*.

And then she passed out.

Portland police patrolmen arrived at the parking
garage to take Sharon Wood's statement about the
crime, which was listed as "aggravated assault." Tragically, no connection was made at the time between the
attack on Sharon in Portland and the dead girls found
floating in the river near Corvallis.

Of the two officers responding, one told Sharon,
"Don't you think you took a hell of a chance—fighting

a man with a gun?" His partner disagreed, "I think you did the right thing."

In this instance, of course, she had. She would not know for years the details of her attacker's other crime. Sharon Wood was left with a pounding headache, wrenched muscles, scrapes, bruises, torn clothing, and nightmares.

But she was alive.

She was one of Jerry Brudos few failures.

He'd had to get out of there quickly. He had kept his head, though. If he'd run, somebody would have been suspicious. He'd forced himself to walk away casually—fast, but casually. He climbed the ramp to the next floor and walked to his car. Nobody stopped him. But his thumb throbbed for the rest of the day.

It was humiliating to have something like that happen, and he'd still been so full of the urge for a woman. He'd tried again the next day, right in Salem. That girl was a young one, not more than fourteen or fifteen, and he'd thought he was lucky to find a schoolgirl out of school at ten-thirty in the morning on a Tuesday. She was just hurrying along the Southern Pacific Railroad tracks headed for Parrish Junior High when he spotted her.

He'd tried to act like it was urgent when he said, "I want you to come with me. I won't hurt you," and then he'd grabbed at her coat at the shoulder and pulled her between two houses, and showed her the gun.

She'd been scared, all right, and he'd told her, "I won't rape you. I wouldn't do that."

"Let go of me," she'd said, as if she wasn't afraid of him at all.

Then he'd led her toward the borrowed sports car and told her to get in, and the little bitch had broken away from him and run screaming for help to a woman who was working in her yard.

He'd had to run too, get in his car, and gun the motor before somebody got a glimpse of the license plate.

Two failures had hurt his ego some, and made him determined that he'd be successful the next day.

He smiled. He had been perfectly successful. He'd walked right into the parking garage at Lloyd Center and found the pretty girl in the beige coat. He'd caught her before she could get into her red Volkswagen and he'd held out the little tin police badge—and she'd fallen for it.

And now he was okay again. The secret was to learn from his failures, not to dwell on them.

There were so many girls around. Even though the police had found the two he'd left in the river, he didn't worry that anybody was close to him; they had no idea who he was. He thought about all the girls there were on college campuses—more than any other place. They were all young, and most of them were pretty.

He developed a new plan. It worked beautifully. All he had to do was call one of the dorms and ask for a common name—"Susan" or "Lisa" or "Mary." Somebody always came to the phone, and he pretended that a friend had given him her name. Some of them wanted to know *which* friend and hung up on him when he couldn't come up with a name. But he managed to get three dates that way. He took them out for coffee and talked with them. None of them were exactly his type, but he enjoyed bringing up the newspaper articles about the dead girls in the river, and it turned him on to see how nervous it made them. Talk about jumpy! When he reached out to touch them on the shoulder, they practically leaped out of their skin.

Seeing them afraid and nervous was so stimulating that he'd been driven to steal more underwear for his collection. He had an improvement on his "panty raids," too; he wore women's underwear when he crept through the dorms, and a pair of large-sized women's pedal pushers. It made his forays more exciting when he dressed that way.

He had no doubt that his "blind" telephone calls would soon win him a coffee date with a girl who *was* his type. When he found the next one, he would take her with him. . . .

— 12 —

Jim Stovall, Jerry Frazier, and Gene Daugherty were living and breathing the cases of Karen Sprinker and Linda Salee. They did not delude themselves into thinking that the girls' deaths were the final acts of a pattern. They knew it would continue if the killer wasn't caught, and it made everything else in their lives take a back seat.

During the day, Stovall and Frazier plodded through junkyards in Salem and Portland with Lieutenant Daugherty, trying to get a line on the origin of the auto parts used to weight the girls' bodies. The parts had come from a Chevrolet, a model produced between 1953 and 1962. The engine head had weighed sixty pounds. The task of tracing the parts to one particular car from the hundreds of thousands that came off assembly lines in a nine-year period was almost hopeless. There were no serial numbers to compare, no way at all to follow the history of the junked vehicle back to Detroit and then through a series of owners. But there was the faintest of possibilities that some junkyard owner would remember selling the parts. And there was more likelihood that the auto parts could be traced than that the origin of the mass-produced mechanic's cloths could. The nylon cord and the copper wire used to fasten the engine parts to the bodies was also mass-produced, available from uncountable sources. The black bra was old, purchased years before, and had been sold through outlets all over America.

It was quite possible that there were more than one killer or that the murderer had had an accomplice. It would have taken a man of Herculean strength to lift both the bodies and the heavy auto parts and carry them to the riverbank. No average man could have done it.

Where the man actually lived was another puzzle to be worked out. Linda Slawson and Linda Salee had disappeared from Portland's city limits, and Detective James Cunningham of the Portland police was assigned to those cases, but Linda Salee had been found in Benton County and Linda Slawson had never been found at all. Karen Sprinker had been reported missing from Salem and had been found in Benton County. Jan Whitney's case was being investigated by the Oregon State Police, and only God knew where her body was.

Stovall and Frazier traveled continually, accompanied by Daugherty, checking in with police departments in the Willamette Valley to be sure they weren't missing any clues, information that, taken alone, meant nohing, but when added to the growing file of facts and leads, might mean everything.

Stovall typed the missing and dead girls' names on a small file card and tacked them up over his desk. He was looking for a common denominator. "What kind of spook are we looking for?" he asked himself again and again.

Since he had no face, and no name, and precious little physical evidence to help him find the killer, he tried a technique that had worked for him before. He drew on his background in criminal psychology, on the few facts he knew for certain, and on the "gut feelings" that every superior detective hooks onto when there is nothing else to do.

Stovall placed a clean sheet of paper on his desk and picked up the felt pen he always favors. In his distinctive printing, he wrote a question mark, and then began to fill the page with the thoughts that came tumbling into his head.

? Killer is . . .
1. Between twenty and thirty—because all victims are young.

2. Of at least average intelligence—knots used to tie parts to bodies skilled.
3. An electrician—copper wire on the bodies wound one turn around and broken, then wound twice as electricians do—twisted in fashion common to electrical wiring.
4. Probably from broken home—with one parent gone . . . or the child of a strong mother and weak father . . . strong dislike for mother shown by desecration of female bodies. HATES WOMEN.
5. Probable record of antisocial behavior going far back.
6. Not participant in contact sports—women strangled but not beaten. Strangulation required little force.
7. Not a steady worker. No reason, beyond girls' disappearances at odd hours of day.
8. Driven by a cycle of some sort—possible pseudomenstrual? All girls vanished toward end of month:
    Slawson: January 26
    Whitney: November 26
    Sprinker: March 27
    Salee: April 23

Even with his training and experience taken into account, it is eerie to see just how close Stovall came to visualizing the man he sought. He could not actually *know* these things at the time, for his list, although based on the few facts known, was almost entirely the creation of a subliminal awareness—as if the detective had, indeed, locked into the murderer's mind.

Stovall searched in May 1969 for his "common denominator"—some way to tie a specific suspect to the pattern of deaths.

He assumed that the killer had to be someone familiar with the area from Corvallis to Portland. His origins or recent living arrangements had to have been centered at one time around the Long Tom River. It was too isolated a waterway for someone to have stumbled on it accidentally. Undoubtedly the bodies had been left in the river during nighttime hours by someone who could literally find his way to its banks in the dark. A stranger would have fallen in himself with one misstep.

The man had to be very, very strong. Stovall felt that it was only one man. Incidents of serial murder—lust murder—rarely involve more than one killer; that kind of killing results from a solitary aberration, a secret compulsion that the killer cannot, will not, share with anyone else. No, he was looking for a large man, because a small man could not have carried the bodies and their heavy weights.

The killer undoubtedly looked normal—as most sexual criminals do. The maniacal rapist, frothing at the mouth, is a fiction writer's killer. Most actual rapists are average-looking—even attractive—and usually have some manner of relationship with a woman. They rape and kill because of an inner rage, because they are driven compulsively to do so. If the killer's black side was obvious, Stovall doubted that he would have been able to get close enough to the victims to abduct them.

Jim Stovall studied a map of Oregon. Since the killer had roved from possibly as far south as Eugene and as far north as Portland, his residence was probably somewhere in between the two cities, a "safe house" to run to when the heat was on after each disappearance. The most likely city for the killer's home base would be Corvallis or Salem.

Karen Sprinker had spent most of her time in Corvallis while she attended Oregon State University; she was seized in Salem. Was there a connection? Was it possible that she had known her killer . . . or that he might have watched her for some time, and stalked her to Salem?

Daughtery and Stovall agreed that the obvious place to begin intensive questioning was Callahan Hall, where Karen Sprinker had lived. There were hundreds of coeds rooming in Callahan and in other dorms on the Corvallis campus.

Gene Daugherty packed up and moved to Corvallis to organize a massive interviewing program. He would literally live there until a break came—if it did. Daugherty found the Corvallis Police Department and the college authorities magnificently cooperative. The police department provided two detectives, B. J. Miller and "Frenchie" De Lamere, who joined in the search for the killer. The interview teams would work each day and every evening, talking to coeds at fifteen-minute intervals.

"First, we talked with all the girls who had known Karen even slightly. We asked them about her dates, and then we asked them about their own dates. How many dates did they have, and who were they with? Had any of them received peculiar phone calls? Had they been taken to strange places? Had they been in contact with any strange or unusual people? Anything that might have been out of the ordinary—no matter how unimportant it might have seemed. Then we talked to the girls who had not known Karen, and asked them the same questions."

The girls interviewed were subdued, sometimes frightened when they talked of Karen. It could have happened to any of them, and they knew it. Yes, most of them had dated frequently, and it seemed okay to date men they had met on campus. A campus atmosphere seemed safer somehow; it wasn't as thought you were dating strangers you'd met in a city.

Now all of the women interviewed tried to remember anything that had happened to them that had seemed a little off-center. Some of them were embarrassed, but most of them were quite frank in their eagerness to help. Not surprisingly, many of them had had dates with college boys who were sexually aggressive—but not peculiar about it, and none of them had used force.

After interviewing dozens of girls and filling countless yellow legal pads with notes, Daugherty and the interview teams began to get a little discouraged. It was such a long shot, really, to hope that one of the coeds was going to give the killer to them. Perhaps there *was* no good information to be gleaned at Oregon State.

But asking questions is a major part of a detective's work. A million answers may be utterly useless, and a thousand possible witnesses have to be dismissed with

a "thank you for your time." But the right answer
cannot be jarred free unless a concerted effort is made.
When that one answer shines through, it is worth all
the tedium.

And so the detectives worked each day in the stuffy
little room off the main lounge of Callahan Hall. Outside, students threw Frisbees on the green, and the
lilacs grew in thick clusters, their blooms filling the air
with fragrance. Occasionally, laughter carried through
the open window, making the grim investigation seem
incongruous. And also reminding the detectives that
Karen Sprinker could never again return to this campus.

With each new girl, the same questions. "Who have
you dated in the last three months?"

And mostly, the same answers. Boys from the dorm
next door, boys they'd known in their hometowns.
There were a few oddballs in the bunch. One girl had
dated a man who wanted to do nothing but have her
sit quietly while he played his flute—"very badly"—for
her. "I turned him down the next time he called."

There were a couple of girls who'd dated a fellow
who wanted to go to Portland and seek out porno
movies. "He was kind of weird—but not that weird,"
one said. "He didn't try anything."

Despite the girls' evaluations of the men they mentioned as harmless, detectives checked out all the ones
who had been in any way peculiar, and they all cleared.

And then three or four young women mentioned
receiving phone calls from a stranger. He had asked
for them by their first name, but none of them had
ever met the man before. One girl tried to remember
what he had talked about. "Let's see . . . it was a
couple of weeks ago. This guy said that he'd been a
prisoner in Vietnam for three years. Then he started
in on this garbage about how he possessed extraordinary powers in ESP—that kind of thing. Like he was
supposed to be clairvoyant or something. He wanted
me to meet him for a Coke, but I said no."

"Did he give you a name?" Daugherty asked.

"No . . ." The girl shook her head slowly. "Or if he
did, I can't remember. I just wasn't interested. I mean,

I didn't know him, and his conversation was a little odd."

After hearing about the same "Vietnam vet" from three more girls, Daugherty began to grow a little more enthusiastic about the lead. He was fascinated by the story told by a girl the next day. She too had received an unsolicited phone call from a man who said he was a Vietnam veteran. But, most interesting of all, *she* had agreed to meet the caller in the lounge of her dorm!

"He wasn't offensive when he called; he didn't say anything suggestive or raunchy," she explained. "He said he was really lonesome because he'd been away in the war for years, and he just wanted to meet a girl who would have a cup of coffee with him and talk. When I mentioned I was taking some psychology courses, he said that he'd been a patient at Walter Reed Hospital. He said he had learned a whole new method of study there and that I might be interested in hearing about it. I guess it was kind of foolish to make a date, but I felt a little sorry for him."

"So he did come over to your dorm?"

"Yes. He came over." She laughed nervously. "He turned out about like most blind dates do. He was a lot older than I expected—about thirty. He wasn't very good-looking. Kind of tubby, and he was losing his hair. I mean, he wasn't exactly a knight on a white horse or anything."

"What did you talk about?"

"At first we stayed in the lounge and just talked about general things—the weather, and studying, although he never did tell me about whatever that special method of study was. Just dumb stuff, the way you do when you don't really know a person. Oh, there was something . . ."

Daugherty looked up sharply. "What?"

"Well, he put his hand on my shoulder and began to massage it . . . and then he said—I don't know how to explain it—he said, 'Be sad.' "

" 'Be *sad*'?"

"Yes. Wasn't that peculiar? He wanted me to be sad or look sad or something, and I laughed and said I didn't feel sad about anything. Then he said, 'Think of those two girls they found in the river. Those girls who got killed. That was an awful thing that happened to them.' "

"That must have frightened you a little."

"No, not really. Everybody on campus had been talking about it, because it was in all the papers and because one of the girls was a student here. But I guess I just wasn't thinking too much about it. He asked me if I would go out with him and get a Coke, and I did."

"He didn't say or do anything else that seemed odd?"

"Well, kind of," the girl told Daugherty and Jerry Frazier and B. J. Miller, who had moved closer to listen to this most interesting incident. "He was telling me all about self-defense. He said most girls think that they should kick a man in the groin, but that's wrong. He said you might miss and make the guy mad and you'd be off balance. He said you should kick him in the shins first, and then in the groin."

"Anything else?"

"Well, I told him that I had heard it would take at least two men to carry an auto part and a body down to the river bank, and he said he agreed with me—but when he was leaving, it was kind of creepy, what he said. . . ."

"What was that?" Miller asked.

"He said, 'Why did you change your mind and come with me?' And I said I guessed I was curious. And he said, 'How did you know I would bring you back home and not take you to the river and strangle you?' Wasn't that kind of weird?"

That gave the detectives pause. Frazier cleared his throat and asked the girl about her blind date's car.

"Oh, he had an old junker of a car, and it was dirty and there were kids' clothes in it. I thought he might have been married, but he didn't mention that he was. He did say something about having had to replace the motor in his car recently."

"Can you describe the car?"

"Not really. I'm really bad on cars. It was so dirty,

and it was night, so I can't even tell you the color. It was a station wagon, and I think it had Oregon plates."

"Tell me again what he looked like. Describe him as if I had to pick him out from a crowd of people on the street."

"Okay. He was tall, close to six feet. And heavy. Not fat . . . but soft around the middle. His hair was blondish-red, and like I said, it was thinning on top—he kind of combed it forward. Let me see . . . His eyes slanted down at the corners. Bad dresser. Oh, and his complexion was pale and he had freckles."

"That's very good," Daugherty complimented her. "That helps. Have you seen him again?"

She shook her head. "He said he would be back in two days, but he never called. I didn't really care. A lot of guys will say they're going to call you. It's just something to say, and I wasn't interested in him anyway."

"I want you to do something for me, if you will," Daugherty said. "If he calls again, tell him you'll see him."

"Oh . . ." The young woman looked alarmed. "I . . ."

"No, you won't have to meet him alone. Make a date, but give him some excuse why you can't see him right away. Then call this number." He handed her a card with the number of the Corvallis police on it. "They'll be alerted. They'll be here before he gets here. Under no circumstances go anyplace with him. Say you'll meet him in the lounge. Okay?"

"Okay. But he might never call again. I think he could tell I wasn't that crazy about him."

"Maybe he will. Maybe he won't. Just be sure you delay him if he does, and call the police."

Freckles. That part of the description rang a bell in Jim Stovall's carefully compartmentalized brain when he heard the coed's description. There weren't that many men who had freckles, especially in the spring before the sunburn season. Salem detectives had been going through all complaints that had come into their department since the first of the year, looking for something that might resemble the Karen Sprinker case. Among other incidents, they had pulled the attempted-kidnaping complaint made by fifteen-year-old Liane Brumley. Stovall had reread it, and now he remembered "freckles." He checked the file. Liane Brumley had been terribly frightened by the man who loomed up in front of her as she hurried along the railroad tracks, saved, possibly, by her decision to scream and run for help.

April 22. Ten-thirty A.M. That was only one day before Linda Salee had disappeared from Lloyd Center in Portland. The suspect had said, "I won't rape you. I wouldn't do that." Stovall figured the man was protesting too much: with a gun and his orders to the Brumley girl to get into his car, what *had* he planned to do with her? Neither Linda Salee nor Karen Sprinker had been shot, but a gun would have been a strong convincer to force a girl to go with the killer without screaming. Stovall was grateful that Liane Brumley *had* screamed; it could well have saved her life.

He ran his finger under the physical description. "Tall, over six feet." That difference was negligible—witnesses are off on height estimation more than any other factor in identification. "Sandy hair. *Freckles.*"

For a moment, he felt exhilaration. Was it possible that all the days spent interviewing and going through car graveyards and driving between one police department and another—all those hundreds of man-hours worked by himself and dozens of others—would come down to something as simple as freckles?

There they were. Two incidents. Both in Salem—but with a connection, however tenuous, in Corvallis now.

Could this really be a break, or was it only wishful thinking?

— 13 —

It was nearing the end of the third full week in May, a time bracket that made Jim Stovall and Gene Daugherty nervous. If the killer operated under the stress of a pseudo-menstrual cycle as Stovall suspected, his prowling time had rolled around again. Somewhere—in Salem, or Corvallis, or Portland, or maybe some other city in Oregon—the killer would be getting restless. He had taken Karen on March 27, Linda on April 23. His compulsion to stalk and seize a woman might well be at fever pitch, and there was no way in hell they could warn every pretty young woman in the state to be on guard.

It was possible that the discovery of the bodies in the Long Tom and the resultant publicity had made the faceless man cautious—but they doubted it. On the contrary, all the press coverage might have honed his appetite, appealed to some need for fame—or, in his case, infamy. He might feel that a gauntlet had been flung down. He might just want to prove that he was smarter than the cops.

It was Sunday night, May 25. In Callahan Hall, the young woman who had promised to call the police if she ever heard from her scruffy admirer again sat in her room studying. She was a little tense, but not much; it had been eleven days since she'd had her Coke date with a stranger, and she hadn't heard anything more from him.

And then the buzzer next to her door blurted its steady tone, and she jumped. She moved quickly to press down on it to show that she had heard and would go down the hall to the phone. On her way, she told herself it could be anyone—her mother, or a girlfriend, or one of the men she dated casually.

But when she picked up the phone, she recognized the slightly hesitant voice of the big freckled man. And she fought to keep her voice calm.

"How about a Coke and some conversation?"

"I . . . I thought I wouldn't hear from you again. This is kind of short notice."

"Sorry. I've been busy. But I could be over there in, say, fifteen minutes."

"Oh . . ." she delayed, "I'd like to see you, but I can't go anywhere until I wash my hair. It's a mess."

"That doesn't matter."

"Well, it does to me. I could be ready in about forty-five minutes—maybe an hour. If that's okay, why don't I meet you downstairs then?"

She held her breath while he argued that she didn't have to bother getting fixed up, and then she heard him agree to the delay.

As soon as she heard the line go dead, she dialed the Corvallis Police Department. "He called. I managed to stall him by telling him I have to wash my hair. He'll be downstairs in the lounge in about forty-five minutes."

"We'll be there. We'll be waiting when he walks in."

B. J. Miller and Frenchie De Lamere, in plain clothes, sat in the lounge out of the line of vision of anyone coming in the door. They waited. Ten minutes. Twenty minutes. Several young men came in, obviously college boys waiting to pick up dates. Ten more minutes. And then they saw him, a big, hulking man who seemed out of place. He wore a T-shirt and wrinkled "high-water" slacks, topped by a Pendleton jacket of a somewhat garish plaid. He was no kid. He had to be thirty, maybe older. The big man looked around the lounge, failed to see his date, and sat on a couch where he could watch the stairs.

De Lamere and Miller moved over to him and showed their badges. He looked up, hardly startled, and smiled slightly.

"We'd like to ask you a few questions, sir—if you don't mind."

"No, not at all. What can I do for you?"

"We'd like to have your name."

"It's Brudos. Jerry Brudos."

"You live here in Corvallis?"

He shook his head. "No. I live in Salem. I used to live here, but I just came over to mow a friend's lawn and check out his place. He's on vacation."

The answers came quite smoothly, and neither officer could detect any signs of stress in Brudos. No perspiration. No fidgeting. He gave his Center Street address. He said that he was an electrician by trade, and admitted a little sheepishly that he was married and had two young children. He gave the name and address of the friend's property where he'd been working.

There was no legal reason to arrest Jerry Brudos or even to hold him for questioning. The officers thanked him, and he left the lounge. They noted that he drove a beat-up greenish-blue station wagon that was *not* a General Motors product. They jotted down the license number and returned to headquarters to begin a check that might verify what Brudos had told them.

Jerry Brudos' story of doing yardwork for a friend was verified. He did know the occupant of the house whose address he'd given, and the man was on vacation. Neighbors said Brudos often worked there, and had during the daylight hours of Sunday, May 25.

On the surface, he seemed to pass muster.

But that was only on the surface. Jerry Brudos' name was in the hopper and the investigative process had begun. Jim Stovall and Gene Daugherty received the information gleaned by the Corvallis officers, and used it as the bare bones of a dossier on the man—Jerome Henry Brudos.

Brudos' record of commitment to the Oregon State Hospital indicated that he had shown evidence of sexual violence as far back as his teens. There were, however, no recent records of treatment. Either he had gotten well or he had managed to avoid treatment.

He had no arrest record as an adult. That might

mean they were focusing on the wrong man—or it might only mean he was clever.

As Stovall and Daugherty worked rapidly to back-track on Brudos, they found too many "coincidences" to be explained away. In January, 1968 Jerry Brudos had lived in the same neighborhood worked by the young encyclopedia salesgirl—the missing Linda Slaw-son. Brudos had indicated that he'd moved to Salem in August or September 1968 and gone to work in Lebanon, Oregon—hard by the I-5 freeway where Jan Whitney had vanished in November. His current job was in Halsey—only six miles from the body sites in the Long Tom. And, of course, when Karen Sprinker disappeared from Meier and Frank on March 27, Brudos had lived only blocks away. . . .

And he was an electrician.

The investigative team in Salem was anxious to get a look at this Jerry Brudos. Jerry Frazier made the first contact, a casual conversation outside the little house on Center Street. Frazier and Jerry Brudos talked in in the old garage Jerry used for his shop and dark-room. The detective was fascinated with the place, and made a note to tell Stovall about the profusion of ropes, knots, the hook in the ceiling. He couldn't say just why the paraphernalia made the hairs on the back of his neck stand up—but it did.

Jerry Brudos talked obscurely about "problems"—that some problems didn't need to be cured, that some made him feel that he was dipping his hand in a cookie jar and how "You're afraid of getting caught."

But when Frazier pressed him about "problems," Brudos just said he had jobs where he couldn't get along with his fellow workers—that he lived in a world full of people but he was always alone.

When he returned to Salem police headquarters and reported to Stovall, he said, "It looks good. He seems calm enough about being contacted, but I'd like for you and Ginther to go back with me and see what you think."

"Any special reason?" Stovall asked.

"Just a feeling. . . ."

Stovall, Frazier, and Greg Ginther, another member

of the team, drove out to Center Street to talk again with Jerry Brudos. Until now, Stovall had had no image to focus on, nothing more than the Corvallis coed's description of her suitor and a black-and-white picture in the files.

The man they saw did not look overtly dangerous; he looked, instead, somewhat like an overgrown Pillsbury Doughboy. They had expected a huge muscular man, and this man betrayed no evidence of exceptional strength. His lidded eyes sloped at the outer corners and his chin and cheeks were blurred with flesh.

He looked like a loser. The kind of guy who sits at the end of the bar nursing his beer, always a little bloated, with no confidence to start up a conversation. He had to have been the sort of kid who got picked last in sandlot ball. He was clearly no ladies' man, at least not in the accepted sense of the term.

Stovall studied Brudos' speech patterns, his mannerisms, the way he moved and walked. He intended to show Liane Brumley the picture he had of Brudos, and he wanted to be able to "listen" to her recollections of her near-abduction with a solid memory of the man who was Jerry Brudos.

He saw Brudos' old station wagon parked nearby; that didn't seem to match Liane's description of the vehicle her would-be kidnapper had driven. She had said it was a small sports car.

"This your only car?" Stovall asked.

"Yeah."

"You ever drive anything else?"

"My friend's sometimes—it's a Karmann Ghia."

That fit closer. Stovall let it pass without comment.

The investigators asked if they could have another look around the garage. It looked like anybody's garage, divided by some plywood into smaller rooms, except that Frazier and Stovall noted the weights were still hanging from rope there. There was something about the knots that looked familiar—instantly reminiscent of the knots that had bound the auto parts to the dead girls' bodies. The rope was a quarter-inch, and there was some nylon cord that looked to be about three-sixteenths of an inch. Both the right size, the right material.

Brudos half-smiled as he said to Frazier, "You seem to be interested in that knot. Go ahead and take it if you want to."

Frazier moved quickly, cutting two short lengths, and being sure to include the distinctive knot. The rope and cord was common enough stuff; the lab could only give a "very probable" on something so widely distributed—but the knot was special.

Brudos did not ask if they would be back; he re-remained quite calm.

If the probe into the girls' murders and disappearances had seemed to lag before, now it accelerated to a frenzied pace. Stovall obtained the old black-and-white photo of Jerry Brudos and included it in a "lay-down"—a montage of mug shots. He took that lay-down to Liane Brumley and asked her if she recognized any of the men. She studied the photos carefully and then tapped the picture of Jerry Brudos.

"That looks like him—but the man who grabbed me had freckles. This man doesn't."

But he did. They just didn't show up in the photograph.

In fiction, it would be enough—all the pieces falling cleverly into place. In truth, it was only a beginning. To arrest a man, and then to take him before a jury, the state has to be armed with physical evidence—something twelve of his peers can see and touch and feel, or something a criminalist can tell them he has seen under a scanning electron microscope. The old axiom that a criminal always leaves something of himself at the scenes of his crimes, and always takes something of the scene away with him—no matter how minute—is truer than it ever was.

That was what Stovall and Daugherty and Frazier and the rest of the team had to find. What they knew now was that circumstantial evidence was piling up, that probably Jerome Brudos *had* been the man who tried to abduct Liane Brumley. The rest they only suspected. They needed all the bits and pieces of physical evidence that waited—somewhere—to be found. Something they could slip into plastic bags with their own initials added, something they could haul into a courtroom when the time was right.

Despite his placid exterior, Jerry Brudos had begun to feel a little uneasy. He sensed he was being tailed by the police. They hadn't gotten into his workshop, had only glanced at the locked door beyond the garage, but he figured they might come back. As far as he knew, there was nothing in there that would do them any good anyway, but the thought of them pussyfooting around his shop and darkroom was unsettling. Worse, he could not bear to have his movements hampered—and the police were hampering him by following him wherever he went.

He called Salem attorney Dale Drake and asked for an appointment the following day—May 27. When he faced Drake in his office, Jerry Brudos said, "I'm having some problems with the police. I'd like you to investigate and find out. I'll pay you for checking into it."

Drake refused the retainer, telling Brudos not to worry about money for the moment. He would stand by to represent him if, indeed, Brudos did have "police trouble."

The police were having a bit of trouble of their own, or, rather, were walking a very delicate path to be sure that they did not blow a case that was not yet fully formed. They did not yet have their damning physical evidence. They could not arrest Brudos for murder and hope to win a conviction. They wanted no pegs a defense team could hang their hats on. Rather, they wanted to give Brudos enough rope to hang himself, and that meant it was prudent to let him stay free where they could watch his movements. But there was danger there; if he should panic and bolt, they might lose him. They had an ace in the hole: the Liane Brumley case. If an arrest seemed essential, they could get a warrant on that case.

And so, when Brudos pulled out to head down the I-5 freeway to his job in Halsey south of Corvallis, a sneaker car was behind him. When he returned home, he was followed. For the next few days there was not a moment when Jerry Brudos was free of surveillance—subtle, but always there.

Beyond the fear that he might cut and run, there was the possibility that he might harm still another girl; the dangerous time period between the twenty-second and the end of the month was only at the halfway point. If they had the right man, and if they let him slip away from their observation, more tragedy might result.

But Jerry Brudos appeared to be following ordinary everyday patterns. He went to work. He came home, and he seemed to stay home in the evenings. On occasion, the family car pulled out and they saw that it was driven by a small dark-haired woman—Brudos' wife. She seemed unaware that something cataclysmic was happening in her world.

On Wednesday, May 28, at ten minutes to eight, a search warrant was served on the two vehicles available to Jerry Brudos. Brudos signed a Miranda Rights Card with a bland expression on his face. If he was getting more and more nervous, he didn't show it. His green station wagon proved to be spotless. It had been thoroughly washed both inside and out. In fact, it was *damp* inside.

Brudos smiled and said, "I took it through a fifty-cent car wash, and my little boy accidentally rolled down a window."

Jerry Frazier found Jerry Brudos almost too calm.

Later, Brudos would confide in Frazier, "I don't think you got anything out of the car. There's something, but I can't put my finger on it. There is kind of a link missing, having to do with the car. But I wasn't worried about it. I just felt like I wasn't involved. There was no doubt in my mind, until you compared the ropes. If I knew you were going to do that, I would have gotten rid of the rope." (But would he? Hadn't he so much as *offered* the knot to Jerry Frazier, almost begged him to take it into evidence?)

Stovall, Frazier, Greg Ginther, and Lieutenants "Manny" Boyes and Robert Pinnick of the Oregon

State Police Crime Lab searched and processed the 1964 Karmann Ghia, too, and took away almost infinitesimal fragments of evidence.

During the long evening, Jerry Brudos called his attorney three times, but let the searchers continue.

On Friday evening, May 30, 1969, Jim Stovall and Gene Daugherty left Salem for Corvallis, armed with a Marion County District Court Arrest Warrant charging Jerry Brudos with Assault While Armed with a Dangerous Weapon (in the Liane Brumley case). It was 5:05 p.m.

Before they could reach their destination, the stakeout team radioed that the Brudos family had left Corvallis, and was heading north on the I-5 freeway. Jerry Brudos was behind the wheel of the 1963 green Comet station wagon, Oregon License 7P–5777, when they left Corvallis, but enroute they changed drivers, and Darcie took the wheel while Jerry lay in the back seat. But they weren't headed home; Darcie drove right through Salem, and continued north toward Portland.

The waiting was over. Daugherty and Stovall could not risk letting Jerry Brudos escape into the metropolitan area of Portland—or perhaps even farther north into Washington State and then 250 miles to the Canadian border. The two detectives fell in behind the state police "sneaker" cars trailing the green station wagon.

There could be no more holding back and watching. The first car behind the Brudos vehicle pulled nearer and the trooper flicked on the revolving red light. Darcie Brudos saw it and eased into the slow lane, coming to a stop on the shoulder.

It was 7:28 p.m. Daugherty approached from one side, and Stovall and B. J. Miller from the other. They saw the worried-looking woman behind the wheel, the little boy and girl in the front seat. Darcie Brudos reached for her driver's license and started to ask what she had done wrong. Daugherty shook his head slightly and shone his flashlight into the back seat.

Jerry Brudos was there, hidden under a blanket.

"You're under arrest. Get out of the car, please."

With Brudos blinking his eyes in the glare of the phalanx of state police cars, Daugherty read him his rights from a Miranda card.

And then Daugherty and Stovall transported Jerry Brudos to the Salem City Police Station where he was booked, photographed, and committed to jail.

Stovall snapped a picture of the big man in the plaid shirt with his own Leica, catching the image of the man they'd searched for so long. Here, he believed, was the face of the man that fit the list he'd made.

But as Brudos stripped to change into jail coveralls, his clothing no longer resembled a typical Oregon working man's. Jerry Brudos was wearing women's sheer panties. He looked up to see Stovall and Daugherty exchange glances.

Brudos reddened, and explained, "I have sensitive skin."

The detectives said nothing.

Jerry Frazier searched Jerry Brudos' wallet as the prisoner was booked. Tucked deep in one of the leather folds, he found a tiny photograph of a nude woman, a rectangle measuring one inch by one and a half inches. It looked as though it was a Polaroid that had been trimmed from its original size. The head and feet were missing. Frazier could just make out a Sears Crafts-man tool chest behind the girl. He placed it in a glassine envelope and put a property tag on it: #2017.

Who was the girl in the picture? Frazier wondered if she was still alive—whoever she was.

Darcie Brudos' nightmare had begun; she had no idea what was happening. She had watched as her husband was handcuffed and placed in the back seat of a police car. She had quieted her sobbing children, and then she had turned around and followed the police caravan back to Salem.

Darcie waited while her husband was booked into jail. When she finally had a moment to talk to him, she begged, "Jerry, what is it?"

"It's nothing," he said shortly. "They're charging me with carrying a concealed weapon."

"But *why*?"

He turned away. Darcie watched Jerry disappear behind a steel door, and then she took her children home.

—— 14 ——

Jerry Brudos, having lied to his wife again, was led back to his cell, past curious prisoners. He was still not particularly worried. He had expected the police would do something like this—but he was secure that they had no way to tie him into whatever they were accusing him of. He considered that they were just using a desperate ploy, hoping that they could keep him in jail.

He did, however, call Dale Drake and ask that he come to the jail. He was smart enough not to go through this without an attorney. Drake stayed the night at the jail. Later, years later, Jerry Brudos would insist that he had no lawyer in attendance. He would relate that other prisoners "beat the living hell out of me." He would also claim that he had been poisoned in jail. He had always seen things in his own way, shaped them until they fit him; he would view his incarceration the same way.

And yet, there was something quite challenging about his arrest. Jerry considered himself brilliant. He mentioned to several officers and to his lawyer that his I.Q. had been tested at 166—well over genius demarcation. (He had actually tested 105 on the Wechsler-Bellevue scale; possibly the lower figure could be attributed to stress.) He did not believe there was a cop in the country who could outsmart him, and he looked forward to the jousting that would take place in the coming interviews, confident that he would win.

Stovall waited downstairs to interview the prisoner. Stovall is one of the best police interrogators in the country, having refined it to an art.

"It's a cat-and-mouse procedure," Stovall explains. "Always, *always*, the investigating team must withhold facts that place the suspect at the scene of the crime. We know something about him, and he knows—or suspects—that, but he doesn't know what. We form a kind of dialogue. The interrogator is never hurried; he deliberately allows the suspect to lead him away from the main points—but never too far. If the suspect says something incriminating, we never pounce on it right away. We let it slide until we're ready, and only then do we come back to it."

Obviously, a great deal had happened between the times the dead and missing girls had disappeared and the time they were found. Only one living person would know those events—and Stovall was quite sure that the big man before him held all those secrets. He could see Brudos taking his measure, and he himself watched the suspect covertly, evaluating his attitude.

The man was cocky, and seemingly at ease. That was good. Cocky suspects are more likely to spill their guts than those more nervous—they yearn to brag and show off, almost heedless of the fact that they let vital bits of information slip out.

This man—Jerry Brudos—quite likely had things to tell that no man really wanted to hear . . . but not soon, and not without a sound foundation of dialogue.

Stovall would make himself available all weekend; he did not expect to glean much from this first interview. If Brudos should decide he wanted to talk, the interrogator never wanted to be more than five minutes away.

Outside the windowless interview room, one could hear male voices and a few fragments of sound from a small radio, droning out the results of the qualifying laps at the Indianapolis Speedway. Inside, alone with the suspect, Stovall waited out the long silences. Brudos seldom looked directly at Stovall, but the detective could detect no beading of sweat on his forehead, no acceleration of breathing as if the suspect felt panicky.

He almost seemed to be reveling in the attention, anxious for the game of give-and-take to begin.

Stovall asked only the easiest questions. Brudos' full

name. His address. Date of birth. Wife's name. Employment history. Vehicles available to him. It might have been an interview given for a new job.

But it wasn't.

"You never divulge," Stovall comments. "You merely suggest, and wait for the suspect to carry it a little further."

"It's a puzzle," Stovall said quietly. "How something like this—all of this—could have developed. So many women missing.

Brudos nodded slightly.

"It's very complex, shows a lot of planning."

Brudos shrugged.

"Do you have any theories? Any way to make sense of this?"

"My attorney would prefer that I don't go into that."

Stovall pulled back, veering off into a less potent subject. "You ever drive a car, other than your own? Or the Karmann Ghia?"

"I drive my mother's sometime."

There was something there, a flicker of disgust in Brudos' eyes. *This man did not like his mother.*

"What kind of a car is that?"

"Rambler, 1964."

"One of those blue jobs? They all seem to look like boats—nautical."

"No. It's light green."

"Do you want a cigarette? A cup of coffee?"

"I don't smoke. I seldom drink, either. No bad habits." Brudos smiled.

Stovall smiled back.

"I think I'll go back to my cell. Those cops woke me up when they arrested me. I worked hard all day."

Stovall stood obligingly and signaled for a jailer.

The first contact was a draw, and Brudos seemed to think that he had handled it well.

"I'll be around if you want to talk more," Stovall said easily.

He watched the big man shamble down the hall on his way back to jail, and knew he might have to wait hours—days maybe—but that Brudos would be wanting to talk again.

Stovall had a cup of coffee and began to organize what would become voluminous notes. In front of the prisoner, he would take few notes, but when he was alone, he would jot down everything that seemed pertinent, and index the answers. That way, he would have a starting point with each new confrontation.

Hours later, the word came from the jail: "He wants to talk again."

"Bring him up."

They began again. The first tentative innocuous remarks. Brudos did not like his cell. It was a "closet." The only window, by his own measurement, was four inches by ten inches and closed up. The light was turned off too much.

Stovall commiserated. "Jails aren't built for comfort."

"Do you know where my wife is?"

"She went home hours ago."

Stovall could detect real concern for the prisoner's wife; his attitude when he spoke of her was nothing like the loathing he evinced when he talked about his mother.

"How do you do this business?" Brudos asked. "I mean, how do you know things—if you have no proof?"

"It's a matter of our knowing some things and other people knowing other things—and eventually they usually come together and we get the whole picture."

"So you don't know everything going on, do you?"

"Nobody claims that. As I said, it's a puzzle. You think of somebody doing all of this . . . and you wonder. You have the pieces of the puzzle, maybe, but you don't have the box with the picture of what it's supposed to look like. You have a thousand-piece puzzle, and all you can do is put the pieces together by color to begin with. We separate the blues from the greens and the browns, for example. So we form the borders, and we keep working toward identifying other pieces—keeping the color scheme of things in mind. Blue. Green. Brown."

Brudos seemed to like that analogy. Stovall didn't

fill him in on the rest. The trial and the error and the hard work, and sometimes losing track of the most important piece because it hadn't fit when you first tried it. Gradually the whole picture always does begin to form. The crime-scene evidence, and the interviews, and the countless hours of follow-up reports.

"Without the picture, it sounds impossible to me," Brudos commented. "I guess you get discouraged."

"Not necessarily."

The silence yawned.

"I know you picked me up because you thought I was guilty of something or other . . ."

"You're charged with assault with a deadly weapon."

"Yeah."

"You're an electrician. Are you pretty skilled at that?"

"I guess you could say that. Electricity . . . electronics, that stuff."

"Who did you work for when you lived in Portland in 1968?"

"Osborne. . . ."

"You worked many places around Salem?"

"Over in West Salem, and out in Lebanon, and then in Halsey."

"That's a long commute."

"It's not bad—almost all freeway."

"You had a little trouble when you lived in Corvallis back in the fifties."

"I was a kid. They sent me out to the hospital here. That was a long time ago."

"Yes. You must have been in high school then."

Brudos shifted. "I can't see how you'd know if I did something . . . with those girls. I can't see how there'd be any way to prove it."

"Do you want to discuss that?"

Brudos shook his head and looked away. "Drake said I didn't have to talk about any of that. He's my attorney, and I think I should do what he says. Did you know I went to high school with him? At least, he says we did—he says he remembered my name because we were in the same homeroom. Small world, huh?"

Stovall nodded. Brudos was avoiding direct questions, and he was adroit at changing the thread of conversation. Stovall wasn't going to push him.

The rest of that interview went the same way. Every time the detective veered too close to something Brudos didn't want to talk about, the conversation switched gears. He saw that Brudos was dying to know what the investigating team had found but that he would not come right out and ask. Nor would the suspect offer any new information.

Again, they had come to an impasse. Brudos was returned to his cell.

They were to continue their abortive discussions for three days, and each new confrontation touched a little closer on the girls' murders. Stovall's notes were becoming more defined. He spent half an hour or more after each session correlating and indexing. Brudos *had* been in the vicinity of every abduction. That was clear. And he'd had the means. The guy was strong; his soft layer of fat hid power. Opportunity. Means. Motive? Motive was becoming more apparent, an underlying madness in a man who clearly detested his mother, and that hatred had ballooned until it included all women—all women except Darcie Brudos.

The mother—Eileen Brudos—seemed to still control her son as if he were only a child. The loan of her car, the frequent loans of money to a man who could not hold a job. Every time the suspect mentioned his mother, there was a concurrent tightening in his jaw in apparent loathing.

Stovall sensed that he himself had passed some kind of test. Brudos seemed to respect him, considered him a fit adversary. The suspect obviously saw himself as a major intellect, and it was essential that he accept his interrogator as someone worthy.

The dialogue had been formed. If it meant that Stovall would have to home in on a kind of madness, he was prepared to do that. And yet he dreaded the denouement of the puzzle almost as much as he sought it. He had to keep reminding himself that the helpless victims were long dead and beyond pain. Even so, whatever had happened would have to be relived in the quiet interview room. . . .

Shifts changed. First Watch. Second Watch. And then Third Watch, and it began again. Stovall drank too much coffee, grabbed fragmented bits of sleep, and took quick showers. Upstairs in his cell, Brudos slept too.

He did, in fact, sleep well. He had called Darcie and told her what she must do. She had always obeyed him, and he counted on that now.

Darcie Brudos was in a state of shock. She kept trying to work back through her mind to make some sense of what had happened. One minute they had been heading off to Portland for the holiday weekend with friends. She had been happy and relaxed, looking forward to three days with people she liked, to break up the gloom of her relationship with Jerry.

But the next . . . The police had moved up behind their station wagon so swiftly, their voices disembodied then behind the glare of flashlights in her face. They scared her, and they scared the kids. She was still scared, alone in the house.

She had no idea what Jerry might have done. She knew he had some guns, but as far as she knew, he never carried them around with him; they were for hunting or for trading. She wondered why the police would follow them halfway to Portland and stop them on the freeway for something like possession of a weapon.

She would not let herself imagine what else might be involved; she would not allow other thoughts to creep in. Jerry was strange, and he'd been stranger lately, but that was only because he was so sensitive. That was only because people—herself included—kept disappointing him. He was the father of their children. He was her husband.

She sat in the darkened living room and stared out at the cars that crawled down Center Street, seeing their headlight beams creep across the far wall.

When the phone rang, she practically jumped out of her skin. It was Jerry, calling from jail. He sounded like himself, a little tense, but in control. He would not wait to listen to her questions; he had something important for her to do.

"Darcie . . ."

"Yes, I—"

"Just listen. I want you to do something for me. I want you to go out to my workshop. There's a box out there, and it's got some old clothes in it."

"What kind of clothes?"

He paused. "They're women's clothes, just some junk I had out there. I want you to burn them. And there's a box of photographs there too. Destroy both those boxes."

"Jerry . . . *why?*"

"The police might try to use them against me. They're asking a lot of questions. Just go out there and get them and burn them."

She could not do it. There were so many things that Jerry wasn't telling her. In the morning she called Dale Drake and asked him what she should do. He told her it would be illegal for her to destroy anything that might be construed as evidence. "If you do, it might tend to incriminate *you.*"

She didn't go out to Jerry's workshop at all; she was afraid to, and she was afraid to tell him that she hadn't done what he asked.

Instead, she took a few clothes for herself and the children and drove to Corvallis to stay with her parents. When they asked questions, she couldn't answer. She called Jerry's brother in Texas and told him Jerry was in trouble, but she couldn't answer his questions either.

She remembered the sight of Jerry dressed up in the bra and girdle, the photograph of him grinning, wearing the black lace slip and high heels, and the ones of Jerry lying on the bed in female lingerie.

Maybe that was it. Maybe that was against the law, and someone had found out.

—— 15 ——

Brudos wanted to talk again.

Jim Stovall stacked his notes carefully in an outer office and walked into the interview room. Jerry looked a little tired, but he wanted to continue their discussion. He was more anxious now to ferret out what the police knew.

"How would you know if I did it?"

"What exactly are you talking about, Jerry?"

"The girls. If you thought I killed those girls, how would you know anything if I didn't tell you?"

"Certain things we know. Certain things you know. . . ."

"What kind of things?"

Stovall was silent for a moment, and then he said slowly, "Well, for instance, if it ever came to pass that you know something about clothing . . ."

"Like what clothing?"

"Items of clothing found . . . items that seemed out of place."

"*My* clothing?"

"No."

"Clothing that was out of place?"

"Yes."

The answer popped out of the suspect's mouth swiftly—a slip, or deliberate? "You must mean the bra . . ."

Stovall kept his own breathing steady and forced himself to continue casually doodling on his scratch pad. The answer was right, an answer that no one but Karen Sprinker's killer would know. That black long-line bra with six hooks and eyes had been described to Karen's mother. And Mrs. Sprinker was positive that

Karen had never had such a garment. It was too big, and totally different from Karen's own bras.

Stovall would not pounce on the throwaway remark. If he did, Brudos might retreat and say nothing more. He would wait and let it drift back into the conversation later. He nodded slightly and went on to other areas. Brudos wanted to talk; he wanted to tell it all, but it had to be drawn out slowly.

They talked about the girl in the dorm in Corvallis; that was known to the police, and Brudos knew that. She was just "someone to talk to," and not his type.

What was his type?

"Women who dress nicely and wear high-heeled shoes. I like shoes."

Stovall agreed. "They look better than sneakers or flat heels, don't they?"

Brudos nodded enthusiastically. "A lot better. I try to get my wife to wear high heels all the time, but she says they hurt her back."

It was clear that talk of shoes excited Brudos and that he assumed that the detective had put no importance on the mention of the bra. "I collect shoes."

"Where would you get shoes? You mean you buy them?"

Brudos shook his head impatiently. "No . . . no. I take them from women."

"How would something like that be accomplished?"

"My lawyer doesn't want me to talk to you, you know."

Stovall nodded, and waited. He could see that a wall of lawyers wasn't going to stop Brudos from bragging.

"There was this one girl in Portland. Back a couple of years ago—maybe 1967. She lived out on South East Pine Street. I was working at Qeco-Osborne Electric Company then, and I was just driving around one day and I saw her. She was wearing a pair of high-heeled shoes. I guess I fell in love with her shoes. I started to follow her, and I noted the address of the apartment where she lived. I went back later—maybe it was early in the morning. It was dark. I didn't want her; I wanted her shoes."

"How would you get in to take her shoes?"

"I took off the window screen—it was already loose. I was only trying to get her shoes when she woke up and started to move. I had to choke her so she couldn't see me. She was wearing a two-piece pajama outfit. I unbuttoned the top and took off the bottoms and had sex with her. She was okay. She woke up when I finished, and I grabbed three pairs of her shoes—and a black bra—and left."

"Did you take anything else?"

He seemed surprised. He was not a thief. He only took underwear and shoes. "No, nothing else."

"That's how you collect your underwear and shoes?"

"Sometimes I find them on the clotheslines. Sometimes I have to go inside and steal them."

"Was that the black bra we were talking about—is that where you got it?"

"No, that was different. The one we were talking about was wide." Brudos held his hands six to eight inches apart to demonstrate. "It caught my attention on a clothesline in Portland a couple of years ago, and I took it."

"And you saved it—kept it someplace?"

"Yes. With the others."

Brudos apparently felt quite safe. They had talked of such a minor thing as stealing underwear from clotheslines, and he had explained away the rape in Portland as only something that happened almost "accidentally" as part of his "collecting."

Stovall had been careful not to evince shock or express judgment on any of the activities. The whole story of the long black bra would be more threatening to the prisoner, and he let it wait for the moment.

"While you were living in Portland, did anything else happen?"

"You mean the girl with the encyclopedias?"

Bingo. "Yes. Her name was Linda."

"She came to my house and I was out in the yard. I thought she was a boy at first—her hair was so short. She said she had an appointment with somebody at our house. I took her around to the rear door and into the basement and told her I wanted to buy the books."

Stovall waited. "Was anyone else home?"

"I told her we had company, but we didn't. My mother was upstairs with my little girl. She sat on a stool in the basement workshop trying to talk me into buying the encyclopedias. . . .

"I walked around behind her. There was a two-by-four about four feet long there. I hit her with it and she fell off the stool. She was unconscious. Then I choked her and she died."

Jerry Brudos had just admitted his first murder. Jim Stovall accepted it calmly, and Brudos continued describing the death of Linda Slawson.

"My wife was out, but my mother was there. I went upstairs and told her to get some hamburgers. I went back downstairs, and then I heard this friend of mine from Corvallis calling out to me."

"What was his name?"

"Ned Rawls. I went out the back door again and around to the front. I told him I was making nitroglycerin in the basement and I couldn't talk, and he went away. I went back to the basement and took the girl out from where I hid her under the stairs."

"Do you remember what she was wearing?"

It had happened eighteen months earlier. Stovall knew that if the woman could be found, there would be nothing left but her clothing and her bones. A specific description of clothing or jewelry would be important.

"Her outer clothes? No. She had a blue brassiere, slip, and girdle—and red panties. I dressed her and undressed her, like she was a big doll. I tried on some of my other things—from my collection.

"I couldn't keep her there. There was my mother and my wife, and they would have found out."

"So what did you do?"

"Early in the morning, about two A.M., I loaded her into the car and took her to a bridge over the Willamette. I took the jack out of the car so it would look like I had a flat, and I threw her over."

"She was never found."

"No. I didn't think she would be. I weighted the body down."

"With what?"

Brudos paused for a moment. If he answered, he would be really getting into it. And then he answered: "With the head of a car engine."

"Is there anything else you want to say about Linda Slawson?"

"I cut her foot off."

"You cut her foot off? When was that?"

"Just before I threw her over. I couldn't keep her, but that was a small part I could save. I had a hacksaw and I cut her left foot off because I'm right-handed. I took it home and put it in the freezer and used it for a photography model and to try shoes on."

"Do you still have it?"

Brudos shook his head. "I couldn't. The women might have found it. After a while, I weighted it down too and threw it in the river."

"Do you remember anything else about that girl? That would be Linda Slawson."

"She had a ring. A class ring from some school back east. A Catholic school, I think."

"She was not afraid of you?"

"No. She was just sitting there trying to sell me books, and then she didn't see me with the board. After I hit her, she was unconscious."

The floodgates were open, but there were three more cases—possibly others—to be got through. Jerry Brudos' demeanor had changed as he told of his crimes. He was cockier and more confident now. He had pulled off abductions that had baffled hundreds of police officers, and he seemed proud to be able to lay out the details of his plans.

It would be a long, long day.

"You know, Jerry, we're attempting to find out what happened to Jan Whitney. We found her car near the I-5, but we never did find her. Would you know what happened to her? It would have taken a lot of planning, I would think, to make a woman just disappear like that."

Brudos smiled slightly.

"Did you ever know Jan Whitney?"

"Not really."

"You encountered her in some way. Would that be it?"

Brudos said nothing. The time sequence was closer; it was almost as if Linda Slawson's murder was not as threatening because it was so far back in his memory. But Jan Whitney had been missing only six months.

"That's a long time back—back to last year," Stovall said. "A person could forget."

That annoyed Brudos, apparently. "I remember."

"You were living in Salem last November, weren't you? Were you working then?"

"I was working in Lebanon."

"That day Jan Whitney disappeared was a Tuesday. You worked that day?"

"Yes. . . . Her car was broken down on the freeway. I saw it on my way home that night."

"What color was it?"

"It was a red-and-white Nash Rambler. It was sitting on the shoulder about two miles south of Albany. She was standing there, and two guys. Two hippie guys."

That was a surprise to Jim Stovall. Jan Whitney hadn't been alone! If two men had been with her, they certainly hadn't come forward to aid in the investigation. But Brudos seemed adamant that there were two young men with her. "She was there with two other individuals? What did they look like?"

Brudos shrugged. "Hippies. They all look alike. Long hair. Young. Jeans and headbands. Kids."

"Were they with her, or had they come along?"

"I gathered that she'd given them a ride, and her car broke down and they didn't know how to fix it. I offered to fix her car, but I didn't have my tools with me. I gave the three of them a ride to Salem and let the hippies off at an on-ramp so they could go on north."

"She was willing to go on with you?"

"Sure. I said I'd take her back and fix her car. I drove to my house on Center Street and pulled into my garage. I told her to wait there in the car while I told my wife I was going back to fix her car, and she did. I told her my tools were in the house.

"My wife wasn't home. I came back and told the girl that I couldn't get into the house, that we'd have to wait a few minutes until my wife came home—made some excuse about where my wife was."

"Did you expect your wife home in a few minutes?"

Brudos shook his head. "Not for a couple of hours. She was over at her friend's house."

"What did you do then?"

"I got in my car and sat behind the girl. I said it was a funny thing to ask someone to close his eyes and try to explain how to tie a shoe. You know, without using your hands to show how, when you can't see."

Brudos gestured with his hands, and Stovall saw that his fingernails were bitten to the quick, like a child's hands can be. It looked peculiar on a grown man.

"And she did? She told you?"

"She looked at me and started using her hands, and I told her that wasn't what I meant. That she had to turn her head around and look toward the front and tell me what to do without moving her hands. So she turned around, and she's saying, 'You take the right lace and you pass it over the left and underneath . . .' and I took a mailman's leather strap I'd got from the house and made a loop over her head and pulled it tight around her throat. Then I opened the rear car door and put my end of the strap through it and closed it. She was pulled back and bent backward over the seat."

"She was dead, then?" Stovall asked quietly.

"She didn't move. She couldn't move. I went in the house to check to be sure my wife wasn't home, and she wasn't. I went back to the car, and she—the girl— was dead. I turned her around on the seat and had sex with her body from the rear."

Jim Stovall had fully expected that the killer he had sought was a sexual psychopath. Jerry Brudos was not the first psychopath he had encountered, but he was the most monstrous. He was a sadist and a necrophile, his sexual desires fulfilled by engaging in erotic acts with women who were either unconscious or dead.

Stovall felt sick; he could not betray his feelings or act on his natural desire to leave the room and get some fresh air. The process had begun. He was hearing what he had sought to hear when he began the dialogue two days ago. It seemed like two months.

"Did you dispose of Jan Whitney's body? I would wonder how you managed that."

"Not then. I took her into the workshop, and later I had sex with her again. I dressed her in some of my clothes collection and took pictures of her. I have a hook in my workshop, and I hoisted her up on a rope."

"You couldn't keep her there forever."

"No. I left her hanging there each day, and after work I would go out there and dress her and have sex with her. I was not sure what to do with her. I wanted something—something to keep."

"You had pictures."

"Something more. I thought I could make paperweights out of her breasts. I cut off her right breast and I was going to make a plastic mold and then I could make lead paperweights. I skinned out the breast and stretched the skin over a sawdust mound, and then I tacked the edges onto a board. I used plastic to make a mold, but it didn't work. I added too much hardener, and it didn't turn out like I wanted."

Jim Stovall thought of the few killers in history whose fetishes had extended to mutilation and subsequent preservation of the bodies. It was a blessedly rare phenomenon. Until Brudos, Ed Gein of Wisconsin was the best known—and the little recluse who had hated his mother so much that he had killed her and other older women and made vests of their dried flesh. But Ed Gein had been a lifelong bachelor, absolutely ruled by his hated mother; this man had a wife, children, an education, and a brilliance in his work. And still he recounted the acting out of his terrible fantasies in a voice as commonplace as if he were describing how to rewire a lamp.

Brudos' voice cut into Stovall's thoughts. "You guys almost caught me on Jan Whitney. I was scared to death."

"What do you mean?"

"The wife and I went to Portland around Thanksgiving, and I left the girl hanging in my shop. Some guy drove his car into my garage and left a hole in it. The police came out, and they wanted to get into the garage, but it was locked. That was close.

"When I got home, I found their card and so I took the girl out of the workshop and put her in the pumphouse in the backyard and covered her with a sheet of plastic. Then I called the cops and they came out and checked my workshop. They never suspected anything, and there was this wide-open hole there. If they'd shone a light in, they maybe could have seen her hanging there. . . ."

If only. If only. Those thoughts came up so often in a homicide investigation. If the victim had not gone where she had—if she had not somehow crossed the path of a killer ready to strike. If *this* had happened, then the tragedy would not have happened. For those who believe in fate, it is easier to fathom. If only Jan Whitney's body had been discovered in November 1968, then Brudos would have been stopped. Then Karen Sprinker and Linda Salee would be alive.

Stovall easily kept Brudos going on his monologue, so caught up was the prisoner in revealing his terrible scenario. "You did dispose of the body then?"

"I threw her in a river. I weighted her down and threw her in a river. The water was very high."

"Which river?"

"The Willamette."

"Where was that—at what point on the river?"

"I don't care to say."

"Was it in Portland?"

"No."

"Was it the Long Tom—and not the Willamette?"

"I told you it was the Willamette. That's enough. It was a long time ago. It doesn't matter."

Stovall wondered at Brudos' sudden reluctance; he would give the most minute and horrific details, and then balk at something that seemed simple. He seemed to believe that, without a body, he could not be convicted of killing Jan Whitney. He did not know that "corpus delecti" is not a human body at all, but rather "the body of the crime." He knew little of the law, obviously, despite his superior attitude.

"Was it at Independence?"

"I can't say."

Stovall mentioned other bridges in the Salem area, but he thought Brudos' reaction to the suggestion of the bridge at Independence was the most telling. No body had been found there, and it might never be after six months without discovery.

"Jan Whitney's car was not on the freeway when it was found. It was somewhere else."

"I went back and moved it after I had her hoisted up in my shop. I tied it to mine with a tow bar and pulled it into the rest stop at Santiam. I was going to get rid of it entirely, but I saw three state police cars while I was towing it—two going south and one going north. I couldn't take the chance that one of them might stop me and ask about her car. So I just towed it into the Santiam rest stop, locked it, and left it."

"What would you have used to weight Jan Whitney's body down? Whatever it was, it must have been effective."

"Scrap iron. I had scrap iron out in the pumphouse."

Jim Stovall considered the information he had elicited from Jerry Brudos thus far. He had two confessions—verbal confessions—on homicides whose victims might never be found. Jerry Brudos certainly had knowledge that no one else could have known; he had mentioned details that had been withheld from the news media. He knew the dates, the places, and the manner of death. Or did he? Without the bodies, no one could say what the manner of death had been. One thing was certain: Brudos' confessed acts against nature had grown increasingly violent. First the theft of undergarments and shoes, then the choking of women, then rape, and then murder.

The homicide of Linda Slawson had, according to Brudos, not involved rape—only the dressing and redressing of the body. Jan Whitney's body had been violated again and again after death. It was as if the obsessive perversions that drove Brudos grew like a cancer within him, demanding always new horrors to satisfy and titillate that malignancy.

With every sensational murder case, there are a half-dozen or more men who confess to the crimes. They want attention, a sense of importance at being, however briefly, in the limelight—or they gain some erotic stimulation from lying about the details of crimes they never committed.

At this point in the interrogation, Stovall had to look at the two confessions with suspicion. Ninety percent of him thought he had the right man, and he was positive he had the man who had threatened Liane Brumley and tried to abduct her. But Stovall had to be careful in correlating what the suspect had said about Whitney and Slawson. It was possible that Brudos was only a weirdo, a student of newspaper accounts of sexual crimes, who had concocted his own fantasy stories.

Each bit of information gleaned in the interview was thoroughly checked, even as Brudos' statements continued. Each time Stovall stepped from the room, he handed notes to Frazier and other members of the team for follow-up.

Brudos had said that Jan Whitney's car had been broken down on the I-5 on the evening of November 26. Frazier called the Albany station of the state police and asked them to check back through their logs during late November 1968 for a possible corroboration of that information.

"Yes," the answer came back. "One of our troopers noted a red-and-white Nash Rambler parked on the east shoulder of I-5 at seven minutes after ten P.M. on November 26—at milepost seventy, two miles south of Albany. No driver or passengers in the area. It was noted, and the trooper on the next shift would have tagged it for towing if it had still been there. But it was gone by the next shift."

That information fit exactly with what Brudos had said. That spot at milepost seventy was just about ten miles from the spot in the Santiam parking lot where the car was eventually located. Someone *had* moved it in the wee hours of the morning. . . .

Frazier did a tedious hand check through all the Salem Police department's accident reports for the Thanksgiving weekend of 1968. He found the report of a car that had skidded off Center Street into a garage at 3123 Center. Minor damage reported. Occupants not at home.

Frazier located the traffic investigator who had left his card at the little gray house and who had subsequently interviewed Jerry Brudos. Yes, there had been a hole in the workshop portion of the garage, a gap in the splintered siding. It had seemed a routine investigation, with nothing to make him suspicious. He had seen only a family home, a few children's toys cluttering the back porch. Nothing at all to indicate there was a virtual abattoir within the garage, a torture chamber. Brudos had seemed anxious to get the place fixed so the rain wouldn't get in. The officer had been in the garage and workshop to check the damage from the inside, and it had looked just like anybody's garage. No body. Nothing strange in there at all.

But of course by then Brudos had, according to his statement, hidden Jan Whitney's mutilated body in the pumphouse.

The facts were beginning to mesh perfectly with the suspect's almost unbelievable confessions.

There was something else that Brudos could not have known without having been there. The long-line black bra found on Karen Sprinker's body. The mention of that bra had been Brudos' first slip, the initial fissure in the wall the suspect had built up.

If Brudos had killed Karen Sprinker, she would have been his third victim, according to his own recital of facts. Each case had been a little worse than the one before. Jan Whitney had allegedly had one breast amputated; Stovall knew that Karen Sprinker's body had been missing both breasts.

The detective truly dreaded hearing the next confession, but he would have to listen. The dialogue was an established thing now, and the original duo of players would continue. There could be no substitution of interrogators.

—— 16 ——

"It was in March . . ." Stovall said. "When Karen Sprinker disappeared . . ."

"The twenty-seventh."

"Yes. A weekday. It always seemed to be on a weekday."

"I spent weekends with my family," Brudos said.

"Had you ever seen Karen Sprinker before?"

"No. It wasn't that girl who attracted me. She just happened to be there."

"Where would that be?"

"Meier and Frank, of course. Everybody knows that—it was in all the papers. I have clippings at home that say that."

"That's true. You weren't working that day?"

"I had a sick day. I had a bad headache in the morning, and I didn't go to work."

"You didn't stay at home, though."

"No. I was just driving around. I drove by Meier and Frank, and I saw this girl."

"Was it Karen?"

"I told you it wasn't."

Brudos was cocky now. He seemed proud of the fact that he had managed his crime in broad daylight in the midst of a crowd of shoppers.

"I was just driving around, as I said, and I saw a girl near Meier and Frank. She was wearing a miniskirt and high heels. It was about ten in the morning. I watched her and she went into the store. The way she looked, her clothing and her shoes, turned me on. I had to have her.

"I drove into the parking garage and I parked on the third floor. I looked for the girl in the miniskirt inside the store. I must have spent an hour or more looking for her—but she was gone. Maybe she went out another door or something. Anyway, I couldn't find her and I went back to my car. I mean, I was walking back toward my car when I saw the other girl."

"Karen Sprinker?"

"I guess so. I didn't know her name. She had on a green sweater and a matching skirt. I didn't like her shoes, but she was a pretty girl with long dark hair. I watched her while she locked her car and then came down the steps toward the door into the store."

The description sounded so familiar to Stovall. Of course. This was the way the investigating team had pictured Karen's abduction. Standing there in the empty parking garage, they had visualized the way it must have been—ghost images left behind, almost palpable in their intensity.

"She reached to open the door, and I grabbed her by the shoulder. She turned around, startled-like, and saw the pistol I was pointing at her. I said, 'Don't scream and I won't hurt you. Come with me and I won't hurt you.' "

"Did she scream?"

"Of course not. She said she would do whatever I wanted if I just didn't shoot her. She kept saying that—several times—as if she was trying to convince me. I walked her to my car and put her inside. Nobody was in the parking garage."

Brudos continued in his monologue, intent now on recreating what had occurred two months before. "I drove to my house and into the garage."

"Was your wife home?"

"No. She was over at her girlfriend's house. She was always over there visiting. The girl—Karen—was still telling me that she would do anything to keep me from shooting her. I asked her if she had ever had a man before, and she said 'No.' She said she was in her period. That was true; she was wearing a Tampax."

Stovall knew this was correct information, and a detail withheld from anyone but the investigating team.

"I raped her—there on the floor of my workshop."

"Did she resist you?"

"No, she was afraid of the gun. Afterward she said she had to use the bathroom, so I took her into the house and allowed her to do that."

"That would have been out the side door of the garage and through the breezeway there to the back door?"

"Yes. She didn't try to run away or anything. I still had the gun. Then I took her back out to the workshop. I wanted some pictures of her. I took some in her clothes, and some in her underwear, and some in underwear I had out there. I had her wear the black patent-leather high heels that I have, because hers were very plain and low. I took a lot of pictures."

Stovall thought of the brilliant, gentle girl, trying to reason with a maniac, believing that she could keep him calm by going along with his orders. She would have been so frightened, and yet hoping desperately that he would set her free when he had finished with her. If she had fought him, what would have happened? Maybe she would have had a chance while she was in the parking garage, or even when she walked from the garage to the house—only twenty feet or so from a busy street. Maybe not. And yet Stovall doubted that Brudos would have had the guts to shoot her where there was a possibility that someone would hear.

So many female victims made the mistake of thinking that reason can temper madness. The odds are always better if a woman screams and kicks and draws attention in a public place. If a rapist or kidnapper shows enough violence to approach a woman and attempt to take her away by force, there is every possibility that he will show no mercy at all when he gets his victim alone in an isolated spot. Captivity and torture are the thrust of his aberration. Pity and compassion have no place in the makeup of a sexual criminal.

Too late for Karen.

"I tied her hands in back of her and told her I had to do that to keep her from going away. She said that wasn't necessary, but I couldn't trust her. Then I put

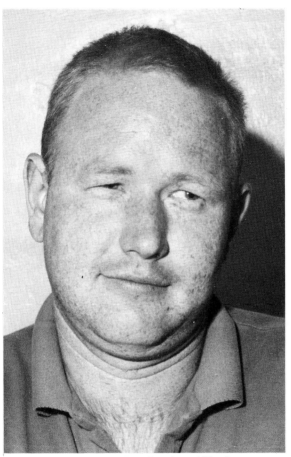

Jerome Brudos, the "Lust Killer,"
as he was being arrested
(photographed by Detective Jim Stovall).

Karen Sprinker, a 19-year-old freshman at Oregon State University at Corvallis, was kidnapped from a Salem, Oregon, department store.

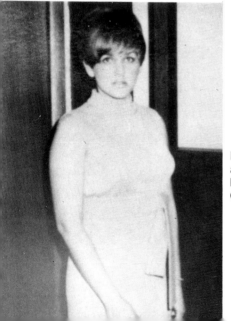

Linda Salee, a petite, athletic 22-year-old, was kidnapped in Portland, Oregon.

Sharon Wood, a 24-year-old secretary, was attacked by
Brudos in the parking garage at Portland State University.
She fought him and escaped, battered but alive.

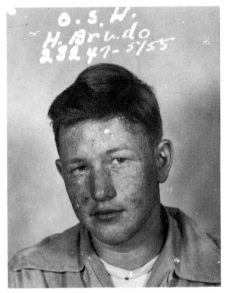

Jerry Brudos at 17. His attack on two teenage girls led him to be committed to the Oregon State Hospital for the treatment of sexual deviation and fetishism.

Detective Jim Stovall of the Salem, Oregon, police department discovered the shocking details of the Brudos murders.

Detective Jerry Frazier, standing, and Jim Stovall, seated, search Brudos' house after his confession. Frazier and Stovall had been up for days, questioning Brudos, searching for evidence.

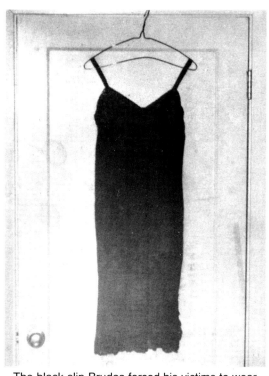

The black slip Brudos forced his victims to wear.

Salem Police Detective Jerry Frazier spotted this rope with its very distinctive knot in Brudos' garage, and thought it matched the knots found on the victims' bodies. Brudos offered Frazier this knot—which subsequently helped convict him.

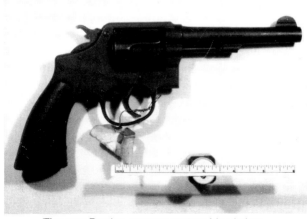

The gun Brudos used to abduct his victims.

SURVEYOR

Brudos on his way to court. (Photo credit: Gerry Lewin)

a rope around her neck. I had it attached to a 'come-along.'

"I swung the rope up on the hoist, and tightened it around her neck. I asked her if it was too tight, and she said it was."

Jerry Brudos, who had never had control over women, had been in absolute control of Karen Sprinker's life.

And he chose to end it.

"I gave the 'come-along' about three more pulls and it lifted her off the ground. She kicked a little and she died."

Stovall's hand tightened around his pen, but he betrayed no other feelings. It was far too late to help Karen; there was nothing to do now but see that this man was off the streets forever—that he would no longer have a chance to act out his sick fantasies.

Brudos described how he had violated the girl's body after death, after taking time out to go into the house to be with his family.

"I went back out later and had sex with her. Then I cut off both of her breasts to make plastic molds. I couldn't get the percentage of hardener right this time either, but they turned out a little better than with the girl from the freeway."

"Jan Whitney."

"Yes. Her. I dressed the girl from Meier and Frank—Karen—in her own cotton panties and the green sweater and skirt. But I used the wide bra instead of her own. I stuffed it with paper towels so it looked all right and so she wouldn't bleed on my car."

"Where did you get that bra?"

"From a clothesline in Portland a couple of years ago. No, wait. Maybe it was one that belonged to my wife. I have a lot of them, so I can't be sure."

"Did you keep Karen's body for several days—the way you kept Jan Whitney's?"

Brudos shook his head. "No. I waited until my wife and the kids had gone to bed, and I took off about two A.M. for the Long Tom River. I weighted the body down with a cylinder head I had for a car. I tossed her into the river on the upstream side."

"Where did you get the cylinder head?"

"I had the stuff around; I fix cars a lot."

"Where are the pictures you took of Karen?"

Brudos smiled, secure that he could count on Darcie's absolute obedience to his wishes. "Gone. They've all been destroyed."

The two men had been cloistered in the little interview room for a long time. Neither smoked, but the air was heavy—perhaps from the weight of the words that had been spoken. Outside, it was spring and the huge magnolia trees on the courthouse lawn opened their waxy white blooms. Parks around Salem were filled with picnickers, some of them on the banks of the Willamette River. Inside the jail complex, there was no season at all, and certainly no sense of holiday.

There was a break in the interrogation; what had been said was too horrific to continue on endlessly. There would be more; Jerry Brudos seemed consumed with the need to pour it all out. He showed no regret at all about what he had done; he whined instead about his cell and the food, and asked for his wife. He talked to Dale Drake, his attorney. What was said in that conversation was privileged communication, but Drake was pale and his jaw was set when he emerged from the conference.

"Did you get anything?" Stovall's fellow investigators asked the detective, and he nodded grimly. He moved to a worktable where he could transcribe what he had heard onto the yellow legal pad, pages and pages of unbelievable cruelty. So many victims who had never had a chance. He indexed, and he correlated, and he saw that all the pieces had fallen into place. All but Linda Salee's murder.

And that would be covered in the next interview.

Brudos ate. Stovall could not. An hour or two later, they began again. Slowly. Easing back into the intimate revelations.

"We're into April now, Jerry," Stovall commented. "Can you recall your activities in April?"

"I remember everything. I have an excellent memory."

"Linda Salee disappeared on April 23, a Wednesday. Would that be the first . . . activity that month?"

"No. You know about the girl on the rail tracks. That was Tuesday. Before that—on Monday—I went to Portland, and I went out to Portland State University . . ."

Were there more? Were there other girls who had not yet been found? It was possible. Considering all the rivers coursing through the state of Oregon, there could be other bodies drifting there, unknown to the investigators. Stovall waited.

"I went up there to find a girl. I saw one in the parking complex at Portland State. She was older, maybe twenty-two to twenty-four years old. I had the pistol—it wasn't real; it was a toy, but it looked real. She fought me. She grabbed for the gun and she tried to twist it out of my hand. She was screaming and she caught my finger in the trigger guard and damn near broke it. She was attracting attention, and I knew I had to get away from there. I managed to get loose of her, and I walked up to the next floor of the parking garage, where my car was—I didn't run because that would have made people suspicious. I got in and drove away."

He was a coward, obviously. Fight him in public, and he ran like a rabbit. Stovall wondered if the girl from Portland had any idea of what she had escaped.

"You drove on home, then?"

"Yeah. The next day, I was driving around in Salem and I saw this young girl on the Southern Pacific tracks. I showed her the plastic pistol and told her that she was to come with me. I had her by the shoulder and I pulled her between two houses. She said she could walk by herself. I had her almost into the car—I had my friend's car that day—when she balked. She took off running. There was some woman working in her yard, and the girl ran to her, and I got in the car and took off."

"Two days in a row, you struck out. That might have made you a little angry—a little disappointed."

"A little."

"You might have been afraid that you had been seen, that you could be identified by someone."

"No. I got away easily both times. I didn't worry."

"You plan well. You probably worked out another plan that would work."

"Yes. I always had another plan, a backup plan. I went back to Portland the next day."

"That would be the twenty-third, then?"

"That's right. I had a badge, looked just like a real police badge—you can buy them, you know. I bought it right there in Lloyd Center; it was a toy, but you'd have to look real close to be sure. I started looking for a girl."

"You found a girl?"

Brudos nodded. "I saw this girl in the parking garage. She was walking toward her car and she had her arms full of packages. I went up to her and showed her the badge and told her I was taking her into custody for shoplifting. I said I was a special police officer assigned to Lloyd Center and would have to take her downtown with me. She believed me, but she said she hadn't stolen anything—that she had the sales slips to prove it. But she came with me quietly. She didn't fight me at all. She just got in my car."

"Did she ask questions when you went by downtown Portland and got on the freeway for Salem?"

"No. It was funny; it was like she wanted to go with me. She didn't say anything at all. She just rode along nicely."

"You drove with her all the way to Salem? That would have meant she was in the car with you for an hour."

"That's right. I got to my house and I drove into the garage and closed the doors. I told the girl to follow me, and I started for the house. I didn't know my wife was home. She walked out on the back porch just as I left the garage. I held my hand back and warned the girl not to come out, and she stopped. My wife didn't see her. I told Darcie to go back into the house and stay there because I had something important to do in the shop.

"My wife said that dinner was almost ready, and I

told her I'd be in in a minute. Then I tied the girl up with a rope and I went into the house for dinner. The girl was out there waiting in the garage. My wife said she was going to the health spa that night and that a baby-sitter was coming. That was okay, because she wouldn't bother me out in my workshop."

"You're telling me that Linda Salee was out there in the garage alone while you went in and ate dinner?"

"Yes. But she was tied up. Funny thing, though. When I went back out there to check on her after I ate, she'd gotten loose of the rope. She hadn't tried to leave the shop, and she hadn't even used the phone out there. She was just waiting for me, I guess."

It *was* odd, Stovall thought. But there might have been a close time element; the woman might have struggled free just as Brudos walked in the door. More likely, she had been terrorized into immobility. Just as a mouse tormented by a cat will simply give up, unable to run any longer, paralyzed by fright and indecision.

Or perhaps it was all a delusion in Brudos' mind, his surface ego demanding that the women he kidnapped should find him attractive and would seek out his company.

There was no way to tell now.

"I got the leather strap out—the postal strap that I used on the woman from the freeway—and I put it around her neck and pulled her off her feet. She was a little woman—short and light. She turned around, kind of, and she said, 'Why are you doing this to me?'

"I pulled the strap tighter and she went limp. I put her on the floor and got on top of her. I think I was inside her when she died."

"She just waited for you in the shop? She didn't try to fight you at all?" Stovall asked.

"Well . . . after I went back out there, I guess she did fight me. I don't know why—because she'd been so quiet all the time coming down and when I first put her in there. She fought me pretty bad until I managed to get the strap around her neck. I didn't like her—the way she kicked and scratched when I told her not to."

It was clear that Brudos felt a great deal of resent-

ment toward Linda Salee, the girl who had resisted
him. She was the first one; the others had gone down
gently, but this athletic little woman had tried to live,
pitting her strength against the hulking killer. If she
only had fought earlier . . .

Still angry, Brudos had chosen to punish Linda Salee
after her death. Mercifully, it no longer mattered.

"I hung her up by her neck from the hook in the
ceiling where I'd hung the others. I had this experiment I wanted to try, using electricity."

Stovall tensed inwardly. There had been those strange
marks on Linda Salee's body, the tissue near her ribs
showing evidence of burns—something that had baffled both him and Medical Examiner Brady.

"An experiment?"

"Yeah. Once I had her up on the hook, I took her
clothes off—having the hook there made dressing and
undressing them easier. I took these two hypodermic
needles and I stuck them on each side of her rib cage,
and then I had electric leads attached to the needles.
Then I plugged in the leads to see what she would
do—if she would dance, or what. It didn't work; it just
burned her."

"You kept her there for a while?"

"One day and one night. I raped her again, but I
didn't like her body. Her breasts were all pink—the
nipples weren't dark like they should be; they just all
blended in together I didn't cut them off because they
didn't appeal to me. I made some circular paper cones
and put them over her breasts to make plastic molds,
but the epoxy set up hot and it didn't work. I wasn't
able to get a really perfect mold from any of them.
When you salt a breast down and dry it, it shrinks to
about a third of its normal size. I'm sure there's a way
to do it so it will work, but I never could."

Thank God he would not have another chance to
try.

"When did you take the girl's body out of your
shop?"

"The second night. I tied the overdrive unit to her
and put her in the Long Tom."

Jim Stovall went over all the versions of the murders

again and again. He would approach the vital points from one angle, and then come back from another angle. The facts never changed; they were entrenched in the suspect's mind—as if he had cherished his secret killing games and relived them until he knew every facet of them perfectly.

The thought of what Jerry Brudos had done was so despicable that a normal man could scarcely contemplate it without feeling a sickness in the gut. Jim Stovall had no doubt at all that if Brudos had not been caught, he would have continued to kill month by month until he himself grew old and died.

Brudos was taken back to his cell, and Stovall walked past the reporters who had clustered around the jail all weekend, eager for a headline story. The Associated Press had got wind of the arrest in the dorm at Corvallis, and printed that. They did not have the name of the suspect, or any details; they only knew that something big was in the wind. They would get nothing at this point of the probe.

Stovall stepped outside and thought the air smelled wonderful, but he was exhausted after three days of the most intense and macabre interrogation he had ever participated in.

Still, he wondered if he could sleep.

— 17 —

The headlines came on Monday morning. On June 2, 1969, an anxious public pored over this slight information:

> Marion County District Attorney Gary Gortmaker announced this morning that Jerome Henry Brudos, 30, a Salem electrician, has been charged with first-degree murder in the death of an Oregon woman. The victim listed in the charge is Karen Sprinker, 19, of Salem.

District Attorney Gortmaker declined to give the press any further information. Nor would he say where Brudos was being held: public feeling ran hot and vengeful; in the old days when the area was Oregon Territory, a man suspected of the crimes that rumor attributed to Brudos would have been summarily hung by an angry mob. Oregon had become a "civilized" state where a man accused must go through the due process of law. And yet . . . Officials feared what might happen if they revealed Jerry Brudos' location.

"Due process" meant that there were many legal and investigative procedures to be accomplished. A search warrant for Brudos' home and workshop, for his vehicles, a further check on facts elicited through Stovall's interviews, and then formal arraignment. In the face of cruel madness, calm, sane steps must be taken.

Detectives checked with Portland police to see if there had been a rape complaint in 1967 that resembled the case Brudos had discussed—a sleeping woman being throttled and sexually attacked. There was. Portland police records indicated their case, #67-35144, had occurred on May 18, 1967—"Assault, Possible Rape." The victim, Joyce Lynn Cassel, had given a statement that correlated almost exactly with what Jerry Brudos had described.

She had lost three pairs of shoes and a black bra. When she had regained consciousness, she'd found her window screen had been removed and set aside. She lived in an apartment on South East Pine. She had not really seen her attacker, because she had been wakened from a deep sleep and attacked in a darkened room.

Had Janet Shanahan also been one of Brudos' victims? Stovall thought not. He had questioned Brudos about the woman murdered in Eugene and left in her car, and Brudos had appeared to be totally unfamiliar with that case. Since he had freely admitted the other four homicides, there was no reason to think he would omit that case from his smug recital. He had also looked blank when Stephanie Vilkco was mentioned.

Brudos balked at reducing his verbal statements to written form, as if he felt his words had no substance that could harm him if they were not down in black and white in a formal statement.

There was now probable cause for a search warrant. Until the verbal statements, probable cause could not have been proved absolutely. A search warrant is a precise document; the items sought must be listed. The preservation of citizen rights in America does not allow lawmen to swoop down upon premises to seek out whatever may be there; the officers must list evidence they seek before they can obtain a search warrant. And if they should find items outside the sphere of an original search warrant, the premises must then be secured until an additional warrant is issued.

At this point, Stovall was able to list items that might well be found in the Brudos home: pictures, underwear, shoes, auto parts, copper wire, rope, the hook in the workshop ceiling, the "come-along," a leather postal strap, possessions belonging to the victims—and possibly even the molds made from the victims' breasts. Brudos had apparently not suspected that his arrest was so near, and the man who had hoarded all manner of bizarre paraphernalia might well have failed to dispose of it.

The first two elements of a solid case were now present. The circumstantial evidence. The confession. And still, there was a third element yet to be discovered: the physical evidence.

The physical evidence went back again to the placard over Jim Stovall's desk: "THE ELEMENTS OF SCIENTIFIC PROOF MUST BE PRESENT TO ESTABLISH AND SUBSTANTIATE A SCIENTIFIC CONCLUSION."

Marion County Circuit Court Judge Val D. Sloper issued a search warrant for the premises of the Brudos home early Tuesday morning, June 3. Armed with the search warrant and accompanied by Attorney Dale Drake and Larry Brudos, the defendant's brother, a group of investigators met at the gray shake house on Center Street. Larry Brudos unlocked the doors, and Stovall, Frazier, D.A. Gortmaker, and Lieutenant Robert W. Pinnick of the state crime lab and his assistants entered.

Nothing had been destroyed. Darcie Brudos had disobeyed her husband overtly for the first time in their marriage. And so all the grotesque tools of Jerry Brudos' crimes remained.

The men worked carefully, moving with excruciating slowness through the empty structures, a foot at a time, and then further once they had determined that they had obtained all evidence from each portion. They could not risk destroying evidence with a single thoughtless step. They photographed constantly, preserving the original appearance of the home and workshop.

Given other circumstances, many of the tools and much of the equipment might be considered ordinary. Given *these* circumstances, they took on macabre meaning.

There was a hook in the workshop ceiling; there was a thirty-foot three-sixteenth-inch rope and a "come-along" to winch an object upward. There was a leather postal strap with a cinch. There was more nylon cord. There were a vise and a locked tool chest. There were hundreds of keys, including a key ring in a brown case bearing numerous keys that seemed to be for cars and for house locks.

The searchers observed full scuba gear and fins, and reloading equipment for ammunition. They found a chest full of women's shoes—including spike patent-leather heels, other high heels, and a pair of low, laced shoes. There were ashes in a green plastic waste-basket that looked to be the residue of burned film or photographs.

There was a large blue shag rug on the floor of the workshop, a rug that seemed out of place in the area.

The investigators moved on to the main house and up into the dusty attic; it smelled of sun-baked wood, and cobwebs wafted in the slight breeze from the open door.

Most of Jerry Brudos' collection was in the attic. There were forty pairs of high-heeled shoes in all sizes from four to ten. White shoes. Brown shoes. Red shoes. Calf. Suede. Straw. Patent-leather. Open-toed sandals. Pumps. All of them slightly worn, and some of them curved to the shape of their original owners' feet.

And of course there were soft piles of undergarments, stolen by Brudos over the years, all the thefts managed when Brudos' compulsion gripped him. They found fifteen brassieres—fancy bras of lace and satin and sheer black nylon, and more utilitarian bras of cotton. They ranged in size from 30 A to 38 D. Some still smelled faintly of perfume; some were freshly laundered.

There were lacy slips and panties. There were dozens of girdles, all of them small-sized.

Some of the dust in the attic was thick and untouched, and there were clear spots where the big man had crouched as he pawed through his treasures, stimulating himself with his fantasies—all of this part of his hidden sex life.

The house itself seemed the home of an average young family—the children's toys still scattered where they had been left when Darcie Brudos abandoned the house to take comfort with her family. The kitchen was neat; there was still food in the refrigerator. But over the counter there was a roll of brown paper towels—towels that would prove to be identical in class and characteristics with those wadded lumps taken from the black bra Karen Sprinker wore.

In the living room, Criminalist Pinnick ran his hands along a high shelf over the fireplace. He touched an object and lifted it down.

It was a metal mold, formed in an exact replica of a female breast. The breast was full, and perfectly shaped. It was too perfect to have been fashioned from clay.

It was real.

There were photos on the shelf too—pictures of Brudos in a black lace slip.

When a further search of the house netted nothing more of evidentiary value, the men returned to the shop. They looked in a dim corner of the shop and saw—on a bench there—another breast mold. This breast was small; it had obviously come from a different source than the lush mold in the living room.

It looked real too—resin had coated human flesh, and taken on its form.

The toolbox lock was forced open. There were tools in the lower portion of it. In the upper-right-hand drawer there was a thick packet of pictures. Pinnick lifted them out carefully.

"Oh, my God . . ."

The investigators saw the glossy black-and-white shots, the pinups of a madman. Jan Whitney and Karen Sprinker—helpless in the lens of their captor.

It was deathly quiet in the shop as Pinnick slowly revealed each photo, holding them by the edges where no fingerprints could cling. The men gazed at the pictures, feeling a sense of personal intrusion on the privacy of the lost girls. Not one of them spoke; it was an experience they had never had before, and hoped devoutly never to have again.

There was a picture of a nude woman suspended from the ceiling by the damnable hook and its intricate pulley arrangements. Her face was obscured by a black hood. It would prove to be the body of Jan Whitney.

That would tie in with the verbal statements given to Stovall. Jan Whitney had not lived to get out of

Brudos' car, had died there with the leather postal strap around her neck.

Karen Sprinker had endured captivity in this very workshop. She stared mutely into the camera, and it was almost impossible to describe the expression on her face. Fear, yes. But something more—a kind of resignation, as if she had detached herself from the proceedings, as if her essence was gone and only her body submitted to the demands of the man behind the camera.

She wore different garments in the pictures. A bra and girdle that had not been her own. Another shot with a different brassiere and girdle. There was a photo where she wore only panties, and another where she had on just a bra. Her feet were encased in the spike-heeled black patent-leather pumps; her own plain flats rested on the fluffy blue rug.

"Damn him," one officer breathed. "Damn him."

Yes, damn him.

There was a black three-ring binder full of more photographs, variations on the other pictures. Many, many photos of nude female torsos, their heads snipped away by scissors.

It was obvious that all the pictures had been taken in the garage workshop; the blue shag rug showed in all the photos, and the Craftsman tool chest could be seen just behind the victims. It seemed impossible to think that Jerry Brudos could have held his captives here, torturing them and then killing them within feet of neighboring homes, just a breezeway removed from his own home. Yet the pictures established that. They substantiated the terrible confessions he had made to Jim Stovall.

Why hadn't the girls screamed for help? It seemed incomprehensible that they had not. And yet there is an explanation. There is profound shock in any kidnapping or hostage situation, a kind of denial. *This can't be happening to me.* Torn from their normal activities in situations that seemed safe, Brudos' victims had to have been instantly plunged into ultimate fear and denial. Studies done of prisoners in concentration camps—the survivors—elicited the theory that those who survived were the individuals who were able to override their shock and terror early on. Instead of "this can't be happening," they knew that it *was* happening, that it was true—and they fought back. Those who could not deal with reality, however terrible it was, died.

And so had Linda Slawson and Jan Whitney and Karen Sprinker and Linda Salee. Before they had time to accept their danger, they were killed.

The investigators had found so many pictures, and they found too the ashes of what seemed to be burned photographs, charred bits of proof sheets in the wastebasket and in the backyard. What had those pictures shown?

Lieutenant Pinnick spotted the corner of still another photograph, a photo caught between a workbench and a wall. He pulled it out of the spot where it had apparently been overlooked.

It was an awful picture. A girl's body, clothed in a black lace slip and panties with garters, hung suspended from the ceiling. The camera angled up to her crotch—reflected in a mirror on the floor. The ropes swirled surrealistically, and the girl's muscles were relaxed. Her face didn't show, but clearly, she was dead.

"Look," Stovall said quietly. "Look at the bottom."

"What *is* that?"

"It's him."

It was. In the lower corner of the photo, there was the frozen image of a killer, caught unawares in the mirror. Brudos had photographed himself as he focused on the body of his victim, capturing his own lust-filled, slack face. He would not have dared to keep such a picture. But he had apparently lost track of this one last print when it slipped behind the workbench. It was as if an unseen hand had secreted it there so that justice would be done.

The monster had photographed himself at the apex of his madness.

The searchers had been in the house and garage for hours, and they were finally convinced they had found all that they had sought. They cleared the property after changing the locks, and left it cordoned off with ropes and signs that forbade trespassing. All the physical evidence found was removed to the state crime lab for testing and evaluation.

Without the rest of it, that single picture would be enough. There was no way Jerry Brudos could explain that away, no chance for him to call back his confession. He had killed, and he had photographed himself in the very midst of his killing frenzy.

There was the matter of the hundreds of keys Jerry Brudos had collected. Where were the locks that they fit? Was there still more corroborating physical evidence among them that would tie him to his victims? Checking them all would be a monumental task, but Stovall, Frazier, and Daugherty did it.

The three investigators went first to McMinnville, where Jan Whitney's Rambler was in storage. The keys on the brown leather key ring opened the trunk of that car. Next they tried the ignition, and the lock turned. To be absolutely sure, the detectives installed a new battery in the Nash and tried the key again.

The engine turned over immediately.

The other keys did not work in Jan Whitney's McMinnville apartment. But the probers learned that Jan had lived previously in an apartment building near Portland State University. They had to hurry; even then, the buildings were being torn down to make way for a freeway. They located Jan's old apartment and found it had not yet been slated for the wrecking ball. Just in time. Two of the keys they had found worked. One opened the main entrance to the apartment building, and the other opened the apartment door to the unit where she had lived. They removed the locks, and those mechanisms, along with Jan Whitney's car, became three more items listed in the growing inventory of physical evidence.

Ned Rawls, Jerry Brudos' friend who had worked on cars with him for years, came to the state crime lab. Before he was shown the engine head that had been tied to Karen Sprinker's body, Rawls described to Lieutenant Pinnick a General Motors head that he had worked on with Brudos in early 1969. Several valves had been bad on the part, and Rawls remembered which of them had needed to be reground. To the nonmechanically minded, an engine head is an engine head; to Ned Rawls such parts were highly individual units. He told Pinnick where each flaw would be if this was the head that he and Brudos had worked on, which Brudos had kept at his house on Center Street.

Pinnick noted Rawls's specific descriptions. And then the two men went to where the engine head in question was stored. When the grease covering was wiped away, *every single specific detailed was present.*

It was another piece of physical evidence that was well-nigh irrefutable.

— 18 —

Salem attorney George Rhoten, one of the finest legal minds in Oregon, had joined the Brudos defense team when Jerome Henry Brudos was arraigned on June 4, 1969. He was still charged with only one murder, Karen Sprinker's, but charges in the Whitney and Salee cases were filed within a week.

Rhoten and Dale Drake had seen "the picture." A defense team composed of F. Lee Baily, Percy Foreman, Melvin Belli, and Clarence Darrow himself could not have formulated a defense on the basis of total innocence after seeing that.

Nor did Rhoten and Drake try. When Judge Sloper said, "You are charged with first-degree murder in the death of Karen Elena Sprinker. How do you plead?" Jerry Brudos answered, "Not guilty, and not guilty by reason of insanity."

Was Jerry Brudos insane, and insane under the law? According to the M'Naghten Rule, the legal guideline in most states in America, a defendant must be proved to have been unable to determine the nature and consequences of his act *at the time of the commission of the crime*. In layman's terms, had Jerry Brudos known the difference between right and wrong when he killed his victims?

Since no psychiatrist has ever been present to observe a killer at the time of his crimes, psychiatric evaluation must be done sometime after those crimes. The doctors' value judgments must be done then in retrospect, an imprecise and iffy method—but the only way possible.

One basic rule of thumb used by a prosecuting attorney to convince a jury that a defendant was *not* insane

161

during the crime is to show that he made efforts to cover up his crimes and to escape arrest. The only shoo-in for mental commitment rather than prison is the killer who is found babbling nonsense next to the corpse of his victim.

That doesn't happen often.

Jerry Brudos made elaborate preparations before his crimes, plotted them with cruel cleverness, and hid his guilt deftly thereafter. And still, the details of his crimes were so perverse that it was hard for some to believe he was, indeed, sane.

The teenage Jerry Brudos had been dismissed from an Oregon state hospital on the supposition that he only needed "to grow up." Well, he had grown up, and during all those years his perversions had multiplied and grown to grotesque proportions. Now seven different psychiatrists would interview Brudos separately and present their conclusions to the court. Drs. George R. Suckow, Gerhard Haugen, Roger Smith, Guy Parvaresh, Ivor Campbell, Colin Slade, and Howard Dewey examined the defendant individually.

They observed a man who was agitated and tense now; Brudos could not sit still for an interview, but rose frequently to stride around the interview room. He often stared at objects in the room with intense scrutiny. His fingernails were bitten to the quick.

Brudos characterized himself as a loner, and yet he seemed quite affable and talkative. He spoke with grandiosity and immaturity, and peppered his conversation with unnecessary detail, avoiding issues.

On an emotional level of response, he seemed quite normal—except when he talked of the deaths of his victims. He showed no emotion at all then. No remorse. He recited his litany of murder time and time again for each psychiatrist and each psychologist, and they all saw it—he was not sorry his victims were dead. Their lives were negligible to him.

Brudos described himself to one of the doctors: "I'm a friendly person who would give you the shirt off my back if you ask for it." And yet, a few minutes later in the examination, the defendant said: "I act the way I do because everybody takes advantage of me."

He had difficulty correlating dates in his past life with events, perhaps blocking out a childhood that had been miserable. Brudos' dislike of his mother was apparent to all the men who examined him. He loved women's clothing, but he declared he had never worn his mother's clothing—had never even thought of it. Her shoes were ugly. She favored his brother . . . always. She always made *him* take second place.

Jerry Brudos' hatred for his mother seemed to color all his thinking, and examiners detected a secondary hatred for all women—except Darcie.

"She won't dress up like other women do, and that makes me feel sorry for myself," he said with tears in his eyes. "But that's the only thing wrong with her."

Jerry Brudos cried—yes—but he cried for himself. When he talked of killing the four young women, his voice was flat and precise:

" . . . I stuffed the black bra with paper—because she was bleeding so much and I didn't want to get blood in my car."

". . . her breasts had pale pink nipples and they didn't show up well so I didn't take any pictures. I couldn't get a good cast of them, so I threw them away. Then I threw her in the river."

"I had sex with her and strangled her at the same time with the postal strap."

Hours-long interviews during which Jerry Brudos cried for himself, and for his wife—but never for his victims.

Asked to describe the sort of person he was, Jerry Brudos put forward some thoughts:

"I don't like to be told what to do. I live in a world full of people, but I feel all alone. I don't know if I knew right from wrong at the time of the deaths of those girls, but I know I didn't think about it. The thing that bothers me most right now is that I'm stuck here and that means I can't maneuver or work things out for myself. Before this, I could always control things and plot out what moves I wanted to make."

Jerry asked for treatment in a hospital. He felt sure he could become a useful member of society and raise his own children. . . .

It was obvious, however, that Brudos had never before sought out treatment for his mental problems; he had given the idea lip service only when he was trapped.

Jerry Brudos was given an electroencephalograph to determine if his bizarre fantasies were the result of brain damage, and he tested normal in brain function. He tested above average in intelligence and cognitive thinking.

He was not insane under the law. Not one of the seven doctors found him to be psychotic. They deemed him fully able to participate in his defense.

Dr. Guy Parvaresh summed up his evaluation of Jerry Brudos in a letter to Brudos' attorneys:

> In psychiatric examination, he was obviously anxious, agitated, and depressed. He cried frequently, saying he was sick and that he could not have help. Throughout the detailed discussion of the crimes, he appeared very preoccupied, emotionally detached, and quite certain that "These things had to be done." There was a prevailing impression throughout the interview that basically this man had been threatened all his life with his emotional and physical existence—so much so that he has developed a well-organized paranoid thinking in that at no time after he began to get involved with a crime would he have doubt as to whether or not he should proceed. "There was no doubt they [the murders] had to be done whether I wanted it or not."
>
> In general, I did not find any evidence of a psychotic process or evidence of perceptual disturbances. His cognitive processes are well-maintained, and he is able to give details of past and recent events. Based on clinical assessment, his intellectual capacity is above average. He shows poor and faulty social judgment and certainly has no insight into his basic emotional problems. It is my clinical opinion that Mr. Brudos understands the nature of the charges against him and can assist in his own defense. This man

has a paranoid disorder and his behavior is a product of this disorder. Despite this, I believe he can differentiate between what is morally and socially right and wrong. A review of his past and the current examination make me believe this man is a menace to himself and society.

Dr. George R. Suckow, examining Jerry Brudos for the state, said virtually the same things in slightly different words:

Overall, this man describes a history going back to childhood of progressively increasing assaults upon young females, starting with fetishism for shoes and undergarments in very early childhood. One is reminded of the person who writes bad checks and does not get caught and then continues, getting worse and worse because no one draws a line showing him where appropriate behavior begins. At the point where he first came to Oregon State Hospital, essentially a line was drawn and for several years, if Mr. Brudos is to be believed, he reverted to fetishism only—but he ultimately began to progress and require increasingly bizarre things for sexual gratification. Interestingly, his sexual relationship with his wife, by his report, deteriorated over the past two years until recently it has simply been a mechanical act on her part at his insistence and not particularly satisfying to either.

Running throughout is a consistent thread of hostility toward his mother which generalizes to most women—but apparently not his wife at an overt level. On all three occasions that Mr. Brudos has requested psychiatric help, he has been in difficulty with the law. It is interesting that in the intervals between, when no one is after him, he does not require help. Though he does describe some rather elaborate fantasies of a sadistic nature toward women in particular, none of these is extensive enough or involved enough to qualify in my opinion as being delusions, since he clearly understands that they are not real, and even will discuss them in terms of how impractical they are.

In my opinion, Mr. Brudos has been aware of the nature and consequences of his actions on each and every one [crime] of which we spoke, and further he has been aware that they were wrong in the view of others.

In my opinion, his diagnosis is 301.7, Antisocial Personality, manifested by fetishism, transvestism, exhibitionism, voyeurism, and, especially, sadism. It is further my opinion that he is an extremely dangerous person to young females when not in confinement and, finally, it is my opinion that he shows little evidence of treatability, if any, for his personality disorder.

In the convoluted medicalese of the psychiatrist, Jerome Henry Brudos was quite sane, and eminently dangerous.

In the language of the man on the street, he was a monster. He would always be a monster.

Darcie Brudos never went back to live in the house on Center Street. Emotionally, she could not bear to; after reading the papers and seeing the story of her husband's alleged crimes featured on the news channels from Portland, she could not imagine living in the house again. It was a moot point anyway, because she was almost out of money and couldn't pay the rent.

She was led through the police barrier and allowed to pack her clothes and the children's, to pick up a few toys. Almost everything else had been seized for evidence, even her records. Everything. She was told that she could have some of the things later—if they proved to have no importance in the case.

Darcie and the children went first to her parents' home in Corvallis, but there wasn't much room there. Her parents agreed to care for Megan and Jason, and Darcie moved in with a cousin.

She talked to the psychiatrists, trying to answer

their questions. "He was always sensitive," she told them. "And he was strange. I was afraid of him."

"Why were you afraid?"

"Because I was all he had, and if I crossed him, I didn't know what he would do."

She answered questions about her sex life, her perceptions of what Jerry had been doing. And always she remained in shock—unable to assimilate the horror of it all. She had not known.

She had not known.

Jerry wanted her to visit him all the time. He wanted the children to visit. She went to see him, and he seemed the same—but nothing was the same, and nothing would ever be the same again. She didn't know what the police had found in Jerry's workshop, and he wouldn't tell her anything about it. But it had to be something or they wouldn't have charged him with killing Karen Sprinker and the other girls.

Darcie had nightmares, and woke with her nightgown soaked with perspiration. Her daytime thoughts weren't much better. The papers were saying that young women had been murdered in Jerry's workshop.

She could avoid visiting him for only a week or so, but then he called and was so insistent that she come. She went, but she wouldn't take Megan, no matter how he argued about it.

She wrote him a letter:

> I'll be seeing you today in about four hours. Sweetheart, I hope you will forgive me for not bringing the kids today. Please understand, because it is tearing me apart, but I really feel I'm right. Megan knows what happened, but she doesn't understand. She gets tears in her eyes every time she talks about you.
>
> Darcie Brudos

Darcie had always been easily swayed by her husband's arguments. He had controlled her life for almost eight years, telling her what to do and where to go. He did not seem angry with her that she'd failed to burn the things in his shop—maybe he didn't know. It was still very, very difficult for her to turn her back on him.

Like all the other victims, Darcie was shocked by the suddenness of the disaster that had befallen her. She too kept thinking: "This can't be happening to me."

— 19 —

On June 26, 1969, the subpoenas went out for a preliminary hearing before Jerry Brudos stood trial. The trial would be a long one, according to rumor. There were more charges now, and more victims listed. The initial list of potential witnesses included: Dr. Robert Paschko, the Salem dentist who had identified Karen Sprinker's body from dental X rays; Salem policemen Lieutenant Elwood "Hap" Hewitt, Sergeant Jim Stovall, and Detective Jerry Frazier; state policemen Lieutenant Gene Daugherty, Sergeant William Freel; Dr. William Brady, State Board of Health—the medical examiner; and Dr. Lucas Sprinker, Karen Sprinker's father. In addition, Ned Rawls's name was on the roster—Jerry Brudos' friend who had stumbled unaware into the middle of Brudos' first murder, and been turned away with a hurried lie about nitroglycerin.

Rawls had told Stovall and Daugherty about the trips to junkyards with Brudos to buy auto parts. He had also mentioned how strong Jerry Brudos was. "He could take all the weight of a three-hundred-pound freezer and never sweat. I'm strong, but his strength exceeds anything I've ever seen."

The witness list was growing longer, and Brudos' attorneys, George Rhoten and Dale Drake, foresaw a terrible macabre circus in court. They had their psychiatrists' evaluations and the reports of the state's psychiatrists. They knew that the insanity plea would not hold up; Jerome Brudos had been adjudged sane within M'Naghten's parameters. They did not relish such a trial—either for their client or for the victims' families, who would have to go through the ordeal.

Jerry Brudos had talked quite openly with Rhoten

169

and Drake, going over the murders, albeit a trifle less
specifically than he had with Jim Stovall and the psychiatric evaluators. They were convinced almost from
the beginning that their client was guilty of murder.
He had told them so himself.

A criminal defense attorney works within restrictive
bonds—both legal and ethical. He cannot reveal what
his client has said to him in privileged communication.
Yet he cannot misrepresent or falsify to the court. No
responsible criminal defense attorney would seek to
free a man of Brudos' killing propensities. When Rhoten
and Drake had reviewed the possibilities of a defense
from every angle, they saw that the *only* way to try for
a not-guilty defense was to pursue a not-guilty-by-
reason-of-insanity plea. They had approached Brudos
with their conclusions, and he had not been particularly amenable to their advice. An insanity plea warred
with his vastly overrated perception of his superior
mental abilities. He argued that it would demean him
to be portrayed as "crazy," and they countered that it
would save him from prison. And so they had convinced him and entered original pleas of not guilty,
and not guilty by reason of insanity, but Brudos had
gone along only grudgingly, taking still another opportunity to remind Rhoten that he, "the crazy man,"
had an I.Q. of 166, that he was close to or surpassing
genius.

Now, toward the end of June 1969, Rhoten and
Drake found themselves between a rock and a hard
place. Not a single psychiatrist or psychologist could
testify that Jerry Brudos was insane at the time of his
crimes—or at present. Whatever basis there might have
been for an insanity defense had crumbled as the
psychiatric reports came in.

The defense attorneys had a client whose burgeon-
ing ego made him resistant to suggestion. And still
they had to counsel him that he must now change his
plea to one of guilty—or risk being flayed in court
with the specific revelations of what he had done. If
the details of his crimes came out in open court, he
would be vilified by the media.

There was no question of the death penalty; it had

been outlawed in Oregon years earlier. The last killer to die in the gas chamber in Oregon was Albert Carnes. He was executed in the early 1950s for the ax murder of a widow in her eighties named Litchfield. A woman had been *sentenced* to die for the murder of her lover's two small children in the 1960s—but emotion ran so high at the thought of the execution of a woman that then-Governor Mark Hatfield commuted her sentence to life in prison. (She was paroled in 1985.) Jerry Brudos did not have to worry about being put to death for his crimes.

In the last week of June, George Rhoten and Dale Drake had an hours'-long conference with Jerry Brudos. They explained to him that he would undoubtedly be incarcerated—either in a mental hospital or in the state prison—and that, given their knowledge of the facilities at the Oregon state mental hospital, he might fare better in prison.

"Jerry, you will have to be separated from society— both for your own good and for the good of society. Do you understand that?"

Brudos nodded.

"I don't consider that you are insane," Rhoten said. "And neither do the experts."

Brudos answered that he did not think he was insane or that he lacked any mental capacity to participate in decisions about his case.

"Mr. Drake and I are obliged to extend you every legitimate defense that can be brought to bear on your behalf. You are entitled to the constitutional guarantees that are afforded defendants. But you have told me certain things you say are fact, and you have told me that what you told Dr. Suckow was true." (Brudos' statements to Suckow were detailed and damning—as much as or more than the statements made to Jim Stovall.) "You have told me that what you told Sergeant Stovall can probably be used against you, and I feel there is independent evidence strong enough to convict you."

They talked for many hours, discussing over and over again the possibility that an insanity plea would fail, and the tremendous amount of physical evidence that the police had that was incriminating to Brudos.

Brudos was hesitant to plead guilty. He had been so sure that he would beat the police and the court.

"Now, Jerry Brudos," Rhoten said quietly, "you have told me that these things were done, and I believe you. I believe that you're telling me the truth, but I want to have some further corroboration. I want to know, in my own mind, whether or not there is something, by some quirk, that you are telling me to mislead me, so I am going to ask that this physical evidence be shown."

And so the two attorneys representing Brudos went to the evidence room and looked at the pictures, the rope, the breast molds, the leather postal strap, all of the wealth of damning evidence that had come from Brudos' home or had been attached to the victims' bodies in the river.

A miasma rose from the clothing, permeating the room. As they gazed at the evidence, it was difficult for Rhoten and Drake. At length, Rhoten returned to his client and said, "Well, this is correct; these facts are true."

There could be no denying that all Brudos' confessions were true—not after seeing his insanely lustful face in the photograph with one of his victims' bodies.

"I would like to talk to my wife—before I make a final decision to plead guilty," Brudos said.

Drake left the interview room and made arrangements for Darcie to be brought to the jail. Pale and trembling almost imperceptibly, Darcie walked into the room an hour later.

When she was through talking to her husband, she had no more illusions. It was over. Her marriage. Her life, it seemed. She had no home for her children. She had no money.

Jerry was guilty of murder, and he was going to say so in court.

She did not know what she was going to do.

— 20 —

If Salem courtroom observers expected to spend a good part of their summer in the Marion County Courthouse hearing all the details of Jerry Brudos' crimes—closeted there in the isolation and drama of a shocking murder trial—they were to be disappointed—at least for the time being.

There would be no trial for Jerry Brudos.

Attorneys George Rhoten and Dale Drake notified Judge Val Sloper that they had a motion to entertain in the late afternoon of June 27, 1969. Only a few of the principals gathered there in the quiet courtroom: Judge Sloper, Rhoten, Drake, District Attorney Gary Gortmaker, Jim Stovall, Gene Daugherty—and, of course, Jerry Brudos himself. Brudos, who had heretofore taken direction from no other human being, had listened to the sage advice of his attorneys. Going in, he had not had the chance of a snowball in hell of winning acquittal. Stovall, Daugherty, and their crew of investigators had gathered evidence and confessions that marked him as a mass killer, and even he could see that.

It was four-fifteen on that warm Friday afternoon when Brudos' plea was entered.

Judge Sloper began with the district attorney. "Mr. Gortmaker?"

"May it please the Court, in the matter of the State of Oregon, plaintiff, versus Jerome Henry Brudos, defendant, case number 67640, the defendant is in court with his attorneys, Mr. Dale Drake and Mr. George Rhoten. This defendant was previously indicted by the Marion County Grand Jury and charged with the crime of murder in the first degree involving

Karen Elena Sprinker allegedly occurring on March 27, 1969. The defendant appeared in court and with his attorneys on the fourth day of June 1969 and entered a plea of not guilty and a plea of not guilty by reason of insanity to the charge alleged in the indictment. I have been informed by the attorneys for the defendant that they desired to appear in court and have a request of the court at this time.

"Also, your Honor, I believe the defendant and his attorneys would like to appear before the court on two other cases, case number 67698, a charge of first-degree murder of Jan Susan Whitney, allegedly occurring on the twenty-sixth day of November 1968; and case number 67700, a charge of first-degree murder of Linda Dawn Salee, allegedly occurring on the twenty-third day of April 1969.

"The defendant appeared in court and with his attorneys on both of these charges and case number 67698 and 67700 on the thirteenth day of June 1969, and entered a plea of not guilty and not guilty by reason of insanity. I believe they have a request of the court in those two cases also."

Judge Sloper turned to Dale Drake. "All right. What is it, Mr. Drake?"

"Yes, your Honor. At this time, the defendant would like to make a motion before the court that he be allowed to withdraw the plea of not guilty by reason of insanity previously entered in case numbers 67640, and 67700, and 67698, the three cases of first-degree murder. The reason for this motion, your Honor, is that subsequent to the entry of said pleas on the dates stated by Mr. Gortmaker previously, the defendant has been examined by the following psychiatrists, all of whom were appointed by the court to examine the defendant. These psychiatrists were Dr. George Suckow, of Oregon state hospital; Drs. Ivor Campbell, Gerhard Haugen, Roger Smith, and Guy Parvaresh, all of Portland, Oregon."

"All right," Sloper said.

"He was examined by Colin Slade and Howard Dewey too, who are two well-known psychologists from Portland. Also, an EEG test was run at the

Oregon state hospital and that was scored by Dr. Phillip Reilly. We have also examined the prior medical histories of the defendant which were present for our examination at the Oregon state hospital when the defendant was incarcerated there in 1956 and 1957.

"Based upon these reports and our own discussions with our client, we are certain at this time that the defendant is able to assist us in his defense. I might say, your Honor, that all of the reports and the examinations and diagnoses by each psychiatrist was substantially the same, and therefore, at this time, we would like to have this report by Dr. Guy Parvaresh marked as Defendant's Exhibit 1, and we would offer it at this time in aid of this motion."

Jerry Brudos sat implacably while the list of doctors who had found him eminently sane was read to the court. At length Judge Sloper asked the defendant himself to rise. Asked if he agreed with Drake's motion to plead guilty, he said that, yes, he had discussed the question with Rhoten and Drake and found that a guilty plea was "the most reasonable approach." He was quite willing to stipulate that he was able to intelligently assist his attorneys.

Indeed, Brudos seemed oddly pleased to be considered so sane and intelligent; it was what he had always wanted people to know.

Drake rose to formally withdraw the not-guilty-by-reason-of-insanity pleas. Sloper listened without expression and then asked, "And what would be the subsequent plea if you are permitted to do so?"

Drake's words dropped like stones in the quiet courtroom. "Guilty, your Honor."

"Mr. Drake, have you and Mr. Rhoten had the opportunity, and have you examined all of the—so far as you are aware—the state's files and the state's evidence?"

Dale Drake explained that he had been available to Jerry Brudos since the Friday night of his arrest—May 30—and that he had been formally appointed to represent Brudos the following Monday morning.

"From Friday night forward, I have been associated with this case, and I have examined the evidence at the time it was taken into custody by the state. Since that time, Mr. Rhoten and myself have examined this morning all of the evidence held by the state, the results of the crime-lab tests, and many pictures and physical evidence of that nature. The state has been most cooperative in this matter."

Sloper turned to the district attorney. "Mr. Gortmaker, have you as a matter of fact disclosed to the defendant's attorneys your complete files and all of the evidence that has been accumulated for the prosecution of these three cases?"

"Yes, your Honor. There was, by Detective Sergeant Stovall of the Salem City Police Department, and Lieutenant Eugene Daugherty of the Oregon state police, assembled at my request all of the exhibits anticipated for trial, together with the statements of witnesses, and a list of anticipated witnesses to be called by the state, and all of this evidence was made available to the defendant's attorneys. They did examine each exhibit, talked to the officers concerning the effect of physical evidence, where it was found and how it was acquired, and so far as I know, all of the evidence we anticipated using in the trial next Monday was made available. . . ."

It is a necessary paradox, inherent in the law, that what begins with such profound emotions as terror and panic must come down to the dry, stolid language of the courtroom. Jerry Brudos' victims had had no chance; he, now, had every chance to understand the ramifications of his guilty pleas.

Did he understand the penalty for conviction of murder in the first degree?

"Yes, your Honor. Life imprisonment."

Sloper wanted to be sure he *really* understood the penalties. It was unlikely that cases so heinous would be punishable at a bargain rate—three for the price of one. "Do you understand that the court has the right in a situation, such as here, where there are multiple charges, that it can direct that the sentence imposed may run consecutively to one earlier imposed, and that it is possible that the maximum penalty in this case could be to sentence you to the Oregon State

Penitentiary for an indeterminate period of time, the maximum of which is your life, three different times, and two of them to run consecutively to the first, and to each other? Are you aware of that?"

"No, your Honor, I wasn't. That's something that didn't come up in the discussion."

"All right, that's good. Would that make a difference to you in expressing a desire to withdraw your plea of not guilty and enter another plea at this time?"

"No, your Honor."

"Has anybody threatened or coerced or intimidated you in any manner at all, in order to coerce you to ask the court's permission to change your plea from not guilty to guilty?"

"No, sir."

"Has anybody promised you anything by way of reward or leniency by the court or anything of that nature to induce you to plead guilty?"

"No, sir."

"Are you aware that under your plea of not guilty, you have a right to require the State of Oregon to establish your guilt to the satisfaction of twelve jurors beyond a reasonable doubt of the truth of the allegations of each of these indictments, or you would be entitled to have the indictments dismissed?"

"Yes, sir."

"Are you also aware that you have a right to remain absolutely silent concerning these charges, and that you cannot be compelled to be a witness in any of the three cases against yourself?"

"Yes, sir."

"And are you also aware of the further right that you have to compel the State to produce here in open court, in the event of a trial, the persons who testified against you, and to face your accuser face to face?"

"Yes, sir."

Judge Sloper picked up a copy of the document entitled "Petition to enter plea of guilty" and went over it paragraph by paragraph with Jerry Brudos. It was the guilty plea in the first case—in the death of Karen Sprinker. It too reduced horror to a few paragraphs, executed in perfect legalese.

Judge Sloper read the third paragraph to Brudos:

"The third paragraph states that, 'I have received a copy of the indictment, being called upon to enter a plea. I am able to read and write and I have read the indictment and I have discussed it with my lawyer. I fully understand every charge made against me. The following is the name of the offense: Murder in the first degree. The elements of the above crime are: That I, Jerome Henry Brudos, on or about the twenty-seventh day of March 1969, in the county of Marion, state of Oregon, purposely and with deliberate and premeditated malice did kill one Karen Elena Sprinker, by strangling and smothering her to death.''

Judge Sloper asked a few more questions, just to be sure that Jerry Brudos understood what he was pleading guilty to. "Why is that you want to plead guilty to these indictments?"

"Well, your Honor, I did it."

"Now, by your plea of guilty and by your saying, 'I did it,' tell me exactly what it is that you did in connection with this indictment, and one Karen Elena Sprinker."

"I abducted her and strangled her to death."

"Did you do this with a deliberate plan in mind?"

"That I don't honestly have an answer for, your Honor."

"Maybe I could define 'deliberate' a little bit for you. You have told me that you killed Karen Elena Sprinker by strangling her and smothering her, after you had abducted her. How long was she in your company—or custody—before you did the act as alleged in the indictment?"

"About an hour."

"And during that time that she was in your custody, a period of an hour, did you during that period of time make up your mind and plan how you were going to strangle or smother her?" Sloper asked.

"No, sir, there was no plan to strangle or smother her—"

Judge Sloper appeared startled at Brudos' bland denial of what he might have had in his mind during the time he kept Karen Sprinker captive. Sloper's words burst out. "There was no *what*?"

"—no plan to strangle or smother her."

Sloper continued his questions, his voice once again free of emotional emphasis. "How did you do the act?"

"Strangled her with a rope."

"Where had you abducted Miss Sprinker?"

"From the Fred Meyer . . . er . . . the Meier and Frank parking lot."

It continued, the same phrases, the legal rituals to be gone through—only this time for Jan Susan Whitney.

"In connection with indictment number 67698, Mr. Brudos, wherein it is alleged that on the twenty-sixth day of November 1968, in Marion County, Oregon, that you purposely and with deliberate and premeditated malice feloniously killed one Jan Susan Whitney by strangling and smothering said Jan Susan Whitney to death, is it your desire to enter a plea of guilty at this time?"

"Yes, sir."

"And why do you want to plead guilty to this indictment?"

"Because I did do it."

"Can you tell me how you did it?"

"With a leather strap . . . strangled her to death."

"Was this after you had first abducted her?"

"Yes, sir."

"And how long was she in your company or custody before you strangled or smothered her?"

"About twenty minutes."

"How did you strangle or smother her with a leather strap?"

"I had a slipknot on it and I put it around her neck and yanked it tight."

"Was that act, then, deliberate?"

"I really don't know. It just happened."

"In connection with indictment number 67700 . . . you are accused of the crime of first-degree murder of one Linda Dawn Salee. . . . Is it your desire to enter a plea of guilty to that indictment at this time?"

"Yes, sir."

"And why do you want to plead guilty to that indictment?"

"Because I did do it."

"And how did you do that?"

"With a leather strap."

"Perhaps if you would give me a little more detail rather than by saying 'with a leather strap,' I could—"

"I had a leather strap with a knot in it and I just put it around her throat and pulled it tight."

"How long was she in your company or custody before the strangulation?"

"About an hour."

"Did you kill Linda Dawn Salee with deliberation and premeditation?"

"Yes, sir."

Brudos' definite answer the third time this question was posed puzzled Judge Sloper a little. The defendant had waffled on deliberation with Karen and Jan—but then Judge Sloper could not have known how angry Jerry Brudos had been with Linda Salee because she fought him to save her life.

"Is there any difference, so far as your deliberate and premeditated acts are concerned, between Linda Dawn Salee, than there was with Jan Susan Whitney?"

"Pardon?" Brudos was puzzled now.

"Is there any difference in the deliberation or the premeditation that was in your mind at the time you strangled Linda Dawn Salee than there was when you strangled Jan Susan Whitney?"

"No, sir."

"One final question, Mr. Brudos. Are you stating to me at this time, in each of these cases, that you did the acts alleged, with deliberation and with premeditated malice?"

"Yes, sir."

Jerry Brudos had now pleaded guilty to killing Karen and Jan and Linda Salee (charges in the death of Linda Slawson, if initiated, would have to come from another jurisdiction, Multnomah County). The confessed killer had the right by law to have sentencing delayed for forty-eight hours. He asked that the waiting period be waived and that his sentence be read immediately.

Three months—to the day—had passed since Jerry Brudos had seized Karen Sprinker in the store parking lot. Starting with no clues at all, Jim Stovall and Gene Daugherty—the whole investigation team—had found the killer, arrested him, and now saw him sentenced for his crimes, the near-impossible accomplished in ninety days.

"Jerome Henry Brudos, in case number 67640, in which you have pled guilty to the first-degree murder of Karen Elena Sprinker, it is the judgment of this Court that you be committed to the custody of the Corrections Division of the Oregon State Board of Control for an indeterminate period of time, the maximum of which is the balance of your natural life.

"In connection with case number 67698, in which you have entered a plea of guilty to first-degree murder in the death of one Jan Susan Whitney, it is the judgment of the Court that you be committed to the custody of the Corrections Division of the Oregon State Board of Control for an indeterminate period of time, the maximum of which shall be the balance of your natural life. It will be the further order of the Court that the sentence shall run consecutively to the sentence just previously imposed in case number 67640."

One more.

"In connection with indictment number 67700, the indictment to which you have just entered a plea of guilty to first-degree murder of one Linda Dawn Salee, it will be the judgment of the Court that you be committed to the custody of the Corrections Division of the Oregon State Board of Control for an indeterminate period of time, the maximum of which is the balance of your natural life. This sentence shall run consecutively to the sentences just imposed in cases numbered 67698 and 67640.

"That will be all. You are remanded to the custody of the warden of the Oregon State Penitentiary.

"Court will be in recess."

* * *

It seemed to be over. The expected circus of horror in the courtroom stopped before it began. Jerome Henry Brudos had three life sentences. Of course, "life" does not mean *life*, actual life, when it is a word in a prison sentence. With good behavior, a lifer in Oregon can expect to be out in about twelve years. Jerry Brudos worked, however, under the burden of *three* consecutive life sentences. If he were to serve them all—even with good-behavior credits—he could not hope to be free for thirty-six years. He would be sixty-six years old at least if, and when, he ever got out.

Brudos had a new address: 2605 State Street—the Oregon State Penitentiary. He had become Number 33284.

He thought a lot about his situation, and the more he thought about it, the more unfair it seemed.

Hell, it had always been that way. People pushed him around and took advantage of him. It wasn't fair.

It wasn't fair at all.

— 21 —

Darcie Brudos still lived with her cousin; she was dependent on her relatives financially and embarrassed about it. Her husband was in prison—apparently forever—and that seemed to be the only way it could have ended. Her children remained with her parents, and what possessions she still owned were scattered, some of them in police custody.

On July 1, Darcie Brudos did something she had sworn she would never do: she applied for welfare. She was found to be eligible immediately for an aid-to-dependent-children grant, and Darcie and the youngsters set up a home again. She attempted to look at the future with some optimism, but it was heavy work to do so. Her life—since she had met Jerry—seemed to have progressed in a steady series of descending steps. When she had thought that things could not get worse, they always *had* gotten worse. It was something of a relief for her to know that Jerry was in prison. She believed now that he had done what they had accused him of, but she still could not dwell on it.

It made her too frightened.

Jerry's surprise guilty pleas had caught the press off guard, and they had reacted out of some frustration—printing every detail they could ferret out. Everybody seemed to know about him and about what he had done. She knew that she would divorce him as soon as she could, and that she would change her name—perhaps even move far away where no one had ever heard of Jerry Brudos.

But not right away. The children were too upset, and she had no confidence that she could make a life for them away from her family.

Hers was the common plight of a woman who has never been without a man to tell her what to do. Certainly she had chafed under the restrictions of her father and then her husband, but she had never had the fortitude to defy either of them. Alone now, she moved through her days tentatively. When she was strong enough, she would get a job, and then the divorce, and then the name change. . . .

If Darcie Brudos felt disbelief and shock, so did the public. Armed with the printed details of Jerry Brudos' crimes that had been gleaned by the somewhat disappointed media, bereft of the expected trial, the public had a field day whispering about Darcie Brudos. It seemed inconceivable that any woman could be so submissive and unaware that her husband could have carried on a series of killings in their own home without her knowledge. The rumormongers were busy.

The general consensus of the public was that Jerry and Darcie Brudos had surely engaged in kinky sex—sex that eventually demanded the presence of other women to fulfill their bizarre scenarios. After all, breast molds and women's underwear had been discovered right in the Brudos home. What woman could have ignored those items? What decent woman would have put up with it without asking questions?

The words and insinuations became almost palpable entities, and rumors and tips flooded the Salem Police Department and the Oregon Children's Protection offices.

The public had not had its full revenge on Jerry Brudos; he had pleaded guilty without a trial, and he had somehow robbed the public. There was the prevailing feeling that the whole story had not been revealed, that something was being held back.

Jim Stovall had never felt that Darcie Brudos had any guilty knowledge of her husband's crimes. He had talked to the man for days, and he had seen a kind of gentleness in Brudos toward his wife—an almost protective sense. The man *was* devious and cruel, but he had also seemed to hold Darcie, however neurotically, above the rest of the world. Stovall doubted that she could have played any part at all in the acting out of her husband's fantasies. His impression of Darcie was that she was truly naive, frightened . . . and innocent.

He had seen, of course, the nude photos of Darcie that Jerry had kept—and he saw that she appeared to wear the same black patent-leather shoes that Karen Sprinker had worn in her last pictures. He did not believe that indicated she had guilty knowledge.

Others did not agree with him.

Mrs. Edna Beecham was convinced that she had important information to tell the police. The more she thought about it, the more she knew she must go to someone and tell her story.

Edna Beecham's sister lived in the house that abutted the Brudos garage, and Mrs. Beecham visited her sister often. She had occasionally had coffee with Darcie Brudos—and she'd liked her well enough. Then.

But Edna Beecham became convinced she had seen something on the afternoon of March 27. It became quite clear in her mind. She talked it over with her sister, and she talked about it with other friends, and they all urged her to go to the police.

And she did.

"I saw something," she began. "I saw something on the afternoon of March 27—about one-thirty P.M. I have to tell . . ."

Life was going to continue to get worse for Darcie Brudos.

On July 17, Jim Stovall and Detective B. J. Miller, accompanied by Salem police Detective Marilyn Dezsofi, drove to Corvallis. Their destination was the home of Darcie Brudos' parents; the grandparents had had custody of Megan, now seven, and Jason, twenty-three months old for several weeks. Now the youngsters were to be placed, at least temporarily, under the custody of the Oregon State Childrens' Services Division.

Jim Stovall carried Jason to the car and Megan took Marilyn Dezsofi's hand. It was a sad errand for the detectives, but necessary. Darcie Brudos had now become the focal point of an ongoing investigation.

Megan Brudos was a smart little girl, and Dezsofi was astounded when the child commented matter-of-factly, "My daddy killed three . . . I mean, five women."

Dezsofi, Miller, and Stovall said nothing, and Megan continued to chatter. "I don't like policemen very well—they came and got my Daddy and put him in that place. Are you policemen?"

Dezsofi nodded.

"Was that man one of them that got my daddy?" she asked, pointing to Jim Stovall. Stovall nodded slightly.

Apparently, conversation about the case had not been soft-pedaled around Megan by her mother and grandparents. "My daddy's sick in the head," Megan confided. "He was sick in the head when he was a little boy and he got sicker and now he is so sick, he will never get well. My mom says we're going to have to change our last name."

Megan babbled quite freely to Dezsofi on the way to a foster home in Jefferson. "You know, my brother is too young to know what Daddy did!"

The little girl said that she knew many secrets, and she might tell them later.

But she didn't. The next time the detectives talked with her she blurted, "I forgot all my secrets."

It would always be questionable how much Megan truly knew, and how much of her knowledge had come from overhearing bits and pieces of conversation. She did not recognize pictures of any of the victims, and she laughed out loud when Dezsofi asked her if her father ever put on ladies' shoes for fun.

"Daddy wear women's shoes?" she chortled, as if the idea was absolutely ridiculous.

In the end, Jim Stovall was convinced that Megan had no valuable information. Further, he didn't want to subject the youngster to detailed questioning on matters concerning her father's crimes. Her life would be difficult enough from here on.

Darcie Brudos was stunned almost to inaction when her children were placed in foster care, and she asked Salem attorneys Charles Burt and Richard Seideman to represent her. She was not sure why her children had been taken from her.

Early on the morning of August 7, the reason was quite clear. Richard Seideman called Darcie and told her that she was being charged with first-degree murder, *i.e.*, aiding and abetting Jerome Brudos in the murder of Karen Sprinker. "You will be arraigned in half an hour."

The wait was not half an hour, but four hours long, and Darcie left the arraignment to walk the gauntlet past the strobe lights of cameras. Reporters described her in print later as "emotionless," "calm," and "stolid." In reality, she had been too numb to react. She moved through her weeks in jail in a kind of dream. *This* was the worst thing, the thing that had been waiting for her all along . . . but something she had never dreamed in her worst nightmares might happen.

The burden of the state was predictable. To prove that Darcie Brudos was guilty of aiding and abetting her husband in the death of Karen Sprinker, the case against Brudos himself must be presented. All the evidence would have to be brought out, all the ugliness paraded before a jury. Whatever the final verdict, the decision would be something of a legal landmark.

It began—this final ordeal—in September 1969.

Since he had presided over Jerry Brudos' hearings, Judge Sloper disqualified himself and Judge Hay would preside. The opposing attorneys were well-matched, perhaps the most outstanding criminal lawyers in Marion County. For the state, Gary D. Gortmaker, tall, confident, his prematurely silver hair perfectly cut—an almost constant winner in court. For the defense, Charlie Burt. Burt is a man of short stature, slightly crippled by a childhood bout with polio, somewhat irascible, gruffness hiding his innate kindness. Both men were in their early forties.

The courtroom had 125 seats for spectators, and there were hundreds of would-be observers waiting outside the locked doors each morning, all vying for a seat. Spectators' purses and packages were searched before they were allowed into the courtroom; threats against Darcie Brudos' life had been voiced.

Those who were lucky enough to get a seat would not budge, even during recesses. They watched Darcie Brudos, and commented in stage whispers that she did not "look like a murderess." She did not; in her white blouse and neat dark suit, her short hair tousled, she looked very young and very frightened. She was much thinner than she was when Jerry was arrested. The pounds she'd fought for years had slid away with the tension of the past four months.

She was only twenty-four, a very young twenty-four. She could hear them talking behind her. She heard muffled laughter and a constant undertone of conversation, as if the gallery believed she could not hear their comments.

"If anybody dies, just prop him up—and keep your seat. We don't want to miss anything."

She saw a hugely pregnant woman who seemed about ready to deliver, and thought how uncomfortable she must be sitting all day on a hard courtroom bench. And then the woman said, "I hope I have the baby over the weekend so I can be back here by Monday morning. . . ."

She saw the armed deputies leaning against the back wall, and realized with a shock that they were there to protect *her* from the possibility of attack by someone who had already judged her and found her guilty.

The first panel of prospective jurors—forty in all—was exhausted by noon of the first day of jury selection; they had all read about the "Brudos case," and they had all formed opinions as to her guilt or innocence. It would take two and a half days to select a jury. Eight women and four men. And then she wondered. It was such a toss-up. She knew women could judge another woman far more harshly than men did. Would they understand? Would they believe her?

It was time to begin. District Attorney Gortmaker rose to make his opening remarks to the jury. Gortmaker assured the jury that he would prove that Darcie Brudos had helped her husband when he'd killed Karen Sprinker. He said he would produce an eyewitness who had *seen* Darcie assist Brudos in forcing a person wrapped in a blanket into their home. . . .

Charlie Burt spoke next. He stressed that Darcie had had no reason at all to aid her husband. He pointed out that Darcie had refused to destroy evidence, had actually saved physical evidence for the police to find. "This is hardly the act of a woman trying to protect herself!"

On the first morning of the trial, Megan Brudos was called into the courtroom so that Judge Hay could determine if she would be a competent witness. A witness against her mother. . . . Darcie had not seen her daughter for over two months. Seeing Megan walk timidly into the courtroom was almost more than she could bear. Megan was only seven years old; she seemed so frail, thinner than she had been, and quite frightened.

The testimony of a child under ten in a court of law is always suspect. Some children are mature enough to relate facts accurately; others are not. Judge Hay leaned toward Megan and smiled as he spoke softly to her.

"What is your name?"

"Megan."

"What do you think happens when you don't tell the truth?"

"You get in trouble."

"Do you believe in God?"

"Yes."

"How are your marks in school?"

"I got some bad marks . . ."

"But some good ones too?"

"Yes, they balance out."

"Do you think you could answer questions honestly—if someone should ask you in this courtroom?"

"Yes."

Both the defense and prosecution declined to question Megan at this time. The child looked around the courtroom for the first time, and she saw her mother. She began to cry.

And so did Darcie.

Megan was led from the room—but she had been accepted as a potential witness against her mother.

On Thursday morning, September 25, the prosecution's case began in earnest. Lieutenant Robert W.

Pinnick of the state crime lab took the stand to identify clothing removed from Karen Sprinker's body.

"Were there articles of clothing that you removed from the body of the deceased?" Gortmaker asked.

"I removed from the badly decomposed body of Karen Sprinker . . . white panties, a black long-line bra, a green skirt . . . a green sweater."

The courtroom was very quiet as Pinnick broke the seal on the bags holding the clothing, and there was a concurrent odor that insinuated itself into the close air. (When Darcie Brudos' trial was over, the courtroom would retain the stench, a stench removed only by having all the benches stripped and revarnished.)

Each garment was displayed after Pinnick identified his own initials on the labels of the bags that held them.

"Did you find anything inside the strapless brassiere?"

"Yes, sir."

"What was that?"

"Brown—or tan—paper towels had been stuffed into the cups."

"When the body was examined—on autopsy—were the breasts intact?"

"They were not. They were absent."

There was no carnival atmosphere now. There were only shocked gasps, and Darcie felt the force of eyes staring behind her.

She had not known. This she had not known.

Burt and Seideman had tried to warn Darcie what the physical evidence would be like; she had listened and nodded, but she had not foreseen how awful it really was. The defense team had tried to keep the evidence out of trial, but all two thousand pieces of it were allowed, trundled into the courtroom by deputies before each session.

Lieutenant Pinnick described the manner in which Karen Sprinker's body was weighted down with an engine head from a Chevrolet, the mass of it attached with nylon rope—microscopically identical in class and characteristic with the nylon rope taken from Jerry Brudos' workshop.

"Did you form an opinion on whether the victim had been undressed . . . or redressed?"

"Yes, sir. She apparently had been. The black brassiere was not hers."

"Did you go to 3123 Center Street on June 3, 1969,
to participate in a search of the premises?"

"Yes, sir."

"And did you seize certain items of evidentiary value
from those premises?"

"Yes, sir."

Darcie watched as piece after piece of evidence was
introduced, identified by Pinnick, and accepted. Here
in the courtroom, it all seemed to have a macabre
air—although some of the items were quite familiar to
her: the blue shag rug (that Jerry had said he needed
to keep his feet warm in the workshop), his tool chest,
the vise, a gas can, a green plastic wastebasket, a
reloading device for ammunition, his rock tumbler, a
blue wooden box and a gray metal kitchen stool. She
had seen all those things on the rare occasion that he
allowed her into the workshop. She was not sure what
they might possibly have to do with his crimes.

For the rest of the day, the morass of evidence grew,
and as it grew, Darcie began to feel physically ill.

There were the shoes—she had seen none of them.
The women's low shoes with laces she had never seen
before. Were they Karen Sprinker's? The prosecution
said they had been. And all of the others. Where had
he gotten them, and how had he kept them so secret
from her?

All the things the police had found in the attic.
Gortmaker lifted packages from a huge box, packages
to be opened to show that they contained so many
brassieres . . . and girdles. Jerry had obviously stolen
these things, and she had had no idea.

Her attorneys had warned Darcie that there would
be terrible pictures, and now they were handed to
Lieutenant Pinnick for identification, passed to the
defense table for Darcie's perusal, and then given to
the jury. She was afraid she was going to vomit.

She saw the hanging body of a woman who hung as
still as death from a hook in Jerry's workshop, her
face covered with a black hood. The next girl, who
had to be Karen Sprinker—she recognized her face

from newspaper stories—gazed into the camera with
an awful kind of fear in her eyes. She wore only
panties and shiny black pumps, and she stood on Jerry's blue rug. . . .

There was a black notebook—she had never seen it
before—and it held pages of pictures of naked female
torsos. The women photographed had no heads; they
had been snipped from the photos. Why? To avoid
identification? Or as a symbolic gesture of violence?
Darcie studied the headless nude photos and wondered who they were—or who they had been.

There were pictures of Jerry. Jerry dressed grotesquely in women's underclothing—wearing a black slip,
stockings, and high heels. She had seen him like this,
but she had put it out of her mind.

And then the worst picture of all. The dead girl
hanging from the ceiling by the rope around her neck.
And Jerry. Her husband's face was there, too; he had
leaned too far over the mirror on the floor, photo-
graphing himself along with the dead woman when he
snapped this terrible picture.

Darcie looked up at the jury and saw that their faces
were gray and sickened as they passed the pictures
down the line. She saw a woman look at one of the
pictures, shut her eyes against the image, and swallow
hard.

What else would they show? Darcie knew she was
living in a nightmare now. How could she have been
in the same house with Jerry and not have realized
how sick he was? How could she convince anyone that
she had not known?

She opened her eyes and saw that Lieutenant Pinnick
was holding up the breast paperweight that Jerry had
explained away so blithely. Now she could see it for
what it was. A life model of a full female breast,
almost five inches across.

"Where was this mold located?" District Attorney
Gortmaker asked.

"In the home."

"*In* the home?"

"Yes, sir. It was on a shelf above the fireplace."

Darcie felt the jurors' eyes turn toward her. She

knew they were wondering how she could have avoided seeing this exhibit. She bent her head toward the yellow legal pad Mr. Burt had given her. He had told her she could take notes if she liked—but it was really only something to do with her hands when she could no longer bear the stares and whispers.

When the long day in court was finally over, the clerk's desk was piled with the evidence. Not against Jerry—not really now—because Jerry was in prison.

She was the one on trial.

Darcie Brudos had seen Edna Beecham's name on the state's witness list, and she'd been confused by it. She could not imagine what Edna Beecham might have to say. Edna Beecham was a friend, although not a close friend. Just a talkative, slightly gossipy woman who'd been pleasant over coffee.

Edna Beecham would not look at her now; she seemed too eager to plunge into her testimony. So eager, in fact, that Judge Hay had to caution the witness to slow down and tell only those things that were responsive to the questions Gortmaker posed to her.

"Please tell the jury what you remember of March 27, 1969."

"I was at my sister's house that day."

"Can you point out on the map behind you where your sister's home is located, please."

Edna Beecham took the pointer and indicated a house whose yard touched the Brudos garage.

"Mark it with an X if you will, Mrs. Beecham."

Darcie waited while Edna Beecham made a careful cross on the map and then took her seat again.

"What time was it that you were visiting your sister?"

"All day. I was visiting from over in Bend. I was looking out the dining-room window about one-thirty P.M. I saw Mr. Brudos. He was pushing something—someone—with a blanket around them toward the garage toward the kitchen door. The kitchen door was open. There were three cement steps that went up to the porch . . . it's a kind of cement platform there. Mrs. Brudos was standing there on the porch part . . ."

Darcie's mouth fell open in shock, and she turned to whisper to Mr. Burt, but he only shook his head slightly. Mrs. Beecham was still talking.

". . . The girl tried to jerk away. But Mrs. Brudos helped Mr. Brudos push the person in the blanket into the house."

Edna Beecham spoke with conviction. She had seen what she had seen, and she seemed anxious to tell it all. She was adamant that she had seen the Brudoses— both of them—struggling to get the blanket-wrapped form into their house.

It was finally time for cross-examination from the defense. Charlie Burt rose easily and walked toward Mrs. Beecham with a disarming smile. She smiled back nervously.

"Mrs. Beecham . . . you say that you saw Mr. Brudos push someone from the garage to the kitchen door?"

"Yes." She got up from her witness chair and demonstrated. "She was pushed up against Mr. Brudos' chest. He had his arms around the girl's body in front. The girl had a gag in her mouth—"

"Oh? She had an adhesive-tape gag?"

"I didn't say adhesive tape—"

"If she had—as you said—a blanket over her head, how could you see the gag?"

"There was an opening there. I saw the gag."

"What color was the blanket?"

"I don't know."

"Are you color blind?"

"No . . . but I don't know. The blanket had a binding on it."

"What color was the binding?"

"I don't know."

"The binding is stitching around the edge?"

"No . . . no, it's material."

"How do you know the blanket-covered figure was a girl?"

"I could tell by the outline. I could see the legs and the shoes."

"What color were the shoes?"

"I don't know."

"Were they red?"

"I do not know. I do know her nylons were cocoa beige."

Sound rippled through the gallery; the woman's memory was oddly selective.

"What was Mr. Brudos wearing?"

"I don't know."

"How is it, Mrs. Beecham, that you could see the Brudos home so clearly, given that there is a tall evergreen hedge between that property and your sister's property?"

The witness had been fingering a rosary in her lap throughout her testimony. Now she threw up her left hand dramatically and cried, "As God is above, I *saw* it!"

"Mrs. Beecham," Burt said quietly. "If you saw Mr. Brudos, assisted by Mrs. Brudos—saw them forcing a young woman with . . . cocoa-beige stockings, and wrapped in a blanket whose color you can not now recall—if you saw them forcing her into their home, why didn't you call the police?"

"My sister asked me not to."

"I see. Your sister asked you not to. Did you tell anyone else?"

"My husband."

Burt allowed Mrs. Beecham's time lapse in calling the police to sink into the jury's minds before he gathered photographs of views of the Brudos home taken from the witness's sister's home.

"These pictures were taken from your sister's dining-room window," he said. "This doesn't appear to be a good vantage point."

Mrs. Beecham studied the pictures and looked up. "This picture doesn't look right to me."

"Wasn't there something that cut your view of the Brudos house off—something in the way?"

"Nothing cut my view. I was up high. Yes, there was this cedar hedge and trees—but I saw everything."

"Did you see the back door of the Brudos home?"

"I'm getting mixed up about the door," she answered. "I could see the cement platform—I couldn't see the kitchen door."

"How about in this angle," Burt asked, handing her another picture taken from her sister's home.

Mrs. Beecham grew more confident. "Branches were not on the trees—I mean, leaves—and I saw the door close. I just don't know much about trees."

"Do you know that evergreen trees—such as cedar—do not lose their leaves?"

"Yes," she said shortly. "I know that much."

"But you say you saw the incident clearly *through* the cedar hedge?"

"I saw it."

"When did you reconstruct your . . . view for the Salem police?"

"Last month."

Jim Stovall listened to Edna Beecham on the stand, just as he had listened to her when he had traveled to Bend, Oregon, at the request of the district attorney's office. Her story had not entirely convinced him then, and it didn't now. "But," he recalls, "when you testify before a grand jury, nobody asks your own opinion; they only ask about what witnesses told you."

Burt's cross-examination of Edna Beecham had shown the woman's confusion and pointed out that she had done nothing whatsoever after allegedly seeing something that demanded action. She simply could not have seen what she said she had.

Darcie felt slightly better.

But she felt worse again when the next prosecution witness was called: Megan Brudos.

Megan entered the courtroom slowly, a tiny figure all dressed in blue with her coat over her arm. She seemed on the edge of tears, but she walked bravely to the witness stand.

She looked up at District Attorney Gortmaker and waited for him to question her. He asked her name again, asked a few casual questions to help her relax, and then he began the hard questions.

"Megan, did your mommy and daddy tell you not to tell anybody what happened in the workshop?"

"I . . . can't remember."

"Did you hear crying coming from the workshop a couple of times that day—that day last March?"

"I can't remember."

"Did you meet a girl about the time of spring vacation named Karen that your daddy took into the workshop while your mother was home?"

"Yes."

The courtroom buzzed again, and Darcie shook her head slightly.

"While Karen was there, did your mother go into the workshop and start crying—and then come out of the workshop and go into the bedroom and lie on the bed and cry?"

"I can't remember."

Darcie had cried so many times over the past months. She had tried not to, tried not to let the children know how desperate and sad she felt. Megan had seen her cry. But Megan could never have seen her cry under the circumstances Gortmaker had described.

"Isn't it true, Megan," the district attorney continued, "that Mommy didn't like to help Daddy when the girls were in the workshop because your daddy wanted to take pictures of them and your mommy didn't want him to?"

"I don't know."

Gortmaker gave it up. As a witness for the prosecution, Megan Brudos had emerged, instead, as a very sad, very confused little girl.

Charlie Burt asked only two questions on cross-examination.

"Megan, did Sergeant Stovall show you some pictures of girls—big girls—and did he ask you if you knew any of them, if you recognized them?"

"Yes."

"The girl we're asking about, the girl named Karen, was in those pictures. Did you tell Sergeant Stovall that you had seen her?"

"No. By the looks of them, I didn't know anyone in those pictures."

The prosecution's presentation was over finally, and it was Charlie Burt's turn to attempt to prove to the jury that Darcie Brudos was in no way connected to her husband's crimes.

Her brother-in-law, Larry, was asked to describe

Jerry Brudos' character. "He is aggressive . . . over-bearing to the point of violence—at least to me and to our parents."

"Who was the dominant partner in the marriage of your brother and Darcie Brudos?" Burt asked.

"I don't think there's any doubt about that. My brother was."

Ned Rawls told the jury of Jerry Brudos' sheer physical strength. He told of Jerry Brudos lifting engine heads and other heavy automobile parts with ease.

"Did Jerry Brudos show you anything when you visited his home on the twenty-ninth of March this year?"

"He showed me photographs of women—nude women's figures."

"What did the women look like?"

"I couldn't tell you. The faces had been snipped out of the photos."

"Did you see anything else on that night that seemed a little strange to you?"

"The breast molds. Lead or something shaped like a woman's breast. He said a friend had asked him to make a paperweight shaped like a breast."

"Did he say who the friend was?"

"No, sir."

Ned Rawls's wife, Lois, was the next witness.

"Mrs. Rawls," Burt asked, "did you have a conversation with Mrs. Edna Beecham in the corridor outside the grand-jury hearing room this past month?"

"Yes, sir."

"What did she say to you?"

"She said she'd seen Jerry and Darcie with a woman with long dark hair who had a blanket wrapped around her. She said they were pushing her on the back porch."

"Did she tell you how she could see the woman's long dark hair when she had a blanket over her head?"

"No, she didn't."

Darcie Brudos' girlfriends Sherrie, Doris, and Ginny Barron—all sisters-in-law—testified that during the months of February and March 1969 Darcie had spent at least four days a week in their homes, from early morning until just before supper. During that period,

Jerry Brudos had telephoned frequently to check on Darcie's whereabouts.

"She was never allowed to go home without calling him first," Sherrie Barron testified. "She couldn't just walk in on him."

None of them, however, was prepared to swear that Darcie had been with them all day on March 27. It had been a weekday, like any other weekday. There had been no reason at the time to mark it as special.

Charlie Burt called a surprise witness: Dr. Ivor Campbell, one of the psychiatrists who had examined Jerry Brudos. He had also spent hours interviewing Darcie Brudos.

Dr. Campbell characterized Darcie Brudos as essentially a normal woman, hardly a dangerous person—and highly unlikely to be motivated to kill another human being.

"Would it, then, Dr. Campbell," Burt asked, "be easy for someone like Jerry Brudos to dominate the defendant—to push her around and make her afraid to even come into her own home without permission?"

"It would."

"How many times have you testified in court, Dr. Campbell?"

"I would say perhaps sixty-five hundred times."

"You examined Jerome Henry Brudos?"

"I did."

"How would you compare Jerry Brudos to other individuals—patients—you may have testified about?"

"I could not."

"You could *not*?"

"No, sir."

"Why is that?"

"My examination of Jerome Brudos indicated a subject whose mental disturbances were so bizarre . . . *so* bizarre that a psychiatrist might just possibly expect to see one personality like his in an entire lifetime of practice."

"One in a lifetime . . . ?"

"And perhaps not then."

—— 22 ——

In television productions of murder trials, the accused invariably takes the witness stand in his own defense. In life, it is the exception rather than the rule. If a defendant testifies, he is automatically vulnerable to cross-examination by the prosecution. Most defense attorneys choose not to give the state that opportunity. Tactically, the choice involved in putting the defendant on the stand is something of a toss-up. If the defendant does not testify, there is sometimes the feeling that he has something to hide. A jury may deduce that silence is an admission of guilt. If a defendant has a prior record of offenses, these can be elicited during cross-examination. But Darcie Brudos had no record at all. Charlie Burt chose to have Darcie testify. It was the best way he could demonstrate her personality—this frightened, passive small woman who had convinced him that she was totally innocent.

The courtroom was packed on Thursday, September 30; the word was that *she* would be on the stand, and everyone wanted to hear what she had to say for herself.

Darcie had agreed to testify, just as she had earlier agreed to go for broke—refusing to plead guilty to lesser charges. She was innocent, and she had chosen to risk a guilty verdict rather than live the rest of her life with a cloud of suspicion around her.

Guilt by association has marred the lives of many women who loved evil men. Darcie studied the women on the jury and wondered if they knew *everything* about the men in their lives. Would they believe that men could have secret lives, dark sides of themselves that their women might never imagine? It was an unsettling thought, a thought most women would reject.

For the first time now, she faced the gallery. She knew the questions would be intimate. She would have to tell this sea of strangers about things that she had discussed with no one else—ever.

Charlie Burt smiled at her, and she trusted him. If anyone could help her, he could.

"Darcie, did you have anything to do with bringing anyone into your home on March 27, 1969?"

"No."

"Did you ever have anything to do with aiding your husband in killing anyone?"

"No."

"How long had you known your husband when you married him?"

"Three months."

"What kind of marriage was it in the beginning?"

She could sense the gallery listening. This would be the "good stuff"—a soap opera right before their eyes.

"I considered it a very good marriage—at first."

"How long were you married before trouble developed?"

"Three or four years."

"What caused the trouble?"

"There were a lot of things. He wasn't working all the time and we seemed to quarrel about so many things."

"Going back to the time you lived in Salem, how were you getting along?"

"Not very good."

"How much did you stay home?"

"Not very often. I didn't enjoy being home when my husband was there."

"What was causing the quarrels with your husband?"

"Different things he wanted me to do . . . and his not working."

"Were there times he would be sick?"

"Several times he would have what he called migraine headaches. He couldn't stand much noise. The headaches put him in a very bad mood."

"You say you quarreled about things he wanted you

to do. Could you tell us what some of those things were?"

She knew that she had to tell it all. Mr. Burt had explained that the prosecution would bring all those embarrassing things out—that her own lawyer could defuse the impact if he asked her first. "I . . . I objected to having Jerry take pictures of me . . . when I was naked."

Darcie heard a buzzing in the courtroom, a few muffled gasps of disapproval.

"Why did you go along with this . . . this picture-taking?"

"He was my husband. He developed his own film and he said he would destroy the pictures after he finished with them."

"Were there other things you argued about?"

"He wanted me to wear high heels all the time. I have back problems, and it was very uncomfortable for me to do that."

"Did you ever see your husband wearing women's clothing?"

"Yes."

"Could you tell us about that?"

"I was . . . kidding him about being overweight. He went into another room, and when he came back he was wearing a girdle and a brassiere and he asked me if he looked thinner."

Darcie looked down at her hands, and the way Jerry had looked in that outfit flashed back across her mind.

"Did you think it was a joke?"

"Yes."

"Did you have any feelings about your husband's mental condition—that maybe something might be wrong?"

"Yes. Just a feeling—but I'd felt something was wrong for the past few years."

"Did you suspect your husband of killing anyone?" Burt asked bluntly.

"No! No, I did not."

"Darcie, can you tell the jury a little of what your home life was like—during the time you were living in Salem?"

"Yes. I—"

"Were you afraid of your husband?"

"He was—is—very large, and he's very, very strong. He kind of dominated everything that went on. He had rules . . ."

"Rules? For instance . . ."

"I was not allowed to go out to Jerry's workshop in the garage. The freezer was out there. I was not allowed to go out to get food from the freezer. If I wanted something for dinner, I had to call Jerry on the intercom and tell him to bring it in. He explained that he had all kinds of photographic equipment out there and I might ruin his pictures if I came into the workshop without warning him."

"When you were away, where did you go?"

"I went to my friends' homes—to the Barrons' houses."

"What happened when you wanted to come home?"

"I had to call my husband and tell him I was on the way."

"Why was that?"

"I don't know. I was just supposed to call. He called my friends too, to see where I was—to check and see if I was with them."

"Did you ever ask him why he did this?"

"Yes, once I did."

"What did he say?"

"He kind of laughed, and he said he wanted to be sure that he got the blonde out of the house before I got home."

There was a sharp gasp in the courtroom. It was too close to the truth.

"Did you think he was joking?"

"Yes, I did."

"Darcie, do you remember finding pictures of women—nude women—in your husband's workshop?"

"Yes. I went out to do the laundry—I had permission—and I asked my husband about some pictures that I saw in a developing tray. He said they weren't his—that they belonged to some college kid he was doing a favor for."

"Do you remember seeing a breast mold?"

"Yes."

"Did you ask your husband what it was?"

"Yes. He said he was making a paperweight."

"Did you believe him?"

"Yes. I had no reason not to."

"Did you ever find other pictures—pictures of your husband wearing women's clothing?"

"Yes."

"Did you take those pictures? Did you ever take pictures of your husband when he was dressed like that?"

"No I did not."

"Do you know whether he had a camera that could be set to take a photo of himself?"

"He had a thirty-five-millimeter he got in Korea, or from Korea."

"Did you ever see him use it?"

"He took a picture of all of us—Jerry, my son, my daughter, and me—by a 'Leaving California' sign once."

"Darcie," Burt said, "did you receive a phone call from your husband on the night he was arrested—on May 30?"

"Yes, he called me from the jail."

"What did he want you to do?"

"He asked me to go out to his workshop and destroy a box of photographs and a box of women's clothing I'd find there."

"Did you?"

"No, sir. I called Mr. Drake, instead. He told me that it would be illegal for me to destroy something that might be evidence."

"What did you do with those things?"

"The police came in and took them later."

"Did you ever go into the attic of your home?"

"No, sir."

"Why was that?"

"Jerry said there were mice . . . and things like that up there. I'm terrified of mice."

"Darcie Brudos . . . if you suspected that people were being killed in your home, what would you have done?"

"I would have moved out . . . I would have left him."

"How do you feel about your husband now?"

"I feel he is a very sick person. I'm afraid to be with him . . . alone."

Darcie Brudos would now have to establish some manner of alibi for her time on the twenty-seventh of March. For the average person, recall of events on what has seemed to be an ordinary day some months previous is a difficult—if not impossible—task. Businesses keep calendars; housewives seldom do. How can one remember what happened on a weekday? Darcie had gone over her days again and again, and she had narrowed down her activities on that Thursday, only because the day had been somewhat unusual. She followed Charlie Burt's instructions to relate what she remembered of the twenty-seventh to the jury.

"That day was a Thursday. I had been at Ginny Barron's from about nine or nine-thirty. I had planned to stay all day, but Jerry called about two and suggested that we drive to Corvallis to see my parents. I went home, and I think we left for Corvallis about three. But when we got to my parents', Jerry just dropped us off and said he had to see friends and would be back for supper. He didn't come back for supper at all. I remember that because my mother had fixed extra food for him, and he didn't even come or call to say he'd be late. He finally showed up around nine—and he had one of his bad migraine headaches."

If Darcie Brudos was telling the truth about that last day of Karen Sprinker's life, it appeared that Jerry Brudos had arranged to have his family far away from their home while he violated his victim's body. Only later, long after midnight, had he secreted the body in his station wagon and driven back to the Long Tom to dispose of it.

On cross-examination, District Attorney Gortmaker questioned the defendant closely about the cameras the family had owned. There had been several—two

movie cameras and three still cameras. The delayed-
timing mechanism had not been found in Brudos' workshop, and Gortmaker suggested that Darcie—and not
Jerry—had taken the gruesome picture of Karen's body
which showed Brudos' face.

Darcie had no idea how the delayed-timing mechanism worked. But she was firm in her response to
suggestions that she had been the person behind the
camera when those terrible pictures were taken.

Gortmaker picked up some glossy eight-by-tens of
different pairs of shoes, including the black patent-
leather pumps.

"Mrs. Brudos, can you identify these shoes? Are
they yours?"

"No."

It was over—for the moment. Darcie Brudos left
the witness stand.

Charlie Burt called her parents to the stand. They
were quite sure of the date that Jerry Brudos had
driven his family to Corvallis. They could not swear to
it.

The next defense witness was Harry Nordstrom, a
man who said he had known Edna Beecham for seventeen years.

"Mr. Nordstrom," Burt asked, "were you ever in a
position to hear a conversation between Mrs. Beecham and her sister—a conversation regarding something Mrs. Beecham had seen from her sister's dining-
room window?"

"Yes, sir. On two occasions."

"What did Mrs. Beecham say?"

"She was trying to convince her sister that she had
seen Jerry Brudos force a struggling girl into their
home—the Brudos home."

"How did she say that was accomplished?"

"One time she said that Jerry carried the girl in—
and once she said she saw him lead her in."

"Carried?"

"Yes."

"And the next time, she had changed her recall. She
said *led* in?"

"Yes, sir."

"Mr. Nordstrom, based on your acquaintance with Mrs. Beecham—for seventeen years—how would you estimate Mrs. Beecham's reputation for telling the truth?"

Nordstrom paused, and then he answered softly. "She tells the truth . . . as she knows it."

Burt had pretty well eliminated the state's prize witness as credible. He still had to attack the prosecution's contention that Jerry Brudos could not have had the strength to carry a weighted body from his station wagon to the bridge rail over the Long Tom River—that *two* people would have had to be present to carry out such a feat.

The combined weight of Karen Sprinker's body and the engine head had been 179 pounds, the weight of an average man. A deadweight. In this context, a macabre term.

Burt called a private investigator who had been hired by the defense to carry out witnessed experiments, and introduced photographs showing that a station wagon like the Brudos' could be backed to within four inches of the bridge rail over the Long Tom.

"Did you carry a weight—weighing 179 pounds—from that station wagon to the bridge rail?" Burt asked the detective.

"I did, several times."

"Without assistance from another person?"

"No, sir. I carried the weight alone."

The jury had heard that Jerry Brudos was strong enough to hold back the weight of a freezer weighing between three and four hundred pounds. It seemed clear that he could have handled a weighted body with some ease.

The defense rested its case.

But District Attorney Gortmaker had something more, something to bring back on rebuttal.

The nude pictures of Darcie Brudos.

Long before, Darcie had feared that technicians in a photo lab might have seen some of the pictures Jerry had taken of her. He had promised her that he had destroyed all those photos. But he had not. He had hoarded them, just as he'd kept all of his other pictures. Now they were introduced into evidence, and Darcie was humiliated to see them passed down the rows of jurors. Her nakedness exposed to the people who would judge her.

Gortmaker pointed out that Darcie wore high patent-leather pumps in the photos—pumps that seemed identical to those apparent in the pictures of Karen Sprinker. It had been such a long time ago. She had not remembered those shoes.

She felt the jury looking at her—glancing at the pictures of her naked body, posing for what she had thought were totally private photos.

Now it looked as if she had lied about the shoes. She had told the district attorney that she did not recognize any of the shoes recovered in the search of Jerry's workshop. But they were there on her own feet in the dozens of slides and photos. She had told the truth as she remembered it.

She had not lied—but it looked as if she had.

The time had come for final arguments. Whichever way it went, the ordeal of the trial was almost over.

On Thursday, October 2, Gary Gortmaker spoke for the prosecution. Darcie heard herself portrayed as a monstrous woman, a woman who had willingly helped her husband torture and kill a helpless girl. A woman who had then accompanied her husband when he disposed of the body. She was depicted as morally loose, someone who posed for photographs that verged on pornographic. She listened, and thought that the D.A. might well be talking about another woman entirely, someone she had never met—and certainly someone she herself would despise.

And she felt trickles of hate aimed from somewhere behind her, and knew. There were those in the gallery who still believed that she was guilty of all these things.

Mr. Burt had told her that each side would have to pull out all the stops, that she must let the legal rhetoric wash over her and not heed it, not allow it to damage her.

But it did.

The words would not wash over her; instead, they penetrated her fragile facade like acid eroding whatever self-esteem she had left. She would never escape them, no matter how far she went. She thought of the little childhood rhyme: "Sticks and stones . . . but words will never hurt me."

And all she could think of was how much words could hurt.

When it was over, Charlie Burt rose and walked to the jury rail.

"Lizzie Borden took an ax,
and gave her father forty whacks.
And when she saw what she had done,
She gave her mother forty-one. . . ."

The poem hung on the air.

"Lizzie Borden was acquitted of both those murders, ladies and gentlemen. Everyone connected with that old case is long dead—the judge, the jury, the lawyers, the defendant. Yet the poem remains—known to every schoolchild. *Why?* Because the public seizes upon the gruesome and the bizarre. Lizzie Borden has been convicted of those crimes by history and folklore."

Burt did not have to equate Jerome Henry Brudos' crimes with the horror of the Borden massacre. It was obvious; there had never been a more gruesome crime in Oregon crime annals than those committed by Jerry Brudos. Burt reminded the jury of the terrible photographs of Brudos' victims, photographs that could not help but revolt anyone who gazed upon them.

"Does the state want the truth . . . or does the state want a conviction? Is Darcie Brudos being prosecuted . . . or is she being persecuted? She was married—is *still* married—to this man. Does that automatically make her guilty by association?"

Burt pointed out again that Darcie had preserved evidence. He took the picture of Jerry Brudos simpering in the black lace slip and handed it to the jury. He took the other picture—the worst picture—of Jerry Brudos staring at his victim's hanging corpse, and held it out for them to see again.

"This is the face of a madman—a monster who inadvertently took his own picture. Do not convict Darcie Brudos because she is *married* to a madman.

"Take Edna Beecham out of the case . . . and it crumbles like a house of cards. If you *believe* Edna Beecham, *convict*. If you do not, *acquit*."

It was 4:09 P.M. on that bleak October afternoon when Judge Hay finished giving his final instructions and the jury retired to debate their verdict.

Darcie was returned to her jail cell to wait. Charlie Burt had told her it might be hours—or it might be days before the jury signaled that they had made their judgment.

The jail matrons were kind to her; they had always been kind to her. Now they brought her two aspirin and a glass of milk. She had never taken tranquilizers, and she would not now. But she was afraid—more afraid than she had been throughout the trial. There were no more words to be said. Whatever would be would be.

Five o'clock. Six o'clock.

At 7:59 P.M. she heard a matron approaching her cell, and she looked up.

"The jury's back. They're waiting for you."

Judge Hay turned to the jury foreman. "Have you reached a verdict?"

"We have, your Honor."

"And how do you find?"

Darcie tried to control her trembling as she faced the jury. She could not read their faces.

"Not guilty."

— 23 —

In the Oregon State Penitentiary, Prisoner 33284 was now dealing with his peers. No, that would be a faulty term; Jerry Brudos' fellow prisoners would never accept him as one of their kind. They were not constrained by the law as the detectives, lawyers, and prosecutors had been. Despite his protestations that he had been treated badly after his arrest, he had been treated with eminent fairness.

Now he was in prison.

There are social hierarchies in prison that are just as clearly defined or even *more* clearly defined than those in other communities. The vast majority of prisoners are basically decent men who have, admittedly, broken laws—but who believe in the sanctity of human life and in the protection of women and children. The upper echelons in prison society are reserved for the "brains"—the safecrackers who can "see" with their fingers, the crafty con men, the bunco artists who are charming and devious and who can sweet-talk anyone out of anything, and, of course, the "paper-hangers," the forgers and counterfeiters.

Brains count inside the walls; the smart cons are the jailhouse lawyers who can give advice on how to get out, or at least how to maneuver for favors inside. They are the elite.

Jerry Brudos was smart, but his crimes had been such that they obliterated any claim he might have had to join those respected for their intelligence.

The social ladder in the joint works on down, then, based on abilities that have no meaning in the outside world. Bank robbers are considered clever if they have managed to get away with a few such crimes before

they were apprehended. Burglars are above robbers—
"cat burglars" getting the nod. Sheer physical strength
is important. If you have no important contacts on the
outside, and you're not that brilliant, you can dominate in prison just by being muscular.

Close to the bottom are the penny-ante crooks. But
at the very, very bottom, according to the general
prison population, are the sex criminals. The rapists.
The child molesters.

And the woman killers.

Cons have women and children whom they love.
And as much as they love their own, they detest the
sex killer. If he did what he did to his victims, he
would be capable of doing the same to their women
and children.

The grapevine at Oregon State Prison had telegraphed
that Jerry Brudos was coming in, whispered intelligence that works faster than anything on the outside.

They were ready for him.

A sex killer on the inside is lucky if he only gets the
silent treatment. He must always be looking over his
shoulder, be aware that whatever punishment he managed to avoid in society may well be waiting for him.

He may lose his mind, or his balls, or his life in
prison.

There is a rule of thumb in prison: never put a
woman-killer in a cell on one of the upper tiers. He
may have an "accidental" fall. Jerry Brudos was housed
in a ground-floor cell.

The cons gave Jerry the silent treatment, declaring
him a nonperson.

When he moved through the chow lines, he kept his
eyes on his tray—watching the piles of starchy stuff for
which he had no appetite. Eating meant that he would
have to find a spot at one of the tables in the vast hall.

It didn't really matter where Jerry Brudos chose a
seat; he would be eating alone within a few moments.
Some one of the other prisoners would give a slight
nod, and the cons would get up en masse and move. It
was an effective way to ostracize him. All the other
tables would be crowded, and Jerry Brudos would be

left sitting alone at a long table, as visible as if a spotlight shone on him.

Jerry Brudos lost his appetite.

The prisoner was no longer overweight. Within a short time his weight had dropped to 150 pounds. Feeling the eyes of his fellow prisoners, hearing their comments directed at him—"Something stinks, I think I'm gonna puke"; "I don't eat with no perverts"; and "Woman killer"—he could only swirl his food around his plate and wait for the bell to clang.

Before—outside—he had had so much control over people; his strength made him respected. His flaring temper frightened them. Now, no one would even talk to him, and Darcie no longer wrote to him. He listened, always, for the sound of footsteps behind him.

On August 13, 1969, someone slammed a bucket of water into the left side of his head. His ears rang from the blow, and he was hustled off to the infirmary. Doctors there found he had a mild inflammation of the eardrum, but no perforation. He complained of pain in his lower back after the incident and was taken "outside" for a visit to a chiropractor.

He was positive that they were out to get him, that somebody—maybe the whole lot of them—only waited for the opportunity to kill him. He began to keep a log recording the dates and details of crimes against him.

He also began to study lawbooks available to him in prison, confident that he would find a way to get out through his intelligence and a clever use of legal procedure.

He did not repent his crimes or grieve for his victims. He only continued to rail at the unfairness of the whole situation.

Jerry Brudos objected to a great many things. He was furious that his children had been removed from him, insisting that he *was* a fit parent, and deserved a hearing. Darcie divorced him in August 1970, changed her name, and moved away. This, too, he found unfair. He had been a good husband, and now she had deserted him. Darcie and the youngsters were together again, and she would spend the years ahead trying to

forget Jerry Brudos and what he had done. Grateful to
Charlie Burt, Darcie would write to him from wherever she was—letters at first, and finally only a re-
membrance at Christmas. The name she chose for
herself and the children is a common name, and there
is nothing to be gained from revealing it here. She
seeks only anonymity and peace after horror.

Jerry began peppering the Oregon court system with
requests and writs, documents which he wrote painstakingly in his own printed hand, following forms he
found in lawbooks. His spelling was often flawed, but
a faithful reproduction of his arguments tells much
about the man's thinking processes.

On September 18, 1970, Brudos submitted a petition for a "Writ of Mandanus, Before the Honorabe
Supreme Court of the State of Oregon." He listed
"exhibits" in his index, and began his seven-page argument:

> Now comes the defendant/petitioner, Jerome
> H. Brudos, who does at this time enter before
> this Honorable Court, to issue a writ of Mandanus,
> directed to the Marion County Circuit Court,
> that NO later than the 15th day of October, 1970,
> to:
>
> 1. Issue to the defendant/petitioner, a com-
> plete, exacting and Itemized reciept, particulary
> describing each and every Iten removed from the
> defendans posession by the Marion County Sher-
> iff's Department, the Marion County District At-
> torney's Office, the Salem City Policce Depart-
> ment, and Any and ALL other oriznations who
> did remove any or all property from the defend-
> ant's/petitioner's House, Garage, Outbuildings,
> Automobiles, and ALL other containers, On,
> About or After the 25th day of May, 1962 [sic].
>
> 2. To order dismissed and declair for Naught,
> the Judgment for the apparent amount of $8,179.00
> against the defendant for totaly unsubstaincated
> and unfounded 'Costs and Disbursments,' against
> him.
>
> 3. To release immediatly all property Not Taken

Upon a Serchwarrent, to the defendant/petitioner
and his agent, one Ned Rawls . . .

—/OR/—

To order immediatly, a Jury trial as is guarnteed
by the 6th or 7th Amendment of the United
States Constitution, which ever shall apply, Also
Artcle I, Section II or, Section 17 which ever
shall apply.

Brudos then listed seventeen "authorities" he had
gleaned from his research. He had forgotten the year
of his crimes, listing instead 1962, but he had what he
considered powerful arguments on his behalf:

—Presentment—
As can be seen from exhibit 1, the Marion
County Circuit Court has apparently given Judgment against the defendant/petitioner, yet the
Court has ignored every inquirey, petition and
ALL Requeats for information by this defendant/
petitioner. This is such an obvious and flagrent,
willful Violation of Constitutional Rights that it
goes with [sic] saying, However, since this Court
is not familiar with this case, this petitioner will
attempt to lay out the full parimiters of the Case
without the aid of an Attorney for the defendant/
petitioner is without funds with which to employ
an attorney.
There is no room for argument for the defend-
ant/petioner has repeadly writen to the Marion
County Circuit Court, the Marion District Attorney's Office seeking information and/or/ a reciept
and yet nether office has responded once with so
much as an acknowlegiment of reciept of the
Letters, Let alone supplied any of the requested
information conserning These matters.
The 5th and 14th Amendment to the United
States Constitution, along with Article 1, Sec-
tion(s) 10 ALL Guarntee "Due Process," but,
Article 1, Section 20 goes on to guarntee that

"No Court shall be secret, but Justice shall be administered openly and without purchase," yet as was seen in exibit 1, That is the only notice the defendant/petitioner, has received and then that was quite by accident out of an old newspaper, and that was after the Judgment was given. The defendant's property was confiscated, the defendent sued, Judgment given, and then a second hearing held which Judgment was given that the defendant/petitioner has no claim upon his own personal property inspite of O.R.S. 23.160 and 23.200.

What was Jerry Brudos so angry about? The state of Oregon has seized his belongings, the tools and gear in his shop, in an attempt to repay the state some of the $8,000-plus that his court costs had totaled. To Jerry Brudos, the law was there to protect him. *And only him.*

To state that this Law is being used indiscrimitly would be so crass and Grossly incorrect for the facts are plain and simple, This law has been used very discrimitly and soley against the defendant/petitioner. . . .

He cited two pages of statutes that he felt applied to himself, and then railed at the court:

Well it goes without saying that if we convict a man of a crime, place him in jail and then stand idely by while His tools of his trade and personal property stolen systematicly and Legaly? We then must have reformed him even if He must turn to a Life of Crime for he no longer has the needed tools with which to work at his ocupation or proper clothing Etc. This further only dimenstrats the Marion County Court Attitude Twards Justice. They don't give a damn about the Laws, Constitution or anything else except, they have a helpless victim who cannot fight Back and Two Court appointed attorneys who will co-operate with the Court or the prosecution's Lest Whim.

*   *   *

A Freudian slip? Or only the man's view of *himself*
as a "helpless victim who cannot fight back"?

Judge Val Sloper had taken exquisite pains to be
sure that Jerry Brudos had understood what he was
pleading guilty to—but a year in prison had clouded
Brudos' memory. Now he was claiming complete innocence of the crimes.

> During the arguments before the Court of Ap-
> peals [sic] upon another facit of this case, it was
> broght out that the Circuit Court Judge ordered
> the defendant's attorneys to Look at the psudo
> evidence compiled. That was on a Friday and the
> defendant was to go to trial the following mon-
> day and yet One attorney had not even bothered
> to look at the evidence. When the defendant
> requested to see the evidence he was told by his
> Attorneys "Oh no you don't get to see the
> evidence." The defendant has since found out
> why. There is photographs that were manifactured
> to make it appear Like the defendant was guilty
> of the Crime and the prosecution could not af-
> ford to Allow the defendant to see these phony
> pictures. They then proceeded to Threatnen the
> defendant's Life along with repurcussions which
> would be effected upon his wife and children.
> Marion County in That respect makes the Com-
> muniust Countrys and their methods Look Like
> Mickey Mouse Culb, for the defendant has the
> prrof and yet the Marion County Courts are
> concerned about a conviction only and could care
> Less that the Victim of this whole thing is in fact
> innosent. It can be seen from Exibit 2, Clearly
> shows that this is in fact the truth yet everybody
> says, "I sincerely doubt that it happened," yet
> nobody bothered to check. A plain and simple fact.
> There is a multitude of witnesses and evidence to
> substaciate this along with his personal testimony.

Brudos' "Exibit 2" was a statement purportedly made
by a fellow prisoner alleging that Brudos had been

treated unfairly, and repeating Brudos' feeling that he had been poisoned in jail! The statement mentioned that Brudos' bedding had been removed during the day and returned only at night. Since the prisoner had threatened suicide, it was a prudent move on the part of the jail staff. Brudos *was* fed separately from the other prisoners; it was for his own protection. In the Marion County jail, there might well have been other inmates who would have delighted in poisoning him, if the opportunity arose. It was hardly information that was new to the courts. Nor was it a legally sound basis for a new trial.

Brudos wound up his "mandanus" writ with an emotional paragraph:

The really teriable part is that the defendant/ petitioner is in fact innocent of The Charges, yet the prosecution did have such a Lever against the defendant they got confessions for Cases that they didn't even have boddies for. Such threats were used that they could obtain such confessions yet the defense attorneys did not even question that. If One Court, Just One would have retained It's impartiality and had attempted to seek the truth and Justice it whould have been exposed, but Marion County Judicial system is so far out upon a Limb they fear of sawing it off Them self, there fore "we" says the Court "Will do nothing without an order stating we must, then we will have to try to get around that then."

The petitioner/defendant does therefore pray this Honorable Court will issue this writ of Mandanus and start to instill some form of Justice in the County that the State Capitol is in and this type of Decay can only spreed if not checked now.

Did Jerry Brudos believe his own arguments? Perhaps.

Perhaps he only wanted out.

The "confessions" had been made by Brudos himself. Yes, he had confessed to killing Linda Slawson and Jan Whitney, knowing that their bodies had not been found. He had chosen to brag about the murders to Jim Stovall.

In the late summer of 1970, the lack of those victims' bodies was a moot point—at least in the case of Jan Whitney. Picnickers along the Willamette River at a spot somewhat below the Independence Bridge saw what they took to be a lamb's carcass caught up in branches near the shore.

It was not a lamb; it was all that was left of Jan Whitney, her body surfacing so many months after she had had the terrible misfortune of meeting Jerome Henry Brudos. Identification was possible only through dental records. Cause of death could no longer be determined.

Brudos was a frequent patient in the prison infirmary. The records are cryptic, and give no details.

On January 1, 1971, he was treated for "rectal bleeding." Perhaps he suffered from hemorrhoids; possibly there were other reasons.

He had lost his battle to recover his property so that he might carry on his occupation. Since he was serving three life terms back-to-back, it was doubtful that his services as an electrician would be soon available to citizens in the Salem area.

A small ad appeared in the Salem *Capital Journal* and the Salem *Statesman* on March 23, 1971:

Sheriff's Sale—March 27, 1971, 1 P.M. Marion County Shops, 5155 Silverton Rd. N.E., Craftsman Roll Cabinet and Tools, Electric Hand Tools, Rifle Re-Loading Equipment, Antique Telephone Insulators, Scuba Diving Equipment, Many Miscellaneous Items. Terms: Cash.

Sales were brisk. The gear taken from Jerry Brudos' grisly workshop netted the state of Oregon something over eleven hundred dollars. The citizens of the state would have to pay for the rest of Jerry Brudos' legal procedures through their taxes.

There were others who attempted to obtain Jerry

Brudos' property. His mother, Eileen, asserted that it
was all rightfully hers—since she had lent him so much
money, by her own reckoning—that had never been
repaid. Ned Rawls and another friend asked for some
of Brudos' tools and guns, and Darcie too laid claim to
the gear left behind.

All of them were denied. Darcie's claims against the
estate had already been satisfied when she signed a
receipt for certain items: a movie screen, a camera,
lawn chairs, throw rugs not used in evidence, a box
fan, two blankets, a box of slides, miscellaneous personal papers, and a BB gun.

These were to be her assets, along with some furniture and clothes—very little after eight years of marriage.

Jerry Brudos continued to suffer "accidents" in
prison. In 1971 his neck was broken, fractured at the
fifth cervical bone, "C-5." He refused to say just how
it had been broken, and it is not explained in his
medical records beyond the terse "Fracture at C-5.
Patient placed in body cast, healed in an acceptable
position."

Brudos frequently complained of migraine headaches,
palpitations, depression, and myriad other symptoms.
He was treated with Meritene and Ritalin and various
combinations of drugs to alleviate his headaches.

He remained a pariah among his fellow prisoners.

He kept up his filing of notices of appeal. In 1972
the basis of his appeal was bizarre; he contended that
the dead girl in one picture was not Karen Sprinker at
all (detectives had asked Dr. Sprinker to look only at
the facial portion of the picture to save him further
pain). Brudos said he had been convicted for killing
someone unknown. With almost unthinkable gall,
Brudos wanted to subpoena Karen Sprinker's father.
He wanted to force Dr. Sprinker to study the grotesque pictures of his daughter, and then he submitted
that he, Brudos, could prove that the girl portrayed
was not Karen, but a stranger, a woman who was a
willing subject he'd photographed years before!

Blessedly for the grieving family, the appeal was denied.

By December 1974 Jerry Brudos had seized upon an entirely new theory, a theory somewhat supported by a psychologist he had been seeing in prison. Brudos had always avoided any responsibility for his crimes; now he had a handle on something that he felt would explain all of it. The psychologist had suggested that Brudos was hypoglycemic. That is, that he had low blood sugar, a condition blamed—rightly or wrongly—for many of modern man's physical and emotional problems.

Not all the prison psychological staff agreed with the diagnosis of hypoglycemia, however. In an evaluation done on December 11, 1974, one doctor wrote of Brudos:

I see Mr. Brudos as a paranoid personality without any real evidence of thought disorder or a psychotic process. He is able to conform his behavior to his environment, and is functioning very efficiently and without difficulty. He is quite an intelligent individual, and, coupled with his paranoia, he is a problem in management. He had a very good relationship in therapy with Dr. B., but the benefit of this relationship was that Dr. B. thought the basic difficulty was that of a physical disease—mainly hypoglycemia. And in this way, Mr. Brudos could escape the responsibility for the heinous crimes. With the present mental status of Mr. Brudos, I see him as a potentially very dangerous individual were he to be released into the community. This situation will continue unless he has intensive and prolonged psychotherapy—not group therapy—but at the present time this does not seem realistic with the shortage of available trained personnel. I strongly recommend there be no change in the current situation concerning Mr. Brudos.

Brudos would not let go of the "hypoglycemic" diagnosis; he saw it as his ticket out of prison and his

vindication. In a hearing in October 1976 he submitted this theory to the court. He had "fired" a
succession of court-appointed attorneys, but his new
lawyer asked for time so that famed Dr. Lendon
Smith, "The Children's Doctor" of television note,
could submit a letter on his evaluation of Jerry Brudos'
condition.

Smith is highly respected in the pediatric field, a
man of great humor and skill. Surprisingly to those
who watch him on television, he also has a background in working with psychotic prisoners and sol-
diers as a psychiatrist in the late forties. He espouses
the theory that poor nutrition often contributes to
antisocial behavior.

Smith wrote on November 1, 1976:

> . . . Violence, headaches, drowsiness, allergies,
> hyperactivity, irrational and even psychotic behav-
> ior may all be due to low blood sugar; the think-
> ing part of the brain simply cannot respond
> rationally to the environment when it is deprived
> of energy.
>
> There is no doubt that Mr. Brudos had hypo-
> glycemia in 1973. The log of his daily jail activi-
> ties can allow for no doubt that he was hypogly-
> cemic in June 1969. People have a potential or
> proclivity to hypoglycemia and they will become
> hypoglycemic when their diet is rich in carbohy-
> drate. I am aware of the high-carbohydrate diet
> in prisons.
>
> I am sure his hypoglycemia was activated by
> the diet he received in jail in June 1969.

And so Jerry Brudos now blamed all of his crimes—if
he should admit guilt—and his confession in June,
1969 on a diet too high in carbohydrates and sugar!

The appeals court took a dim view of the "too many
candy bars and mashed potatoes" theory. Jerry Brudos
remained in prison.

In toto, 1976 had not been Brudos' best year. Darcie
had obtained an order forbidding her children to visit
their father in prison, nor did she want them to corre-

spond with him. She was still afraid of him—for herself, and especially for the children's emotional well-being.

Jerry had also lost his phone privileges—after still another extended hearing. A female employee in the warden's office reported that Brudos had phoned her and told her that "she was cute," instructing her to come to a window so that he could see her better. When this was documented, the prisoner's access to the phone was taken away.

Jerry was becoming angry . . . and frightened. He felt always that someone stalked him, someone inside the prison. His fellow cons had never warmed to him. He had regained the weight he'd lost initially, but he sensed the hatred all around him. He complained, "Sometimes, it appears as though the penitentiary is just bent on trying point-blankly to get me killed."

Not the penitentiary staff certainly. Whatever their private feelings, their mandate was only to keep Brudos away from the public. The prisoners themselves? That was another matter entirely.

The last appeal of record filed in the Oregon State Supreme Court's dusty archives notes the date: May 25, 1977. By 1977, several infamous serial killers had emerged to replace Jerry Brudos in the headlines. Ted Bundy had allegedly murdered young women in Washington, Oregon, Utah, and Colorado, and was currently in the Utah State Prison. In the same prison at Point of the Mountain, Gary Gilmore had faced a firing squad, but only after generating enough newsprint to encircle the world if placed end to end. There was Juan Corona in California. Crime was in the news, and television talk shows were rife with discussions of the efficacy of the death penalty.

Jerry Brudos based this last appeal on a rather convoluted theory. Since *his* alleged crimes were so heinous, and since one of his own attorneys had once compared his crimes to those of Jack the Ripper and the Boston Strangler, he now put forth the premise that media coverage equated recent heinous and sensational crimes with his own. His paranoia had expanded. While he had formerly felt that the prison staff and population were against him, he now insisted that the entire state of Oregon was plotting against him, and that his life was in danger. His next point seemed diametrically opposed to his protestations that he feared for his life. "The extraordinary security measures taken to protect me in prison make the courts unable to be objective on my appeals . . ."

And he reiterated that his hypoglycemic condition in 1969 had made him unable to plead with a clear and unconfused mind.

Again, Jerry Brudos was denied a new trial.

Outside, the world has gone on without Jerry Brudos. His mother, Eileen Brudos, the mother he claimed to detest, died in 1971. Darcie Brudos has a new name and a new life. Her children are almost grown now. The Sprinkers, the Salees, the Slawsons, and the Whitneys have picked up the pieces of their shattered lives. Lt. Gene Daugherty rose to the position of Deputy Superintendent of the Oregon State Police before his retirement in 1980. Jim Stovall is a lieutenant now in charge of Patrol units for the Salem police department.

The horror has diminished with the passage of time, but will never fade entirely.

Afterword

March 1, 1988

Will Jerome Henry Brudos ever get out of prison? The rational answer is no. However, an overview of "lifers" who *have* been released on parole after ten or twelve or fourteen years is not reassuring. In the vast majority of states in America, "life in prison" means somewhere between ten and fourteen years. "Good behavior" generally cuts sentences by a third. In Oregon, a convicted killer can technically apply for parole in six months. While parole has never been granted so soon, most convicted killers in Oregon are back on the streets within a dozen years.

One Portland man, convicted in the early sixties in the mutilation murder of a housewife, served a little over twelve years in the Oregon State Prison in Salem. During his "life" sentence, he was trained to be an apprentice plumber. He was a model prisoner—as most sadistic sociopaths are. Within a month of his parole, he repeated his crime, using an identical M.O. (Modus Operandi). He was arrested for killing and dismembering a woman he met in a bar, although detectives believe his actual new toll is three victims, not one.

The same thing happened with an Oregon City murderer who was released in the late seventies and went to work as a school janitor. He was subsequently arrested and convicted of killing the high school teacher whom he had dated until she discovered his criminal record. When she confronted him, and threatened to tell school authorities, he killed her.

Oregon is no worse than any other state. It is only representative of a profoundly dangerous problem, and this book happens to be about a killer who operated in

Oregon. Prisoners convicted of heinous crimes are released every day in every state *years* before their sentence release date. In some cases, their prison records have been exemplary. In others, infraction slips have mysteriously disappeared before they ever reached the hands of the parole board.

There are many reasons for parole to occur so much earlier than the layman might expect. Prisons are full to bursting, and the cost of keeping one prisoner in a penitentiary for just one year ranges from $6,000 to $15,000. "Old" crimes tend to be forgotten, buried under the mountains of media coverage of new crimes that mount up inexorably year after year. A man whose name has been infamous becomes just another number after he has been in prison for two decades. He becomes a "nobody" in the world of crime.

And sometimes he gets out. *Often*, he gets out. So many killers slip through the cracks of the justice system; only the hue and cry of the media or victims' support groups serves to remind parole boards, prison administrators, and legislators of the crimes that sent him to prison for "life."

Jerome Brudos. Is it possible that he too may one day convince a parole board in Oregon that he is safe to be at large?

Quite.

That possibility is the impetus behind this book. The "monster" may sleep, but he only slumbers—waiting for his chance to roam free once more. He does not get better. There is no psychiatric treatment today that cures a sadistic sociopath. Minor behavior modification is the most studies have been able to promise, and that modification usually disappears when active treatment ceases.

Jerry Brudos had been in the Oregon State Penitentiary for almost twenty years. He has changed little in appearance in those two decades. He has long since regained the weight he lost in his first months in prison, and he is once again a bulky, lumbering giant of a man. He is still freckled, but his hair is much thinner, and the blond is considerably grayed. He is forty-nine years old now.

There is an old saying among convicts: No matter how long your sentence, you only do "hard time" for one year. The literal translation is that human beings acclimate. Prison becomes a little world.

Jerry Brudos has acclimated. Since prison mail is not censored in Oregon, he is able to pursue his over-weening interest. He sends away for—and receives—every catalog he can find featuring, of course, women's shoes. He stacks them up in the corner of his cell for slow perusal and study.

He earns spending money by making leather key fobs. He always liked the touch of leather. Over the years, he has probably turned out hundreds of the key rings stamped with jobs, hobbies, avocations, college logos, and mascots. Prison visitors who choose to can pay a dollar or two for a slightly ghoulish souvenir. A whole display board is filled with leather key fobs that Jerry Brudos once touched and shaped.

The tags read "Jerry Brudos—Box 33284."

Today, with the evolution of electronics into a world that Brudos could only have imagined twenty years ago, he has become totally involved with computers. The man whose writing seems to be that of a near illiterate remains a genius with electronics. The Oregon State Penitentiary has a network of computers and word processors and who would be more adept at keeping them humming than Jerry Brudos? Some informants insist he "runs the whole prison computer system," and others deem him only a technician who helps out.

Were it not for his fetishes and his fantasies, for his obsession with death, Jerry Brudos—on the outside—could probably have made a fortune working with computers.

But, in the end, murder became paramount to Jerry Brudos. To the layman, a killer is a killer is a killer. To the criminologist, there are as many gradations of the violence in murder as there are colors in the rainbow. Humans kill for financial gain. Humans kill because of jealousy. Humans kill one another for revenge or out of fear or even to achieve a kind of infamy. But the lust killer, the sadistic killer, the serial killer, is a breed unto himself.

Little Jerry Brudos, the five-year-old who was transfixed by a pair of women's shoes, and who then evolved through so-called "minor" sex crimes over thirty years to commit multiple murders fits the majority of the guidelines established for the lust killer/serial killer. It is a category which Jerry Brudos resents mightily. He threatened to sue an Oregon newspaper for deeming him a "lust killer." "I'm a killer, yes," he wrote. "But I'm not a *lust killer.*" A matter of pride . . . or semantics? (Brudos withdrew his suit when he was reminded of his psychiatric report.)

Because the number of these murderers has grown alarmingly in America since the early 1960s, the Behavioral Science Unit of the F.B.I. carries on continual research to update our knowledge of them.

During the black years when the big man with the friendly, almost-shy grin acted out his secret fantasies, there was no definitive term to describe his psychopathology. The phrase "serial killer" had yet to be coined. In the 1960s, the press lumped his kind of killer in with all the others who murdered many victims. "Mass murderers" they were deemed. But this freckled giant was not a mass murderer, nor was Albert De Salvo, "The Boston Strangler," whose crimes had taken place 3000 miles away and half a decade earlier. Nor was Jack-the-Ripper a mass murderer as he prowled night after night through the narrow streets of London's red-light district.

They were all serial killers, men who killed their victims one at a time over a long time—men who would never stop until they were arrested or too old—or dead.

How far back in criminal history can we trace serial killers? Possibly to the very beginning. Bob Ressler, of the F.B.I.'s Behavioral Science Unit, suggests that the werewolves of gypsy fables were, in actuality, not murderous mutants at all, but serial killers. Humans, after all, but as deadly as werewolves.

By 1988, the term "serial killer" would be well

known, these killers-by-the-numbers a favorite topic of talk shows, and the concern of law enforcement officials all over America. These are the men who stalk and kill and wait . . . and stalk and kill again and wait.

Jerry Brudos was one of them. Twenty years ago, this man with the broad bland face was as dangerous and deadly as any murderer since time began. But, in 1968, he was tragically ahead of his time. For a long time no one knew he was out there, scheming and trolling for victims.

Even when they found him, he was difficult to categorize. Today, the Jerome Henry Brudos case is used by criminologists, detectives, professors, psychologists, and psychiatrists as one of the classic examples of murderous horror. Infamous, Brudos is nevertheless sought out by experts who would interview him, seeking some way to untangle the bloody threads of his life. He is not only a serial killer; he is a lust killer.

The worst of the worst.

Special Agents R. Roy Hazelwood and John E. Douglas have isolated the profile of this most dreaded killer in their paper "The Lust Murderer."

They might well have been describing Jerome Henry Brudos.

Basically, there are two types of personalities, who commit lust murders: the Organized Nonsocial and Disorganized Asocial (and occasionally, one who possesses characteristics of both). Jerry Brudos' personality fits into the parameters of the first type easily. According to Hazelwood and Douglas, the Organized Nonsocial killer is a person who is completely heedless of the welfare of society; he cares only for himself. Other humans matter *only* in the ways they fulfill—or deny—his needs. While he dislikes other people, he does not avoid them. Rather, he shows the rest of the world an amiable facade. It allows him to manipulate them toward his own goals. He is quite cunning, and he plans well.

The lust killer is a man full of fantasy—Brudos, for example, drew pictures in his mind of the "killing place" where he could imprison captive women, torture them, and then freeze them for his pleasure for-ever. He was fascinated early on with pornography, and used it to build on his own fantasies. Psychiatrists detect a glaring lack of self-confidence in the lust killer. Like Brudos, he can ward off reality by sinking into his cruel fantasies. Therein lies his power over all the women who have rejected him.

For Brudos, the first rejection by a woman is easy to pinpoint: his own mother did not like him. He could never please her in any way.

The true lust killer finds his victims because they come to him. That is, they *cross his path*. He does not choose them ahead of the killing time, but he is always ready. Linda Slawson came to Jerry Brudos' home to sell encyclopedias. Although she had gone to the wrong address, for *him* it was propitious. Jan Whitney's car had broken down on the freeway just moments before Brudos passed by on his way home from work. Karen Sprinker had the misfortune to be in the parking ga-rage of a department store while Brudos was seeking another woman, a woman who had evaded him. And Linda Salee too walked out of a busy store at the most dangerous moment—only to meet Jerry Brudos.

Until the terrible moment when they became his choice, he had never seen any of them before. . . .

They had crossed his path.

The motivations behind the commission of a lust murder are emotions alien to a normal male. The lust killer is a sadist for whom sex and cruelty are so interwoven that, for him, one does not exist without the other. Although he may deny interest in sex when he is arrested, it is quite probably the most intense stimulus in his life. The victim is not a real person to him. Indeed, there *are* no other *real* people in his life. Only himself. His victim is only a vehicle for his own pleasure.

Jerry Brudos has told psychiatrists that, once he began his attacks, there was never any thought of not carrying through. He killed under the influence of an urge that even he himself could not—cannot—define. It was something that was to be done. His victims had been drawn into the fantasies that had become reality to him.

Because Jerry Brudos was really a most inadequate man, a "Casper Milquetoast" among other men, he needed to demean and possess women. He could not seem to possess Darcie, as hard as he tried to control her. She was slipping away from him—at least in his own mind. But he could possess his love-hate objects: women. He could trap them, torture them, confine them, and eventually destroy them. When he did that, his anxiety was assuaged for a time. In Brudos' case, the time seemed to be about a month. Just as Jim Stovall had predicted, Brudos prowled under a pseudo-menstrual cycle.

The lust killer's modus operandi is marked by brutality and sadism, say Hazelwood and Douglas. Invariably the victim's bodies are mutilated, and mutilated in areas that have sexual connotation: the genitals, the breasts, the buttocks. Brudos' fixation was on the breasts; he destroyed them by literally cutting them away from the dead victims.

It is rare for a lust killer to shoot his victims; he requires the direct contact of beating, strangulation, or stabbing. Jerry Brudos used the leather postal strap and his hanging device. As with other lust killers, the main portion of his sexual attack occurred while his victims were unconscious or dead. His innate fear of female rejection continued to such a degree that, even when his victims were helplessly bound, he could not risk their fighting him.

Most lust killers have a scenario that requires they take a souvenir of their killings. Here, too, Jerry Brudos worked in a pattern that was predictable. He saved shoes, undergarments, and photographs, and, exceeding even heretofore infamous lust killers, he saved the severed breasts and attempted to make paperweights out of them.

There is one characteristic common to most lust killers that may be surprising. They seem obsessed by driving, often driving hundreds of miles. They travel long distances trolling for victims, and Brudos was no exception. His battered station wagon was constantly on the I-5 freeway, going to Portland, back to Salem, then to Corvallis. This may be a manifestation of their anxiety, of the need to keep moving. More likely, it is their innate cunning that inspires this; they have learned that they will avoid detection more easily if they commit their crimes in widely separated police jurisdictions. They seek to have their "patterns" known only to themselves.

Agents Douglas and Hazelwood have determined that most lust killers are relatively young—between seventeen and twenty-five years of age. Brudos began his sexual crimes at the age of sixteen, but he managed to avoid serious consequences for his heinous crimes until he was thirty years old. In that way, he was, perhaps, cleverer than most, and in his perverted mind, he considered it something of an accomplishment. When he was finally face-to-face with Jim Stovall, he was eager to brag about his crimes.

Like all lust killers, Jerry Brudos was fascinated with the investigation. He saved newspaper clippings to gloat over, secure that he was smarter than the cops in this deadly game. He was alarmed when police investigated the hole left in his garage after the accident, and yet smug that they could have come so close and still not caught him. When Stovall questioned Brudos, it was Brudos who asked so eagerly, "How can you tell? How can you figure out that I did anything?"

He was still very confident at that point.

Jerry Brudos is Caucasian, and so were all his victims. It is almost unheard-of for a lust killer to cross racial lines. Since his hatred of women appears to stem from women in his own life—a mother, a wife, a sister—he tends to attack within his own race. The victims may resemble physically the women who have rejected him, or, as in Brudos' case, they may be the very antithesis. Eileen Brudos had always worn plain clothing, dull flat-heeled shoes, and little makeup. Her son grew up to kill pretty women who wore pretty clothing. Unlike Brudos, Ted Bundy, alleged to have murdered thirty-six young women, chose victims who were beautiful and who resembled the lost fiancée who had rejected him. Whether the lust killer chooses opposites or doubles for his hate object, he *does* invariably choose victims who fit his particular victim profile.

Few lust killers begin by actually murdering. It is a slow but constantly accelerating process—a juggernaut of perversion, if you will. Many begin with voyeurism: "Peeping Toms." Some are exposers. It is a fallacy that such offenses are not dangerous and will not progress. There is always the constant need for more stimulus, more excitement. Jerry Brudos began by stealing shoes, moving on to the theft of women's undergarments. He was a voyeur. When the theft of lingerie from clotheslines was not enough, he actually entered homes to steal his treasures. Here too was an added excitement. William Heirens, the seventeen-year-old premed student convicted of the mutilation murder of six-year-old Suzanne Degnan in Chicago in the 1940s, and other sex killings, related to arresting officers that he achieved sexual climax only when he crossed over the windowsill of a home where he went to steal undergarments. That his crimes accelerated fatally is well-documented. (Heirens, over fifty today, is still in prison.)

Jerry Brudos found that the theft of shoes and bras and panties was not enough to fill the void in his self-esteem, not enough to quiet his anxiety and rage. And so he raped. When that was no longer enough, he killed and mutilated his victims.

And if he had not been caught . . . ?

The question must always be "Why?" What happens to change a chubby-cheeked, freckled five-year-old into a monster? If there were clearly definitive answers, it might be simpler to explain. But there are certain factors which seem to be present in the history of almost all lust killers.

With the complete records available on Jerry Brudos' past, the reader can easily see the correlations between his case and the accepted profile put together by experts.

Special agents Hazelwood and Douglas offer their opinion based on their studies of scores of cases:

What set of circumstances creates the individual who becomes the lust murderer? . . . It is generally accepted that the foundation of the personality is formed within the first few years of life. While extreme stress, frequent narcotic use, or alcohol abuse can cause personality disorganization in later life, it is the early years that are critical to the personality structure and development.

Seldom does the lust murder come from an environment of love and understanding. It is more likely that he was an abused or neglected child who experienced a great deal of conflict in his early life and was unable to develop and use adequate coping devices. Had he been able to do so, he would have withstood the stresses placed on him and developed normally in early childhood. . . .

These stresses, frustrations, and subsequent anxieties, along with the inability to cope with them, may lead the individual to withdraw from the society which he perceives as hostile and threatening. Through the internalization process, he becomes secluded and isolated from others. . . . This type possesses a poor self-image and secretly rejects the society which he feels rejects him.

Family and associates would describe him as a nice quiet person who keeps to himself, but who never quite realized his potential. During adolescence, he may have engaged in voyeuristic activities or the theft of feminine clothing. Such activities serve as a substitute for his inability to approach a woman sexually in a mature and confident manner.

The individual designated as the organized nonsocial type harbors similar feelings of hostility, but elects not to withdraw and internalize his hostility. Rather, he overtly expresses it through aggressive and seemingly senseless acts against society. Typically, he begins to demonstrate his hostility as he passes through puberty and into adolescence. He would be described as a troublemaker and manipulator of people, concerned only with himself. . . .

Jerry Brudos falls somewhere between the two types. He was a quiet youngster—as far as anyone knew— until his attacks on the two teenage girls, attacks which landed him in the Oregon State Hospital. Would adequate treatment at that time have worked? Perhaps. But he did not receive intensive treatment; he was viewed only as a sissy, lazy, and told he needed to grow up.

It is likely that it was far too late at that point anyway; his fantasies were already formed and they would never leave him.

Have they left him now? After eighteen years in prison? That too is extremely doubtful. The mold was formed so early. Like Kenneth Bianchi (the alleged "Hillside Strangler"), Edward Kemper (Northern California's "Chainsaw Murderer-Coed Killer"), and Wisconsin's infamous Edward Gein, Jerome Brudos is the product of a home with a strong, controlling mother, and with a weak (or absent) father figure (although these men cannot all be considered lust killers).

Jerry Brudos hates women. He has almost always hated women. And, in all likelihood, he will continue to hate women. Like Delilah's hold over Samson, women weaken Jerry Brudos and make him afraid. He can control them only by obliterating them.

Brudos and Bundy and Bianchi and Long and Kemper and the many others who came out of the shadows to kill, and who were finally caught, are in prison. There are other prowlers who are still free. There is virtually no way to spot this kind of danger until it strikes. Women can protect themselves by being constantly aware, by avoiding lonely places.

While there is no sure means of escaping from the control of the lust murderer, fighting him presents the only possible avenue of escape.

Fight. The lust killer is a coward who counts upon his chosen victim to be passive. If his quarry screams and kicks and fights, she may escape with her life.

But, if she allows him to take her away to his isolated killing place, thinking that she can reason with him, she will surely die.

Because he has no mercy in him.

No one who encountered Jerry Brudos has ever forgotten him. The detectives who tracked him and finally caught him will never forget him.

Jim Stovall rose to the rank of Lieutenant, and helped solve dozens of homicide cases long after Brudos was in prison. He retired from the Salem Police Department in the mid eighties, and divides his time between living and skiing in Colorado and his home in Salem. He still studies the criminal mind, and the ever-more-scientific methods devised to track and trap murderers.

Jerry Frazier moved from the Salem Police Department to the Marion County District Attorney's Office where he works as an investigator. Not too long ago, he found himself stopping in front of the *shake* house on Center Street. He talked to the current tenants, who admitted that they would never have moved in— had they known the house's history. No, there were no ghosts; it was just the idea.

"They had a lot of turnover of renters," Frazier recalls. "The place always had people moving in or moving out. That day, I walked into that garage after so many years. The dividers were gone, but the *feeling*—a kind of chill—was still there. Just as much as the day Jerry Brudos offered me that rope knot that was eventually going to help convict him."

In April of 1984, I was presenting a seminar to the Oregon Writers Colony at Gearhart, Oregon, on the Pacific Ocean. Using slides, I moved through the lives of the serial killers I had written about. When I had finished speaking, I looked up to see an attractive red-haired woman standing in front of me. If it is possible to be that color, she was pale gray-green. She looked, literally, as if she had seen a ghost.

"Are you all right?" I asked.

"I was the one . . . who got away," she murmured.
"I was the one he called the 'blonde bitch.' "

"You're in my book," I said. " Have you read it?"

She shook her head. "After I got away, I found out
that he was arrested for murder—but something stopped
me from reading about it. I didn't want to know what
he'd done. I didn't want to know how close I'd come
. . . I guess I didn't want to know the details."

Understandable, after what she had been through.
The woman was Sharon Wood, alive and well fifteen
years after her terrifying few minutes with Jerry Brudos.

However, after our chance meeting in the lodge on
the Oregon beach, Sharon Wood felt a pressing need
to find out more about the man who had tried to
destroy her life. She asked, as she had asked herself
right after the attack, "Why am *I* alive . . . while the
others are dead?"

She thought of her twins born in 1970, Dori and
Christopher, children who would never have been born
if she hadn't escaped from Jerry Brudos. And, in
doing so, Sharon Wood could not help but think of the
children that Karen Sprinker, Jan Whitney, Linda
Slawson, and Linda Salee might have had. Of the
years they might have had.

Wood, a free-lance writer and photographer herself
by 1984, was compelled to learn more about Brudos—
this man whose story she had avoided for so many
years. She sent away to the Portland Police Department for the follow-up report on her own case, and
she visited the Oregon State Penitentiary and interviewed the warden's assistant.

She found that the prison staff considered Jerry
Brudos "a model prisoner," and that he was one of
the small percentage allowed to work in the hobby
shop. Sharon stood in front of the window displaying
Brudos' key fobs, and she felt her spine tighten. One
was stamped "Portland State Vikings": Portland State
is the college where Brudos attacked her; and another
was stamped with a camera.

Grateful that he had never had the opportunity to
take his ghastly pictures of her, she paid one dollar
and bought the leather fob with the camera on it.

Today, Sharon Wood works to help other women learn self-defense. She wholeheartedly supports the Portland Police Department's "Womenstrength" program. It is easy to see that Sharon feels an obligation to victims, and that she is grateful that she was allowed to live out her life.

Although Jerry Brudos is not likely to get out of prison until he is a very old man, there are other killers who thus far have avoided being newsworthy. They are just as dangerous—and they have never been caught; they are still prowling. Their philosophy on the value of a human life can be summed up, just as Jerry Brudos' was, in a short anecdote told by a detective who met him sometime after his arrest.

Jim Byrnes, a Marion County detective at the time of Brudos' arrest in 1969, and now a private investigator, recalls a conversation with Jerry Brudos.

"He liked strawberry milkshakes, and I'd take them to him to try to get him to talk. I wanted to get at how he really felt. One day, I asked him, 'Do you feel some remorse, Jerry? Do you feel sorry for your victims—for the girls who died?'

"There was a half piece of white paper on the table between us, and he picked it up, crumpled it in his fist, and threw the ball of paper on the floor. 'That much,' he said. 'I care about those girls as much as I care about that piece of wadded-up paper. . . .' "